BLACK+DECKER™

THE BOOK OF
HOME
IMPROVEMENT

THE MOST POPULAR REMODELING
PROJECTS SHOWN IN FULL DETAIL

COOL
SPRINGS
PRESS
Home and Garden Experts™

MINNEAPOLIS, MINNESOTA

Quarto is the authority on a wide range of topics.

Quarto educates, entertains and enriches the lives of our readers—enthusiasts and lovers of hands-on living.

www.quartoknows.com

© 2017 Quarto Publishing Group USA Inc.

First published in 2017 by Cool Springs Press, an imprint of The Quarto Group, 401 Second Avenue North, Suite 310, Minneapolis, MN 55401 USA. Telephone: (612) 344-8100 Fax: (612) 344-8692

QuartoKnows.com

Visit our blogs at QuartoKnows.com

Cool Springs Press titles are also available at discount for retail, wholesale, promotional, and bulk purchase. For details, contact the Special Sales Manager by email at specialsales@quarto.com or by mail at The Quarto Group, Attn: Special Sales Manager, 401 Second Avenue North, Suite 310, Minneapolis, MN 55401 USA.

10 9 8 7 6 5 4 3 2 1

ISBN: 978-0-7603-5356-1

Library of Congress Control Number: 2016962896

Acquiring Editor: Mark Johanson
Project Manager: Madeleine Vasaly
Art Director: James Kegley
Layout: Danielle Smith-Boldt

Printed in China

Photo credits

16 (top): Weather Shield
18–19: Guy Cass Architect, AIA, NCARD
20–21: © Susan Teare
42: Shutterstock
57, 402 (bottom): iStockPhoto
136, top: Oshkosh Designs
178: Eric Roth for Thomas Buckborough
294: Sun Tunnel Systems Inc.
352: © Bob Perron
380: © Tony Giammarino, www. tonygiammarino.com

382 (bottom): Cambria Natural Quartz Countertops
383 (top): DuPont Corian
386 (top): Julia Caruso
396, 407 (top), 411 (left): GE Appliances
426, 450: Moen
461: MTI
474 (both), 481 (bottom right), 492 (top): Kohler
481 (top right): Interstyle
481 (bottom left): Duravit
498 (right): Distinctive Design

NOTICE TO READERS

For safety, use caution, care, and good judgment when following the procedures described in this book. The publisher and BLACK+DECKER cannot assume responsibility for any damage to property or injury to persons as a result of misuse of the information provided.

The techniques shown in this book are general techniques for various applications. In some instances, additional techniques not shown in this book may be required. Always follow manufacturers' instructions included with products, since deviating from the directions may void warranties. The projects in this book vary widely as to skill levels required: some may not be appropriate for all do-it-yourselfers, and some may require professional help.

Consult your local building department for information on building permits, codes, and other laws as they apply to your project.

CONTENTS

CONTENTS (CONT.)

Bathroom Projects

Room Addition Projects

INTRODUCTION

For experienced (or maybe just intrepid) do-it-yourselfers, there eventually comes another step beyond the many basic repair and maintenance projects that are so crucial to home ownership. Just keeping a home's systems and structure in good working order is, of course, the goal of any responsible homeowner, but sooner or later most are ready to go to the next level by tackling projects that aim at improving, not just maintaining, their homes. These are projects that qualify as true home remodeling—DIY projects designed to extend the home's usefulness and increase its real-estate value.

That's where *The Book of Home Improvement* comes in. Earlier BLACK+DECKER major references, *The Book of Home How-To* and *The Complete Outdoor Builder*, were devoted to the basic skills and essential projects for keeping your home in good working order, both inside and out. *The Book of Home Improvement* builds on that foundation by offering a great selection of legitimate remodeling projects that can actually add financial value to the home while improving your family's enjoyment of it. Most homeowners will find great satisfaction by owning all three of these major home-improvement encyclopedias, as they are designed to work together.

This book offers well over one hundred fully illustrated remodeling projects, carefully selected for their popularity among homeowners and their value as equity-building improvements. These are the projects recommended by real-estate professionals for improving the value of your home. While some basic skills on your part are assumed—likely because you own other BLACK+DECKER books presenting the core DIY know-how— all the information you need to complete these projects is found right here: lists of tools and materials, building plans, and the unsurpassed step-by-step photography you've come to know from BLACK+DECKER books. With projects ranging from fairly simple replacement of trim moldings to elaborate extension of living space with added room additions, *The Book of Home Improvement* will quickly become an essential addition to your home DIY library.

PLANNING A REMODELING PROJECT

PLANNING A REMODELING PROJECT

The origins of the old idioms "Measure twice, cut once" and "An ounce of prevention is worth a pound of cure" are not definitively known, but we suspect they were coined by someone with rueful experience in home remodeling. Likewise for "Where fools rush in, angels fear to tread." Adequate planning and preparation are crucial to getting good results with home-improvement projects, while hastiness can be the start of disaster.

Planning a major remodeling project is a complex subject that can't be addressed in a single chapter of any book, but the segments of this chapter outline some key ideas for good preparation for any project. Keep the following in mind as you prepare for your project:

- Understand how your planned work fits in with the overall structure and function of your home— whether it is a carpentry project that integrates with the framework of your home or a heating, cooling, wiring, or plumbing project that will blend into an existing mechanical system.
- Review the codes and acceptable building practices authorized by your community. These exist for your safety, and following them can prevent accidents and expensive do-overs.
- Have a clear visual sense of the work you intend to do. A key step here is to have good, detailed plan drawings and practical schedules to organize the steps of your work.
- Use tools and materials safely; review their proper usage, and make sure your skills are honed before tackling a big project. Don't get in over your head.

With careful, meticulous planning, even DIYers of average experience can tackle surprisingly complex remodeling projects with great success.

IN THIS CHAPTER:
- Anatomy of a House
- Building Codes & Permits
- Remodeling Case Studies
- Working Safely
- Tools & Materials

ANATOMY OF A HOUSE

Before you start a do-it-yourself carpentry project, you should familiarize yourself with a few basic elements of home construction and remodeling. Take some time to get comfortable with the terminology of the models shown on the next few pages. The understanding you will gain in this section will make it easier to plan your project, buy the right materials, and clear up any confusion you might have about the internal design of your home.

If your project includes modifying exterior or load-bearing walls, you must determine if your house was built using platform- or balloon-style framing. The framing style of your home determines what kind of temporary supports you will need to install while the work is in progress. If you have trouble determining what type of framing was used in your home, refer to the original blueprints, if you have them, or consult a building contractor or licensed home inspector.

ANATOMY OF A HOUSE WITH PLATFORM FRAMING

Platform framing (photos, right and above) is identified by the floor-level sole plates and ceiling-level top plates to which the wall studs are attached. Most houses built after 1930 use platform framing. If you do not have access to unfinished areas, you can remove the wall surface at the bottom of a wall to determine what kind of framing was used in your home.

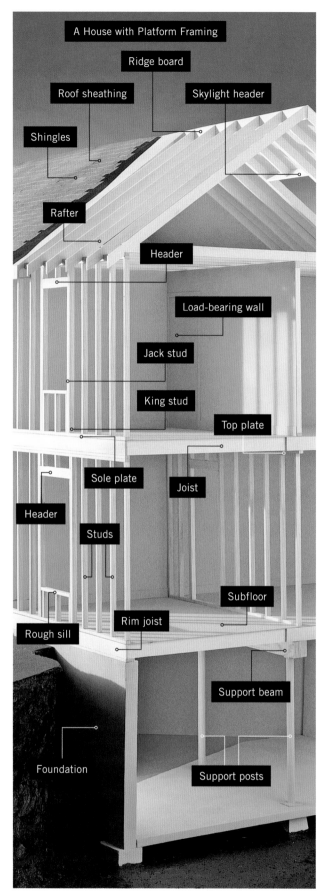

A House with Platform Framing

Ridge board

Roof sheathing

Skylight header

Shingles

Rafter

Header

Load-bearing wall

Jack stud

King stud

Top plate

Sole plate

Joist

Header

Studs

Subfloor

Rough sill

Rim joist

Support beam

Foundation

Support posts

Framing in a new door or window on an exterior wall normally requires installing a header. Make sure that the header you install meets the requirements of your local building code, and always install cripple studs where necessary.

Floors and ceilings consist of sheet materials, joists, and support beams. All floors used as living areas must have joists with at least 2 × 8 construction.

There are two types of walls: load-bearing and partition. Load-bearing walls require temporary supports during wall removal or framing of a door or window. Partition walls carry no structural load and do not require temporary supports.

ANATOMY OF A HOUSE WITH BALLOON FRAMING

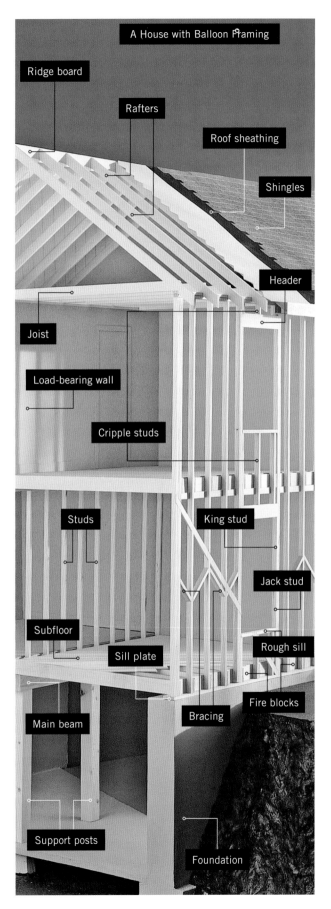

A House with Balloon Framing

Ridge board · Rafters · Roof sheathing · Shingles · Header · Joist · Load-bearing wall · Cripple studs · Studs · King stud · Jack stud · Subfloor · Sill plate · Rough sill · Main beam · Bracing · Fire blocks · Support posts · Foundation

Balloon framing (photos, right and above) is identified by wall studs that run uninterrupted from the roof to a sill plate on the foundation, without the sole plates and top plates found in platform-framed walls (page opposite). Balloon framing was used in houses built before 1930, and it is still used in some new home styles, especially those with high vaulted ceilings.

ANATOMY DETAILS

Many remodeling projects, like adding new doors or windows, require that you remove one or more studs in a load-bearing wall to create an opening. When planning your project, remember that new openings require a permanent support beam called a header, above the removed studs, to carry the structural load directly.

The required size for the header is set by local building codes and varies according to the width of the rough opening. For a window or door opening, a header can be built from two pieces of 2-inch dimensional lumber sandwiched around ⅜-inch plywood (chart, right). When a large portion of a load-bearing wall (or an entire wall) is removed, a laminated beam product can be used to make the new header.

If you will be removing more than one wall stud, make temporary supports to carry the structural load until the header is installed.

Recommended Header Sizes

ROUGH OPENING WIDTH	RECOMMENDED HEADER CONSTRUCTION
Up to 3'	⅜" plywood between two 2 × 4s
3 to 5'	⅜" plywood between two 2 × 6s
5 to 7'	⅜" plywood between two 2 × 8s
7 to 8'	⅜" plywood between two 2 × 10s

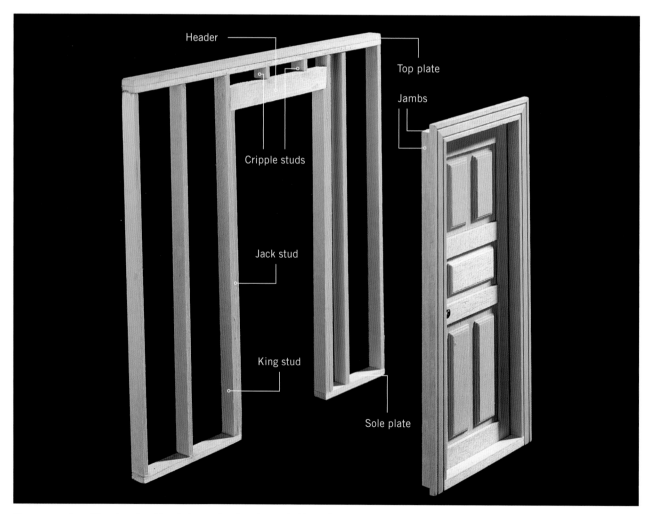

Door opening: The structural load above the door is carried by cripple studs that rest on a header. The ends of the header are supported by jack studs (also known as trimmer studs) and king studs that transfer the load to the sole plate and the foundation of the house. The rough opening for a door should be 1" wider and ½" taller than the dimensions of the door unit, including the jambs. This extra space lets you adjust the door unit during installation.

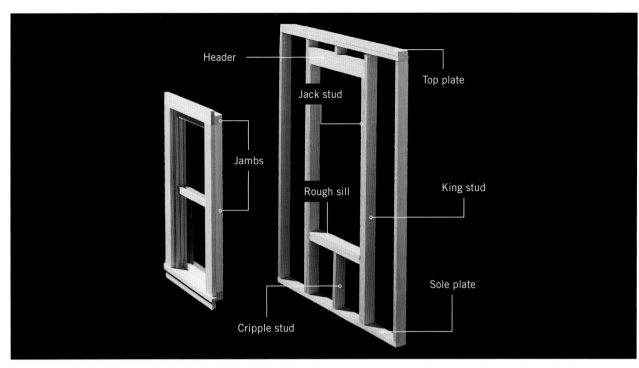

Window opening: The structural load above the window is carried by cripple studs resting on a header. The ends of the header are supported by jack studs and king studs, which transfer the load to the sole plate and the foundation of the house. The rough sill, which helps anchor the window unit but carries no structural weight, is supported by cripple studs. To provide room for adjustments during installation, the rough opening for a window should be 1" wider and ½" taller than the window unit, including the jambs.

FRAMING OPTIONS FOR WINDOW & DOOR OPENINGS (NEW LUMBER SHOWN IN YELLOW)

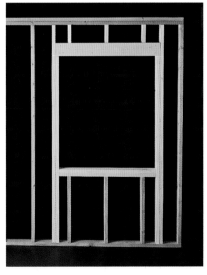

Using an existing opening avoids the need for new framing. This is a good option in homes with masonry exteriors, which are difficult to alter. Order a replacement unit that is 1" narrower and ½" shorter than the rough opening.

Framing a new opening is the only solution when you're installing a window or door where none existed or when you're replacing a unit with one that is much larger.

Enlarging an existing opening simplifies the framing. In many cases, you can use an existing king stud and jack stud to form one side of the new opening.

BUILDING CODES & PERMITS

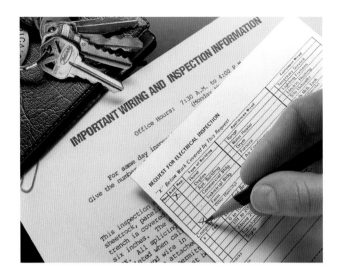

Building permits are required for any remodeling project that involves a change or addition to your home's structure or mechanical systems. Building permits are issued to ensure your remodeling project meets local building codes, which establish material standards, structural requirements, and installation guidelines for your project. In short, they ensure that your (or your contractor's) work is done properly.

The areas outlined on pages 15 and 16— room dimensions, exits and openings, light and ventilation, and fire protection—are usually covered by general building permits. If your project involves major changes to your plumbing, electrical, or HVAC systems, you may be required to obtain separate permits from the respective administration departments.

Building permits are required by law, and getting caught without them can result in fines from the city and possible trouble with your insurance company. Also, work done without permits can cause problems if you try to sell your house.

Most local building codes follow the national codes, such as the National Electrical Code, but are adapted to meet the demands of local conditions and legislation. Keep in mind that local codes always supersede national codes. Always check with your local building department before finalizing your plans.

Before issuing permits, your local building department will require plans and cost estimates for your project. After your plans have been approved, you must pay permit fees, which are based on the cost of the project. You'll also learn what inspections are required and when you should call for inspections.

Once issued, a building permit typically is good for 180 days. You can apply for an extension by submitting a written request showing justifiable cause for the delay.

Tip ▶

Here are some tips to help you prepare for the permit process:

- To obtain a building permit, you must fill out a form from your local building department that includes a description of the project; your home's address, legal description, and occupancy; and an estimate of the project cost.
- The building department may require two to four sets of construction documents or drawings of your project— including floor and elevation plans—to be submitted for inspection and approval.
- A building inspector will examine all construction plans and stamp or send written notification of approval and acceptance.
- One set of approved documents is kept by the building official, one set is sent to the applicant, and one set is displayed at the site until the project is completed.
- Some permits are granted by phase of construction. After the work for one phase is completed and inspected, a permit for the next phase is issued. However, building officials will not guarantee issuance of subsequent permits.
- All work is inspected by a building official to ensure compliance with codes and permits.
- Your project is complete only after the local building inspector makes a final inspection and gives approval of your site.

ROOM DIMENSIONS

- Habitable rooms must be at least 7' wide and 7' deep.
- Ceilings in all habitable rooms, hallways, corridors, bathrooms, toilet rooms, laundry rooms, and basements must be at least 7' 6" high, measured from the finished floor to the lowest part of the ceiling.
- Beams, girders, and other obstructions that are spaced more than 4' apart can extend 6" below the required ceiling height.
- In nonhabitable rooms, such as unfinished basements, ceilings may be 6' 8" from the floor, and beams, girders, and ducts may be within 6' 4" of the floor.
- Habitable rooms cannot have more than 50% of their floor area under sloped ceilings less than 7' 6" high, and no portion of a floor area can be under a ceiling less than 5' high.
- Finished floor is not considered measurable floor area when it is below sloped ceilings less than 5' high or beneath furred ceilings less than 7' 6" high.
- One habitable room in a home must have at least 120 square feet of gross floor area. Other habitable rooms can have gross floor space of 70 sq. ft. minimum.

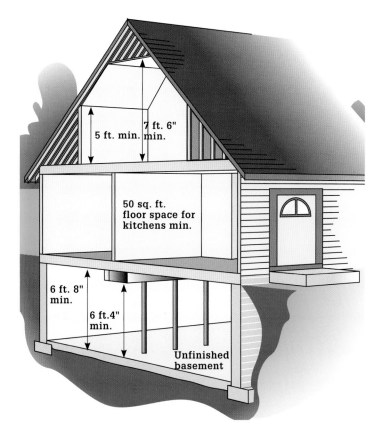

- Kitchens cannot have less than 50 sq. ft. of gross floor area.
- Hallways must be at least 3' wide.

EXITS & OPENINGS

- Sleeping rooms and habitable basements must have at least one egress window or exterior door for emergency escape. Occupants must be able to open the exit from inside the home, without a key or tool.
- An egress window must have a net clear opening of at least 5.7 sq. ft., with a minimum height of 24" and a minimum width of 20".
- Window sills on egress windows cannot be more than 44" above the floor.
- Egress windows below ground level must have window wells. If the wells are deeper than 44", they must have permanent ladders or steps. The steps can project up to 6" into the well but must be usable when the window is fully opened. Steps

must be at least 12" wide and project at least 3" from the wall. Ladder rungs must be less than 18" apart.
- Screens, bars, grills, and covers on emergency exits must open easily and be removable from inside the home, without tools or keys.
- Exit doors must be at least 3' wide and 6' 8" high. They must provide direct outside access and operate without special knowledge or tools.
- Bulkhead enclosures may serve as emergency exits in habitable basements if they provide direct access to the basement and meet the dimension requirements for emergency exits.

NATURAL LIGHT & VENTILATION

- Ventilation includes windows, doors, louvers, and other approved openings or mechanical systems.
- Windows must equal at least 8% of the floor area in habitable rooms. The minimum openable area of a window must equal at least 4% of the room's floor area.
- In bathrooms, windows must be at least 3 sq. ft., and at least half of the window must open.
- Windows must open and operate from inside the room, and they must exit to a street, alley, yard, court, or porch.
- Window light can be replaced by an artificial light if it produces 6.46 lux from 30" above the floor.
- Mechanical ventilation can replace operable windows. In bedrooms, ventilation must supply outside air at a rate of 15 cubic ft. per minute (cfm) for each occupant. In primary bedrooms, the rate is based on two occupants. In additional bedrooms, the rate is based on one occupant per room.
- In bathrooms, intermittent mechanical ventilation rates must be 50 cfm, and continuous rates must be 20 cfm. Bathroom ventilation must exhaust to the outside.

FIRE PROTECTION

- All concealed and interconnected spaces, such as soffits, drop and cove ceilings, stair stringers, and areas around vents, pipes, ducts, chimneys, and fireplaces must be fireblocked to prevent fire spread.
- Exterior walls must be constructed to resist fire for at least one hour, with exposure from both sides.
- Batts or blankets of fiberglass, mineral wool, or other approved material must be secured between wall studs and partitions, at the ceiling and floor level, and at 10-ft. intervals both vertically and horizontally.
- Foam insulation installed in interior walls covered with ½" wallboard or other approved material must have a flame-spread rating of 75 or less and a smoke-developing index of 450 or less.
- Other insulation, including facings, vapor barriers, and breather papers, must have a flame-spread index of 25 or less and a smoke-developing index of 450 or less.
- Loose-fill insulation mounted with screens or supports must have a flame-spread rating of 25 or less and a smoke-developing index of 450 or less.

- Wall and ceiling finishes must have a flame-classification rating of 200 or less and a smoke-developing index of 450 or less.
- Smoke alarms must be installed in bedrooms, in hallways near bedrooms, and on each full story of a home. Multiple alarms must be wired together so one activation triggers all alarms.

Universal Design ▶

Universal design is intended for all people. While standard home and product designs are based on the "average" person—that is, the average adult male—not everyone fits into that category. Some people are short, some tall; some have difficulty walking, while others walk ably but find bending difficult. And physical abilities change constantly, as do family situations. By incorporating universal design into your remodeling plans, you can create spaces that work better for everyone who lives in or visits your home, regardless of their size, age, or ability.

Universal design is simply good design that improves everyday situations. For example, wide doorways make passage easier for a person carrying a load of laundry as well as for someone in a wheelchair; a lowered countertop enables a child to help prepare dinner and allows a person who tires easily to sit while cooking. More a way of thinking than a set of rules, universal design can be applied to any area of your home—from room layouts to light fixtures to door hardware. In all cases, universal design encourages independence by creating a safe, comfortable environment.

Many people take on remodeling projects to accommodate changes in their households. Perhaps you are remodeling because your aging parents are coming to live with you or your grown children or grandchildren

are coming for an extended visit. Or you may be preparing your home for your own retirement years. Considering both your current and future needs is an essential part of a fundamental universal design concept: creating a lifespan home—one that accommodates its residents throughout their lives. A lifespan home enables your aging parents to live comfortably with you now and will allow you to stay in your home as you grow older. And, while universal design makes your everyday life easier, it will also make your home more appealing to a wide range of potential buyers if you choose to sell.

Much of the universal design information in this book comes from universal design specialists, kitchen and bath designers, physical therapists, specialty builders and manufacturers, and organizations such as the National Kitchen and Bath Association (NKBA). Some suggestions are ADA (Americans with Disabilities Act) requirements; while these generally apply to public spaces, they often are used as guidelines for residential design. As always, be sure that all aspects of your project meet local code requirements.

For more help with planning with universal design, contact a qualified professional. Many kitchen and bath designers, home builders, and product manufacturers specialize in universal design.

REMODELING CASE STUDIES

Elevation view
of completed two-story bumpout

This two-story room addition is about outdoor spaces as well as indoor spaces. While the new children's bedroom, Jack & Jill bathroom, and family room were the driving reasons for the addition, the covered patio, balcony, and spa terrace proved to be the real gems created by the project.

Side view of completed two-story bump-out

From the side or from the rear, this carefully planned and meticulously executed room addition meets one of the key tests many designers would put to it: does it look like it has always been there?

Interior view of completed two-story bumpout

A pair of windows in the remodeled master bathroom looks out toward the spa area. The master bath repeats the dark wood tones and buff wall colors featured on the exterior of the house and addition.

REMODELING CASE STUDIES

Side view of completed wing addition

Filled with light-gathering windows, this addition visually opens up an older brick home, modernizing without corrupting the existing historic architecture. The distinctive steel roof effectively unifies the two structures despite different siding styles.

Front view of completed wing addition

The glass-fronted facade of the addition comes to life at night with a cheery, welcoming glow. The planning stage of any addition should consider all aspects, all exposures at all times.

Interior view no. 1
of wing addition

One of the advantages of an addition is that it allows you to incorporate small luxuries you've dreamed about over time, like the light-soaked window seat shown here.

Interior view no. 2
of wing addition

This addition's abundant windows not only let light in, they also exploit the spectacular views surrounding this secluded home. Window placement is key to effectively planning a successful addition.

WORKING SAFELY

Your personal safety when working on carpentry projects depends greatly on what safety measures you take. The power tools sold today offer many safety features, such as blade guards, locks to prevent accidental starts, and double insulation to reduce the risk of shock in the event of a short circuit. It's up to you to take advantage of these safety features. For example, never operate a saw with the blade guard removed. You risk injury from flying debris as well as from being cut by the blade.

Follow all precautions outlined in the owner's manuals for your tools and make sure you protect yourself with safety glasses, earplugs, and a dust mask or respirator to filter out dust and debris.

Keep your work environment clean. A cluttered work area is more likely to result in accidents. Clean your tools and put them away at the end of every work period, and sweep up dust and debris.

Some materials emit dangerous fumes or particles. Keep such materials stored away from heat sources and out of the reach of children; always use these products in a well-ventilated area.

Maintaining safety is an ongoing project. Take the time to update your first-aid kit and evaluate your workspace, tools, and safety equipment on a regular basis. To avoid accidents, repair and replace old and worn-out parts before they break.

Read the owner's manual before operating any power tool. Your tools may differ in many ways from those described in this book, so it's best to familiarize yourself with the features and capabilities of the tools you own. Always wear eye and ear protection when operating a power tool. Wear a dust mask when the project will produce dust.

Some walls may contain asbestos. Many homes built or remodeled between 1930 and 1950 have older varieties of insulation that included asbestos. Consult a professional for removal of hazardous pollutants like asbestos, and if you find asbestos or materials that may contain asbestos, do not attempt to remove them on your own. Even if you determine that no asbestos is present, it is a good idea to wear a particle mask and other safety gear when doing demolition.

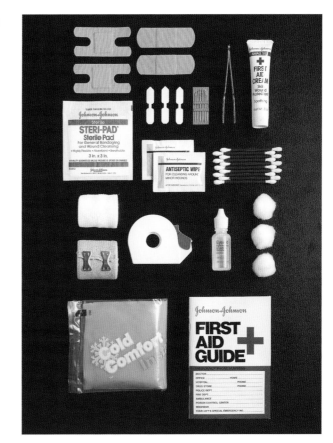

FIRST-AID KITS

Assemble a first-aid kit. Cuts from hand or power tools can be serious and require prompt and thoughtful attention. Be prepared for such situations with a well-equipped first-aid kit that is easy to find. Record any emergency telephone numbers on the first-aid kit or by the nearest phone so they are available in an emergency.

Equip your kit with a variety of items (photo right), including bandages, needles, tweezers, antiseptic ointment, cotton swabs, cotton balls, eye drops, a first-aid handbook, a chemical-filled cold pack, elastic bandages, first-aid tape, and sterile gauze.

For puncture wounds, cuts, burns, and other serious injuries, always seek medical attention as soon as first aid—such as washing and wrapping of cuts—has been provided.

SAFE PRACTICES

Keep your tools sharp and clean. Accidents are more likely when blades are dull and tools are filled with sawdust and dirt.

Use a GFCI receptacle, adapter, or extension cord to reduce the risk of shock while operating a power tool outdoors or in wet conditions.

Check with a neon circuit tester to make sure the power is off before removing cover plates, exposing wires, or drilling or cutting into walls that contain wiring.

23

TOOLS & MATERIALS

Building shelves and built-ins is a challenging job that requires patience, attention to detail, and the right tool for each task. Without these basic requirements, the work will be more difficult and the results will suffer.

Start off right by using high-quality tools. Good tools last longer and are generally more accurate than less expensive versions.

Many people buy tools only as they are needed to avoid purchases they will not use. This rationale should only apply to power tools and higher-priced specialty items. A high-quality basic tool set is important for every do-it-yourselfer to have on hand. Doing so avoids improper tool usage and makes your job easier, with improved results.

The hand tools you will need for most finish carpentry jobs can be broken down into two types: layout tools and construction tools. It is common for most people to own construction tools, but to lack necessary layout tools for basic carpentry jobs. Purchase the highest-quality layout tools you can afford. They are crucial for helping you avoid costly measuring and marking mistakes.

LAYOUT TOOLS

Layout tools help you measure, mark, and set up perfect cuts with accuracy. Many layout tools are inexpensive and simply provide a means of measuring for level, square, and plumb lines. However, recent technologies have incorporated lasers into levels, stud finders, and tape measures, making them more accurate than ever before, though at a slightly higher price. Although these new tools are handy in specific applications, their higher price is not always warranted for the do-it-yourselfer.

- **A tape measure** is one of the most common tools around. The odds are good that you already own at least one. (If you are making frequent trips for building supplies, invest in a second tape that stays in your car.) Carpentry projects require a sturdy tape measure with a length greater than your longest stock. A 25-foot tape measure has a wider and thicker reading surface than a 16-foot variety, but either is adequate for most carpentry jobs. If you can't tell the difference between the smaller lines on a standard tape, consider

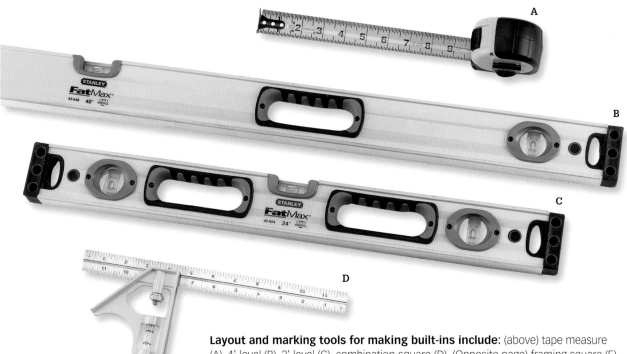

Layout and marking tools for making built-ins include: (above) tape measure (A), 4' level (B), 2' level (C), combination square (D). (Opposite page) framing square (E), chalk line (F), stud finder/laser level (G), T-bevel (H), profile gauge (I).

purchasing an "Easy Read" variety. It is important to read the tape accurately.

- **A framing square,** also known as a carpenter's square, is commonly used to mark wood for cutting and to check for square. Framing squares are also used for laying out stairs and rafters.

- **Chalk lines** are used to make temporary straight lines anywhere one is needed. The case of a chalk line, or the "box," is teardrop-shaped so that the tool can double as a plumb bob. Use a chalk line to mark sheet goods for cutting or to establish a level line in a room. Keep in mind that chalk can be difficult to remove from porous surfaces.

- **A stud finder** is used to locate the framing members in a wall or ceiling. Higher-priced versions also locate plumbing, electrical, or other mechanicals in the wall. Although stud finders are not completely necessary, they are convenient for larger jobs.

- **Levels** are available in a variety of lengths and price ranges. The longer and more accurate the level, the higher the price. The two most commonly used sizes are 2-foot and 4-foot lengths. A 2-foot level is handy for tight spaces, while the 4-foot variety serves as a better all-purpose level. Laser levels are handy for creating a level line around the perimeter of a room or for establishing level lines over longer lengths. They provide a wide range of line or spot placement, depending on the model.

- **A T-bevel** is a specialized tool for finding and transferring angles precisely. T-bevels are generally used in conjunction with a power miter saw to find the angle of non-square corners. This tool is especially handy in older homes where the original states of square, plumb, and level may no longer apply.

- **A profile gauge** uses a series of pins to recreate the profile of any object so that you may transfer it to a work piece. Profile gauges are especially useful when scribing to an irregular wall.

- **A combination square** is a multifunction square that provides an easy reference for 45- and 90-degree angles, as well as marking reveal lines or a constant specific distance from the edge of a work piece.

CONSTRUCTION TOOLS

- **A good quality hammer** is a must for every carpentry project. A 16-ounce curved claw hammer, otherwise known as a finish hammer, is a good all-purpose choice. Some people prefer a larger straight claw hammer for heavy tear-down projects and rough framing, but these hammers are too clumsy and heavy for driving smaller casing and finish nails, and tend to mar the surface of trim.

- **Utility knives** are available with fixed, folding, or retractable blades. This tool is used for a wide variety of cutting tasks from cutting drywall to back-beveling miter joints. Always have additional blades readily available. Folding fixed-blade utility knives offer the durability and strength of a fixed blade with the protection of a folding handle.

- **A set of chisels** is necessary for installing door hardware as well as notching trim around obstacles and final fitting of difficult pieces. Keep a set only for use with wood, and do not use them for screwdrivers or demolition.

- **Block planes** are used to fit doors into openings and remove fine amounts of material from trim. A finely tuned block plane can even be used to clean up a sloppy miter joint.

- **A coping saw** has a thin, flexible blade designed to cut curves, and is essential for making professional trim joints on inside corners. Coping saw blades should be fine toothed, between 16 and 24 teeth per inch for most hardwoods, and set to cut on the pull stroke of the saw to offer you more blade control.

- **A sharp handsaw** is convenient for quick cut-offs and in some instances where power saws are difficult to control. Purchase a crosscut saw for general-purpose cutting.

- **Protective wear,** including safety glasses and ear protection, is required any time you are working with tools. Dust masks are necessary when sanding, doing demolition, or when working around fumes.

- **Pry bars** come in a variety of sizes and shapes. A quality forged high-carbon steel flat bar is the most common choice. Wrecking bars make lighter work of trim and door removal due to their added weight. No matter what type of pry bar you use, protect finished surfaces from scratches with a block of wood when removing trim.

- **Side cutters and end nippers** are useful for cutting off and pulling out bent nails. The added handle length and curved head of end nippers makes them ideal for pulling larger casing nails. Pneumatic brad nails and smaller pins will pull out easier with side cutters. Purchase a nail set for countersinking nail heads. Three-piece sets are available for different nail sizes.

- **A rasp and metal file set** is important for fitting coped joints precisely. The variety of shapes, sizes, and mills allow for faster rough removal of material, or smoother slow removal, depending on the file.

- **Use a putty knife** to fill nail holes with wood filler and for light scraping tasks.

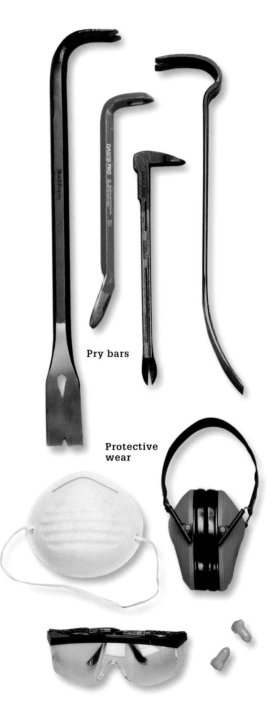

Pry bars

Protective wear

Handsaws

Putty knife

Nail sets

Utility knives

Hammer

Coping saw

Rasp and metal file set

Side cutters and end nippers

Block plane

Chisels

Compound power
miter saw

Circular saw

Jigsaw

Reciprocating saw

Cordless drill

POWER TOOLS

Despite the higher price as compared to hand tools, power tools are a great value. They allow you to work more quickly and accurately than with hand tools and make repetitive tasks like sanding, drilling, and sawing more enjoyable. Basic home carpentry does not require every power tool shown here, but some tools, such as a power miter box, are crucial for professional results. Purchase power tools on an as-needed basis, keeping in mind that while the cheapest tool is not always your best option, the most expensive and powerful is probably not necessary, either. Cheaper tools generally sacrifice precision, while the most expensive tools are made for people who use them every day, not just occasionally.

- **A cordless drill** is one of the handiest tools available. Although drills are not normally used to install trim, they make quick work of installing structural components. Occasionally, trim-head screws are used to install trim, in metal studs, or where extra holding power is needed.
- **A circular saw** is ideal for straight cuts in plywood and quick cut-offs of solid material. Purchase a plywood blade to make smooth cuts in plywood, and a general-purpose blade for other cuts.
- **A jigsaw** is the perfect tool for cutting curves, or notching out trim around obstructions. Jigsaw blades come in an array of designs for different styles of cuts and different types and thicknesses of materials. Always use the right type of blade and do not force the saw during the cut or it may bend or break.

Router

Random orbit sander

Biscuit joiner

Power planer

Finish sander

Belt sander

Tablesaw

- **A biscuit joiner** (also called a plate joiner) is a specialty tool used with glue and biscuits to make strong joints between two pieces of stock.
- **A reciprocating saw** is used for removal and tear-down applications. This tool is especially handy for removing door jambs.
- **A compound power miter saw** will yield professional results. Most have a 10- or 12-inch-diameter blade. A compound power miter saw has a head that pivots to cut both bevels and miters. Sliding miter saws have more cutting capacity but are less portable. A fine-tooth carbide-tipped blade is best for built-in and shelving projects.
- **A belt sander** is not essential but is a handy tool for quick removal of material.
- **Random-orbit sanders** are a good choice for smoothing flat areas, such as plywood, quickly.

Random-orbit sanders don't leave circular markings as disc sanders do, and can sand in any direction regardless of wood grain.

- **Finish sanders** are available in a variety of sizes and shapes for different light sanding applications.
- **A power planer** is used to trim doors to fit openings and flatten or straighten out materials. Power planers are faster to use than manual hand planes, but the results are more difficult to control.
- **A tablesaw** is the best tool for ripping stock to width, and larger models can be fitted with a molding head for cutting profiles.
- **A router** (plunge router is shown here) has many uses in trim carpentry, especially for cutting edge profiles to make your own custom woodwork.

WALL, CEILING & TRIM PROJECTS

Work on walls, ceilings, and trim often comprises essential skills for many major construction-based remodeling projects, some of which will be presented later in this book. You will likely refer to this chapter many times in the course of completing the later projects, and many of the projects here qualify as full-fledged remodeling projects all on their own. Nothing refreshes a home like replacing old trim moldings that were original to your home with new, stylish moldings. Adding some trim flourishes to walls and ceilings where none exist can radically transform the look of your home, making it seem new almost overnight. Removing a wall can create the much-desired "open concept" layout, while framing new walls complete with window and door openings as part of a major basement or attic remodeling or as part of a structural room addition can help add valuable living space to your home, greatly increasing both its functionality and market value.

Pick and choose among these projects at your leisure, or refer back to this chapter for the skills and finishing touches you need for major remodeling projects.

IN THIS CHAPTER:

- Molding Profiles
- Building Walls
- Building a Wet Wall
- Installing Interior Doors
- Installing a Prehung Interior Door
- Framing Basement Foundation Walls
- Removing a Non-Load-Bearing Wall
- Archways
- Preformed Domes
- Soundproofing a Room
- Stool & Apron Window Trim
- Arts & Crafts Casing
- Basement Window Trim
- Basic Casing
- Built-Up Chair Rail
- Built-Up Crown Molding
- Polymer Crown
- Wall Frame Moldings
- Wainscot Frames
- Coffered Ceilings
- Ceiling Medallions
- Jointless Rail-and-Stile Wainscot
- Raised-Panel Wainscot
- Crown Molding
- Decorative Door Header
- Built-Up Base Molding

MOLDING PROFILES

Trim moldings in stock profiles are available off the shelf at most home centers. Most molding manufacturers assign codes such as "WM166," or "HWM127" to every profile and size. However, you will find that the codes are not applied uniformly, making them virtually worthless if you're trying to track down specific molding profiles. The best way to order molding is to obtain a catalog from your molding supplier and use its labeling conventions.

There are a few conventions that are fairly consistently applied. In general, moldings labeled with a code starting with "WM" are paint-grade or softwood moldings. "HWM" designates the trim piece as a hardwood molding. If you like the style of a softwood molding, but would prefer to buy the piece in a hardwood species, ask for the equivalent in hardwood from the lumberyard sales associate.

Even though moldings are commonly found under categories such as "baseboard" or "cove," these categories relate to the style of the trim piece, not necessarily where it should be used. In fact, even among seasoned trim carpenters you'll frequently encounter arguments over which type a particular size or profile belongs to. The similarities are especially apparent when comparing base molding to case molding, as the following photos will confirm.

Mini-Glossary of Molding Shapes & Profiles ▸

Bead—A rounded profile

Chamfer—A 45° beveled edge profile

Dentil—A series of rectangular blocks spaced close together to form a border pattern

Flute—A shallow groove with a round profile, usually running longitudinally on the workpiece in groups of at least three

Frieze—Horizontal banding on the wall at the wall-ceiling joint

Ogee—An S-shape or reverse curve profile

Rosette—A square block with concentric circular carving, usually placed at the intersection of head and side casing

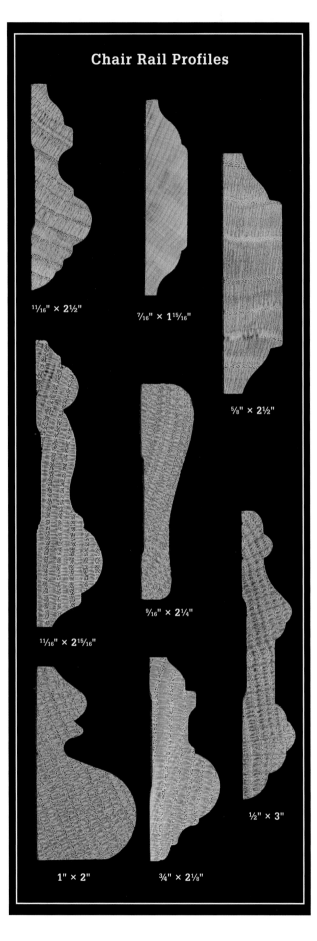

Chair Rail Profiles

$^{11}/_{16}$" × 2½"

$^{7}/_{16}$" × 1$^{15}/_{16}$"

$^{5}/_{8}$" × 2½"

$^{9}/_{16}$" × 2¼"

$^{11}/_{16}$" × 2$^{15}/_{16}$"

½" × 3"

1" × 2"

¾" × 2⅛"

Case Molding Profiles

$\frac{3}{8}$" × $2\frac{11}{16}$" $\frac{3}{8}$" × $2\frac{11}{16}$" $\frac{1}{2}$" × $2\frac{11}{16}$" $\frac{9}{16}$" × $2\frac{1}{2}$" $\frac{11}{16}$" × $2\frac{3}{16}$" $\frac{9}{16}$" × $2\frac{3}{16}$"

$\frac{3}{8}$" × $3\frac{15}{16}$" $\frac{3}{4}$" × $3\frac{1}{4}$" $\frac{11}{16}$" × $3\frac{3}{16}$" $\frac{5}{8}$" × $3\frac{3}{16}$" $\frac{5}{8}$" × $3\frac{7}{16}$" $\frac{9}{16}$" × $3\frac{1}{4}$" $\frac{3}{8}$" × $3\frac{3}{16}$"

Base Molding Profiles

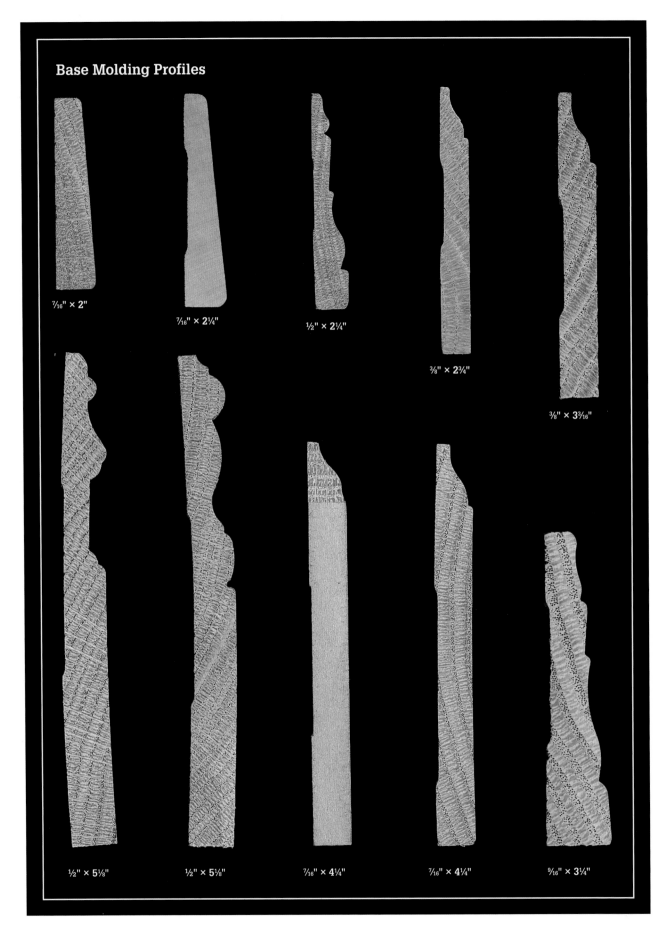

$\frac{7}{16}$" × 2"

$\frac{7}{16}$" × 2$\frac{1}{4}$"

$\frac{1}{2}$" × 2$\frac{1}{4}$"

$\frac{3}{8}$" × 2$\frac{3}{4}$"

$\frac{3}{8}$" × 3$\frac{3}{16}$"

$\frac{1}{2}$" × 5$\frac{1}{8}$"

$\frac{1}{2}$" × 5$\frac{1}{8}$"

$\frac{7}{16}$" × 4$\frac{1}{4}$"

$\frac{7}{16}$" × 4$\frac{1}{4}$"

$\frac{9}{16}$" × 3$\frac{1}{4}$"

Cove Molding Profiles

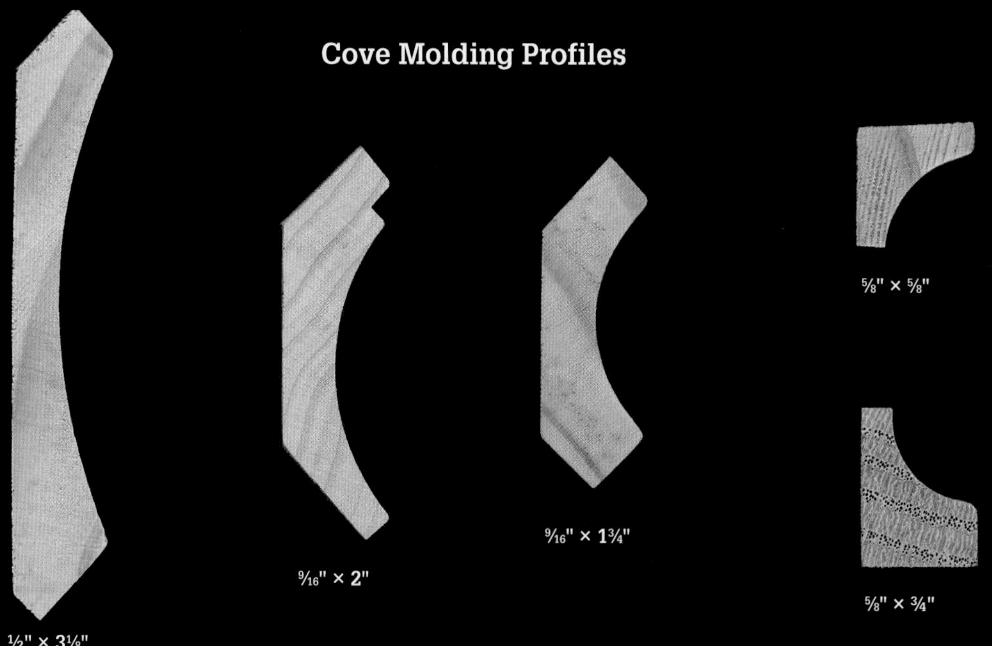
½" × 3⅛"
⁹⁄₁₆" × 2"
⁹⁄₁₆" × 1¾"
⅝" × ⅝"
⅝" × ¾"

Cap Molding Profiles

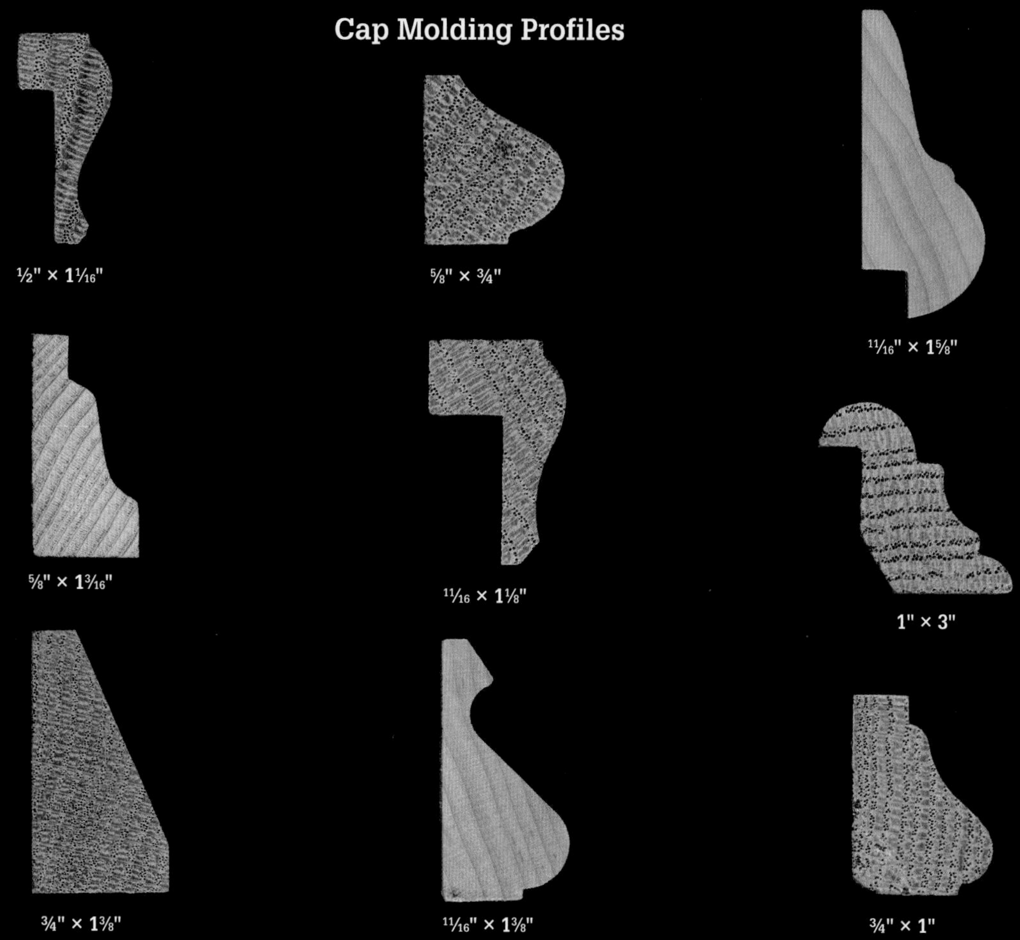
½" × 1¹⁄₁₆"
⅝" × ¾"
¹¹⁄₁₆" × 1⅝"
⅝" × 1³⁄₁₆"
¹¹⁄₁₆ × 1⅛"
1" × 3"
¾" × 1⅜"
¹¹⁄₁₆" × 1⅜"
¾" × 1"

Crown/Bed Molding Profiles

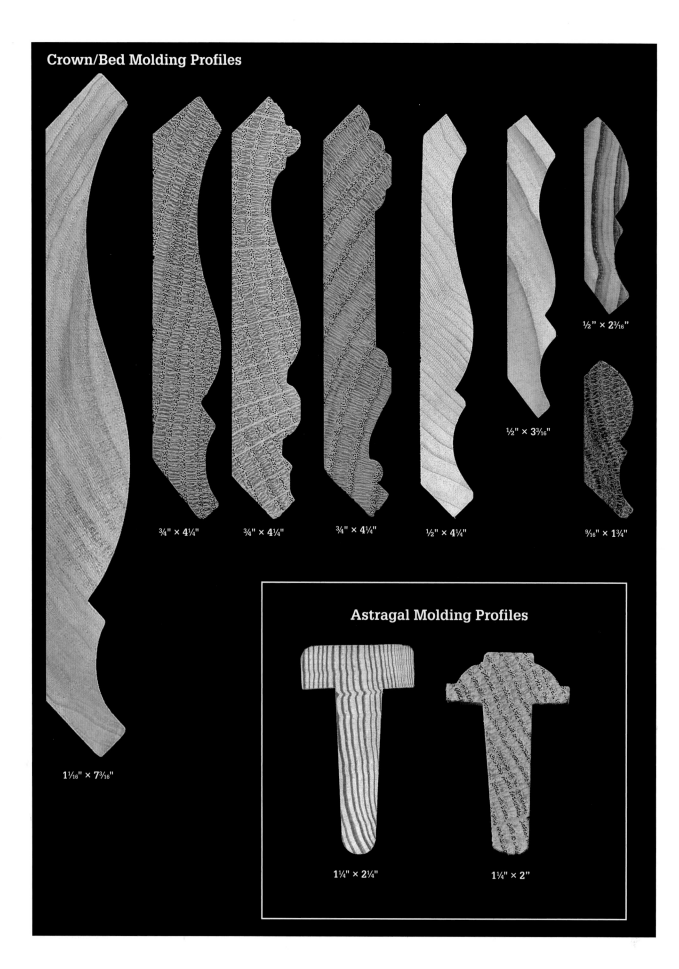

¾" × 4¼"

¾" × 4¼"

¾" × 4¼"

½" × 4¼"

½" × 2³⁄₁₆"

½" × 3³⁄₁₆"

⁹⁄₁₆" × 1¾"

1¹⁄₁₆" × 7³⁄₁₆"

Astragal Molding Profiles

1¼" × 2¼"

1¼" × 2"

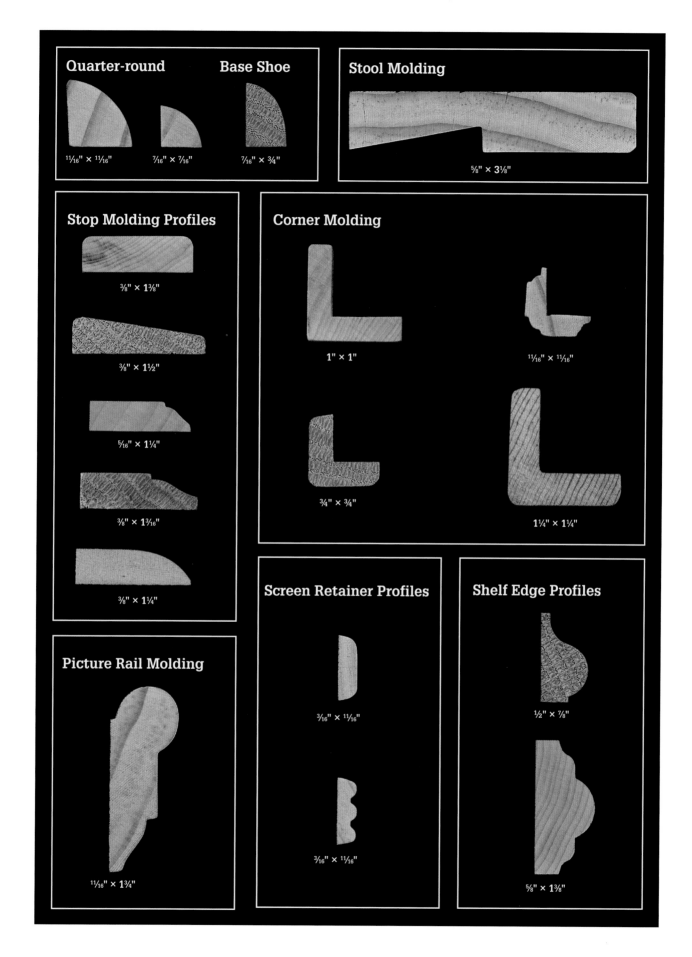

Quarter-round

$\frac{11}{16}$" × $\frac{11}{16}$"

$\frac{7}{16}$" × $\frac{7}{16}$"

Base Shoe

$\frac{7}{16}$" × $\frac{3}{4}$"

Stool Molding

$\frac{5}{8}$" × $3\frac{1}{8}$"

Stop Molding Profiles

$\frac{3}{8}$" × $1\frac{3}{8}$"

$\frac{3}{8}$" × $1\frac{1}{2}$"

$\frac{5}{16}$" × $1\frac{1}{4}$"

$\frac{3}{8}$" × $1\frac{3}{16}$"

$\frac{3}{8}$" × $1\frac{1}{4}$"

Corner Molding

1" × 1"

$\frac{11}{16}$" × $\frac{11}{16}$"

$\frac{3}{4}$" × $\frac{3}{4}$"

$1\frac{1}{4}$" × $1\frac{1}{4}$"

Picture Rail Molding

$\frac{11}{16}$" × $1\frac{3}{4}$"

Screen Retainer Profiles

$\frac{3}{16}$" × $\frac{11}{16}$"

$\frac{3}{16}$" × $\frac{11}{16}$"

Shelf Edge Profiles

$\frac{1}{2}$" × $\frac{7}{8}$"

$\frac{5}{8}$" × $1\frac{3}{8}$"

BUILDING WALLS

Partition walls are constructed between load-bearing walls to divide space. They should be strong and well made, but their main job is to house doors and to support wall coverings.

ANCHORING NEW PARTITION WALLS

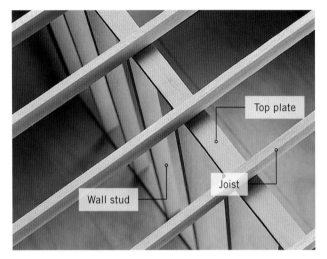

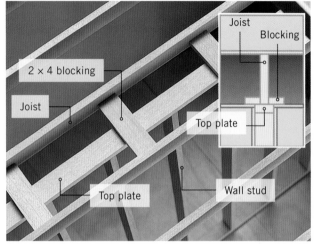

When a new wall is perpendicular to the ceiling or floor joists above, attach the top plate directly to the joists, using 16d nails.

When a new wall falls between parallel joists, install 2 × 4 blocking between the joists every 24". If the new wall is aligned with a parallel joist, install blocks on both sides of the wall, and attach the top plate to the joist (inset).

WALL ANATOMY

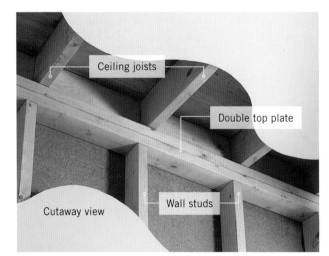

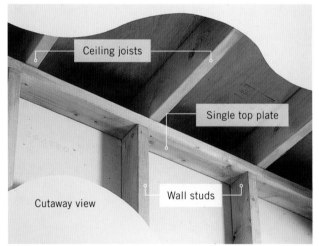

Load-bearing walls carry the structural weight of your home. In platform-framed houses, load-bearing walls can be identified by double top plates made from two layers of framing lumber. Load-bearing walls include all exterior walls and any interior walls that are aligned above support beams.

Partition walls are interior walls that do not carry the structural weight of the house. They have a single top plate and can be perpendicular to the floor and ceiling joists but are not aligned above support beams. Any interior wall that is parallel to floor and ceiling joists is a partition wall.

HOW TO BUILD A NON-LOAD-BEARING PARTITION WALL

1

Mark the location of the new wall on the ceiling, then snap two chalk lines or use a scrap piece of 2× lumber as a template to mark layout lines for the top plate. Use a stud finder to locate floor joists or roof framing above the ceiling, and mark these locations with tick marks or tape outside the layout lines.

2

Cut the top and sole plates to length and lay them side by side. Use a speed square or framing square to draw pairs of lines across both plates to mark the stud locations. Space the studs at 16" intervals, on center.

3

Mark the location of any door framing on the top and sole plates. Refer to the door's rough opening specifications when marking the layout. Draw lines for both the king and jack studs.

4

Fasten the top plate to the ceiling using 3" deck screws or 10d nails. Be sure to orient the plate so the stud layout faces down.

5

Option: Rather than toenailing the studs to the sole plate, some builders prefer to attach them by face-nailing through the underside of the sole plate and into the bottom ends of the walls studs. Then, after the cap plate is installed on the ceiling, they tip the wall up, nail the sole plate in position, and then toenail or toe-screw the studs to the cap plate.

6

Hang a plumb bob from the edge of the top plate at several points along its length to find the sole plate location on the floor. The tip of the plumb bob should almost touch the floor. Wait until it stops moving before marking the sole plate reference point. Connect the points with a line to establish one edge of the sole plate. Use a piece of scrap 2× material as a template for marking the other edge. (continued)

7

Drive the fasteners into the floor framing. For concrete floors, attach the sole plate with a powder-actuated nail gun or with hardened masonry screws. Cut out and remove a section of sole plate in the door opening or openings, if any (see page 50).

8

Measure the distance between the top and sole plates at several places along the wall to determine the stud lengths. The stud length distance may vary, depending on structural settling or an out-of-flat floor. Add ⅛" to the stud length(s), and cut them to size. The extra length will ensure a snug fit between the wall plates.

9

Fasten the end wall studs to adjoining walls. If the new studs do not fall at stud locations, you'll need to install blocking in the old walls.

10

Nail the king studs, jack studs, a header, and a cripple stud in place to complete the rough door framing. See page 49 for more information on framing a door opening. (Inset) An option for attaching wall studs to plates is to use metal connectors and 4d nails.

11

If building codes in your area require fire blocking, install 2× cutoff scraps between the studs, 4' from the floor, to serve this purpose. Stagger the blocks so you can endnail each piece.

12

Drill holes through the studs to create guide holes for wiring and plumbing. When this work is completed, fasten metal protector plates over these areas to prevent drilling or nailing through wiring and pipes later. Have your work inspected before proceeding with drywall.

Joining Sections Using Steel Studs ▸

Steel studs and tracks have the same basic structure—a web that spans two flanged sides—but, studs also contain a ¼" lip to improve their rigidity.

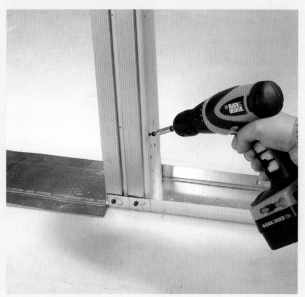

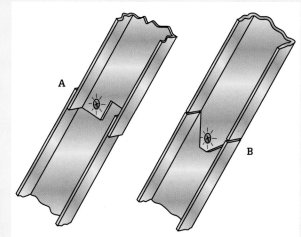

Join sections with a spliced joint (A) or notched joint (B). Make a spliced joint by cutting a 2" slit in the web of one track. Slip the other track into the slit and secure with a screw. For a notched joint, cut back the flanges of one track and taper the web so it fits into the other track; secure with a screw.

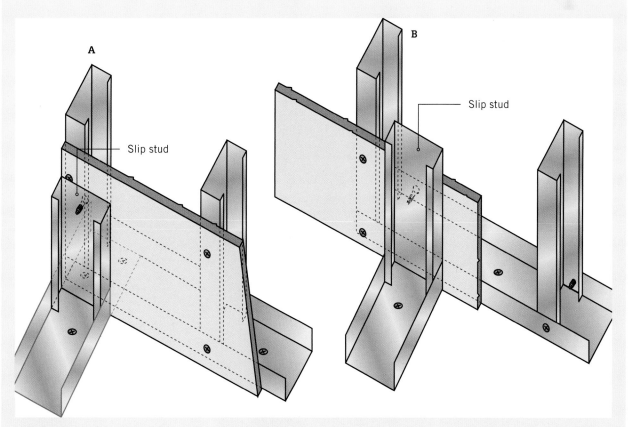

Slip stud

Slip stud

Build corners using a slip stud: A slip stud is not fastened until the adjacent drywall is in place. Form L-shaped corners (A) by overlapping the tracks. Cut off the flange on one side of one track, removing enough to allow room for the overlapping track and drywall. Form a T-shaped corner (B) by leaving a gap between the tracks for the drywall. Secure each slip stud by screwing through the stud into the tracks of the adjacent wall. Also screw through the back side of the drywall into the slip stud, if possible. Where there's no backing behind the slip stud, drive screws at a 45° angle through the back corners of the slip stud and into the drywall.

BUILDING A WET WALL

A wet wall is simply a wall that contains plumbing for water supply and drainage. To accommodate the drain and vent pipes, which range from 1½ to 3 inches in diameter for branch lines, the wall framing needs to be built with 2 × 6 or larger dimensional lumber. You can also attach furring strips (usually 2 × 2) to existing 2 × 4 framing members to increase wall thickness. The chart on the next page describes how deeply you are allowed to notch wall framing members under various load conditions, as well as the maximum-diameter holes you may drill for running plumbing and wiring.

Building a new wet wall or converting an existing wall to house new plumbing requires a building permit and an on-site inspection once all of the hook-ups are made. Do not install any wallcoverings until after your plumbing and wiring have been inspected and approved.

Tools & Materials ▸

Circular saw
Wrecking bar or pry bar
Drill/driver
Caulk gun and adhesive
Hammer
8d common nails

Masking tape
Hole saw
Jigsaw
Basic plumbing tools
Reciprocating saw
Protective plates

Plumbing pipes and hangers
Dust mask
Goggles
Gloves
Ear protection

Maximum Hole & Notch Chart ▸

FRAMING MEMBER	MAXIMUM HOLE SIZE	MAXIMUM NOTCH SIZE
2 × 4 load-bearing stud	1⁷⁄₁₆" diameter	⁷⁄₈" deep
2 × 4 non-load-bearing stud	2½" diameter	1⁷⁄₁₆" deep
2 × 6 load-bearing stud	2¼" diameter	1⅜" deep
2 × 6 non-load-bearing stud	3⁵⁄₁₆" diameter	2³⁄₁₆" deep
2 × 6 joists	1½" diameter	⁷⁄₈" deep
2 × 8 joists	2⅜" diameter	1¼" deep
2 × 10 joists	3¹⁄₁₆" diameter	1½" deep
2 × 12 joists	3¾" diameter	1⅞" deep

The framing member chart shows the maximum sizes for holes and notches that can be cut into studs and joists when running pipes. Where possible, use notches rather than bored holes, because pipe installation is usually easier. When boring holes, there must be at least ⅝" of wood between the edge of a stud and the hole, and at least 2" between the edge of a joist and the hole. Joists can be notched only in the end ⅓ of the overall span; never in the middle ⅓ of the joist. When two pipes are run through a stud, the pipes should be stacked one over the other, never side by side.

Sizing for Water Distribution Pipes ▸

FIXTURE	UNIT RATING
Toilet	3
Vanity sink	1
Shower	2
Bathtub	2
Dishwasher	2
Kitchen sink	2
Clothes washer	2
Utility sink	2
Sillcock	3

SIZE OF SERVICE PIPE FROM STREET	SIZE OF DISTRIBUTION PIPE FROM WATER METER	MAXIMUM LENGTH (FT.)— TOTAL FIXTURE UNITS					
		40	60	80	100	150	200
¾"	½"	9	8	7	6	5	4
¾"	¾"	27	23	19	17	14	11
¾"	1"	44	40	36	33	28	23
1"	1"	60	47	41	36	30	25
1"	1¼"	102	87	76	67	52	44

Water distribution pipes are the main pipes extending from the water meter throughout the house, supplying water to the branch pipes leading to individual fixtures. To determine the size of the distribution pipes, you must first calculate the total demand in "fixture units" (above, left) and the overall length of the water supply lines, from the street hookup through the water meter and to the most distant fixture in the house. Then, use the second table (above, right) to calculate the minimum size for the water distribution pipes.

Sizes for Branch Pipes & Supply Tubes ▸

FIXTURE	MIN. BRANCH PIPE SIZE	MIN. SUPPLY TUBE SIZE
Toilet	½"	⅜"
Vanity sink	½"	⅜"
Shower	½"	½"
Bathtub	½"	½"
Dishwasher	½"	½"
Kitchen sink	½"	½"
Clothes washer	½"	½"
Utility sink	½"	½"
Sillcock	¾"	N.A.
Water heater	¾"	N.A.

TYPE OF PIPE	PIPE SUPPORT INTERVALS	
	VERTICAL-RUN SUPPORT INTERVAL	HORIZONTAL-RUN SUPPORT INTERVAL
Copper	10'	6'
PEX	5'	3'
CPVC	10'	3'
PVC	10'	4'
Steel	12'	10'
Iron	15'	5'

Branch pipes are the water supply lines that run from the distribution pipes toward the individual fixtures. Supply tubes are the vinyl, chromed copper, or braided tubes that carry water from the branch pipes to the fixtures.

Minimum intervals for supporting pipes are determined by the type of pipe and its orientation in the system. Remember that the measurements shown above are minimum requirements.

HOW TO BUILD & PLUMB A WET WALL

1

Clear the work area. If you are remodeling an existing wall to contain plumbing for a new kitchen or bathroom, you'll need to completely remove the wall coverings so you can fur out the wall studs. This project requires a building permit and at least one on-site inspection. Shut off power at the main service panel before cutting into walls.

2

Begin removing wallcoverings on the entire wall. There are many ways to go about this. One is to set your circular saw to a cutting depth equal to the wallcovering thickness and make a few starter cuts. Remove any cover plates on the wall before you start.

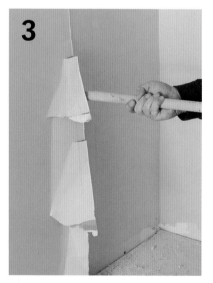

3

Next, use a wrecking bar to pry the wallcovering loose. Work in sections that are large, but manageable. Discard the material you remove immediately.

4

Remove old drywall screws or nails that remain in the wall-framing members.

Cut 2 × 2 furring strips to length. Start with the sole plate of the wall. Apply a bead of construction adhesive to the 2 × 2.

Attach the furring strips to the wall framing members with 8d finish or casing nails. Drive a nail every 12 to 16".

Install the vertical furring strips next, using nails and construction adhesive. Finally, attach furring strips to the wall cap plate. Re-route wiring in the wall according to your plan. If you are keeping receptacles or switches in the same place, you'll still need to move the boxes forward in the wall cavity so the edges will be flush with the new wall surface.

If you are installing a drain for a tub or shower, mark out the location of the drain onto the subfloor. Remove floorcoverings first. Mark a center point for the drainage pipe onto the sole plate. The pipe should align with the location for the drain trap. If your plan calls for it, drill additional holes for fixture drains, such as the wall sink stub-out being installed in this wall.

Drill holes for the drain pipes using a hole saw that's slightly larger than the outside diameter of the new pipe. In most cases, a 2"-dia. pipe is adequate for this type of branch drain (see table, page 43), so a 2½" hole saw is a good choice.

Feed sections of drain pipe up through the holes in the sole plate and floor (if you are tying in to the plumbing on the floor below—the easiest way to tap into the existing plumbing system). Connect the drain line to a drainage stack, maintaining a slope of at least ¼" per ft. It is always a good idea to include a cleanout on the new branch line. (continued)

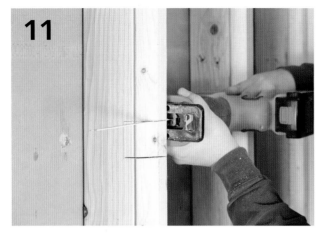

11

Cut notches in the wall-framing members to hold the horizontal plumbing in the drain lines. See chart on page 43. Cut no deeper than needed to hold the pipes.

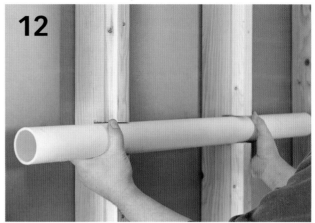

12

Cut the horizontal lines to length and set them into the notches. You can hold them in place with tape if they don't stay put.

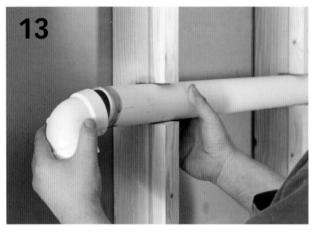

13

Attach a 90° elbow to the end of the new horizontal line so it aligns with the drain pipe coming up through the floor. The other end of horizontal pipe is fitted with a tee fitting so the vent line can be extended up through the cap plate and ceiling.

14

With the drain pipes seated in the fitting below the floor (but not cemented), mark the free ends of the vertical pipes for cutting at the points where they will join the fittings on the horizontal line. Dry-fit this union. Do not cement yet.

15

Remove the subfloor in the section you've laid out for the drain. Cut with a jigsaw, using a starter hole if you need to. If you've planned the drain location wisely it will not fall over a floor joist.

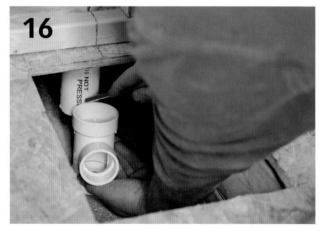

16

Reach into the hole in the subfloor and mark the vertical pipe for cutting to accept a tee fitting. The tee should have a slight sweep downward. Normally, the open end of the tee is sized for a 1½"-dia. drain tube to run from the vertical drain line to the drain trap.

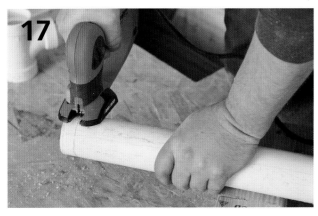

Remove the drain pipes and cut them to the lengths you've marked.

Cement the reducing tee into the drain line for the tub, making sure to orient the sweep correctly and to align the opening with the drain trap location.

Cement a reducing tee into the drain line for the sink stub-out.

Cement the drain lines into the drain fittings from below. Solvent-cement the branch drain line components on the floor below, tying the line into the main drain stack or another large branch drain.

Connect the vent pipe from the wet wall with another vent line in the attic or, if you prefer, run it out through the roof and flash and cover it according to your local plumbing codes.

Install cold and hot water supply lines, connecting from the floor below.

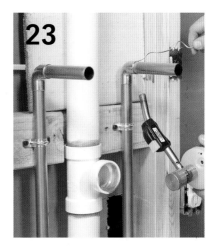

Solder supply stub-outs onto the new water lines. Install protective metal plates on the wall studs to cover pipe (and electrical cable) penetrations. Have your work inspected and, when approved, you may go ahead and install wallcoverings.

INSTALLING INTERIOR DOORS

Creating an opening for a door in a wall involves building a framework about 1 inch wider and ½ inch taller than the door's jamb frame. This oversized opening, called a rough opening, will enable you to position the door easily and shim it plumb and level. Before framing a door, it's always a good idea to buy the door and refer to the manufacturer's recommendations for rough opening size.

Doorframes consist of a pair of full-length king studs and two shorter jack studs that support the header above the door. A header provides an attachment point for wallboard and door casings. On load-bearing walls, it also helps to transfer the building's structural loads from above down into the wall framework and eventually the foundation.

Door framing requires flat, straight, and dry framing lumber, so choose your king, jack, and header pieces carefully. Sight down the edges and ends to look for warpage, and cut off the ends of pieces with splits.

Tools & Materials ▸

Tape measure	10d or pneumatic
Framing square	framing nails
Hammer or nail gun	⅜" plywood (for
Handsaw or	structural headers)
reciprocating saw	Construction adhesive
Framing lumber	Eye and ear protection

Creating a square, properly sized opening for a door is the most important element of a successful door installation project.

HOW TO FRAME A ROUGH OPENING FOR AN INTERIOR PREHUNG DOOR

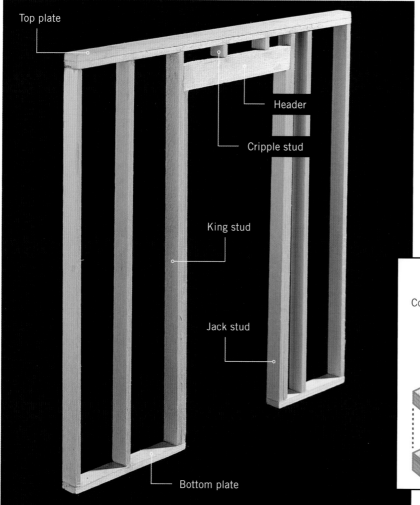

Top plate

Header

Cripple stud

King stud

Jack stud

Bottom plate

Doorframes for prehung doors (left) start with king studs that attach to the top and bottom plates. Inside the king studs, jack studs support the header at the top of the opening. Cripple studs continue the wall-stud layout above the opening. In non-load-bearing walls, the header may be a 2 × 4 laid flat or a built-up header (below). The dimensions of the framed opening are referred to as the rough opening.

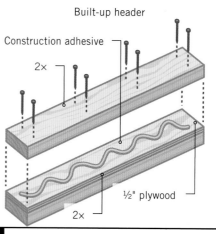

Built-up header

Construction adhesive

2×

½" plywood

2×

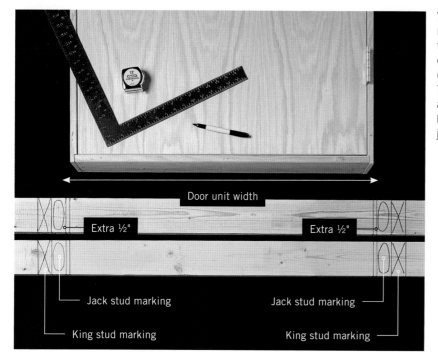

Door unit width

Extra ½"

Extra ½"

Jack stud marking

Jack stud marking

King stud marking

King stud marking

To mark the layout for the doorframe, measure the width of the door unit along the bottom. Add 1" to this dimension to determine the width of the rough opening (the distance between the jack studs). This gives you a ½" gap on each side for adjusting the doorframe during installation. Mark the top and bottom plates for the jack and king studs.

HOW TO FRAME A PREHUNG INTERIOR DOOR OPENING (LOAD-BEARING)

Door framing on load-bearing walls will require a structural header that transfers loads above the wall into the jack studs, sole plate, and down into the house foundation. Build it by sandwiching a piece of ½" plywood between two 2 × 4s. Use construction adhesive and nails to fasten the header together.

Mark layout lines for the king and jack studs on the wall's top and sole plates (see page 39). Cut the king studs slightly longer than the distance between the wall plates, and toenail them in place with 10d nails or 3" pneumatic nails.

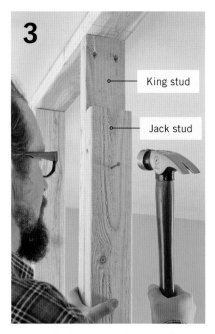

King stud

Jack stud

Cut the jack studs to length (they should rest on the sole plate). The height of a jack stud for a standard interior door is 83½", or ½" taller than the door. Nail the jack studs to the king studs.

Install the built-up header by resting it on the jack studs and endnailing through the king studs. Use 10d nails or 3" pneumatic nails.

Fasten a cripple stud above the header halfway between the king studs for use as a nailing surface.

Cut a sole plate opening for the door with a reciprocating saw or handsaw. Trim the sole plate flush with the jack studs. Install the saw blade teeth-up for better access.

HOW TO FRAME AN OPENING FOR A NON-LOAD-BEARING WALL

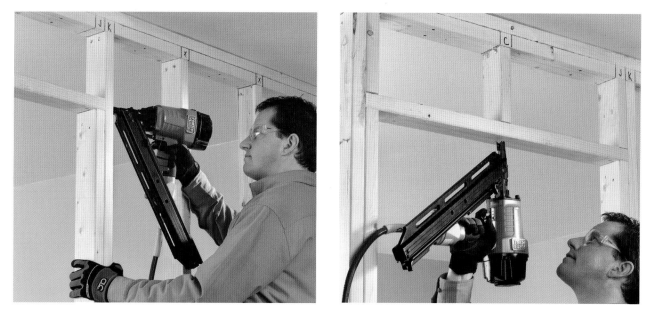

Variation: In a non-load-bearing wall, the header can be a piece of 2× framing lumber that lays flat on top of the jack studs. Cut it to length, and install by endnailing through the king studs or down into the jack studs. Toenail a cripple stud between the top plate and header, halfway between the king studs. It transfers structural loads into the header.

Option: Framing Openings for Sliding & Folding Doors ▸

The same basic framing techniques are used whether you're planning to install a sliding, bifold, pocket, or prehung interior door. The different door styles require different frame openings. You may need to frame an opening two to three times wider than the opening for a standard prehung door. Purchase the doors and hardware in advance, and consult the hardware manufacturer's instructions for the exact dimensions of the rough opening and header size for the type of door you select.

Most bifold doors are designed to fit in an 80"-high finished opening. Wood bifold doors have the advantage of allowing you to trim the doors, if necessary, to fit openings that are slightly shorter.

51

INSTALLING A PREHUNG INTERIOR DOOR

Install prehung interior doors after the framing work is complete and the drywall has been installed. If the rough opening for the door has been framed accurately, installing the door takes about an hour.

Standard prehung doors have 4½-inch-wide jambs and are sized to fit walls with 2 × 4 construction and ½-inch wallboard. If you have 2 × 6 construction or thicker wall surface material, you can special order a door to match, or you can add jamb extensions to a standard-sized door (photo, below).

Tools & Materials ▸

Level
Hammer
Handsaw
Prehung interior door

Wood shims
8d casing nails
Eye and ear protection

Tip: Jamb Extensions ▸

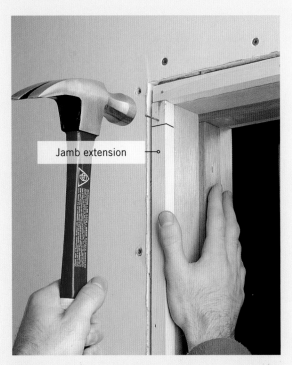

Jamb extension

If your walls are built with 2 × 6 studs, you'll need to extend the jambs by attaching wood strips to the edges of the jamb after the door is installed. Use glue and 4d casing nails when attaching jamb extensions.

HOW TO INSTALL A PREHUNG INTERIOR DOOR

1

Slide the door unit into the framed opening so the edges of the jambs are flush with the wall surface and the hinge-side jamb is plumb.

2

Insert pairs of wood shims driven from opposite directions into the gap between the framing members and the hinge-side jamb, spaced every 12". Check the hinge-side jamb to make sure it is still plumb and does not bow.

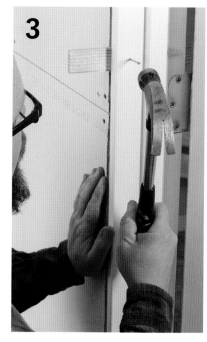

3

Anchor the hinge-side jamb with 8d casing nails driven through the jamb and shims and into the jack stud.

4

Insert pairs of shims in the gap between the framing members and the latch-side jamb and top jamb, spaced every 12". With the door closed, adjust the shims so the gap between door edge and jamb is ⅛" wide. Drive 8d casing nails through the jambs and shims, into the framing members.

5

Cut the shims flush with the wall surface, using a handsaw. Hold the saw vertically to prevent damage to the door jamb or wall. Finish the door and install the lockset as directed by the manufacturer. See pages 73 to 79 to install trim around the door.

FRAMING BASEMENT FOUNDATION WALLS

Tools & Materials ▸

Tape measure	3" deck screws
Plumb bob	10d nails (coated if using
Combination square	treated lumber)
Powder-actuated nailer	or pneumatic
or hammer drill	framing nails
Pneumatic nailer	PAT fasteners
or hammer	or masonry screws
Miter saw or circular saw	Metal protector plates
Staple gun	Rolled insulation
Utility knife	6-mil vapor barrier
Drywall finishing tools	Moisture-resistant
Framing materials	wallboard

You can use conventional wall-framing techniques to turn an unused basement into a warm, inviting living space. Stud walls provide deep bays for insulation and allow you to use ordinary receptacle boxes for wall outlets. Fully framed walls will be stronger than the furring strip method discussed on page 45, and they may be your only option if your basement walls aren't flat and plumb. The downside to framing your basement walls is that the material costs will be greater than using furring strips and foam insulation. Stud walls will also reduce the size of the room, which may be an issue if you have a small basement.

Assembling a stud wall next to a foundation wall is essentially the same process as building a wall elsewhere. However, since there's always the potential for water infiltration through cinder block or poured basement walls, it's a good idea to build your walls about ½ inch away from the foundation to create an airspace. This gap will also be useful for avoiding any unevenness in your foundation walls.

HOW TO FRAME A BASEMENT FOUNDATION WALL

Mark the location of the new wall on the floor joists above, then use a scrap piece of 2 × 4 as a template to draw layout lines for the new top plate. Position the top plate about ½" away from the foundation wall to create an airspace. If the joists run parallel to the foundation wall, nail blocking between them to create attachment points for the new wall.

Hang a plumb bob from the top plate layout lines to mark the sole plate position on the floor. Move the bob along the top plate and mark the sole plate at several points on the floor. Set a piece of scrap 2 × 4 in place on the floor to make sure the sole plate will still allow for an air gap. Draw pairs of lines across both plates with a combination square to mark stud locations.

Fasten the top plate to the floor joists using 3" deck screws or 10d nails (top). Be sure to orient the plate so the stud layout faces down. Attach the sole plate to the concrete floor with a powder-actuated nailer (lower) or with hardened masonry screws. Drill pilot holes for the screws with a hammer drill.

Measure the distance between the top and sole plates at several places along the wall to determine the stud lengths. The stud length distance may vary, depending on structural settling or an out-of-flat floor. Add ⅛" to the stud length(s), and cut them to size.

Toenail the studs in place. Add framing around any basement windows and install fire blocking if local codes require it.

Drill holes through the studs to create raceways for wiring and plumbing. Install these systems and fasten metal protector plates over these areas to prevent drilling or nailing through wiring and pipes later. Have your work inspected before proceeding with insulation and wallboard.

Install rolled insulation in the stud bays. Using plastic encapsulated insulation is a good preventive measure against mold growth. Otherwise, use kraft-faced insulation.

Staple 6-mil plastic sheeting to the wall studs to form a vapor barrier behind the finished wall. Cut holes in the plastic for receptacle openings. *Note: There is considerable debate over whether or not you should employ a vapor barrier on a basement wall, mostly because the barrier can trap water that enters from the exterior. Check with your local building inspector.*

Install your wallcovering of choice. If you choose drywall, finish the seams with drywall compound and tape as usual. Be sure to use moisture-resistant drywall for basement walls (some new drywall products are also mold- and mildew-resistant—ask at your building center).

HOW TO FRAME SOFFITS AND CHASES

Install 2 × 4 blocking between floor joists to form a square framework around the obstruction. Use 3" deck screws to fasten the framework in place.

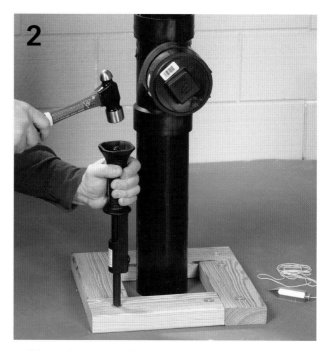

Build another square framework on the floor that matches the size of the top frame. Make this frame from treated lumber, and fasten it to the concrete with a powder-actuated nailer or a hammer drill and masonry screws. Hang a plumb bob down from the top frame to find the exact location of this bottom frame before attaching it.

Toenail four 2 × 4 studs between the two frames to complete the chase framework. Finish the chase with drywall, metal corner bead, and drywall compound.

If the chase encloses a DWV stack or other plumbing with valves or cleanouts, be sure to build an access panel in the chase to keep these areas accessible. Use furring strips or plywood behind two sides of the access opening to form tabs that hold the access panel in place. Attach the panel with screws, and glue on decorative trim to hide the drywall edges.

Where to Use a Soffit ▸

Wall stud

Air duct

Recessed lighting fixture

Fireblocking

Soffit frame

Hide immovable obstructions in a soffit built from dimension lumber or steel and covered with drywall or other finish material. An extra-wide soffit is also a great place to install recessed lighting fixtures.

HOW TO FRAME A FURNACE DUCT

Build a pair of ladder-like frames that match the side dimensions of the furnace duct from standard 2 × 2s. Fasten the parts together with 3" deck screws.

Set the frames against the sides of the duct, and fasten them to the floor joists above with 3" deck screws.

Install 2 × 2 crosspieces between the frames to provide attachment points below the duct for drywall. Then finish the soffit with drywall, metal corner bead, and drywall compound.

WALL, CEILING & TRIM PROJECTS

REMOVING A NON-LOAD-BEARING WALL

Removing an existing interior wall is an easy way to create more usable space without the expense of building an addition. Removing a wall turns two small rooms into a large space perfect for family living. Adding new walls in a larger area creates a private space to use as a quiet study or as a new bedroom.

Be sure the wall you plan to remove is not load bearing before you begin (see page 38). If you need to remove a load-bearing wall, check with a contractor or building inspector first. Load-bearing walls carry the weight of the structure above them. You'll need to install a temporary support wall to take the place of the structural wall you're removing.

Remember that walls also hold the essential mechanical systems that run through your home. You need to consider how your project affects these mechanicals. Turn off electrical power at the service panel before you begin demolition.

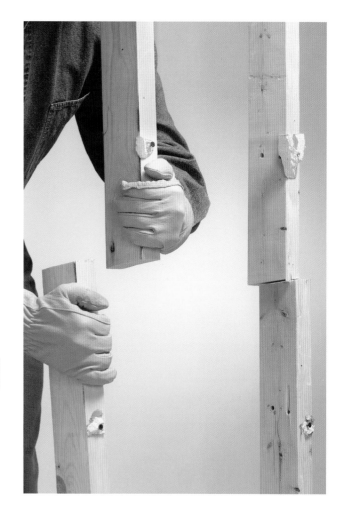

Tools & Materials ▸

Stud finder
Tape measure
Utility knife
Hammer
Pry bars

Reciprocating
   or circular saw
Drill
Eye and ear protection

HOW TO REMOVE A NON-LOAD-BEARING WALL

1

Use a utility knife to score the intersections where the wall you're removing meets the ceiling to keep from damaging it during wall removal. Pry away baseboard trim and remove receptacle plates and switch covers to prepare for demolition.

2

Use the side of a hammer to punch a starter hole in the drywall, then carefully remove the drywall with a pry bar. Try to pull off large sections at a time to minimize dust. Remove any remaining drywall nails or screws from the wall studs.

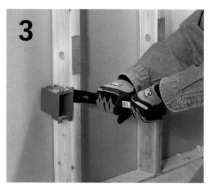

3

Reroute outlets, switches, plumbing, or ductwork. Have professionals do this for you if you are not experienced with these systems or confident in your skills. This work should be inspected after it is completed.

Locate the closest permanent studs on the adjacent wall or walls with a stud finder, and carefully remove the drywall up to these studs. Score the drywall first with a utility knife, then cut through it with a circular saw.

Remove the wall studs by cutting through them in the middle with a reciprocating saw and prying out the upper and lower sections. Remove the endmost studs where the wall meets an adjacent wall or walls.

Cut through the wall's top plate with a circular saw or reciprocating saw. Pry out the top plate sections carefully to avoid damaging the ceiling.

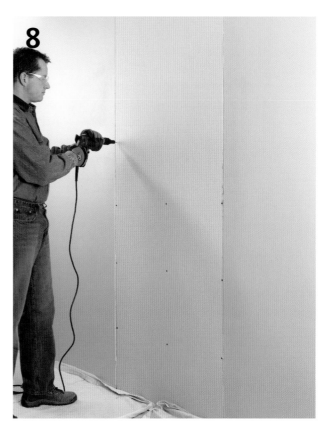

Remove the sole plate just as you did the top plate by cutting through it and prying up the long pieces.

Patch the walls and ceiling with strips of drywall, and repair the floor as needed with new floor coverings.

ARCHWAYS

While an arch may be framed and drywalled on site, polyurethane inserts create a symmetrical arch in the style of your choosing much more easily, making them popular among pros and DIYers alike. This arch was ordered to fit, so no further cutting or fitting was needed. Note that polyurethane products carve and sand like wood, so it's better to run thicker rather than thinner when attempting to match your wall thickness.

Tools & Materials ▸

Work gloves
Eye and ear protection
Framing lumber
Hammer and nails
Drywall panels
Screwgun

Drywall screws
Arch inserts
Panel adhesive
Corner bead
Finishing materials

Where to cut in? ▸

If you are simply adding an arch to an existing passageway, use a hacksaw and utility knife to cut free corner bead in the area that will receive the arch inserts. Prying out bead will leave an indent for tape and mud. Leave enough corner bead at the sides so arch overlaps bead by about ¾".

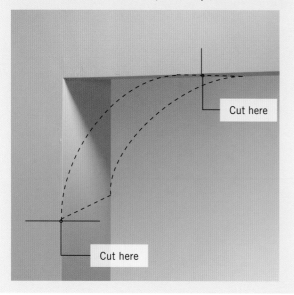

Cut here

Cut here

A framed and drywalled archway divides a large space into smaller, more intimate spaces and makes a dramatic design statement in the process.

HOW TO BUILD AN ARCHWAY

Frame a partition wall with the alcove opening roughed in as a rectangle. Secure the frame so it is plumb and square to the ceiling joists, the adjacent wall studs (if possible), and to the floor.

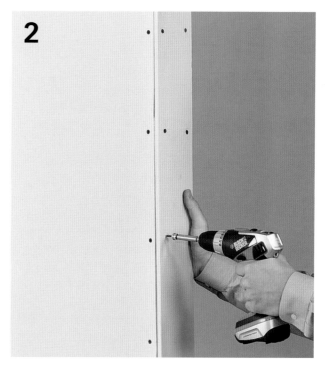

Attach drywall to all surfaces of the framed partition wall except the bottom of the door header. Avoid creating a drywall seam on the king stud.

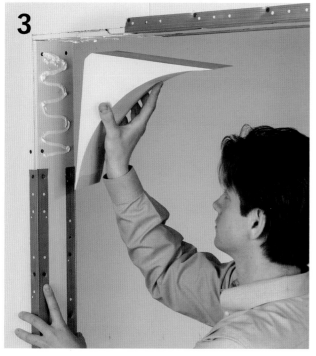

Install corner beads and arches so the arch inserts will overlap the bead by ¾". Typically, arches are secured with panel adhesive and screws.

Tape, fill, and finish all seams, exposed fastener heads, and corners of the partition wall. Trim and finish the arched partition wall to match existing walls.

PREFORMED DOMES

Domes and other three-dimensional features may be ordered preformed. The one we installed here is made of polyurethane. The most difficult and critical steps in dome installation involve the modifications you must make to the ceiling framing. Joists under a roof and the bottom chords of roof trusses are often under tension since the split-leg action of roof rafters pushes out against the walls on which they rest. Joists lower in the building may be supporting tremendous loads that aren't obvious. Therefore, before you cut through structural members, you must have a framing-modification plan drawn up by a qualified structural engineer. In most localities, these drawings need to be approved by a building inspector in order to get a building permit to do the work.

Tools & Materials ▸

Work gloves
Eye and ear protection
Compass
Straightedge
Screwgun
Drywall screws
Framing lumber
Spiral saw
Hole saw
Insulation (if necessary)
Light fixture
Caulk
Finishing materials

A simple domed shape transforms an ordinary ceiling into a grand design statement, especially when the dome is appointed with an attractive ceiling light or chandelier. This Fypon dome is fabricated from urethane foam and installed as one piece.

PREFORMED DOME STYLES

A plain round dome is hard to beat for versatility and ease of installation. This fabricated dome does require that you either remove sections of ceiling joist or create a lower ceiling with a furred-out framework.

Ornate domes add high drama, especially when they include a chandelier or an intricate medallion.

HOW TO INSTALL A PREFORMED DOME

1

Trace the dome onto cardboard in an upside-down position, and transfer four alignment lines onto the outline. Since this outline includes the flange, it's larger than the hole you need to cut in the ceiling.

2

Scribe a second, smaller circle inside the outline by setting a compass or scribe slightly less than the width of the flange and following along the outline. Use a straightedge and marker to connect the opposite alignment marks, forming a cross. Cut out the inside circle to make your template.

3

Screw the cardboard template to the ceiling. The alignment cross may be used to center a round dome or to make an oval dome parallel with a wall. Transfer the alignment marks to the ceiling with a pencil to guide positioning of the domes that are oval or imperfectly round.

4

Cut through the drywall and framing at the edge of the template. Add reenforcement framing as specified by a qualified structural engineer. Add trimmers and blocking to the dome edges at screw locations. Add insulation if necessary, above the dome.

5

Prepare for a fixture box if a light fixture or fan will be hung in the dome. Drill a 1" hole in the center of the dome. Raise framing above the ceiling opening to secure an electric fixture box above the center of the opening. Dome specifications will determine how far to recess the fixture box from the face of the ceiling. Typically, the face of the fixture box should be flush with the finished (visible) face of the dome. You may temporarily attach the dome to help position the fixture box.

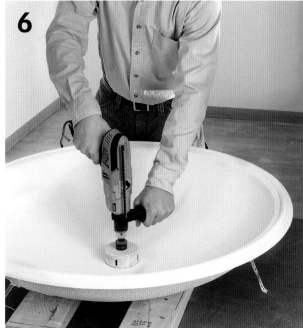

6

Cut a hole for the light fixture wiring in the center of the dome. A hole saw that's slightly bigger than the round electrical fixture box works. For larger or more challenging openings, use a spiral saw to cut the outline of the fixture box in the dome.

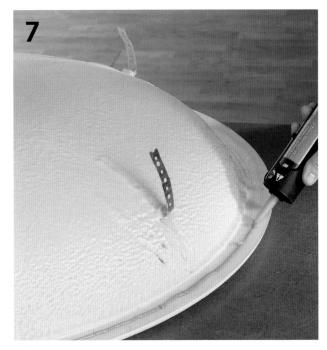

7

Apply polyurethane construction adhesive to the back of the dome flange. Lift the dome into place with helpers, aligning the ceiling and dome alignment marks and fitting the dome around the electrical box. Attach the flange of the dome to the blocking through the ceiling with drywall screws. Countersink the screw heads slightly.

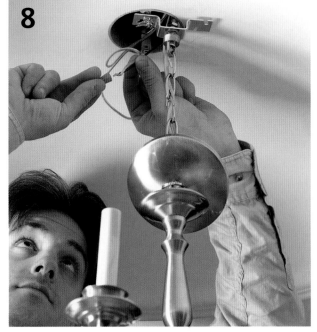

8

Hang your light or fan and caulk all air gaps through and around the fixture box. Caulk the seam where the dome flange meets the ceiling. Cover the fastener heads with joint compound. Finish the dome with ceiling paint.

SOUNDPROOFING A ROOM

Home theaters are quickly becoming a common feature in many homes. And while finding an affordable yet impressive multimedia system is no longer a problem, finding a space within your home to enjoy it may not be so easy. The walls of the average house are not designed to contain extreme sound levels. To combat this issue, there are numerous soundproofing products and materials available to help keep those on both sides of a home theater wall happy.

Engineers rate the soundproofing performance of wall and ceiling assemblies using a system called Sound Transmission Class (STC). Standard partition walls carry STC ratings of 28 to 32. Determining an appropriate STC rating for your home theater is dependent on a number of factors, such as the power of your multimedia system and the type of room opposite the wall. But a minimum of 60 STC is adequate for most. Remember: The higher the STC rating, the more sound is blocked.

But blocking sound is not the only consideration. The low frequencies generated by subwoofers cause vibrations, which in turn create unwanted noise within the room. The most effective approach for soundproofing a home theater is to install both sound barriers to minimize sound escaping and sound absorbers to reduce noise within the room.

Adding mass to walls and ceilings is an effective way to block sound. In new construction, staggered-stud partitions or double stud partitions (two adjacent rows of studs) are possibilities. Hanging soundproofing board, sound-rated drywall, or multiple layers of drywall can increase STC ratings significantly. Two of the most effective systems are resilient channels and mass loaded vinyl (MLV) underlayment, a heavy vinyl sheeting that many manufacturers claim can more than double a wall's STC rating.

For sound absorption, closed-cell acoustical foam matting can be used to insulate between drywall panels and framing. Similarly, padded tape minimizes transmission of sound vibration between wall panels and framing, and can be used to line resilient channels for added insulation. Sound isolation mounting clips contain molded neoprene to provide added insulation between resilient channels and framing. Vibration pads made of cork and closed-cell acoustical foam or neoprene isolate sound vibration to reduce transmission between objects.

When fastening soundproofing and drywall panels to resilient channels, leave a ¼-inch gap between all panels at corners and fill the gaps with acoustical caulk. In fact, all gaps, seams, and cracks should be filled with acoustical caulk. The more airtight a home theater, the more soundproof it is.

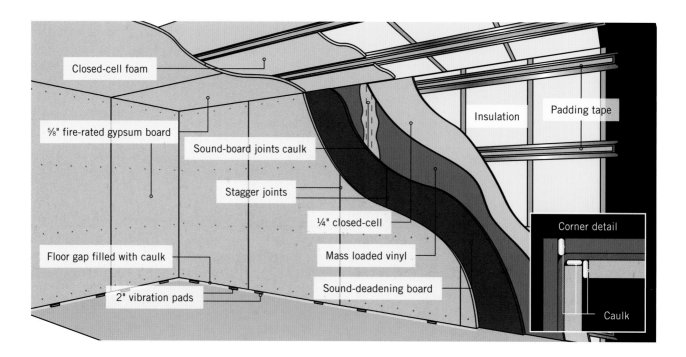

Closed-cell foam

⅝" fire-rated gypsum board

Sound-board joints caulk

Stagger joints

¼" closed-cell

Floor gap filled with caulk

Mass loaded vinyl

2" vibration pads

Sound-deadening board

Insulation

Padding tape

Corner detail

Caulk

SOUNDPROOFING A ROOM

Use contact cement to glue ¼" closed-cell acoustical matting directly to existing wall and ceiling surfaces or to the backside of drywall panels in new construction.

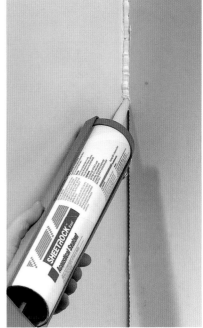

Apply self-adhesive padded tape to resilient channels or directly to the edges of framing members.

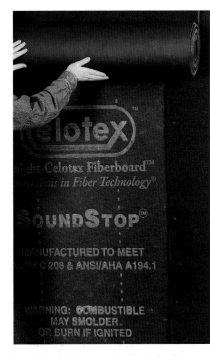

Staple MLV (mass loaded vinyl) underlayment directly to framing members, between layers of drywall and soundproofing board, or directly to existing wall and ceiling surfaces. Overlap seams by at least 6".

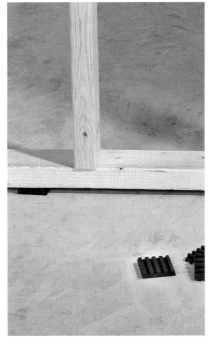

Install 2" vibration pads every 2' between flooring and installed drywall panels. Fasten baseboard into framing only, not into vibration pads.

Seal all gaps between panels and at wall and ceiling joints with acoustical caulk.

STOOL & APRON WINDOW TRIM

S tool and apron trim brings a traditional look to a window and is most commonly used with double-hung styles. The stool serves as an interior sill; the apron (or the bottom casing) conceals the gap between the stool and the finished wall.

In many cases, such as with 2 × 6 walls, jamb extensions made from 1× finish-grade lumber need to be installed to bring the window jambs flush with the finished wall. Many window manufacturers also sell jamb extensions for their windows.

The stool is usually made from 1× finish-grade lumber, cut to fit the rough opening, with "horns" at each end extending along the wall for the side casings to butt against. The horns extend beyond the outer edge of the casing by the same amount that the front edge of the stool extends past the face of the casing, usually under 1 inch.

If the edge of the stool is rounded, beveled, or otherwise decoratively routed, you can create a more finished appearance by returning the ends of the stool to hide the end grain. A pair of miter cuts at the rough horn will create the perfect cap piece for wrapping the grain of the front edge of the stool around the horn. The same can be done for an apron cut from a molded casing.

As with any trim project, tight joints are the secret to a successful stool and apron trim job. Take your time to ensure all the pieces fit tightly. Also, use a pneumatic nailer; you don't want to spend all that time shimming the jambs perfectly only to knock them out of position with one bad swing of a hammer.

The window stool and apron give the window a finished appearance while offering the practical advantage of a window sill.

Safety Tip ▶

Back-cut the ends of casing pieces where needed to help create tight joints, using a sharp utility knife.

Tools & Materials ▶

Tape measure	Pneumatic nailer
Straightedge	(optional)
Circular saw or jigsaw	1× finish lumber
Handsaw, plane, or rasp	Casing
Drill	Wood shims
Hammer	4d, 6d, and 8d finish
Utility knife	nails
Jigsaw	Wood glue
Compass	T-bevel
Combination square	Eye and ear protection

HOW TO INSTALL STOOL & APRON WINDOW TRIM

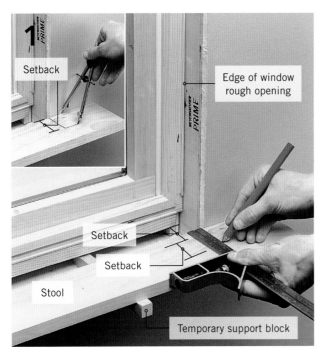

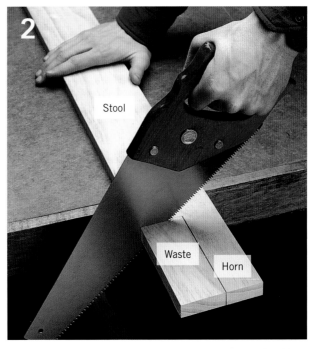

Cut the board for the stool to length, with several extra inches at each end for the horns. Temporarily position the stool in the window opening, pressed against the wall and centered on the window. Use a combination square to measure the setback distance from the window frame to the near edge of the stool. Mark the setback onto the stool at each edge of the window rough opening (if the measurements are different, use the greater setback distance for each end). Then use a compass and pencil to scribe the profile of the wall onto the stool to complete the cutting line for the horn (inset photo).

Cut out the notches to create the stool horns. For straight lines, you can use a large handsaw, but for the scribed line use a more maneuverable saw like the jigsaw or a coping saw. Test-fit the stool, making any minor adjustments with a plane or a rasp so it fits tightly to the window frame and flush against the walls.

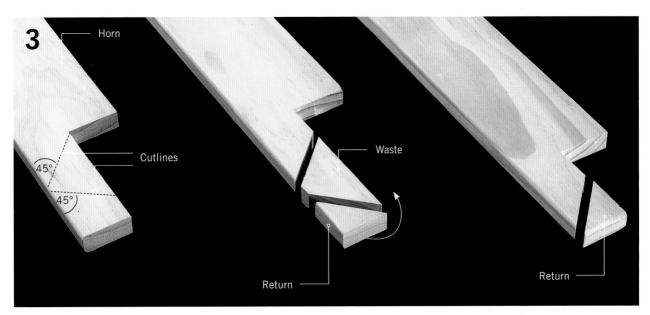

To create a return at the horn of the stool, miter-cut the return pieces at 45° angles. Mark the stool at its overall length and cut it to size with 45° miter cuts. Glue the return to the mitered end of the horn so the grain wraps around the corner. *Note: Use this same technique to create the returns on the apron, but make the cuts with the apron held on edge, rather than flat.*

(continued)

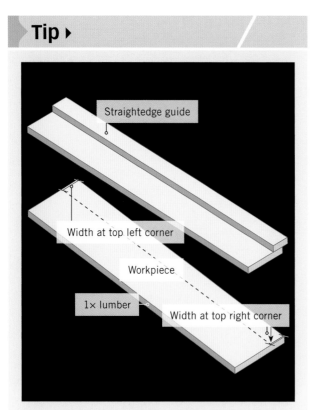

Where jamb extensions are needed, cut the head extension to its finished length—the distance between the window side jambs plus the thickness of both side extensions (typically 1× stock). For the width, measure the distance between the window jamb and the finished wall at each corner; then mark the measurements on the ends of the extension. Use a straightedge to draw a reference line connecting the points. Build a simple cutting jig, as shown.

4

Clamp the jig on the reference line, and rip the extension to width. Using a circular saw, keep the baseplate tight against the jig and move the saw smoothly through the board. Reposition the clamp when you near the end of the cut. Cut both side extensions to length and width, using the same technique as for the head extension (see TIP at left).

5

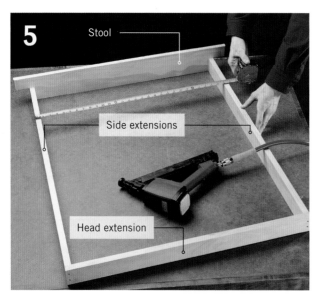

Build a box frame with the extensions and stool, using 6d finish nails and a pneumatic nailer. Measure to make sure the box has the same dimensions as the window jambs. Drive nails through the top of the head extension into the side extensions and through the bottom of the stool into side extensions.

6

Apply wood glue to the back edge of the frame, and position it against the front edge of the window jambs. Use wood shims to adjust the frame, making sure the pieces are flush with the window jambs. Fasten the frame at each shim location, using 8d finish nails driven through pilot holes. Loosely pack insulation between the studs and the jambs, or use minimal-expanding spray foam.

7

Reveal mark

Reveal

On the edge of each jamb or jamb extension, mark a ³⁄₁₆ to ¼" reveal. Place a length of casing along the head extension, aligned with the reveal marks at the corners. Mark where the reveal marks intersect, then make 45° miter cuts at each point. Reposition the casing at the head extension and attach, using 4d finish nails at the extensions and 6d finish nails at the framing members.

8

Head casing

Stool

Cut the side casings to rough length, leaving the ends slightly long for final trimming. Miter one end at 45°. With the pointed end on the stool, mark the height of the side casing at the top edge of the head casing.

9

To get a tight fit for side casings, align one side of a T-bevel with the reveal, mark the side extension, and position the other side flush against the horn. Transfer the angle from the T-bevel to the end of the casing, and cut the casing to length.

10

Test-fit the casings, making any final adjustments with a plane or rasp. Fasten the casing with 4d finish nails at the extensions and 6d finish nails at the framing members.

11

Cut the apron to length, leaving a few inches at each end for creating the returns (step 3). Position the apron tight against the bottom edge of the stool, and then attach it, using 6d finish nails driven every 12".

ARTS & CRAFTS CASING

Tape measure
Straightedge
Power miter saw
Circular saw
  or jigsaw
Handsaw
Plane or rasp
Drill hammer
Pneumatic nailer
Combination square

Compass
Nail set
1 × 4 finish lumber
Back band trim
Wood shims
4d, 6d, and 8d finish
  nails
Finishing putty
Eye and ear protection

Traditional Arts & Crafts casings are made of simple, flat materials with little to no decorative molding trimmed out of the stock. Add nonmitered corners to the mix, and this casing becomes as plain as possible. The back band installed on the perimeter of this project is optional, but it adds depth to the window treatment while maintaining a simple style.

Traditionally, the wood used for this style of trim is quartersawn oak. The term "quartersawn" refers to the method of milling the material. Quartersawn oak is easily distinguishable from plain-sawn oak by its tight grain pattern laced with rays of lighter color also known as rifts. Quartersawn oak is more expensive than plain oak and may only be available at lumberyards or hardwood supply stores, depending upon your area. Either plain-sawn or quartersawn oak will fit the style of this casing.

To begin the installation of this trim style, refer to pages 69 and 71 to read the step-by-step process for installing jamb extensions, if necessary, and the stool portion of this project.

The Arts & Crafts style is similar to the overall look and feel of Mission furniture, as can be seen in this relatively simple oak window casing.

HOW TO INSTALL ARTS & CRAFTS CASING

1

Follow the step-by-step process on pages 69 to 71 to install the stool and jamb extensions. Set a combination square to ³⁄₁₆ or ¼" and mark a reveal line on the top and side jambs.

2

To find the length of the head casing and apron, measure the distance between the reveal lines on the side jambs, and add twice the width of the side casings. Cut the head casing and the apron to length. Install the head casing flush with the top reveal line. Use a scrap piece of trim to line up the head casing horizontally.

3

Measure and cut the side casings to length. Install them flush with the reveal lines. Make sure the joints at the top and bottom are tight. Measure the distance to the end of the stool from the outer edge of the side casing. Install the apron tight to the bottom of the stool at the same dimension from the end of the stool.

4 Back band

Measure, cut, and install the back band around the perimeter of the window casings, mitering the joints at the corners. Continue the back band around the edge of the apron, mitering the corners. Nail the back band in place with 4d finish nails.

BASEMENT WINDOW TRIM

Basement windows bring much-needed sunlight into dark areas, but even in finished basements they often get ignored on the trim front. This is partly because most basement foundation walls are at least 8 inches thick, often a lot thicker. Add a furred-out wall and the window starts to look more like a tunnel with a pane of glass at the end. But with some well-designed and well-executed trim carpentry, you can turn the depth disadvantage into a positive.

A basement window opening may be finished with drywall, but the easiest way to trim one is by making extrawide custom jambs that extend from the inside face of the window frame to the interior wall surface. Because of the extra width, plywood stock is a good choice for the custom jambs. The project shown here is created with veneer-core plywood with oak veneer surface. The jamb members are fastened together into a nice square frame using rabbet joints at the corner. The frame is scribed and installed as a single unit and then trimmed out with oak casing. The casing is applied flush with the inside edges of the frame opening. If you prefer to have a reveal edge around the interior edge of the casing, you will need to add a solid hardwood strip to the edge of the frame so the plies of the plywood are not visible.

Tools & Materials ▸

Pencil	Clamps
Tape measure	Spray-foam insulation
Tablesaw	Finish-grade ¾" oak
Drill with bits	plywood
2' level	Composite or cedar
Framing square	wood shims
Utility knife	1¼, 2" finish nails
Straightedge	1⅝" drywall screws
Miter saw	Carpenter's glue
Router and router table	Eye and ear protection

Because they are set into thick foundation walls, basement windows present a bit of a trimming challenge. But the thickness of the foundation wall also lets you create a handy ledge that's deep enough to hold potted plants or even sunning cats.

HOW TO TRIM A BASEMENT WINDOW

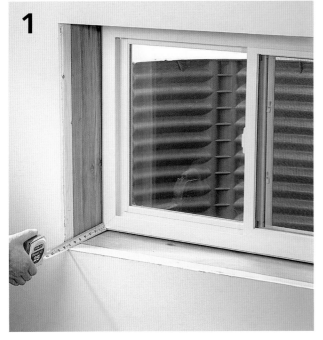

1

Check to make sure the window frame and surrounding area are dry and free of rot, mold, or damage. At all four corners of the basement window, measure from the inside edge of the window frame to the wall surface. Add 1" to the longest of these measurements.

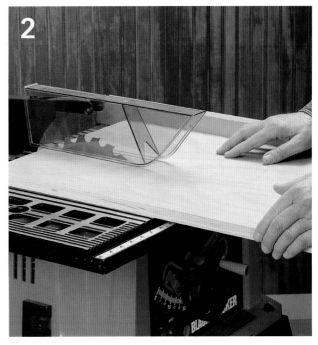

2

Set your tablesaw to make a rip cut to the width arrived at in step 1. If you don't have a tablesaw, set up a circular saw and straightedge cutting guide to cut strips to this length. With a fine-tooth panel-cutting blade, rip enough plywood strips to make the four jamb frame components.

3

Miter gauge

Cross-cut the plywood strips to correct lengths. In our case, we designed the jamb frame to be the exact same outside dimensions as the window frame, since there was some space between the jamb frame and the rough opening.

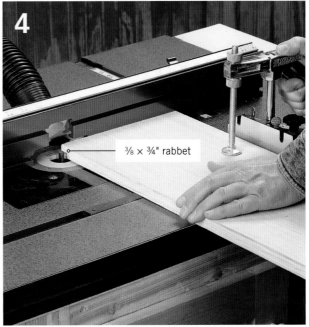

4

⅜ × ¾" rabbet

Cut ⅜"-deep × ¾"-wide rabbets at each end of the head jamb and the sill jamb. A router table is the best tool for this job, but you may use a tablesaw or handsaws and chisels. Inspect the jambs first, and cut the rabbets in whichever face is in better condition. To ensure uniformity, we ganged the two jambs together (they're the same length). It's also a good idea to include backer boards to prevent tearout. (continued)

Glue and clamp the frame parts together, making sure to clamp near each end from both directions. Set a carpenter's square inside the frame, and check it to make sure it's square.

Before the glue sets, carefully drill three perpendicular pilot holes, countersunk, through the rabbeted workpieces and into the side jambs at each corner. Space the pilot holes evenly, keeping the end ones at least ¾" in from the end. Drive a 1⅝" drywall screw into each pilot hole, taking care not to overdrive. Double check each corner for square as you work, adjusting the clamps if needed.

Let the glue dry for at least one hour (overnight is better). Then remove the clamps and set the frame in the window opening. Adjust the frame so it is centered and level in the opening and the exterior-side edges fit flush against the window frame.

Taking care not to disturb the frame's position (rest a heavy tool on the sill to hold it in place if you wish), press a steel rule against the wall surface and mark trimming points at the point where the rule meets the jambs at each side of all four frame corners, using a sharp pencil.

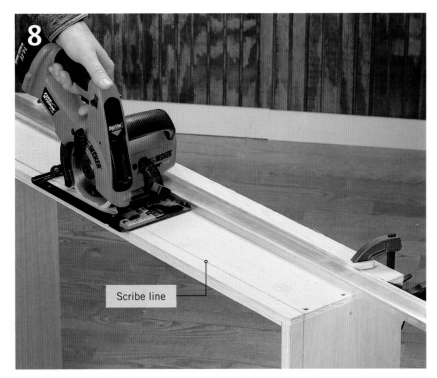

Scribe line

Remove the frame and clamp it on a flat worksurface. Use a straightedge to connect the scribe marks at the ends of each jamb frame side. Set the cutting depth of your circular saw to just a small fraction over ¾". Clamp a straightedge guide to the frame so the saw blade will follow the cutting line, and trim each frame side in succession. (The advantage to using a circular saw here is that any tearout from the blade will be on the nonvisible faces of the frame).

Replace the frame in the window opening in the same orientation as when you scribed it, and install shims until it is level and centered in the opening. Drive a few finish nails (hand or pneumatic) through the side jambs into the rough frame. Also drive a few nails through the sill jamb. Most trim carpenters do not drive nails into the head jamb.

Insulate between the jamb frame and the rough frame with spray-in polyurethane foam. Look for minimal-expanding foam labeled "window and door," and don't spray in too much. Let the foam dry for a half hour or so, and then trim off the excess with a utility knife. *Tip: Protect the wood surfaces near the edges with wide strips of masking tape.*

Remove the masking tape, and clean up the mess from the foam (there is always some). Install case molding. We used picture-frame techniques to install fairly simple oak casing.

BASIC CASING

Stock wood casings provide an attractive border around window and door openings while covering the gaps between the wall surface and the window jamb. Install casings with a consistent reveal between the inside edges of the jambs and the edges of the casings.

In order to fit casings properly, the jambs and wall surfaces must be in the same plane. If one of them protrudes, the casing will not lie flush. To solve this problem, you may need to shave the edges of the jambs down with a block plane. Or you may need to attach jamb extensions to the window or door to match the plane of the wall. For small differences where a drywall surface is too high, you can sometimes use a hammer to compress the drywall around the jambs to allow the casings to lie flush.

Tools & Materials ▸

Tape measure	Miter saw
Drill	Casing material
Pencil	Baseboard molding
Nail set	and corner blocks
Hammer or	(optional)
pneumatic nailer	4d and 6d finish nails
Level	Wood putty
Combination square	Eye and ear protection
Straightedge	

Drywall screws rely on the strength of untorn face paper to support the panel. If the paper around the screws becomes torn, drive additional screws nearby where the paper is still intact.

Simple case molding installed with mitered corners is a very common approach to trimming windows and doors. While it lacks visual interest, it is easy to install and relatively inexpensive.

HOW TO INSTALL MITERED CASING ON WINDOWS & DOORS

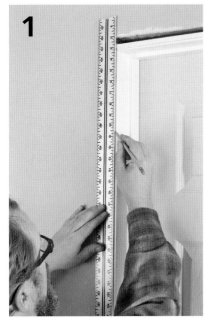

1

On each jamb, mark a reveal line ³⁄₁₆ to ¼" from the inside edge. The casings will be installed flush with these lines.

2

Place a length of casing along one side jamb, flush with the reveal line. At the top and bottom of the molding, mark the points where horizontal and vertical reveal lines meet. (When working with doors, mark the molding at the top only.)

3

Make 45° miter cuts on the ends of the moldings. Measure and cut the other vertical molding piece, using the same method.

4

Drill pilot holes spaced every 12" to prevent splitting, and attach the vertical casings with 4d finish nails driven through the casings and into the jambs. Drive 6d finish nails into the framing members near the outside edge of the casings.

5

Measure the distance between the side casings and cut top and bottom casings to fit, with ends mitered at 45°. If the window or door unit is not perfectly square, make test cuts on scrap pieces to find the correct angle of the joints. Drill pilot holes and attach with 4d and 6d finish nails.

6

Locknail the corner joints by drilling pilot holes and driving 4d finish nails through each corner, as shown. Drive all nail heads below the wood surface, using a nail set, then fill the nail holes with wood putty.

BUILT-UP CHAIR RAIL

Designing and installing a built-up chair rail can be a very creative project that adds a considerable amount of style to any room. For the project shown, five smaller pieces of trim are combined with a 1 × 4 filler strip to create a bold, strong chair rail. If you are considering a larger built-up chair rail, make sure the existing base and crown moldings of the room will not be overshadowed. A good rule of scale to remember is that chair rail should always be smaller than the crown or base.

If you plan to design your own molding, the choices are just about endless. It is a good idea to mimic the style of your existing moldings so that the new chair rail will not look out of place. If the room you are installing in currently has no chair rail, consider new wall finishes as well. Two-tone painted walls will emphasize the transition of a chair rail, as will changing the finish from paint to wallpaper or wainscot.

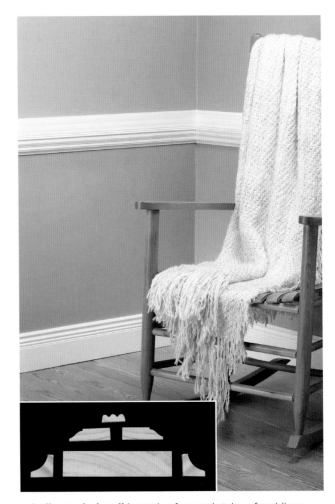

A built-up chair rail is made of several styles of moldings, so the design options are virtually unlimited. The profile shown here features a strip of screen retainer on top of two pieces of profiled door stop. The stop molding is attached to a 1 × 4 filler that is then softened at the top and bottom edges with cover molding.

Tools & Materials ▸

Ladder
Pencil
Stud finder
Tape measure
Combination square
Power miter saw
Coping saw
Pneumatic finish nail
    gun and compressor
4' level or laser level
Drill with bits
Painter's tape
Moldings
Round metal file
Pneumatic fasteners
Hole filler
Finish materials
Eye and ear protection

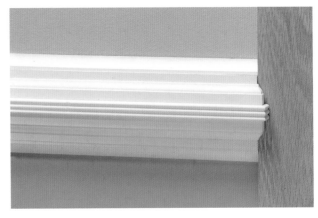

Before you begin installing the molding pieces of the built-up chair rail, decide what type of return you will use. Returns are finish details that occur in areas where different moldings meet at perpendicular angles or quit in the middle of a wall. On some built-up chair rail, you can take advantage of the depth of the molding by butting the back moldings up to the obstructions but running the cap moldings onto the surface.

HOW TO INSTALL A BUILT-UP CHAIR RAIL

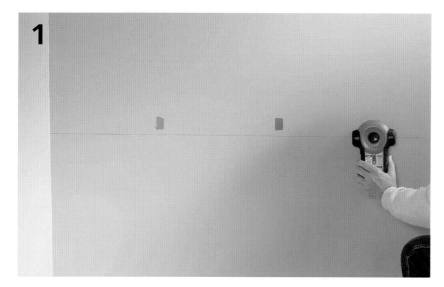

1

On the starting wall of your installation, mark the desired height of the first chair rail component you will install (here, the 1 × 4 filler strip). At this height, mark a level line around the room. Locate all studs along the walls, and mark their locations with painter's tape above the line.

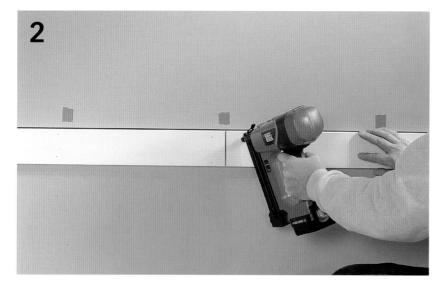

2

Cut and install the 1 × 4 filler strip so that the top edge of the strip follows the level line around the room. Fasten the strip with two 2½" finish nails driven at every stud location. Butt the ends of the filler strip together, keeping in mind that the joints will be covered by additional moldings.

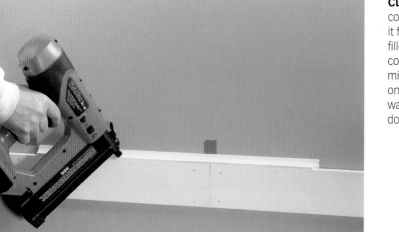

3

Cut and install the upper piece of cove molding around the room, nailing it flush to the top edge of the 1 × 4 filler strip. Use scarf joints on long runs, coped joints at inside corners, and mitered joints on outside corners. Drive one nail at every stud location into the wall and one nail between each stud down into the filler strip.

(continued)

4

Install the lower piece of cove molding flush with the bottom edge of the filler strip. Use the same nailing sequence as with the upper cove molding. Cut scarf joints on long runs, coped joints at inside corners, and mitered joints on outside corners.

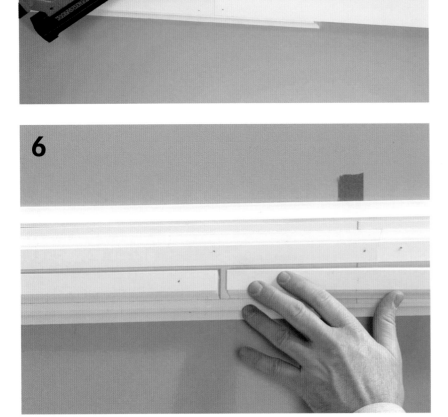

5

Measure, cut, and install the upper piece of stop molding around the room, driving two 1½" finish nails at each stud location. Cut scarf joints, coped joints, and mitered joints as necessary for each piece. Stagger the seams of the scarf joints on the stop molding so that they do not line up with the scarf joints of the cove moldings.

6

Install the lower piece of stop molding around the room, keeping the edge of the molding flush with the bottom edge of the filler strip. Fit each joint using the appropriate joinery method. Drive two nails at each stud location.

7

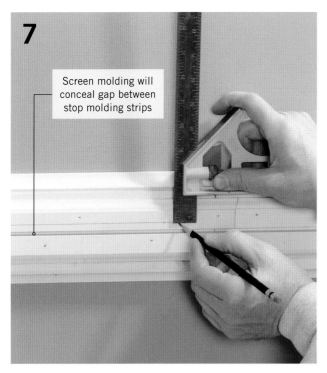

Screen molding will conceal gap between stop molding strips

Set a combination square to 1⅜". Rest the body of the square on the top edge of the upper stop molding and use the blade of the square as a guide to mark a reference line around the room. This line represents the top edge of the screen molding.

8

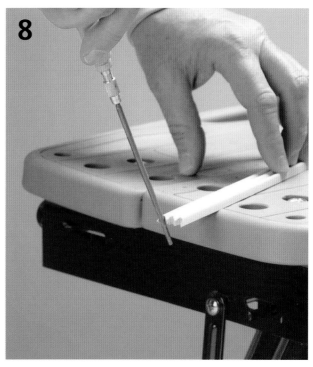

Install the screen retainer molding, as with the other moldings, using the appropriate joints necessary. Fine-tune the cope cuts using a round metal file. Nail the molding in place. Keep the top edge of the molding flush with the reference line from Step 7.

9

Set any nail heads with a nail set, and fill all the nail holes with paintable wood filler. Check for any gaps in the joinery, and fill them as well. Let the filler dry, and sand it smooth with 180-grit sandpaper. Wipe the moldings with a dry cloth to remove any dust.

10

Use a paintbrush to apply a final coat of paint to the moldings. Cover the finished floor with a drop cloth, and protect the lower portion of the wall from drips by masking it off with plastic if necessary.

BUILT-UP CROWN MOLDING

Built-up crown molding is a multi-piece assembly created by joining several trim boards, usually including at least one crown profile, on the wall and the ceiling. Often referred to as cornice molding, these built-up combinations can be truly striking in appearance, especially at and around outside corners. By using careful layout techniques and building simple mock-ups, this complex-looking process can become relatively simple. In large part, this is because the material that is installed both on the ceiling and on the wall can function as a backer, giving the crown molding that's featured in the assembly a secure surface area for nailing. Be creative and experiment with different combinations of trim to come up with a unique design of your own.

Built-up Options ›

Create a mock-up of the built-up molding assembly you're planning to install. Fasten 12"-long pieces of each type together in the intended orientation. If you are undecided among multiple combinations, make a mock-up of each so you can compare them.

Tools & Materials ›

Power miter saw	1½" finish (8d) or pneumatic	Wood glue
Finish nailer	(16-gauge) nails	Utility knife
Tape measure	#2.5 pencil	Eye and ear protection

Built-up crown molding creates a bit of old-world charm in any setting. The three-piece interpretation seen here is made with two pieces of baseboard and a piece of crown.

HOW TO INSTALL A BUILT-UP CROWN

1

Remove any old crown molding in the cornice area. Use a utility knife to cut through old paint and caulk between the molding and the wall or ceiling. Then use a pry bar to work the crown molding loose in small sections. Be sure to brace the end of the pry bar on the inside of the crown and pull downward. Do not pry upwards; this can damage the ceiling.

2

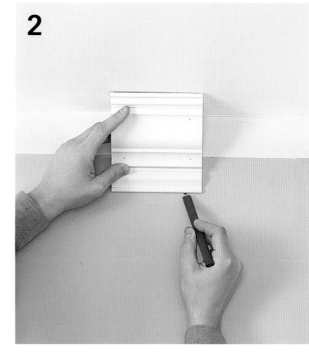

Use a mock-up of the built-up molding as a marking gauge to establish a baseline for the bottom of the assembly on the wall. Start in the corners and work your way around the room. This will allow you to see how the ceiling rises and falls so you know where to install the first piece.

3

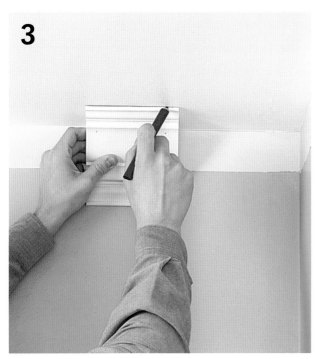

Make a reference line for the top of the built-up assembly, using the mock-up as a gauge.

Tip ▶

To measure a wall when working alone, first make a mark on the wall or ceiling exactly 10" out from one corner. Then, press the tab against the wall at the other end, measure to the marked line, and add 10" to the measurement.

(continued)

4

Install the base (lowest) molding around the entire room first. The bottoms of the base pieces should be flush against the bottom line that was scribed using the mock-up as a gauge. Do not try to push the trim up against the ceiling; it must be flush with the base line. Any gaps at the top will be hidden by subsequent trim pieces.

5

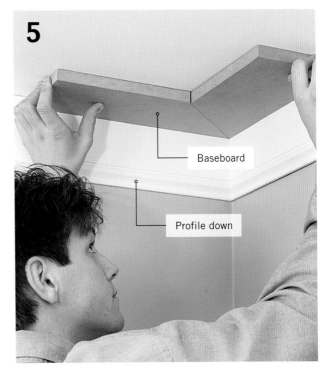

Baseboard

Profile down

Find the correct miter angles for installing the flat ceiling trim. Cut two scraps of stock at 45°, and test how well they fit together in the corner. Adjust the cuts as needed to form a corner that has a neat miter with both sides flush against the wall.

6

Install the second trim profile parts all around the perimeter of the room. Typically, this will be flat moldings (with or without an edge profile) installed flat against the ceiling and mitered at the corners.

7

Install the final piece, which is usually crown molding that fits against the flat wall molding and the ceiling molding. It is best to use coped joints at the inside corners (see page 111). Sand, fill the nail holes, and finish the built-up cornice as desired (if you have not prefinished all the parts).

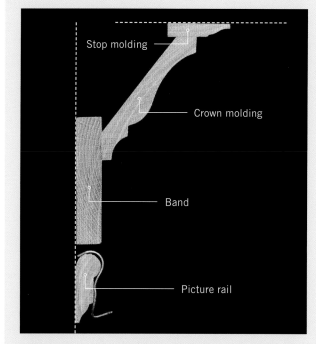

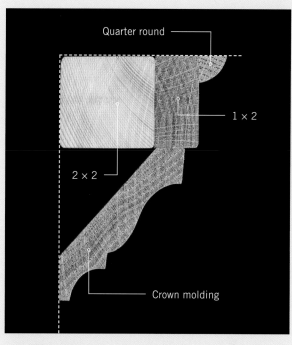

Use picture rail to enhance a cornice molding. Standard height for picture rail is about 10 to 12" below the ceiling, but you can place it at any level. For a simple variation of the project shown, use square-edged stock for the band (since the bottom edge will mostly be hidden), and add picture rail just below the band. Be sure to leave enough room for placing picture hooks.

Install blocking to provide a nailing surface and added bulk to a built-up cornice. In this simple arrangement, a 2 × 2 block, or nailing strip, is screwed to the wall studs. A facing made from 1 × 2 finish lumber is nailed to the blocking and is trimmed along the ceiling with quarter-round. The crown molding is nailed to the wall studs along the bottom and to the nailer along the top.

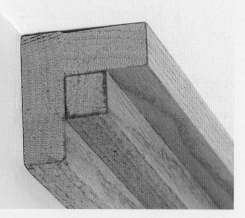

This highly detailed Victorian-style built-up cornice is made of several pieces of stock trim and solid stock ripped down to different widths. The right-angle component of this cornice may be screwed directly to the wall, to serve both a decorative function as well as serve as a nailer for the other trim elements. The screw holes are covered when the crown molding is installed.

Built-up cornice treatments can be as simple or complex as you would like. This Arts & Crafts variation is made of flat solid stock ripped down to specific dimensions. Two pieces of 1 × 2 stock are fastened together to form an L-shaped angle. The angle is then screwed to the wall at the stud locations. An additional piece of 1" wide stock is nailed in place so the top edge is flush with the installed angle. This configuration creates a stepped cornice with a simpler appearance than the traditional sprung moldings. Notice that the L angle is nailed together with a slight gap at the back edge. This is done to compensate for irregularities in the corner joint.

POLYMER CROWN

Polymer moldings come in a variety of ornate, single-piece styles that offer easy installation and maintenance. The polystyrene or polyurethane material is as easy to cut as softwood, but unlike wood, the material won't shrink and it can be repaired with vinyl spackling compound.

You can buy polymer molding preprimed for painting, or you can stain it with a nonpenetrating heavy-body stain or gel. Most polymers come in 12-foot lengths, and some have corner blocks that eliminate corner cuts. There are even flexible moldings for curved walls.

Tools & Materials ▸

Tape measure	Finish nails
Drill with countersink-piloting bit	150-grit sandpaper
	Rag
Power miter saw or hand miter box and fine-tooth saw	Mineral spirits
	Polymer adhesive
	2" drywall screws
Caulk gun	Vinyl spackling compound
Putty knife	Paintable latex caulk
Crown molding	Eye and ear protection

HOW TO INSTALL POLYMER CROWN MOLDING

Plan the layout of the molding pieces by measuring the walls of the room and making light pencil marks at the joint locations. For each piece that starts or ends at a corner, add 12 to 24" to compensate for waste. If possible, avoid pieces shorter than 36" because short pieces are more difficult to fit.

Hold a section of molding against the wall and ceiling in the finished position. Make light pencil marks on the wall every 12" along the bottom edge of the molding. Remove the molding, and tack a finish nail at each mark. The nails will hold the molding in place while the adhesive dries. If the wall surface is plaster, drill pilot holes for the nails.

To make the miter cuts for the first corner, position the molding faceup in a miter box. Set the ceiling side of the molding against the horizontal table of the miter box, and set the wall side against the vertical back fence. Make the cut at 45°.

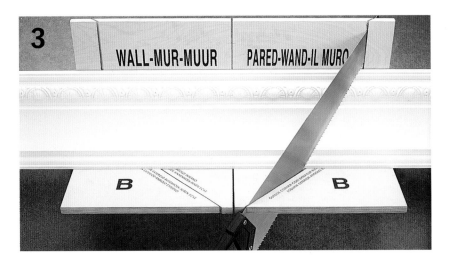

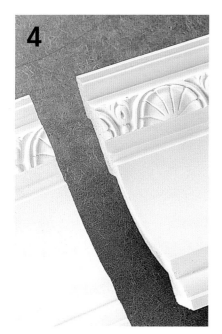

4

Check the uncut ends of each molding piece before installing it. Make sure mating pieces will butt together squarely in a tight joint. Cut all square ends at 90°, using a miter saw or hand miter box.

5

Lightly sand the backs of the molding that will contact the wall and ceiling, using 150-grit sandpaper. Slightly dampen a rag with mineral spirits, and wipe away the dust. Run a small bead of polymer adhesive (recommended or supplied by the manufacturer) along both sanded edges.

6

Set the molding in place with the mitered end tight to the corner and the bottom edge resting on the nails. Press along the molding edges to create a good bond. At each end of the piece, drive 2" drywall screws through countersunk pilot holes through the flats and into the ceiling and wall.

7

Cut, sand, and glue the next piece of molding. Apply a bead of adhesive to the end where the installed molding will meet the new piece. Install the new piece, and secure the ends with screws, making sure the ends are joined properly. Install the remaining molding pieces, and let the adhesive dry.

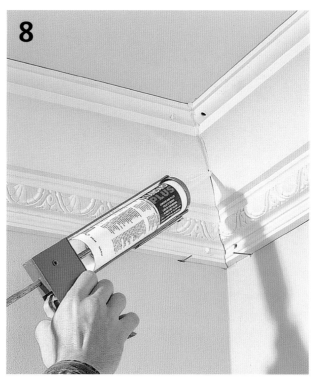

8

Carefully remove the finish nails and fill the nail holes with vinyl spackling compound. Fill the screw holes in the molding and any gaps in the joints with paintable latex caulk or filler, and wipe away excess caulk with a damp cloth or a wet finger. Smooth the caulk over the holes so it's flush with the surface.

WALL FRAME MOLDINGS

Adding wall frame moldings is a traditional decorative technique used to highlight special features of a room, divide large walls into smaller sections, or simply add interest to plain surfaces. You can paint the molding the same color as the walls or use a contrasting color. For even greater contrast, paint or wallcover the areas within the frames.

Decorative wood moldings with curved contours work best for wall frames. Chair rail, picture rail, base shoe, cove, quarter-round, and other suitable molding types in several wood species are readily available at home centers and lumberyards.

To determine the sizes and locations of the frames, cut strips of paper to the width of the molding and tape them to the wall. You may want the frames to match the dimensions of architectural details in the room, such as windows or a fireplace.

Install the molding with small finish nails driven at each wall stud location and at the ends of the pieces. Use nails long enough to penetrate the studs by ¾ inch. If there aren't studs where you need them, secure the molding with dabs of construction adhesive.

Tools & Materials ▸

Level
Framing square
Level
Miter box and backsaw
Drill and bits
Hammer and
   finishing nails
Nail set

Paper strips
Tape
Wood finishing
   materials
Construction adhesive
Paintable latex caulk
   or wood putty
Eye and ear protection

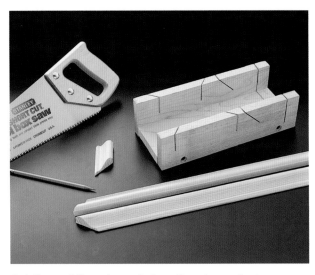

Cut the molding pieces to length, using a miter box and a backsaw (or power miter saw) to cut the ends at 45°. The top and bottom pieces should be the same length, as should the side pieces. Test-fit the pieces, and make any necessary adjustments.

Wall frame moldings use ordinary trim pieces to create frames with mitered corners that give the illusion of frame-and-panel construction.

HOW TO INSTALL WALL FRAME MOLDINGS

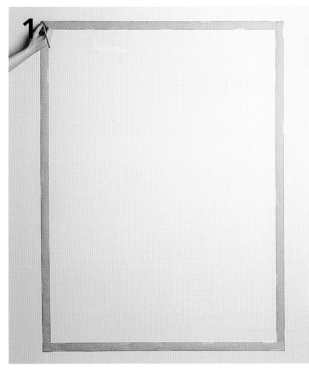

Cut paper strips to the width of the molding, and tape them to the wall. Use a framing square and level to make sure the frame is level and the strips are square to one another. Mark the outer corners of the frame with light pencil lines.

Paint or stain the moldings as desired. Position the top molding piece on the placement marks, and tack it in place with two finish nails. If necessary, drill pilot holes for the nails to prevent splitting.

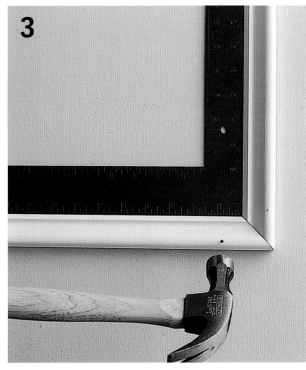

Tack the side moldings in place, using the framing square to make sure they are square to the top piece. Tack up the bottom piece. Adjust the frame, if necessary, so that all of the joints fit tightly, and then completely fasten the pieces.

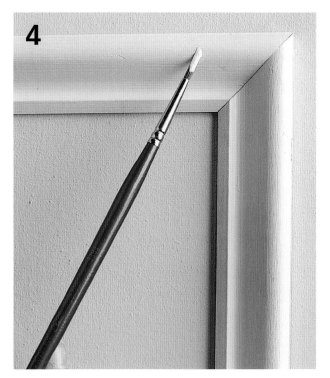

Drive the nails slightly below the surface, using a nail set. Fill the nail holes (and corner joints, if necessary) with wood putty. Touch up the patched areas with paint or stain.

WAINSCOT FRAMES

Frame-and-panel wainscot adds depth, character, and a sense of old-world charm to any room. Classic wainscot was built with grooved or rabbeted rails and stiles that captured a floating hardwood panel. In the project shown here, the classic appearance is mimicked, but the difficulties of machining precise parts and commanding craftsman-level joinery are eliminated. Paint-grade materials (mostly MDF) are used in the project shown; however, you can also build the project with solid hardwoods and finish-grade plywood if you prefer a clear-coat finish.

Installing wainscot frames that look like frame-and-panel wainscot can be done piece by piece, but it is often easier to assemble the main frame parts in your shop. Not only does working in the shop allow you to join the frame parts together (we use pocket screws driven in the backs of the rails and stiles); it generally results in a more professional look.

Once the main frames are assembled, they can be attached to the wall at stud locations. If you prefer to site-build the wainscot piece by piece, you may need to replace the wallcovering material with plywood to create nailing surfaces for the individual pieces.

We primed all of the wainscot parts prior to installing them and then painted the wainscot (including the wall sections within the wainscot panel frames) a contrasting color from the wall above the wainscot cap.

Tools & Materials ▸

Laser level
Pencil
Tape measure
Circular saw or
    tablesaw
Straightedge guide
Power miter saw
Drill with bits
Carpenter's square
Pocket hole jig with
    screws
Pry bar
Hammer
Pneumatic finish

nail gun with
    compressor
Caulking gun
¾"-thick MDF
    sheet stock
3" drywall screws
1¹⁄₁₆" cove molding
½ × ¾" base shoe
⁹⁄₁₆ × 1⅛" cap molding
    (10' per panel)
Panel adhesive
Paint and primer
Eye and ear protection

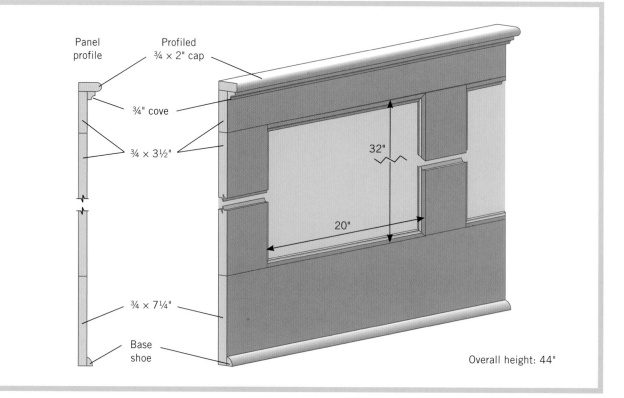

Panel profile
Profiled ¾ × 2" cap
¾" cove
¾ × 3½"
32"
20"
¾ × 7¼"
Base shoe
Overall height: 44"

HOW TO INSTALL WAINSCOT FRAMES

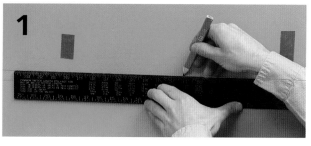

Use a laser level and a pencil to mark the height of the wainscot installation directly onto all walls in the project area. Also mark the height of the top rail (¾" below the overall height) since the cap rail will be installed after the rest of the wainscot is installed. Mark stud locations, using an electronic stud finder.

Plot out the wainscot layout on paper, and then test the layout by drawing lines on the wall to make sure you're happy with the design. Try to use a panel width that can be divided evenly into all project wall lengths. In some cases, you may need to make the panel widths slightly different from wall to wall, but make sure to maintain a consistent width within each wall's run.

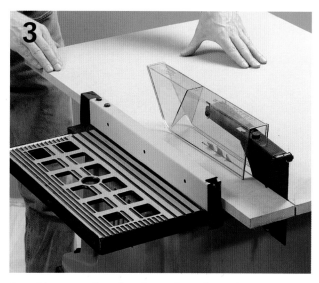

Based on your plan, rip a sheet of MDF into strips to make all of the wainscot parts except the trim moldings. In our case, that included the cap rail (2" wide), the top rail and stiles (3½" wide), and the base rail (7¼" wide). *Note: These are standard lumber dimensions. You can use 1 × 4 and 1 × 4 dimensional lumber for the rails and stiles. Use 1 × 2 or rip stock for the cap rail.*

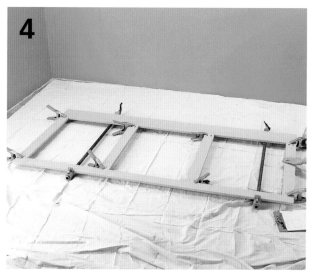

Cut top rails, base rails, and stiles (but not cap rails) to length, and dry-assemble the parts into ladder frames based on your layout. Plan the layouts so wall sections longer than 8' are cut with scarf joints in the rails meeting at a stud location. Dry-assemble the pieces on a flat worksurface.

(continued)

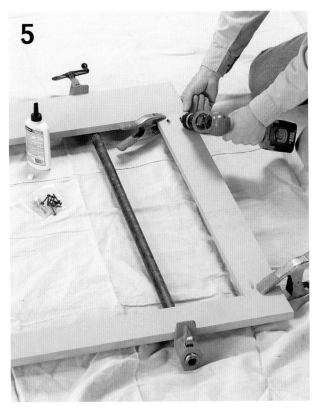

5

Assemble the frames using glue and pocket screws or biscuits. Clamp the parts together first, and check with a carpenter's square to make sure the stiles are perpendicular to both rails.

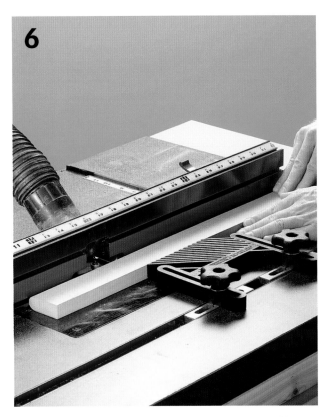

6

Mount a ¾" roundover bit in your router or router table, and shape a bullnose profile on the front edge of your cap rail stock.

7

Prime all parts on both sides, including the milled moldings and uncut cap rail stock.

8

Position the frames against the wall, and shim underneath the bottom rails as necessary to bring them flush with the top rail marks on the wall (¾" below the overall height lines). Attach the wainscot sections by driving 3" drywall screws, countersunk, through the top rail and the bottom rail at each stud location. If you are using scarf joints, be sure to install the open half first.

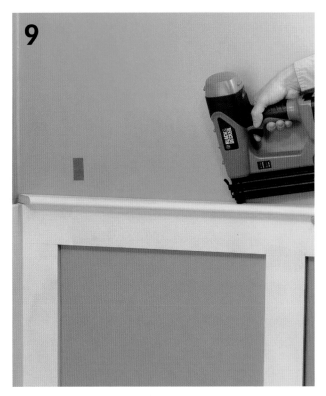

Cut the cap rail to length, and attach it to the top rail with panel adhesive and finish nails. Drive a 3" drywall screw through the cap rail and into the wall toenails style at each location. Be sure to carefully drill pilot holes and countersink holes for each screw. Miter-cut the cap rails at the corners.

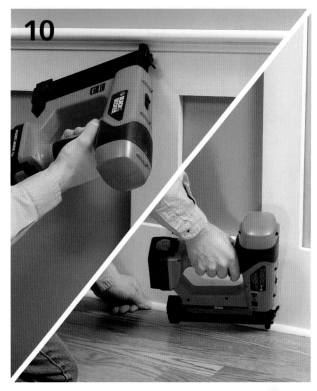

Install cove molding in the crotch where the cap rail and top rails meet, using glue and a brad nailer. Then nail base shoe to conceal any gaps between the bottoms, rails, and the floor. Miter all corners.

Cut mitered frames to fit around the perimeter of each panel frame created by the rails and stiles. Use cap molding.

Mask the wall above the cap rail, and then prime and paint the wainscot frames. Generally, a lighter, contrasting color than the wall color above is most effective visually.

COFFERED CEILINGS

Installing a coffered ceiling is one of the most lavish treatments you can perform on a ceiling. It adds both beauty and character and is a great way to cultivate a more formal atmosphere in a room. Coffered ceilings, sometimes referred to as box beams, consist of recessed panels or individual cells of intersecting beams that are trimmed with moldings.

These individual cells can either be squares or rectangles: the precise shape is dictated by the layout of the room they are being installed in. The types of moldings used, the depth of the individual cells, and the reveals can all change the look of the coffer to make it resemble a particular style, such as Craftsman, Federal, or Victorian. Creating a coffer depth too big in a smaller room can be overwhelming. Taller ceilings (above 9 feet) should have deeper cells of around 5 to 8 inches, while a traditional 8- to 9-foot ceiling would have a depth anywhere from 2 to 5 inches.

The method that is shown in this chapter will create the illusion that heavy solid beams were used,

but in fact simple, lightweight three-sided hollow boxes are all you need. Once the boxes are installed to the ceiling, planks of MDF are used to complete the box. When affixing these to the ceiling, plenty of good quality construction adhesive is used, along with nailing securely into joists wherever possible.

Tools & Materials ▸

¾" MDF panels	Drill
1 × 6 pine	16g (or 8d) finish nails
5" base molding	Carpenters square
4⅝" crown molding	Glue/construction
Power miter saw	adhesive
Tape measure	Caulk
#2.5 pencil	Finish materials
Finish nailer	Eye and ear protection
Deck screws	

The rich architectural appeal of a coffered ceiling can be achieved with some strips of MDF and a little crown molding.

Alternate Method: Beams ▸

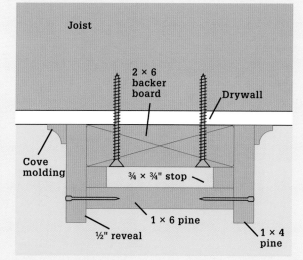

Exposed beams lend a feeling of strength and structure to a room, even if they're really just hollow shells like the beams seen here. Because they can be attached directly to the ceiling surface, installing decorative beams is a relatively easy trim carpentry project (as long as you're comfortable working at heights).

A cross section view of the exposed beams shown being installed here reveals that they are hollow inside and actually quite simple in structure. You can install beams in any direction, but perpendicular to the ceiling joists (as shown above) is the easier orientation to work with.

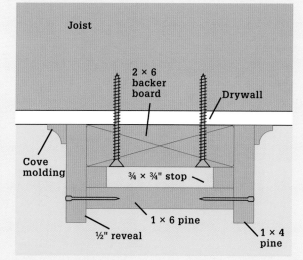
Labels: Joist; 2 × 6 backer board; Drywall; Cove molding; ¾ × ¾" stop; ½" reveal; 1 × 6 pine; 1 × 4 pine

HOW TO INSTALL A COFFERED CEILING

1

Take measurements and plan your layout. Divide the ceiling into square or rectangular sections that are proportional to the overall size. The general idea is to install series of plus-shape nailers to establish each point of intersection, and then connect the nailers with strips of MDF.

2

Mark the layout lines for the ceiling and snap chalk lines to establish the grid you'll be basing your layout on.

(continued)

3

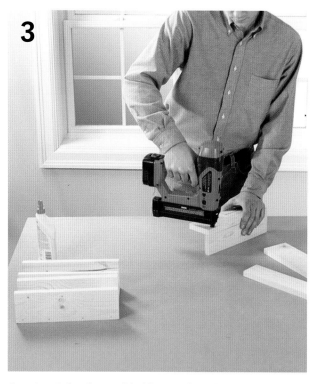

Construct the three-sided boxes that will create the nailer unions that define each coffered section. The boxes are made from 1 × 6 pine.

4

Hang the nailer union assemblies from the ceiling according to your layout plans. Use deck screws driven up through the boxes and into ceiling joists where possible. If no joists are available in the installation area, use toggle bolts.

5

Hang T-shaped nailer union assemblies next to the walls according to your installation plan.

6

Cut strips of MDF to make the beam covers. Allow an extra 1½" of width so the beam covers will conceal the bottom edges of the beam sides after they are installed. Also rip the stock for the beam sides (this should be equal in width to the depth of the nailer boxes).

7

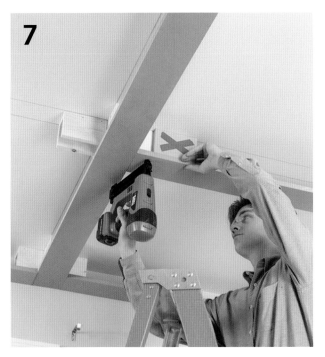

Attach the MDF strips to the bottoms of the nailers and then to the sides, using panel adhesive and 16-gauge pneumatic finish nails. Then install the beam side strips, making adjustments as needed to ensure that the surfaces of the sides are flush with the edges of the beam covers.

8

Measure the inside dimensions of each coffer so you can make a crown molding frame that is preassembled on the ground and then simply lifted up into place and secured.

9

Cut crown molding and assemble it into a square frame on the ground. Short each dimension by about 1/32" to make sure the frame will fit inside. You'll have the best chance for success if you measure and build each frame individually.

10

Lift the finished crown molding frames up into the coffer opening and secure with pneumatic finish nails. Caulk all gaps, fill nail holes, and then paint and prime. Add ceiling medallion and other ornamental millwork if you wish, but use discretion.

CEILING MEDALLIONS

A ceiling medallion is an elegant style accent that can highlight a light fixture or establish the visual focal point of a room all on its own. Most medallions today are made of polyurethane and are available at home centers off the shelf in various styles and sizes. Specialty restoration dealers carry extensive lines of medallions as well.

In the project shown, a medallion is installed over a light fixture. Depending on the style of medallion you choose, a hole may need to be cut in the center to allow access to the electrical mechanicals in the ceiling. If you are installing the medallion over a light fixture, turn off the power at the main service panel before you begin.

Tools & Materials ▸

Screwdriver
Adjustable wrench
Pencil
Drill with bits
   and circle cutter
Caulk gun
Medallion

150-grit sandpaper
Polyurethane adhesive
Threaded nipple
Drywall screws
Paintable latex caulk
Eye and ear protection

Ceiling medallions are classic trim accessories, and most sold today are designed to be installed in conjunction with a ceiling light fixture. Some medallions come as solid discs (carved wood, cast plaster, or more commonly, urethane) and others are two-piece assemblies that can be slipped between the light and the ceiling and snapped together.

HOW TO INSTALL A CEILING MEDALLION

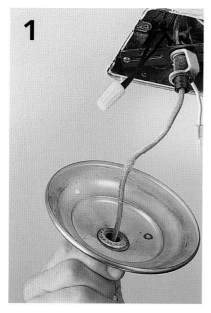

1

Turn the power off at the main service panel. Remove the cover plate of the light fixture. Disconnect the fixture wires, taking note of the color of the wires of each connection. If necessary, unscrew the supporting nipple in the center of the electrical box and set the fixture aside.

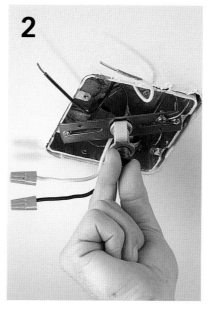

2

Compensate for the added thickness of the medallion by adding a longer nipple to the center of the electrical box. If a nipple is not used, purchase longer screws to reattach the cover plate to the mounting strap once the medallion is installed.

3

Cut a hole in the center of the medallion using a circle cutter and a drill. The hole should be smaller than the cover plate, but large enough to access the screw holes on the mounting strap. Lightly sand the back of the medallion with 150-grit sandpaper.

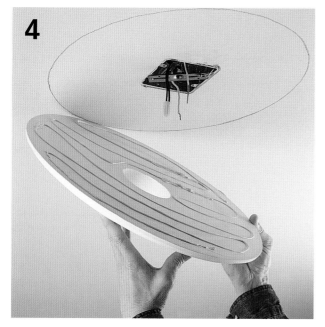

4

Position the medallion on the ceiling centered over the electrical box. Trace the outline with a pencil. Apply adhesive to the back of the medallion, staying 1" away from the outer edge. Align the medallion with the pencil line and press it to the ceiling.

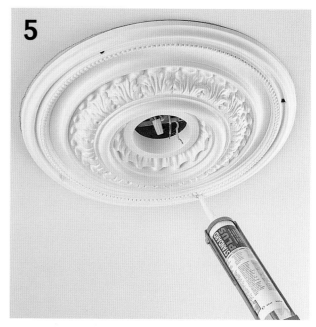

5

Drill countersunk pilot holes in inconspicuous areas of the medallion and drive drywall screws through the holes to hold it in place until the adhesive dries. Fill the holes with paintable latex caulk, smoothing the holes with a wet finger. Paint the medallion as desired, and reattach the light when the paint is completely dry.

JOINTLESS RAIL-AND-STILE WAINSCOT

Some forces of nature that affect carpentry cannot be avoided, but they can be controlled. One is the natural movement of wood that occurs from changes in temperature and humidity. Many a trim job that is perfect when it is installed in the summer suffers from opened miters and other signs of shrinkage when the humidity drops during the fall and winter heating seasons.

By creating a layout and cutting out panels from a 4 × 8-foot sheet of MDF, you can control the number of joints and greatly reduce the affects of wood movement. MDF is a manmade material composed of sawdust and resins and formed without a grain pattern under extremely high pressure, which makes it one of the most dimensionally stable wood products. Although all materials will be affected somewhat by humidity changes, MDF is affected the least.

After careful planning and measuring, the design and layout of the room can be transferred directly to a story pole stick. This can be transferred to the 4 × 8 sheet so layouts can be consistent. After cutting out the center panel, the remaining material becomes the rails and stiles. The panel itself is squared up and run through a router bit, creating the raised panel. Bolection molding is then cut and used to trim out each panel.

Tools & Materials ▸

Circular saw	Clamps
Cutting guide	Jigsaw
Tape measure	MDF
Laser level	8d nails
Straightedge	Finishing materials
Router (optional)	Eye and ear protection
Sander (detail or	Work gloves
random orbit)	

These wainscot frames are cut from full sheets of MDF, so they require virtually no joinery.

HOW TO INSTALL JOINTLESS WAINSCOT

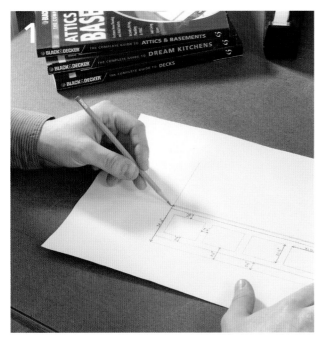

Plan your layout. Measure the length of each wainscot run and calculate a plan that minimizes the number of vertical joints. The goal is to have all of the panel inserts the same width. Do not have panels meet in vertical joints in the stile areas. Butt the "rails" against a full-width stile in the adjoining panel.

Mark a layout line on the wall at the planned wainscot height. Generally, 36" to 42" is the typical height range, although on older homes, full-height or nearly full-wall height wainscot coverage was not uncommon. Use a laser level to mark the height if you have access to one.

Lay out the cutting lines on your MDF panels, following your plan. For uniform results, create and use a layout stick to mark the locations of the margins and panel widths.

Set up for the panel cutouts. To get the straightest possible line when removing the panel from the frame material, use a circular saw and a straightedge cutting guide. Clamp the guide to the panel so the saw foot setback has the blade falling just inside the layout line. Set the saw cutting depth to about ⅛" deeper than the thickness of the stock (⅞" for ¾" MDF panels).

(continued)

5

6

Make a plunge cut. Position the saw so the blade will come down well within the start of the waste area. Press the foot firmly against the straightedge guide. Hold the saw so the blade is slightly above the worksurface. Turn on the saw. Once the blade is rotating at full speed, carefully lower the saw onto the workpiece, holding onto the handle with a firm grip. This is called a plunge cut. Without pressing down too hard and forcing the blade, let the blade cut into and through the workpiece.

Set up for the panel cutouts following the straightedge guide. Be careful, but don't proceed too slowly or the blade may cause some burning. Stop cutting an inch or so before the blade reaches the cutting line. Make all internal plunge cuts on all frame sections.

7

8

Finish the cutouts with a jigsaw. Make sure the workpiece and the waste are well supported from below, and use a jigsaw to compete the cutouts at the corners.

Sand the corner smooth with a detail sander or a random orbit sander. Hand sanding is also an option.

Ogee bit with bead

Option: Cut a decorative edge profile on the frame cutouts using a router and a piloted profiling bit, such as the ogee bit seen here (inset). Exercise some care, particularly around the corners. If you are planning to shape and install insert panels, you generally should not profile the frame, too.

9

Prime and paint the frames. Use a small brush to paint the profiled areas and use a small roller sleeve to coat the rail and stile areas. Also paint the cap molding and base trim with a small paint roller.

10

Prepare the walls. You have many design options here. The simplest is to paint the wall the same color as the wainscot frames. Or, you can paint it a contrasting color. By using a paintable, embossed wallpaper you can add some interesting texture. Or you can apply natural wood paneling, mirrored glass panels—there is virtually no limit to the possibilities.

11

Install the frame with panel adhesive and pneumatic nails or 8d finish nails driven at stud locations. Cut biscuit slots at the stile-and-rail joints and use biscuits to assist in the alignment. Add base and cap molding as desired.

RAISED-PANEL WAINSCOT

By definition, wainscot is a treatment to the lower half of a wall. Designs can range from simple architecturally applied moldings directly to the drywall to elaborate rail and style construction with raised-panel centers. Aside from the traditional look of raised-paneled wainscot, these raised panels can be installed on any part of a wall; the lower third, the full wall, or the ceiling.

Tools & Materials ▸

Circular saw
Framing square
Tape measure
Clamps
Pneumatic nailer
16-gauge or 18-gauge
   pneumatic nails

Panel adhesive
High-tack wood trim glue
Finishing materials
Raised-panel router bit
Recessed router
Eye and ear protection

Raised-Panel Bits ▸

Raised-panel router bits generally require a router table with a powerful ½"-collet router or a shaper to run them successfully. The bit cuts the edge profile into the panel inserts. If you are making traditional raised-panel frames, you'll also need a sticking bit set to cut the edge profiles for the frame rails and stiles.

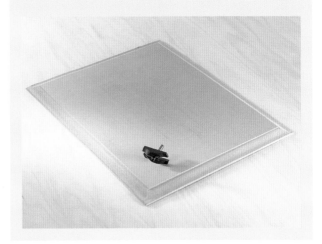

Genuine raised-panel wainscot has depth and substance that can be mimicked with trim moldings, but never duplicated.

HOW TO INSTALL RAISED-PANEL WAINSCOT

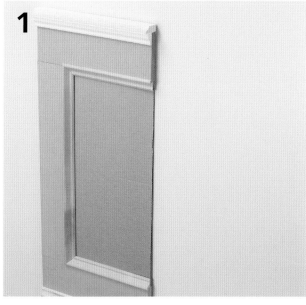

1

Plan your layout and make a mock-up of the wall treatment, including base molding, shoe molding (if you'll use it), lower rail, panel insert, upper rail, bolection moldings and cap moldings.

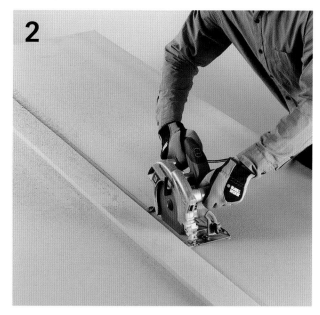

2

Cut the panel inserts, making sure they are square. If you have access to a tablesaw or a panel-cutting saw, use it. If the panel has a finish-grade side, make sure the blade is cutting down into the finished side to limit any tearout to the back surface. Allow for ¼" clearance between the panels and the frames.

3

Cut the panel edge profiles. After all the raised panels are cut to the proper size, install a panel cutting bit in your router table and cut the edge profiles. One great way to accomplish this is to attach a series of thin auxiliary fences to your router table fence. After making one pass on each side of all the panels, remove one of the sacrificial pieces of MDF to expose more of the panel bit and make another pass. This process is repeated until the full profile has been cut. When complete, you will have a perfectly profiled raised panel.

(continued)

4

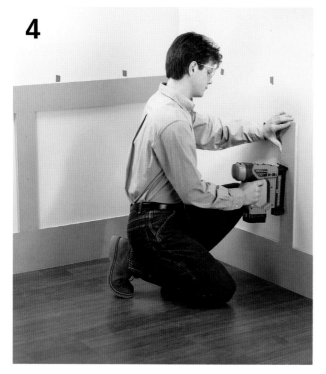

Make and install frames for the panels. Here, ¾"-thick MDF is ripped into 4"-wide strips and formed into frames that are mounted on the room walls. See pages 92 to 95 for more information on making and installing wainscot frames.

5

Cut ¼"-wide spacers from thin stock—about the same thickness as the edges of the panel inserts. Tack the spacers around the edges of the panel openings in the frame—use at least two spacers at each edge. You can use double-sided tape to hold the spacers, but hot glue from a hot-glue gun is a better choice.

6

Insert raised panels into openings so the panels fit inside the spacers. Test the fit and make any adjustments as needed.

7

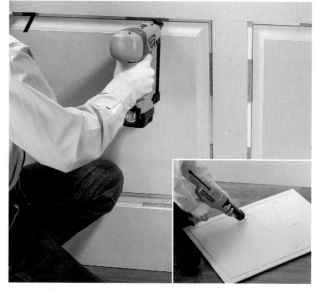

Fasten the raised panels in the frame openings. Use small (18-gauge) pneumatic brads to secure the panels, preferably driven close enough to the edges that the bolection molding will cover the nailheads. *Option: Apply panel adhesive to the back of the panel (inset) before tacking it in place. The adhesive will greatly improve the holding power of the bond, but it also complicates removal of the panels if you need to make an adjustment at some point.*

8

Remove the panel spacers and the top and sides of the opening, prying them loose with a flat screwdriver. Leave the bottom spacers in place as an auxiliary support for the panel, which is fairly heavy.

9

Install base molding according to your trim plan and mock up. Miter or cope the molding at inside corners and miter it at outside corners. Use panel adhesive and pneumatic nails (16-gauge) or 2½"-finish nails to secure the moldings, driving nails at stud locations where possible. Attach base shoe molding if you plan to use it, making sure to fasten it to the base molding and not to the floor.

10

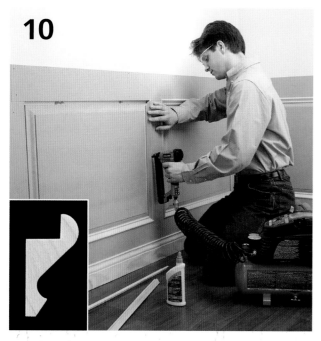

Miter-cut the corners and fasten bolection molding to cover the gaps between the raised panels and the frames. Use high-tack wood trim glue and pneumatic brad nails to attach the bolection molding. Bolection molding (inset) resembles cap molding but is intended to cover gaps and create a shadow line because it stands out from the surfaces to which it is attached.

11

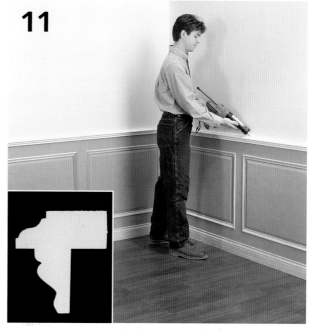

Install the cap molding to cover the tops of the frames, using finish nails or pneumatic nails. Fill nail holes with putty throughout the project and prepare for finishing by sanding lightly and by filling the gap between the cap molding and the wall with a thin bead of paintable caulk. Apply your finish of choice. We used primer and paint, since MDF is not suited for clear finishing.

CROWN MOLDING

Simply put, crown molding is angled trim that bridges the joint between the ceiling and the wall. In order to cover this joint effectively, crown moldings are "sprung." This means that the top and bottom edges of the molding have been beveled, so when the molding is tilted away from the wall at an angle, the tops and bottoms are flush on the wall and ceiling surfaces. Some crown moldings have a 45-degree angle at both the top and the bottom edges; another common style ("38-degree crown") has a 38-degree angle on one edge and a 52-degree angle on the other edge.

Installing crown molding can be a challenging and sometimes confusing process. Joints may be difficult for you to visualize before cutting, and wall and ceiling irregularities can be hard to overcome. If you have not worked on crown molding joints before, it is recommended that your first attempt be made with paint-grade materials. Stain-grade crown is commonly made of solid hardwood stock, which makes for expensive cutting errors and difficulty concealing irregularities in joints.

Inside corner joints of crown molding should be cope-cut, not mitered, except in the case of very intricate profile crown that is virtually impossible to cope (and must therefore be mitered). While mitering inside corners may appear to save time and produce adequate results, after a few changing seasons the joints will open up and be even more difficult to conceal.

Installing crown molding in a brand-new, perfectly square room is one thing, but what happens when the walls and ceilings don't meet at perfect right angles? In most houses that have been around for more than a couple of seasons, walls have bulges caused by warped studs or improper stud placement that's causing the drywall to push out into the room. Ceilings have issues caused by warped joists or drywall that has loosened or pulled away from the ceiling joists. Corners may be best finished with extra-thick layers of joint compound that has been applied a bit heavily, causing an outside corner piece to sit further away from the corner bead. These are just a few of the issues that can work against you and cause even an experienced carpenter to become frustrated.

Tools & Materials ▶

Hammer
Utility knife

Scrap of wood
Eye protection

Basic crown molding softens the transitions between walls and ceilings. If it is made from quality hardwood, crown molding can be quite beautiful when installed and finished with a clear top coat. But historically, it is most often painted, either the same color as the ceiling (your eye tends to see it as a ceiling molding, not a wall molding) or with highly elaborate painted-and-carved details.

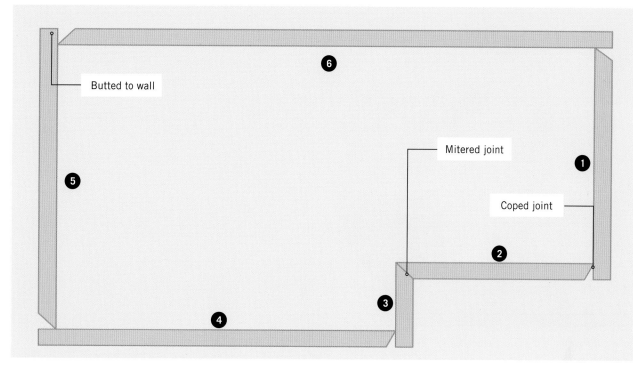

Plan the order of the installation to minimize the number of difficult joints on each piece, and use the longest pieces for the most visible sections of wall. Notice that the left end of first piece is cope-cut rather than butted into the wall. Cope-cutting the first end eliminates the need to cope-cut both ends of the final piece and places the cuts in the same direction. This simplifies your installation, making the method to cut each piece similar.

HOW TO INSTALL BASIC CROWN MOLDING

Cut a piece of crown molding about 1' long with square ends. Temporarily install the piece in the corner of the last installation wall with two screws driven into the blocking. This piece serves as a template for the first cope cut on the first piece of molding.

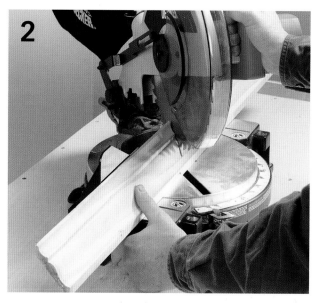

Place the first piece of molding upside down and sprung against the fence of the miter saw. Mark a reference line on the fence for placement of future moldings, and cut the first coped end with an inside miter cut to reveal the profile of the piece.

(continued)

3

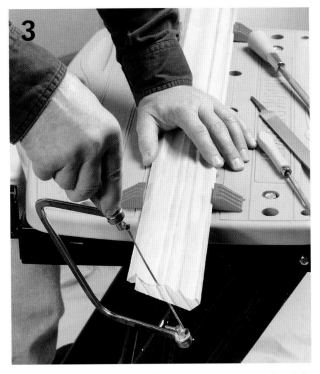

Cope-cut the end of the first piece with a coping saw. Carefully cut along the profile, angling the saw as you cut to back-bevel the cope. Test-fit the coped cut against the temporary scrap from step 1. Fine-tune the cut with files and fine-grit sandpaper.

4

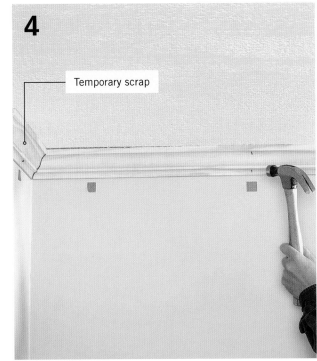

Temporary scrap

Measure, cut to length, and install the first piece of crown molding, leaving the end near the temporary scrap loose for final fitting of the last piece. Nail the molding at the top and bottom of each stud location.

5

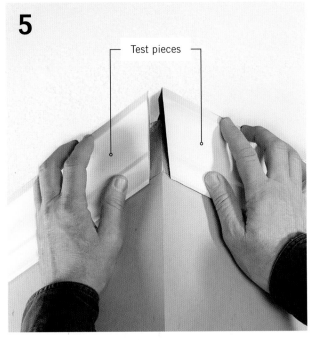

Test pieces

Cut two test pieces to check the fit of outside corners. Start with each molding cut at 45°, adjusting the angles larger or smaller until the joints are tight. Make sure the test moldings are properly aligned and are flush with the ceiling and walls. Make a note of your saw settings once the joint fits tightly.

6

Position the actual stock so a cut end is flush against the wall at one end and, at the other end, mark the outside corner on the back edge of the molding. Miter-cut the piece at the mark, according to the angles you noted on the test pieces.

7

Measure and cut the third piece with an outside corner miter to match the angle of your test pieces. Cut the other end squarely, butting it into the corner. Install the piece with nails driven at stud locations. Install the subsequent pieces of crown molding, coping the front end and butting the other as you work around the room.

8

Temporary spacer removed

To fit the final piece, cope the end and cut it to length. Remove the temporary scrap piece from step 3, and slide the last molding into position. Nail the last piece at the stud locations when the joints fit well, and finish nailing the first piece.

9

Fill all nail holes. Use spackling compound if painting; wait until the finish is applied, and fill with tinted putty for clear finishes. Use a putty knife to force spackling compound or tinted wood putty into loose joints, and caulk gaps ⅛" or smaller between the molding and the wall or ceiling with flexible, paintable, latex caulk.

10

Lightly sand the filled nail holes and joint gaps with fine sandpaper. Sand the nail hole flush with the surface of the moldings, and apply a final coat of paint to the entire project.

DECORATIVE DOOR HEADER

Adding a decorative head casing to a door is a simple way to dress up your existing trim. Although head treatments are more common over doors, this project will work for window trim as well. Designing your own decorative molding can be creative and fun, but try not to overwhelm the room with an elaborate piece, or it may detract from the décor.

Standard stock door casings have an outer-edge thickness of approximately $^{11}/_{16}$ inch. Build your custom header around this thickness. Use it to create a reveal line to a thinner piece of trim, or build out from the edge for a bolder, more substantial appearance. In the project shown, a bed molding, or smaller piece of crown molding, is used to build out the header away from the wall. The ends of the molding are returned to the wall, and the entire piece is capped with a piece of lattice molding. Installing a decorative header of this style on an interior door may require the installation of additional blocking. For installation over an exterior door or a window, nail the pieces in place directly to the load-bearing framing in the wall above the opening.

Tools & Materials ▸

Pencil	2½" finish nails
Tape measure	Moldings
Power miter saw	Wood glue
Finish nail gun	Finish materials
Brad nail gun	Eye and ear protection
1 and ⅝" brad nails	

Replacing plain head casing on a door or window with a decorative built-up version is a quick and easy way to add some sophistication to any ordinary feature of your home.

HOW TO INSTALL A DECORATIVE DOOR HEADER

1

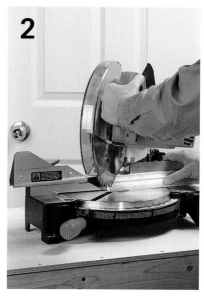

2

Measure the width of your door casing and rough-cut a piece of bed or crown molding 6" longer. Use the casing width dimension to lay out cut marks on the bottom edge of the molding. Start the marks 2" from the end to allow space for cutting the mitered ends.

With the molding upside down and sprung against the fence, cut a 45° outside corner miter angle at each end, on the casing reference marks from step 1.

3

4

5

Cut mitered returns for the molding using the leftover piece. Set the angle of the power miter saw to the opposing 45° angle and cut the returns with the molding upside down and sprung against the fence. Dry-fit the pieces, recutting them if necessary. Apply glue to the return pieces and nail them to the ends of the head molding with 1" brad nails.

Nail the new header in place with 2½" finish nails driven at an angle through the bed molding and into the framing members of the wall.

Cut lattice molding 1" longer than the length of the bed molding and nail it in place with ⅝" brad nails so that it has a uniform overhang of ½". Fill all nail holes with spackle and sand them with fine-grit sandpaper. Apply the final coat of finish.

BUILT-UP BASE MOLDING

Built-up base molding is made up of several strips of wood (usually three) that are combined for a particular effect. It is installed in two common scenarios: (1) to match existing trim in other rooms of a house or (2) to match a stock one-piece molding that is not available.

Installing a built-up base molding is no more difficult than a standard one-piece molding, because the same installation techniques are used. However, built-up base molding offers a few advantages over standard stock moldings. Wavy floors and walls are easier to conceal, and the height of the molding is completely up to you, making heat registers and other obstructions easier to deal with.

In this project, the base molding is made of high-grade plywood rather than solid stock lumber. Plywood is more economical and dimensionally stable than solid lumber and can be built up to any depth, as well as cut down to any height. Keep in mind that plywood molding is less durable than solid wood and is only available in 8- and 10-foot lengths, making joints more frequent.

Tools & Materials ▸

Pneumatic finish	Tape measure
nail gun	Sandpaper
Air compressor	Power sander
Air hose	¾" finish-grade oak
Miter saw	plywood
Hammer	Base shoe molding
Nail set	Cap molding
Tablesaw or	1¼" brad nails
straightedge guide	2" finish nails,
and circular saw	wood putty
Pencil	Eye and ear protection

Built-up base trim is made by combining baseboard, base shoe, and another molding type, typically cap molding.

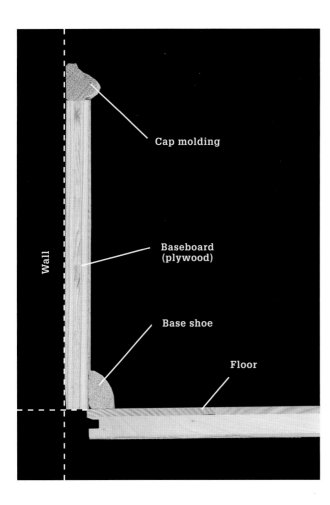

Cap molding

Wall

Baseboard
(plywood)

Base shoe

Floor

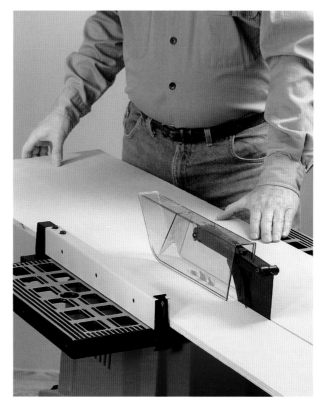

Cut the plywood panel into 6" strips with a tablesaw or a straightedge guide and a circular saw. Lightly sand the strips, removing any splinters left from the saw. Then apply the finish of your choice to the moldings and the plywood strips.

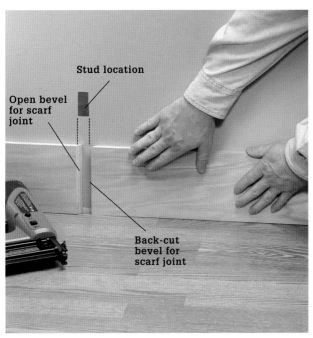

Stud location

Open bevel
for scarf
joint

Back-cut
bevel for
scarf joint

Install the plywood strips with 2" finish nails driven at stud locations. Use scarf joints on continuous runs, driving pairs of fasteners into the joints. Cut and install moldings so that all scarf joints fall at stud locations.

Base Trim Spacers ▸

Baseboard can be built up on the back with spacer strips so it will project farther out from the wall. This can allow you to match existing casings or to create the impression of a thicker molding. However, the cap rail needs to be thick enough to cover the plywood edge completely or the core of the panel may be visible.

INSTALLING BUILT-UP BASE MOLDING

Test-fit inside corner butt joints before cutting a workpiece. If the walls are not square or straight, angle or bevel the end cut a few degrees to fit the profile of the adjoining piece. The cap molding will cover any gaps at the top of the joint. See illustration, page 117.

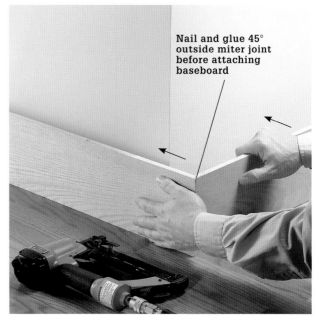

Nail and glue 45° outside miter joint before attaching baseboard

Miter outside corners squarely at 45°. Use wood glue and 1¼" brad nails to pull the mitered pieces tight, and then nail the base to the wall at stud locations with 2" finish nails. Small gaps at the bottom or top of the base molding will be covered with cap or base shoe.

Use a brad nailer with 18-gauge, ⅝" brads to install the cap and base shoe moldings along the edges of the plywood base. Fit scarf joints on longer lengths, coped joints on inside corners, and miter joints on outside corners. Stagger the seams so that they do not line up with the base molding seams. Set any protruding nails with a nail set and fill all nail holes with putty.

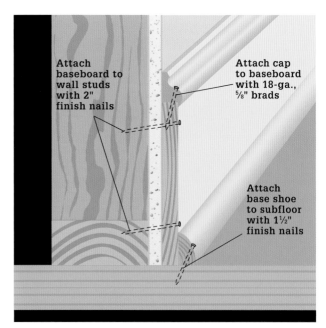

Attach baseboard to wall studs with 2" finish nails

Attach cap to baseboard with 18-ga., ⅝" brads

Attach base shoe to subfloor with 1½" finish nails

Built-up baseboard requires more attention to the nailing schedule than simple one-piece baseboards. The most important consideration (other than making sure your nails are all driven into studs or other solid wood), is that the base shoe must be attached to the floor, while the baseboard is attached to the wall. This way, as the gap between the wall and floor changes, the parts of the built-up molding can change with them.

OPTIONS WITH HEAT REGISTERS

Installing base molding around heat registers and cold-air returns can sometimes be challenging. Register thickness and height vary, complicating installation.

Here are a few methods that can be employed for trimming around these obstructions.

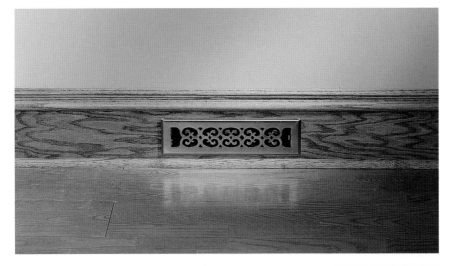

Adjust the height of your baseboard to completely surround the heat register opening. Then cut a pocket out of the base for the heat register to slide into. Install the base shoe and cap trim molding continuously across the edges of the baseboard.

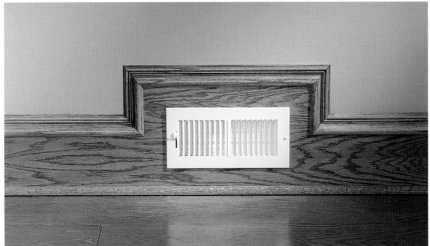

Install a taller backer block to encompass larger register openings. Cut a hole the same size as the duct opening in the backer block and cover the edges of the plywood with cap rail, mitering the rail at the corners. Butt the base molding into the sides of the register. Cut and install returns for the base shoe flush with the ends of the register.

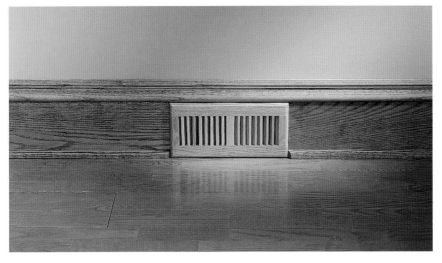

Install a wooden heat register for a less noticeable appearance. Wooden registers can be finished to match your trim and are available through most hardwood floor retailers. Butt the base molding into the ends of the register cover and bevel the front edges of the base shoe to match the depth of the register.

FLOOR PROJECTS

Floors are the hardest-working component of most homes, taking the brunt of foot traffic and also serving as a major decorative element—generally they are the largest unbroken surface area of any room. Because they are constantly in use, most flooring surfaces need to be refreshed at least once if you own your home for many years.

This chapter includes six representative flooring projects of the types that aren't usually covered in standard flooring books. Among these are some purely decorative projects that you might tackle as part of cosmetic remodeling when old surface flooring is removed in favor of new flooring that freshens your home's style statement. Also included is structural flooring work, such as installing underlayment panels during a major attic, basement, or room addition project, and the kind of system upgrade represented by installing an underfloor heating system for a bathroom or kitchen.

This chapter will be a helpful resource if you're looking for the kind of unique flooring improvement that truly sets your home apart.

IN THIS CHAPTER:

- Planning Overview
- Floor Anatomy
- Installing Raised Subfloor Panels
- Installing Laminate Flooring
- Underfloor Radiant Heat Systems
- Laying a Decorative Floor Medallion
- Bonded Bamboo Strip Flooring
- Cork Tile
- Mosaic Tile

PLANNING OVERVIEW

Afloor is one of the most visible parts of your decor, which is why appearance is a primary consideration when choosing floor coverings. Start your search by collecting ideas and inspiration from magazines and books, and visit retail flooring showrooms and home centers to get a sense of what your options are.

As important as appearance is, there are many other considerations that will go into your flooring decision. You'll no doubt put your budget near the top of the list, but you should think about how easy the floor will be to install, how comfortable it is underfoot, its longevity and durability, its resistance to moisture, and how easy it is to clean. You'll also need to assess the demands of the space, including moisture, heavy traffic, and other conditions.

When estimating materials for your project, always add 10 to 15 percent to the total square footage to allow for waste in installation (some carpet installations may require even more). And always save extra flooring materials just in case you ever need to make a repair.

Measure the area of the project room to calculate the quantity of materials you'll need. Measure the full width and length of the space to determine the overall square footage, then subtract the areas that will not be covered, such as stairways, cabinets, and other permanent fixtures.

Checklist for Planning a Flooring Project ▸

Use this checklist to organize your activities as you start your flooring project.

- Measure the project area carefully. Be sure to include all nooks and closets, as well as areas under all movable appliances. Calculate the total square footage of the project area.
- Use your measurements to create a floor plan on graph paper.
- Sketch pattern options on tracing paper laid over the floor plan to help you visualize what the flooring will look like after you install it.
- Identify areas where the type of floor covering will change, and choose the best threshold material to use for the transition.
- Estimate the amount of preparation material needed, including underlayment sheets and floor leveler.
- Estimate the amount of installation material needed, including the floor covering and other supplies, such as adhesive, grout, thresholds, tackless strips, and screws. Add 10 to 15% to your total square footage to allow for waste caused by trimming. For some carpet installations you will need to add even more. *Tip: For help in estimating, go to a building supply center and read the labels on materials and adhesives to determine coverage.*
- Make a list of the tools needed for the job. Locate sources for the tools you will need to buy or rent.
- Estimate the total cost of the project, including all preparation materials, flooring, installation materials, and tools. For expensive materials, shop around to get the best prices.
- Check with building supply centers or flooring retail stores for delivery costs. A delivery service is often worth the additional charge.
- Determine how much demolition you will need to do, and plan for debris removal through your regular garbage collector or a disposal company.
- Plan for the temporary displacement of furnishings and removable appliances to minimize disruption of your daily routine.

FLOOR ANATOMY

A typical wood-frame floor consists of layers that work together to provide the required structural support and desired appearance. These parts include:

1. Joists. At the bottom of the floor are the joists, 2 × 10 or larger framing members that support the weight of the floor. Joists are typically spaced 16 inches apart on center.
2. Subfloor. The subfloor is nailed to the joists. Most subfloors installed in the 1970s or later are made of ¾-inch tongue-and-groove plywood; in older houses, the subfloor often consists of 1-inch-thick wood planks nailed diagonally across the floor joists.
3. Underlayment. On top of the subfloor, most builders place a ½-inch plywood underlayment. Some flooring materials, especially ceramic tile, require cementboard for stability.
4. Adhesive. For many types of floor coverings, adhesive or mortar is spread on the underlayment before the floor covering is installed. Carpet rolls generally require tackless strips and cushioned padding.
5. Floorcovering. Other materials, such as snap-fit laminate planks or carpet squares, can be installed directly on the underlayment with little or no adhesive.

Asbestos & Flooring ▶

Resilient flooring manufactured before 1980 may contain asbestos, which can cause severe lung problems if inhaled. The easiest method for dealing with asbestos-containing flooring is to cover it with a new floorcovering. If the asbestos flooring must be removed, consult an asbestos-abatement professional or ask a local building inspector to explain the asbestos handling and disposal regulations in your area.

CUTAWAY OF A TYPICAL FLOOR

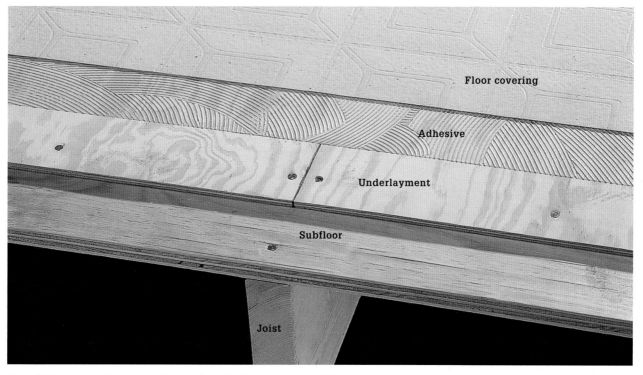

Floor covering

Adhesive

Underlayment

Subfloor

Joist

Not all floor covering materials require adhesive; some materials, such as snap-fit laminate, are installed directly on the underlayment.

INSTALLING RAISED SUBFLOOR PANELS

Raised subfloor panels are an excellent choice as a base layer when installing wood or laminate floors over concrete slabs, such as in a basement. The raised panels do an even better job of protecting against moisture than simple plastic vapor barriers.

Do not expect a raised subfloor to eliminate problems in a basement with severe water problems, however. The system works very well for combatting the normal moisture that is always present in an otherwise water-secure basement, but a basement that frequently has puddled water must be corrected in a more aggressive way before flooring can be laid over the slab.

The raised subfloor panels fit together securely with simple tongue-and-groove edges, and for best results the concrete slab must first be examined for dips or cracks, and leveled out before laying the subfloor panels.

Tools & Materials ▶

Long board
Floor leveler and trowel (if needed)
Tape measure
Circular saw
Jigsaw
Carpenter's square
Tapping block and pull bar
Hammer
¼" wall spacers
Particle mask
Eye and ear protection

HOW TO INSTALL RAISED SUBFLOOR PANELS OVER A CONCRETE SLAB

Clean the concrete floor and install temporary ¼" spacers along all walls. Starting with the longest wall, measure the length of the wall, and calculate the number of panels needed by dividing this length by the width of the panel (most products are 2 × 2'). If necessary, trim the starting panel to ensure that the last panel in the first row will be at least 3" in width.

Check the first corner for square, using a carpenter's square. If it is not square, the first panel will need to be angled in the back corner to ensure the first row will fit flush against the wall along its entire length.

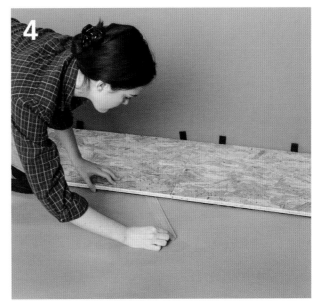

Lay the first panel with the tongue side flat against the wall spacers. Slide the next panel into place by connecting its tongue into the groove of the preceding panel. Using a tapping block, snug up the tongue-and-groove joint. For the last panel in the first row, measure the gap between the last installed panel and the wall spacer, and cut the last panel to this measurement. Install by inserting the tongue of the cut panel into the groove of the preceding panel, and levering it down into place. Pull it into place so the joint is secure using a pull bar.

Before beginning the second row, check the first row for flatness, and if there are any areas with "give" or bounce, adjust them with leveling shims inserted under the panels.

As you start the second row, cut the first panel in half, so that seams will be staggered between rows. Begin with the half panel, and install the second row as you did the first, sliding the tongues into the grooves of the preceding row, and snugging them up with the tapping block. Install the subsequent rows, so that the first panels alternate, with odd number rows matching the pattern of the first row, even numbered rows matching the pattern of the second row.

At the last row, trim the wall side of the panels to fit the space between the previous row and the wall spacers, and snug up their joints with the pull bar. Remove all spacers.

INSTALLING LAMINATE FLOORING

Most big-name flooring manufacturers now feature dozens if not hundreds of laminate flooring options among their catalogues, for a very simple reason: laminates are favorites among DIYers and value-conscious shoppers.

Laminate flooring is a multilayer synthetic product in which the layers are fused (laminated) together. The core of the flooring is usually a high-density fiberboard (HDF) that is tightly bonded with resins. To this core, a photo appliqué layer is bonded—this layer is not wood at all, but a plastic layer that can be made to look remarkably like any kind of wood. Over the plastic photo layer is a clear protective surface layer that protects against wear.

The technology makes it possible for the flooring to closely resemble any desired wood simply by varying the photo appliqué layer. Recent advances even allow the laminate products to be textured in a way that closely mimics actual wood grain. Laminate flooring products are very stable and easy to install, making them an excellent choice for DIYers.

Laminate flooring products have few drawbacks, but they can be susceptible to scratching, especially in high traffic areas, and they are not always the best choice for high moisture areas, such as bathrooms or laundry rooms. And there have been cases of lower-quality, non-brand-name flooring products that delaminate over time.

You can minimize the chances for problems by buying a quality product from a well-known, reputable manufacturer, and checking the product specifications to make sure it is appropriate for your planned location. Most manufacturers offer products marketed as "waterproof" or "water-resistant" for bathrooms and other wet locations, though you should be aware that these will never be quite as genuinely waterproof as ceramic tile or vinyl floor.

Early laminate flooring products were installed with a full glue-down bond to the subfloor, and while some of these products are still available, the vast majority of laminate floors are now installed with a "floating" system that require no glue. A locking channel system holds the planks together both along the length and at the ends, and simple gravity holds the flooring down.

Because laminate floors float, foot traffic can create a hollow sound as the flooring flexes under footsteps. This is one reason why all manufacturers require that the flooring be installed on a special underlayment that deadens the sound and minimizes the flexing of the floor. Some flooring products have the resilient foam underlayment already attached to the bottom of the flooring planks.

HOW TO INSTALL A FLOATING LAMINATE FLOOR

Tools & Materials ›

Eye & ear protection
Work gloves
Utility knife
Tape measure
Power miter saw
Circular saw
Flush-cutting handsaw
Shop vacuum
Framing square
Pry bar
Jigsaw
Pull bar
Tapping block
Rubber mallet
Hammer
Chisel
Level
Caulk gun
Liquid floor leveler
  (if necessary)
Nails (as needed)
Sheet underlayment
  kit with clear tape
Laminate flooring
Wood glue
Flooring spacers
Finishing putty
Mildew-resistant
  silicone caulk
T-moldings

Inspect each plank, and reject any that are scarred or that have damaged tongues or grooves. For the first row of planks along the wall, remove the tongues along the long sides of the planks using a circular saw or tablesaw. *Note: If you are ripping the first row down to accommodate a partial plank, then make sure to cut away the tongue-side of the plank.*

2

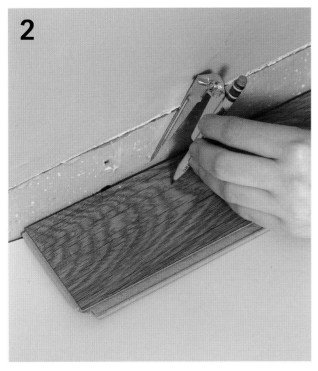

Variation: If your wall is irregular, using a compass to trace the wall outline on the plank, then use a jigsaw to cut the plank to conform to the wall's contours.

3

Cross-cut a plank into ⅓- and ⅔-length segments. These pieces will be used to start the second and third rows, respectively.

4

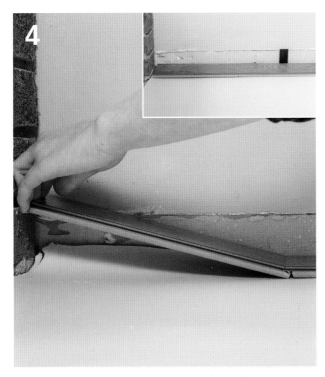

Begin laying the first row using the planks with the tongues cut away, beginning with a full-length piece in the corner. Make sure to maintain a ⅜" gap along both walls. For the second piece, align the end tongue-and-groove, and snap into place. At the last plank in the row, cut the plank to fit with a miter saw, maintaining the ⅜" gap to the wall (inset).

5

Install the subsequent rows of planks, alternating full plank, ⅔-length plank, and ⅓-length plank, so that joints are staggered in a repeating pattern. To fit each plank, first insert the tongue into the edge groove of the previous row of planks, then slide it laterally until the new plank butts up to the end of the preceding piece. Snap downward to lock into place.

(continued)

6

If necessary, tap on the opposite end of the plank with a tapping block to snug up the joint. Take care, though, not to damage the plank.

7

At the last piece in the row, cut length to size, then fit the piece into the edge groove, and use the pull bar and hammer to lightly draw the piece back to secure the end joint.

8

As you install the last row, lay each full piece against the wall on top of the last installed piece, with a scrap plank positioned vertically against the wall as a spacer. Trace the wall contour onto the plank.

9

Cut along the scribed lines of the last planks using a jigsaw.

10

To install the pieces of the final row, slide the long-side tongue into the groove of the previous row, with the ends aligned. Use the pull bar and hammer to work along the length of the plank, pulling toward you to gently secure the joint.

11

Reinstall the trim moldings that were removed, covering the gaps between the flooring and the wall. Remember the floating floor needs to expand and contract, so make sure to drive finish nails at an angle into the wall, not into the flooring.

HOW TO CUT LAMINATE FLOORING FOR OPENINGS & OBSTACLES

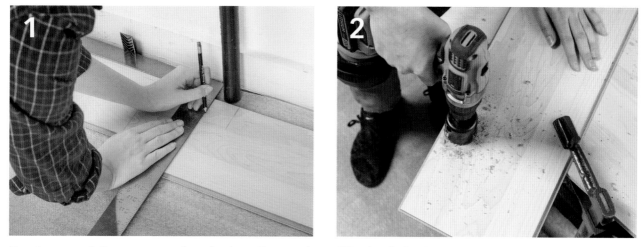

For pipes, carefully measure and mark where the opening will be, by aligning the piece to be installed against the obstacle and marking with a pencil. Make sure to add a ⅜" expansion gap around all sides. Then, cut the opening with a hole saw. Extend the notch to the edges of the plank using a jigsaw.

For internal cutouts, such as those required for floor ducts, first outline the opening on the laminate plank. Drill small corner holes as pilot openings, then use a jigsaw to cut out the opening.

UNDERFLOOR RADIANT HEAT SYSTEMS

Floor-warming systems require very little energy to run and are designed to heat ceramic tile floors only; they generally are not used as sole heat sources for rooms.

A typical floor-warming system consists of one or more thin mats containing electric resistance wires that heat up when energized like an electric blanket. The mats are installed beneath the tile and are hardwired to a 120-volt GFCI circuit. A thermostat controls the temperature, and a timer turns the system off automatically.

The system shown in this project includes two plastic mesh mats, each with its own power lead that is wired directly to the thermostat. Radiant mats may be installed over a plywood subfloor, but if you plan to install floor tile you should put down a base of cementboard first, and then install the mats on top of the cementboard.

A crucial part of installing this system is to use a multimeter to perform several resistance checks to make sure the heating wires have not been damaged during shipping or installation.

Electrical service required for a floor-warming system is based on size. A smaller system may connect to an existing GFCI circuit, but a larger one will need a dedicated circuit; follow the manufacturer's requirements.

To order a floor-warming system, contact the manufacturer or dealer. In most cases, you can send them plans and they'll custom-fit a system for your project area.

Tools & Materials ▸

Vacuum cleaner	Trowel or rubber float
Multimeter	Conduit
Tape measure	Thinset mortar
Scissors	Thermostat with sensor
Router/rotary tool	Junction box(es)
Marker	Tile or stone floorcovering
Electric wire fault	Drill
indicator (optional)	Double-sided carpet tape
Hot glue gun	Cable clamps
Radiant floor mats	Eye and ear protection
12/2 NM cable	

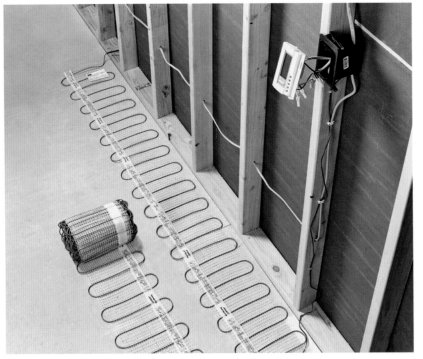

A radiant floor-warming system employs electric heating mats that are covered with floor tile to create a floor that's cozy underfoot.

Installation Tips ▸

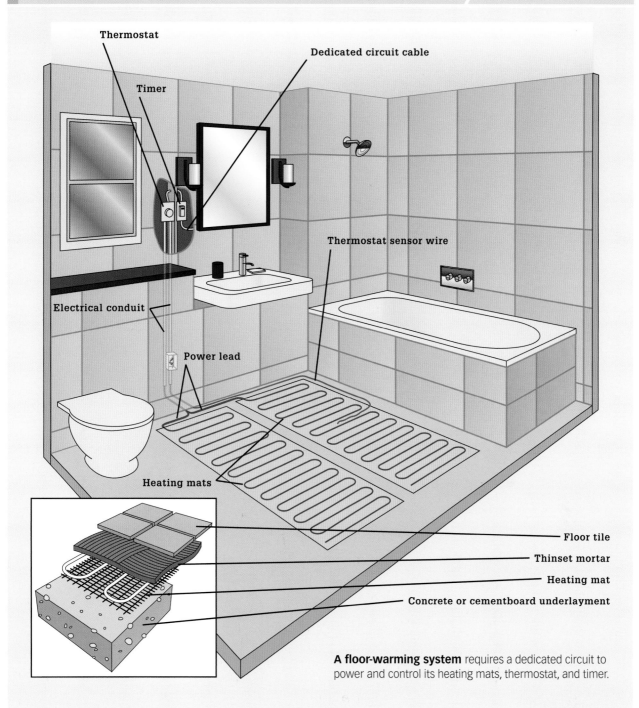

Thermostat

Timer

Dedicated circuit cable

Thermostat sensor wire

Electrical conduit

Power lead

Heating mats

Floor tile

Thinset mortar

Heating mat

Concrete or cementboard underlayment

A floor-warming system requires a dedicated circuit to power and control its heating mats, thermostat, and timer.

- Each radiant mat must have a direct connection to the power lead from the thermostat, with the connection made in a junction box in the wall cavity. Do not install mats in series.
- Do not install radiant floor mats under shower areas.
- Do not overlap mats or let them touch.
- Do not cut heating wire or damage heating wire insulation.
- The distance between wires in adjoining mats should equal the distance between wire loops measured center to center.

INSTALLING A RADIANT FLOOR-WARMING SYSTEM

Floor-warming systems must be installed on a circuit with adequate amperage and a GFCI breaker. Smaller systems may tie into an existing circuit, but larger ones need a dedicated circuit. Follow local building and electrical codes that apply to your project.

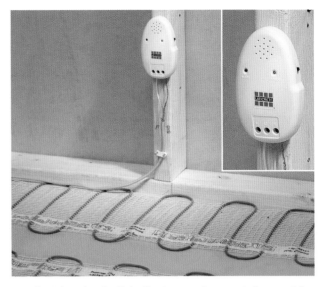

An electric wire fault indicator monitors each floor mat for continuity during the installation process. If there is a break in continuity (for example, if a wire is cut) an alarm sounds. If you choose not to use an installation tool to monitor the mat, test for continuity frequently using a multimeter.

HOW TO INSTALL A RADIANT FLOOR-WARMING SYSTEM

1

Install electrical boxes to house the thermostat and timer. In most cases, the box should be located 60" above floor level. Use a 4"-deep, 4"-wide double-gang box for the thermostat/timer control if your kit has an integral model. If your timer and thermostat are separate, install a separate single box for the timer.

2

Drill access holes in the sole plate for the power leads that are preattached to the mats (they should be over 10' long). The leads should be connected to a supply wire from the thermostat in a junction box located in a wall near the floor and below the thermostat box. The access hole for each mat should be located directly beneath the knockout for that cable in the thermostat box. Drill through the sill plate vertically and horizontally so the holes meet in an L-shape.

3

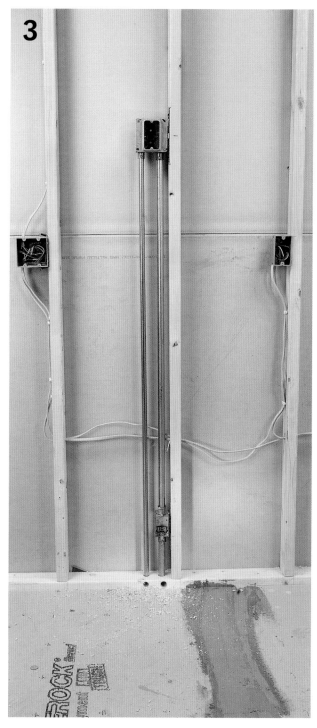

Run conduit from the electrical boxes to the sill plate.
The line for the supply cable should be ¾" conduit. If you
are installing multiple mats, the supply conduit should feed
into a junction box about 6" above the sill plate and then
continue into the ¾" hole you drilled for the supply leads. The
sensor wire needs only ½" conduit that runs straight from
the thermostat box via the thermostat. The mats should be
powered by a dedicated 20-amp GFCI circuit of 12/2 NM cable
run from your main service panel to the electrical box (this is
for 120-volt mats—check your instruction manual for specific
circuit recommendations).

4

Clean the floor surface thoroughly to get rid of any debris
that could potentially damage the wire mats. A vacuum cleaner
generally does a more effective job than a broom.

5

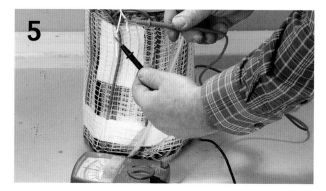

Test for resistance using a multimeter set to measure
ohms. This is a test you should make frequently during
the installation, along with checking for continuity. If the
resistance is off by more than 10% from the theoretical
resistance listing (see manufacturer's chart in installation
instructions), contact a technical support operator for the kit
manufacturer. For example, the theoretical resistance for the
1 × 50' mat seen here is 19, so the ohms reading should be
between 17 and 21.

6

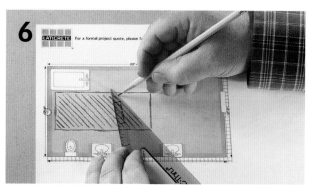

Finalize your mat layout plan. Most radiant floor warming
mat manufacturers will provide a layout plan for you at the
time of purchase, or they will give you access to an online
design tool so you can come up with your own plan. This is
an important step to the success of your project, and the
assistance is free.

(continued)

7

Unroll the radiant mat or mats and allow them to settle. Arrange the mat or mats according to the plan you created. It's okay to cut the plastic mesh so you can make curves or switchbacks, but do not cut the heating wire under any circumstances, even to shorten it.

8

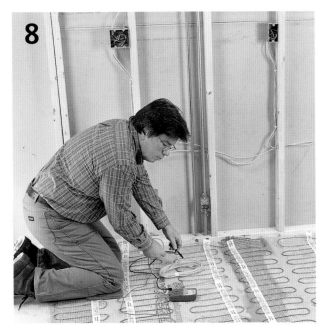

Finalize the mat layout and then test the resistance again using a multimeter. Also check for continuity in several different spots. If there is a problem with any of the mats, you should identify it and correct it before proceeding with the mortar installation.

9

Run the thermostat sensor wire from the electrical box down the ½" conduit raceway and out the access hole in the sill plate. Select the best location for the thermostat sensor and mark the location onto the flooring. Also mark the locations of the wires that connect to and lead from the sensor.

Variation: If your local codes require it, roll the mats out of the way and cut a channel for the sensor and the sensor wires into the floor or floor underlayment. For most floor materials, a spiral cutting tool does a quick and neat job of this task. Remove any debris.

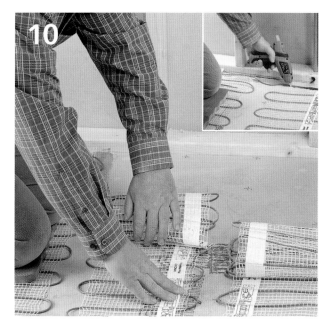

Bond the mats to the floor. If the mats in your system have adhesive strips, peel off the adhesive backing and roll out the mats in the correct position, pressing them against the floor to set the adhesive. If your mats have no adhesive, bind them with strips of double-sided carpet tape. The thermostat sensor and the power supply leads should be attached with hot glue (inset photo) and run up into their respective holes in the sill plate if you have not done this already. Test all mats for resistance and continuity.

Cover the floor installation areas with a layer of thinset mortar that is thick enough to fully encapsulate all the wires and mats (usually around ¼" in thickness). Check the wires for continuity and resistance regularly and stop working immediately if there is a drop in resistance or a failure of continuity. Allow the mortar to dry overnight.

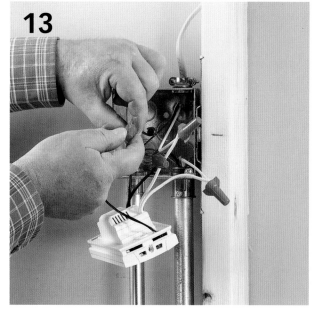

Connect the power supply leads from the mat or mats to the NM cable coming from the thermostat inside the junction box near the sill. Power must be turned off. The power leads should be cut so about 8" of wire feeds into the box. Be sure to use cable clamps to protect the wires.

Connect the sensor wire and the power supply lead (from the junction box) to the thermostat/timer according to the manufacturer's directions. Attach the device to the electrical box, restore power, and test the system to make sure it works. Once you are convinced that it is operating properly, install floor tiles and repair the wall surfaces.

A medallion made from wood strips and veneers makes a beautiful design highlight when inset into a wood floor. Flooring retailers and online flooring sellers should have access to many designs. A local craftsman can also make a custom medallion for you.

INSTALLING A DECORATIVE MEDALLION

If anything is more beautiful under your feet than a newly installed hardwood floor, it's a decorative centerpiece that complements the rest of the surface. Ready-made hardwood medallions, such as the one shown in this project, are relatively easy to install and provide a focal point for the entire room.

Tools & Materials ▸

Medallion	Eye and ear protection
Installation jig	Pry bar
Hammer	Wood putty
Nails	Trowel
Notched trowel	Urethane flooring adhesive
Router	

HOW TO INSTALL A FLOOR MEDALLION

Place the medallion on the floor where you want it installed. Draw a line around the medallion onto the floor.

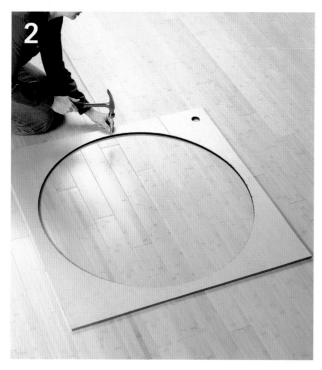

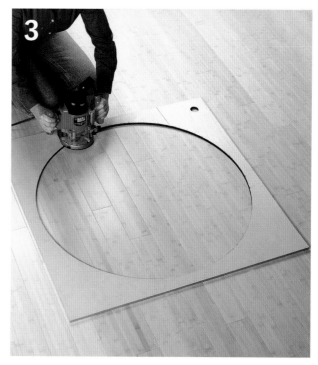

Nail the installation jig to the floor so the opening is aligned with the outline you drew in the previous step. Drive the nails into joints in the floor.

Using the router bit that came with the medallion, place the bearing of the router bit on the inside edge of the jig opening and make a ¼"-deep cut. Remove any exposed nails or staples. Make repeated passes with the router, gradually increasing the depth.

Use a pry bar to remove the flooring inside the hole. Remove all nails. Dry-fit the medallion to ensure it fits. Remove the jig and fill nail holes with wood putty.

Apply urethane flooring adhesive to the subfloor where the hardwood was removed. Spread the adhesive with a trowel. Set the medallion in place and push it firmly into the adhesive so it's level with the surrounding floor.

BONDED BAMBOO STRIP FLOORING

It looks like hardwood, and is available in traditional tongue-and-groove form and in laminate planks. But bamboo is not wood. It's really a grass—and one of the most popular flooring materials today.

Bamboo flooring is made by shredding stalks of the raw material, then pressing them together with a resin that holds the shreds in their finished shape. Not only is bamboo a fast-growing and renewable crop, the companies that make bamboo flooring use binders with low emissions of volatile organic compounds (VOCs). The result is tough, economical, and ecologically friendly. In other words, it's just about perfect for flooring.

If you choose tongue-and-groove bamboo, the installation techniques are the same as for hardwoods. Bamboo is also available as a snap-fit laminate for use in floating floors. In this project we show Teragren Synergy Strand in Java (see Resources, 000): thin, durable planks that are glued to the underlayment.

Bamboo flooring can mimic the appearance of classic hardwood, but is a much more sustainable resource that produces less harmful chemicals during the production process.

Tools & Materials ›

Adhesive	Moisture level meter	Bamboo flooring material	Weights
Carpenter's level	Notched trowel	Hammer	Trim
Carpenter's square	Rubber mallet	Drill	Floor leveler (if necessary)
Chalk line	Scrap lumber	Screws	Sandpaper
Cleaning supplies	Shims	Nails	Eye and ear protection
Marking pen or pencil	Straightedge	Circular saw	Work gloves
Tape measure	Weighted roller	Butcher paper	

Tips for a Successful Installation ›

60° 70°
RECOMENDED
TEMPERATURE
RANGE

40% 60%
RECOMENDED
HUMIDITY
RANGE

Bamboo plank flooring should be one of the last items installed on any new construction or remodeling project. All work involving water or moisture should be completed before floor installation. Room temperature and humidity of installation area should be consistent with normal, year-round living conditions for at least a week before installation. Room temperature of 60 to 70ºF and a humidity range of 40 to 60% is recommended.

About radiant heat: the subfloor should never exceed 85ºF. Check the manufacturer's suggested guidelines for correct water temperature inside heating pipes. Switch on the heating unit three days before flooring installation. Room temperature should not vary more than 15ºF year-round. For glue-down installations, leave the heating unit on for three days following installation.

HOW TO INSTALL BAMBOO STRIP FLOORING

1

Give the bamboo time to adjust to installation conditions. Store it for at least 72 hours in or near the room where it will be installed. Open the packages for inspection, but do not store the planks on concrete or near outside walls.

2

Even though thin-plank bamboo is an engineered material, it can vary in appearance. Buy all planks from the same lot and batch number. Then inspect the planks to make sure they match. Use the same lighting as you will have in the finished room.

3

Inspect the underlayment. Bamboo planks can be installed on plywood or oriented strandboard at least ¾" thick. The underlayment must be structurally sound; wood surfaces should have no more than 12% moisture.

4

Make sure the underlayment is level. It should not change by more than ⅛" over 10'. If necessary, apply a floor leveler to fill any low places, and sand down any high spots. Prevent squeaks by driving screws every 6" into the subfloor below.

5

Sweep and vacuum the surface, then measure all room dimensions.

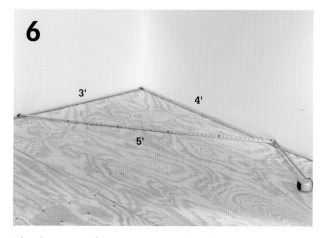

6

Check corners for squareness using the 3-4-5 triangle method.

(continued)

7

The planks should be perpendicular to the floor joists below. Adjust your starting point if necessary. Snap a chalk line next to the longest wall. The distance from the wall should be the same at both ends, leaving ½" for expansion.

8

Lay the first course of planks with the tongue edge toward the wall. Align the planks with the chalk line. Hold the edge course in place with wedges, or by nailing through the tongue edge. This row will anchor the others, so make sure it stays securely in place.

9

Once the starter row is in place, install the planks using a premium wood flooring adhesive. Be sure to follow the manufacturer's instructions. Begin at the chalk line and apply enough adhesive to lay down one or two rows of planks. Spread the adhesive with a V-notched trowel at a 45° angle. Let the adhesive sit for the specified time.

10

When the adhesive is tacky and ready to use, lay the first section of bamboo planks. Set each plank in the adhesive by placing a clean piece of scrap lumber on top and tapping it down with a rubber mallet. Check the edge of each section to make sure it keeps a straight line.

11

After you finish the first section, cover the next area with adhesive and give it time to become tacky. Waiting for the adhesive to become tacky is necessary, even though it slows your work down—and it allows the section you just finished to set up.

12

When the adhesive is ready, lay down the next section of planks. Fit the new planks tightly against the previous section, taking care not to knock the finished section out of alignment. If the planks have tongue-and-groove edges, fit them carefully into place.

13

Continue applying adhesive and installing planks, one section at a time, to cover the entire floor. When adhesive gets on the flooring surface, wipe it off quickly.

14

At the edges and around any fixed objects, such as doorways or plumbing pipes, leave a ½" gap for expansion. Use shims to maintain the gaps if needed. These spaces can be covered with baseboards, base shoe, and escutcheons.

15

As you finish each section, walk across it a few times to maximize contact between the planks and the adhesive. When all the planks are in place, clean the surface and use a clean weighted roller. Push the roller in several directions, covering the entire surface many times.

16

In places that are difficult to reach with a roller, lay down a sheet of protective material, such as butcher paper, and stack weights on the paper. Let the finished floor sit for at least 24 hours, then clean the surface and remove any spacers from the expansion gaps. Finally, install the finishing trim.

CORK TILE

Cork flooring has all kinds of benefits. It dampens sound, resists static, insulates surfaces, and provides visual warmth like no other floor covering. Cork is a renewable natural product—tree bark—that can be harvested once a decade without cutting down the tree.

Natural cork tiles complement most furnishings and decorations, and can be found in every shade from honey yellow to deep espresso brown. Left in its original color or stained, cork has beautiful patterns that range from burls to spalting. Every tile is different, which means no two installations will look the same.

The tiles may seem fragile, but they take on the strength of the underlayment below. In fact, once a cork floor is installed and properly sealed, it can withstand normal household use just as well as any other material.

Tools & Materials ›

Tape measure	Scrap lumber	Paint roller and tray	Paper
Chalk line	Rubber mallet	Recommended flooring adhesive	Vacuum
Utility knife	Joint sealer	Level	Floor roller
Cork tile	Sander	Straightedge	
Notched trowel	Floor sealer	Eye and ear protection	

Tips for a Successful Installation ›

Before you work with any cork flooring material, remove it from the package and leave it in the room where it will be installed. This lets the material adjust to the room's temperature and humidity. Manufacturers recommend acclimating cork for at least 72 hours.

Cork is a renewable material that is comfortable underfoot and dampens sound. Cork is also available in many shades and has a striking natural texture.

HOW TO INSTALL CORK TILE

1

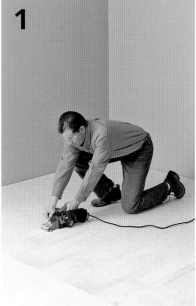

If you plan to install the cork on plywood underlayment or a similar material, make sure the surface is clean and dry, with no more change in level than ⅛" over 10'. Fill any low spots and sand down any high spots.

2

Measure the outside edges of the room, and snap chalk lines across the center. Dry-lay a row of tiles from the center to each wall.

3

If the last row will be less than ¼ the width of one tile, adjust the center point to balance the layout.

4

Apply a recommended adhesive, using the method specified by the manufacturer. Some adhesives are best applied with a paint roller, others with a notched trowel. Put down only as much adhesive as you can use in the time allowed.

5

Cork adhesive needs to set for 20 to 30 minutes before you can begin laying the cork tiles. After that, the working time is roughly one hour. Check the setting time specified by the adhesive manufacturer.

6

Begin at the intersection of the two center guidelines, and set the first tile in place. Check to make sure the adhesive holds it firmly. Continue laying tiles in the first quadrant along your layout lines.

(continued)

7

Fill in the first quadrant, one tile at a time, working from the row laid next to the layout lines. Cork tile colors and patterns will vary. Use this to your advantage by mixing batches for greater variety.

8

To fit each new tile in place, hold a piece of scrap lumber against the edge and tap it gently with a rubber mallet. If the humidity is high during installation, fit the tiles together tightly so they won't pull apart in drier weather.

9

As you complete each row, check to see that all edges are straight. If a row has gone out of line, remove as many tiles as necessary and start again. It's frustrating to make corrections now, but it's difficult or impossible later.

10

To fit tile around an object, such as a pipe or drain, cut a tile-sized piece of paper. Work the paper into the space, cutting as needed until it fits. Then lay the paper on a tile and use it as a cutting guide. Cut tiles with a utility knife.

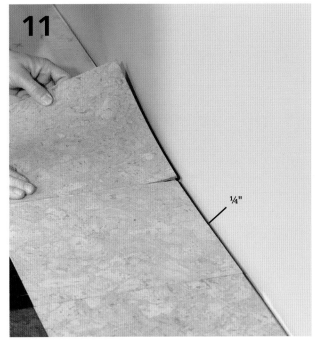

11

¼"

Like other natural materials, cork will expand and contract as the temperature and humidity change. To allow space for varying conditions, leave a ¼" gap between the finished floor and all walls, thresholds, water pipes, and other vertical surfaces.

12

If your cork floor measures more than 30' in any direction, install a ⅝"-wide expansion joint—either in a continuous surface or where the cork meets another flooring material. This allows the cork to flex with changing conditions.

13

Once all the tiles are in place, vacuum the surface to remove all dust. Make several passes across the entire surface with a 100-pound floor roller. Move the roller in different directions to press every tile down securely. Let the finished floor sit overnight, then roll it again.

14

After rolling the surface, clean it once more and apply a recommended sealer. The most common is a water-based polyurethane. Make sure the sealer penetrates all joints so it prevents moisture from entering and damaging the finished floor. Allow the sealed floor to cure for another day before you use it. Install molding, trim, and other finishing pieces.

MOSAIC TILE

Mosaic tile is an excellent choice for smaller areas. It requires the same preparation and handling as larger tiles, with a few differences. Sheets of mosaic tile are held together by a fabric-mesh base. This makes them more difficult to hold, place, and move. They may not be square with your guidelines when you first lay them down. And mosaic tiles will require many more temporary spacers and much more grout.

A few cautions: variations in color and texture are just as likely with mosaic tile as with individual tiles, so buy all your tile from the same lot and batch. Different types of tiles will require different types of mortar and mastic. Finally, if the finished project will be exposed to the elements, make sure you have adhesive and grout suitable for outdoor use.

Tools & Materials ▸

Carpenter's square
Chalk line
Cleaning supplies
Coarse sponge
Grout sealer
Marking pen
   or pencil
Tape measure
Notched trowel

Recommended adhesive
Rubber mallet
Sanded grout
Scrap lumber
Tile nippers
Tile spacers
Mosaic tile sheets
Grout float
Eye and ear protection

Mosaic tiles come in sheets (usually 12 × 12") and can be made from ceramic, porcelain, glass or any number of designer materials. Normally installed for their appearance, mosaics are relatively high maintenance and prone to cracks because of all the grout lines.

HOW TO INSTALL MOSAIC TILE

Clean and prepare the area as you would for individual tiles, with reference lines beginning in the center. Beginning at the center intersection, apply the recommended adhesive to one quadrant. Spread it outward evenly with a notched trowel. Lay down only as much adhesive as you can cover in 10 to 15 minutes.

Select a sheet of mosaic tile. Place several plastic spacers within the grid so that the sheet remains square. Pick up the sheet of tiles by diagonally opposite corners. This will help you hold the edges up so that you don't trap empty space in the middle of the sheet.

3

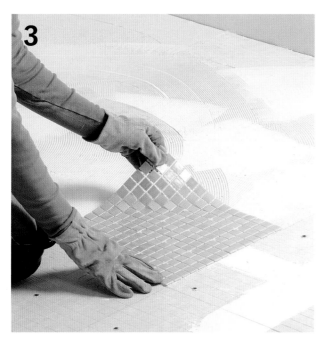

Gently press one corner into place on the adhesive. Slowly lower the opposite corner, making sure the sides remain square with your reference lines. Massage the sheet into the adhesive, being careful not to press too hard or twist the sheet out of position. Insert a few spacers in the outside edges of the sheet you have just placed. This will help keep the grout lines consistent.

4

When you have placed two or three sheets, lay a scrap piece of flat lumber across the tops and tap the wood with a rubber mallet to set the fabric mesh in the adhesive, and to force out any trapped air. *Note: Staple scrap carpet material to the lumber to protect the tile surface.*

5

At the outer edges of your work area, you will probably need to trim one or more rows from the last sheet. If the space left at the edge is more than the width of a regular grout line, use tile nippers to trim the last row that will fit. Save these leftover tiles for repairs.

6

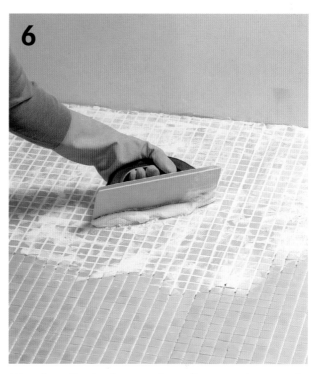

After the adhesive has cured, usually 24 to 48 hours, apply grout as you would for individual tiles. With many more spaces, mosaic tiles will require more grout. Follow the manufacturer's instructions for spreading and floating the grout. Clean up using the instructions for individual tiles (see page 389).

CABINETS, COUNTERTOPS & STORAGE PROJECTS

Cabinets, countertops, and storage elements are very often one aspect of a major remodeling or renovation project—many of the projects in this chapter might be part of such an overreaching renovation. But they also can serve as great standalone projects for when you want to do a bit of cosmetic face-lifting or upgrade with a custom add-on or two. You can install a new countertop in just a weekend, and it can make a kitchen or bathroom look brand new again. Even more ambitiously, adding an impressive custom storage unit, such as a formal bookcase or laundry center, can transform a fairly ordinary home into one that looks like a fine, custom-crafted structure.

But the best time to consider adding some of these unique features is during major remodeling, such as when you are converting an attic or basement to living space, when you are doing an overall kitchen or bathroom remodel, or when you are pulling out all stops by adding a structural room addition to your home. This is a chapter you'll want to consult carefully in conjunction to the later sections dedicated to major remodeling.

IN THIS CHAPTER:

- Materials
- Understairs Bookcases
- Basement Stairway Shelving
- Basement Storage Wall
- Custom Laundry Center
- Double-Bowl Vanity Top
- Butcher Block Countertops
- Concrete Countertop
- Granite Tile Countertops
- Banquette
- Recessed Cabinet
- Window Seat
- Wall Niche
- Formal Bookcase
- Box Beam Shelves
- Media Bar
- Club Bar

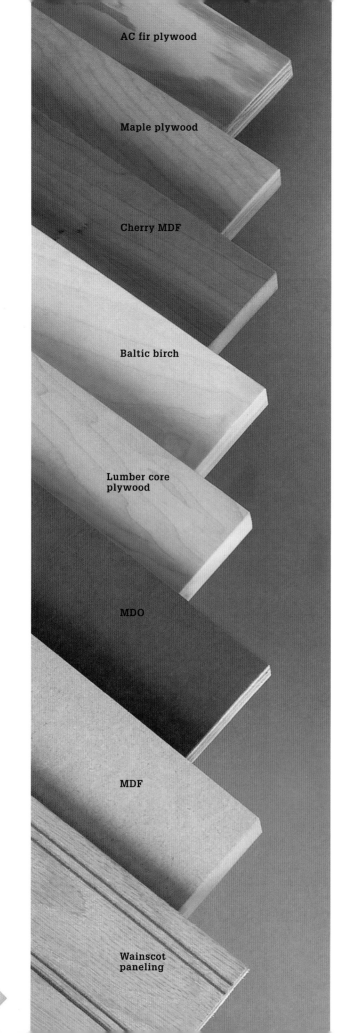

AC fir plywood

Maple plywood

Cherry MDF

Baltic birch

Lumber core
plywood

MDO

MDF

Wainscot
paneling

MATERIALS

SHEET GOODS

There are many different types of plywood for a wide array of uses. For built-in and shelf projects, finish-grade or paint-grade plywood is commonly used. Each type is made up of thinly sliced layers called plies. These layers are made of solid hardwood, softwood, or wood products. The more plies a sheet good has, the stronger it will be. This is only true for veneer-based plies. Medium density fiberboard, or MDF, is made of wood fibers that have been glued and pressed together. These panels are extremely stable and rarely shrink or warp, but will expand when wet. Plywood thicknesses range from ⅛ to 1 inch. Many species of wood are available for the outer plywood veneers. The core, or inner plies, give the panel its structural characteristics.

AC plywood has a finish-grade face on one side and a utility grade on the other. Standard AC plywood is made of seven plies of softwood, such as spruce or pine. This plywood is a good choice for paint-grade moldings. Hardwood veneer plywood is available in red oak and maple or birch at most home centers. Its inner core is basically the same as AC plywood, but it has a hardwood outer face. MDF oak veneer plywood is made up of three layers: two outer oak veneers and a solid core made of MDF. This plywood tends to be less expensive than a veneer core product and has a smoother face, but is heavy and does not hold fasteners as well.

MDF is available with or without an outer veneer. Baltic birch plywood is made up of equal size plies, all without voids, so the edges are attractive and can be left exposed. This panel is commonly used in Modern-style furniture and cabinets and with a clear finish. Lumber-core plywood has strips of solid wood edge-glued between outer veneer plies. Medium density overlay, or MDO, plywood has a plywood core with a resin-coated paper face. This panel is moisture resistant, unlike MDF, and has the fastening strength of a solid veneer core. The face is perfect for paint-grade applications. Wainscot paneling is available in several thicknesses from ³⁄₁₆ to ⅝ inch.

LUMBER

Solid hardwood is available at most home centers in varying widths. Species vary, depending on your location. These boards make good solid stock material to combine with or mill into new trim moldings because they are already planed to a uniform thickness. If you can't find the type of lumber you need at a home center, check with a lumberyard or a woodworking store in your area. Most lumberyards will charge a nominal flat fee to plane the boards for you. You can also order almost any type of wood online.

Common Defects ▸

Whenever possible, do a quick inspection of each board before you purchase it. Because hardwood lumber is often stained, carefully take note of cosmetic flaws such as splits, knots, checks, and wanes. These issues can sometimes be cut around, but once the finish is applied, the imperfection will show through. Lumber that is twisted, cupped, or crooked should be avoided. If a board is slightly bowed, you can probably flatten it out as you nail it. In any case, always choose the straightest, flattest lumber you can find.

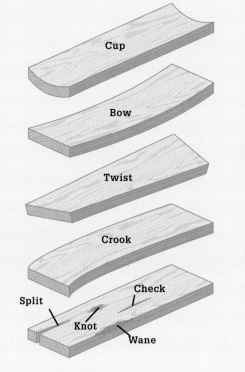

UNDERSTAIRS BOOKCASES

If your home has a staircase with open space below, chances are you've wondered how to make the most of that oddly configured square footage. This bookcase project could be the answer. Behind the two pairs of gently rising birch-frame doors you'll find a bank of birch plywood shelves that are designed for use as a formal bookcase. Because the door panels are created with Plexiglas, the shelves are also quite suitable for display purposes.

While the bookcase cabinets must be custom-fit to your space, the basic design of the individual units is quite simple. Each cabinet is essentially a plywood box with an angled top. The boxes fit side by side in the understairs area, flush with the wall surfaces. The shelves in each unit incorporate birch 1 × 2 shelf edge to improve their appearance and stiffen the shelf boards.

A birch face frame is wrapped around the perimeter of the project, concealing the plywood edges. The

swinging doors are also made of birch. The secret to building the face frames and the doorframes is a clever woodworking technique known as the pocket screw joint made with angled screws driven into the back sides of the mating pieces.

Understairs storage units are often made with slide-out shelving or pull-out drawers. This strategy allows for efficient use of space since the pull-out units can be nearly as deep as the total stair width. The drawback is that the drawers or slide-out shelves can be a bit rickety, especially if you're not an experienced cabinetmaker. When designing your project, you can increase the storage space by deepening the shelves and using them as storage cubbies. If your staircase is bounded by another interior wall, you can add a bookcase on the other side, with the two bookcases sharing a divided panel or wall.

A rich formal bookcase inhabits the previously wasted space underneath a staircase. The books are protected by birch doors with Plexiglas panels that have a soft, contemporary design feeling.

Tools & Materials

Tools

Work gloves
Eye and ear protection
Respirator
Stud finder
Level
Pencil
Utility knife or wallboard saw
Pry bar
Drill
Router (and rabbet bit)
Pilot bits
Chisel
Large pipe clamps
Framing square
Tablesaw
Pneumatic brad nailer
HVLP sprayer (optional)
Hammer
Nail set

Materials

2 × 4 lumber
Plywood stock (¼", ¾")
Wood glue
Brads
150- or 220-grit sandpaper
Desired finish
Pocket screws
6d finish nails
1¼" drywall screws
Coarse-thread drywall screws
Wood putty; frosted glass
Plexiglas

Glazier's points
Latches
Pulls
1 × 2 hardwood
Shims
Hinges
Stain, or other
    finish materials

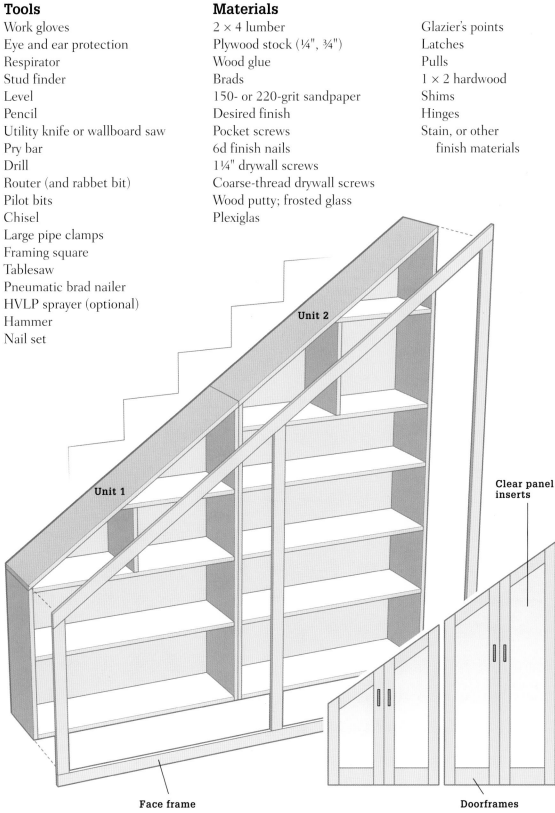

Unit 2

Unit 1

Clear panel inserts

Face frame

Doorframes

HOW TO BUILD THE UNDERSTAIRS BOOKCASE

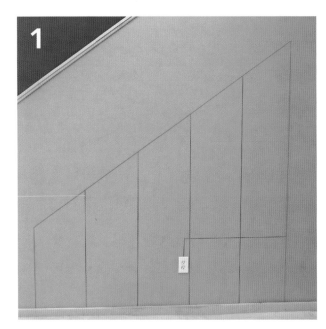

Lay out the planned project on the walls. Be sure to identify and label all stud locations as well as any wiring, plumbing or ductwork in the project area. Try to plan the opening in the wall so it will be bordered by existing studs, and with the wall covering cut up to the studs but not beyond.

Cut and remove the wall covering with electrical service. First shut off electricity at the main service panel. To minimize dust, use a utility knife or wallboard saw to cut the wall covering along the cutting lines. Pry off the wall covering, taking care not to damage surrounding walls surfaces.

Install 2 × 4 sleepers on the floor after you've thoroughly cleaned up the project area and disposed of all debris properly. Sleepers should butt against the wall's sole plate and run back in a perpendicular fashion slightly farther than the planned project depth. Install a sleeper at the end of the project area, beneath the midpoint, and at 16" intervals.

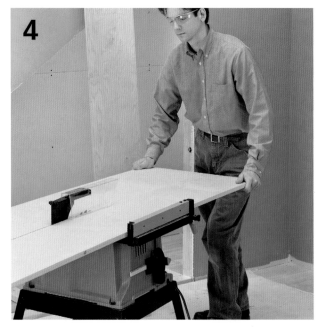

Rip plywood stock into strips for making the cabinet frame and shelves. We used ¾" birch-veneer plywood to match the birch that is used for the face frame and doorframes. The cabinet frame pieces are ripped to 12" wide but the shelves should be only 11¼" wide to allow for the ¾"-thick shelf edge strips. Cut all parts to length.

5

Assemble the unit frames with wood glue and coarse-thread drywall screws driven through the outer faces and into the edges of the mating boards. Drill countersunk pilot holes for the screws. Work on a flat surface and check the joint with a framing square to make sure they are square. If you have large pipe clamps, use them to clamp the workpieces before driving the screws. Make both the Unit 1 and Unit 2 frames (tops, sides, and bottom panels).

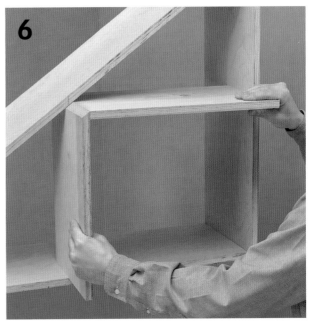

6

Install shelf boards in the cabinet frame. The shelves should be flush with the back edges of the frame, leaving a ¾" reveal in the front. Draw shelf layout lines on both faces of the frame pieces so you can center the screws. Install the full-width shelves first. Assemble the shorter shelves and their divider supports into L shapes, and then install them as a unit. Cut back panels from ¼" plywood and attach them with brads.

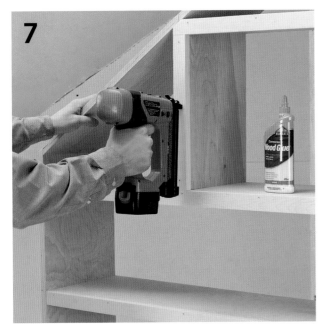

7

Attach hardwood shelf edge to the shelves and the divider support edges. The tops of the 1 × 2 edge boards should be flush with the top surfaces of the shelves. The vertical edging pieces should be flush with the outside edges of the dividers.

8

Apply a finish to the cabinet units. Sand all wood surfaces with 150- or 220-grit sand paper, wipe down with mineral spirits, and then apply two to three light coats of water-based polyurethane. We used an HVLP sprayer to apply the finish, but wipe-on polyurethane works just fine if you don't have spraying equipment.

(continued)

CABINETS, COUNTERTOPS & STORAGE PROJECTS

155

9

Install the first unit in the project opening. The front edges should be flush with the room-side surface of the wall. Check with a level and shim between the frames and sleepers as needed. Attach by driving 6d finish nails through the base panel and into the sleepers and also through the side panel and into the wall stud.

10

Install the second unit in the project opening, shimming as needed to make sure it is level and the top panel continues in alignment with the top of the first unit. Before securing the panels to the sleepers and stud, drive 1¼" drywall screws to join the units' side panels at each corner where they meet. Countersink the pilot holes and cover with tinted wood putty. Attach the other side panel to the wall stud and nail the bottom panel to the sleepers with 6d finish nails.

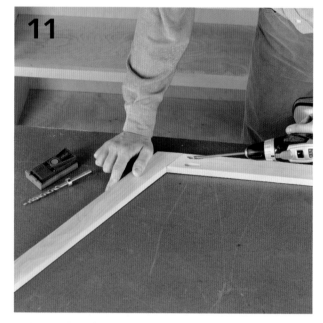

11

Make the face frame. It's possible to cut the pieces of the face frame and nail them individually to the cabinet units, but you'll get more professional-looking results with cleaner joints if you assemble the face frame, finish it, and then attach it to the cabinet as one piece. We used pocket screws to make the joints, but you can use dowels or biscuits instead. Apply a finish.

12

Attach the face frame to the cabinet frame edges with brads or pneumatic finish nails. Use plenty of nails, since the face frame will support the swinging door hinges. Set all nail heads and conceal with tinted wood putty.

13

Make the doorframes. The frames will look best with the vertical stiles running full height and capturing the rails between them. As you work, lay each completed frame on a flat surface next to the previous one and make sure the line formed by the top rails follows the same angle as the top face frame rails. The joint options are the same for the doorframes as for the face frames (we again used pocket screws). Make sure to leave at least 1" of clear stock on each corner so the router won't cut into any fasteners when cutting rabbets.

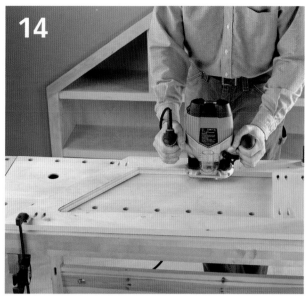

14

Cut rabbet recesses for the door panel inserts. Use a piloted rabbet bit and router. The rabbets should be ⅜" deep and ½" wide. Make the cuts in multiple passes of increasing depth— don't try to remove all the material in a single pass. Once all rabbets have been cut around the perimeter of each doorframe back, square off the corners of the cuts with a sharp wood chisel. *Note: In most cases, to create clearance you will need to cut a ½" chamfer on the top inside edge of the two doorframes where the hinges are on the side with the point.*

15

Install the door panels. You can use frosted glass (tempered is best), ¼" plywood, or Plexiglas. We used Plexiglas because of the risk of breakage. It is possible to cut both glass and Plexiglas to size yourself, but given the high cost of materials and relatively low cost of custom cutting, you'll be glad you chose to have the pieces cut to size at the store. Panels should be about ¼" smaller than the opening (including the rabbet widths) in each direction. Use glazier's points to secure the panels.

16

Hang the doors and attach latches and pulls. Take great care when hanging the cabinet doors to make sure that the line created by the door tops is straight and parallel to the face frame, with a consistent reveal. Orient the cabinet door pairs so they close together in the center of each unit. Attach the door pulls roughly midway up each cabinet door. Add latches or catches so doors will stay closed. *Note: You may need to bevel the inside faces of the frames on the hinge side.*

BASEMENT STAIRWAY SHELVING

In many homes, the basement stairs offer two easy options for convenient and out-of-the-way storage. One utilizes the stud cavities along the stairwell wall. The other occupies that large yet awkward triangular area underneath the staircase. In both places, a simple lumber shelving system lets you take advantage of underused space without sacrificing valuable square footage.

Adding shelves along a stairwell wall couldn't be simpler. All it requires is notching a 2 × 6 shelf board to fit over the wall studs, then screwing the shelf in place. This gives you a 5½-inch-deep shelf space between the studs, plus a 2-inch-deep lip in front of each stud. Of course, the stairwell wall must be unfinished on one side for this type of shelving. If the stairwell wall isn't an option, perhaps you have an open wall in the basement or garage—any wall with exposed framing will work.

Utility shelves for the understairs space are made with a 2 × 4 support frame and plywood shelf surfaces. The stair structure itself provides support at one end of the shelves. Like the stud-wall shelves, you can set the understairs shelving at any height or spacing that you like. In the project shown on pages 160 to 161, the shelf system includes a low bottom shelf that's built with extra supports, good for keeping heavy items off of the basement floor.

Shelves along an open stairwell wall (left photo) can accommodate loads of smaller items. If your basement door is near the kitchen, these shelves are great for backup pantry storage. Shelves underneath the staircase (right photo) are ideal for basement workshop storage and for long pieces of lumber and other materials.

Tools & Materials ▸

For Stairway Shelves:

Work gloves	Circular saw
Eye and ear protection	Mallet
Level	
Handsaw	
Square	
Wood chisel	
Drill with countersink bit	
2 × 6 lumber	
3½" deck screws	

For Understairs Shelves:

Work gloves
Eye and ear protection
Circular saw
Level
Drill with bits
Tape measure
2 × 4 pressure-treated lumber (for posts and struts)

2 × 4 standard lumber (for shelf supports)
2½" deck screws or coarse-thread wood screws
¾" AC (paint-grade on one side) plywood
2" coarse-thread drywall screws

HOW TO BUILD STAIRWAY WALL SHELVES

Mark the desired height for each shelf, then use a level to transfer the mark across the front edge of each stud. Measure from your level lines to mark the location of the next shelf up or down. The lines will represent the top face of the shelves.

Measure along each level line and cut the 2 × 6 shelf stock to length. Hold each shelf in place on its lines and mark the side edges of each stud for the notches. *Tip: If a stud is out of square to the wall plane, make the notch big enough so the shelf will fit straight on.*

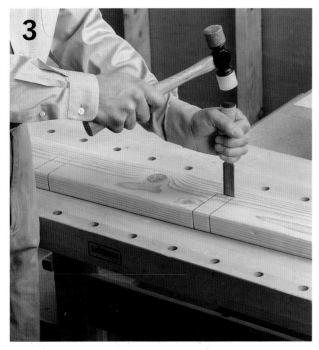

Use a square to mark the notch depths at 3½". Make notch marks on both sides of the shelf. Cut the sides of the notches with a handsaw. Complete the notches by chiseling straight down from both sides of the board along the seat, or base, of the notch marks.

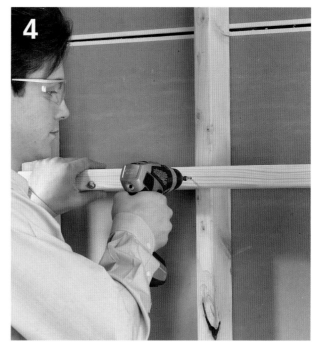

Position each shelf on its lines and make sure the shelf is level from front to back. Drill a pilot hole at the center of each stud location using a countersink bit. Fasten the shelf to each stud with a 3½" deck screw.

HOW TO BUILD UNDERSTAIRS BASEMENT SHELVES

Mark the locations of the two 2 × 4 posts onto the floor. The posts must be equidistant from the bottom end of the staircase. Cut each post a little longer than needed. Position the post plumb next to the floor mark, and trace along the stair stringer to mark the angled top cut for the post.

Cut the post ends with a circular saw or power miter saw. Set each post on its floor mark and fasten the top end to the bottom edge of the stair stringer with three 2½" deck screws or wood screws driven through pilot holes.

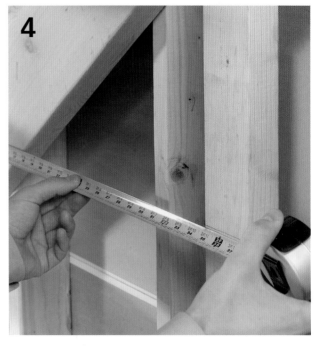

Mark the desired location of each shelf onto the stair stringers. Use a level—and a long, straight board as needed—to transfer the height marks to the inside faces of the posts.

For each shelf, measure and cut two 2 × 4 side supports to span from the outside edges of the posts to the back sides of the steps (or as far as practical). Also cut one 2 × 4 end support to span between the outside faces of the posts.

5

Fasten the side supports to the posts and stair stringers with four 2½" screws at each end. Fasten the end supports to the outside edges of the posts with two screws at each end. The end supports should be flush with the top edges of the side supports, with their ends flush with the outside faces of the posts.

Option: For long shelves that will hold heavy items, add midspan supports between the side supports. Reinforce a bottom shelf with 2 × 4 struts cut to fit between the side supports and the floor. Note: Very heavy items should go on a reinforced bottom shelf, since stair structures aren't designed for significant extra weight loads.

6

Cut the shelf panels to fit from ¾" plywood. The edges of the panels should be flush with the outside face of the side and end supports. Fasten the panels to the supports with 2" drywall screws.

Variation: If your staircase has a center stringer, notch the plywood shelf panels to fit around the stringer. Cut the sides of the notches with a circular saw or handsaw, and then make the seat cuts with a chisel to complete the notches.

BASEMENT STORAGE WALL

Storage space in a basement can be a mixed blessing. On one hand, there's usually plenty of room in a basement, and you can stash all kinds of stuff down there, out of view from your living areas. On the other hand, basements tend to be dusty, sometimes damp, and often a good home for insects and other critters, so you have to be careful what you store, especially if it's going to be there for awhile. Finished basements are more hospitable environments; however, most finishing projects leave little room for general storage, and things ends up getting crammed next to the hot water heater.

Here's a storage solution that makes any basement a great place for storage, whether the space is finished, unfinished, or something in between. In essence, this project is a floor-to-ceiling wall of simple wood cabinets with plywood doors. The doors help keep

out dust and critters, while the 2 × 4 base of the unit protects stuff on the bottom shelves from a damp floor or even minor flooding. As shown here, the cabinets are just under 24 inches deep, but you can make them any size you need. You can also reconfigure the shelves, doors, and cabinet dimensions to fit your space and your stuff.

How much you put into the look of the storage wall is up to you. For a nicely finished basement, you'll probably want to use cabinet-grade, hardwood-veneer plywood or medium-density fiberboard (MDF) for all of the cabinet parts and the doors. Covering the side gaps and the base and top frames with matching ¼-inch plywood completes the finished, built-in look. For an unfinished basement, you can simplify the project and save money by using paint-grade plywood.

The storage wall looks best when it runs from corner to corner in a basement room or alcove. But because it's anchored at top and bottom, it can also go next to a wall on only one side or be "freestanding" with open space on both sides.

Tools & Materials

Tools

Work gloves
Eye and ear protection
Chalk line
Tape measure
Plumb bob
Circular saw and straightedge guide or tablesaw
Level
Caulk gun
Drill with bits and drill guide (or use drill press)
Depth stop
Clothes iron
Sand paper
Ladder
Hammer
Clamps
Portable drill guide

Pneumatic brad nailer

Materials

2 × 4 pressure-treated lumber (for base frame)
2 × 4 standard lumber (for top frame)
16d galvanized common nails
Tapered cedar shims
Construction adhesive
Plywood (¼", ½", ¾")
Veneer edge tape (optional)
Pegboard with ¼" holes
Coarse-thread drywall screws (1¼" and 2")
2½" galvanized deck screws
1 × 2 lumber
Wood glue
1" brads
Door handles or pulls
Shelf pins
European-style (cup) hinges
Finishing materials

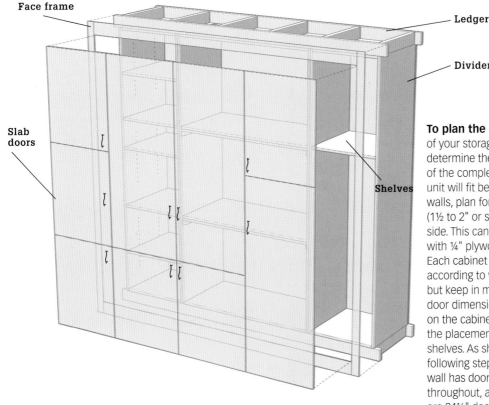

Face frame

Ledger

Divider panels

Slab doors

Shelves

To plan the dimensions of your storage wall, first determine the overall width of the completed unit. If the unit will fit between two side walls, plan for a small space (1½ to 2" or so) at either side. This can be covered with ¼" plywood trim pieces. Each cabinet can be sized according to what it will hold, but keep in mind that the door dimensions are based on the cabinet width and the placement of the fixed shelves. As shown in the following steps, the storage wall has doors of equal width throughout, and the cabinets are 24¼" deep.

HOW TO BUILD A BASEMENT STORAGE WALL

1

Mark the location of the base frame onto the floor. Measure out 24¼" from the back wall and make a mark at each end of the project area. Snap a chalk line between the marks. *Note: When the cabinets are installed (step 12), they will overhang the front edges of the frames by ½" and be ½" from the back wall.*

2

Use a plumb bob to transfer the chalk line location from the floor to the joists above, snap a chalk line across the joists. If the joists run parallel to the back wall, you may need to install 2 × 4 blocking between joists to support the top frame.

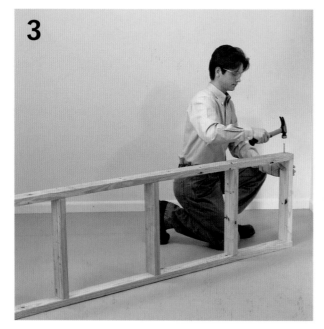

3

Build the base and top frames with 2 × 4 lumber and 16d galvanized nails, adding crosspieces spaced 24" on center. Use pressure-treated lumber for the base frame. Make the frames 23¾" wide (or ½" narrower than the cabinet depth) and their length equal to the total cabinet width.

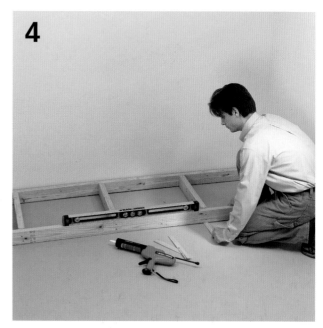

4

Install the frames with their front edges on the chalk lines. Use cedar shims as needed so the frames are perfectly level in both directions. Secure the base frame to a concrete floor with construction adhesive. Fasten the top frame to the joists with nails or screws.

5

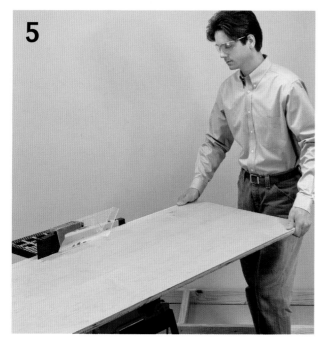

Measure between the top and base frames to find the cabinet height. *Tip: Leave yourself ⅛" or so of wiggle room for getting the cabinets into place.* Cut the cabinet side panels from ¾" plywood at 23¾" wide × the overall cabinet height. Use a tablesaw or a circular saw and edge guide to ensure straight cuts.

6

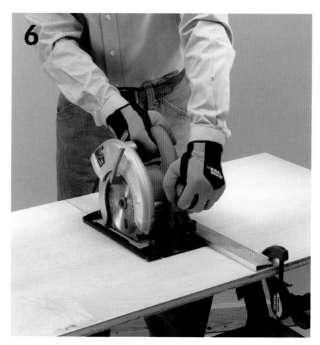

Cut the top and bottom cabinet panels and the fixed shelves at 23¾" deep, with the length equal to the overall cabinet width minus 1½". Cut the adjustable shelves to the same dimensions minus ⅛" in both directions. Cut the back panel from ½" plywood, equal to the overall cabinet dimensions.

7

For the cabinet(s) with adjustable shelves, drill a row of shelf-peg holes 2" from the front and back edges of the side panels using a template cut from ¼" pegboard. Make the holes ⅝" deep using a depth stop on the drill bit. Orient the template carefully so the holes are even from side to side.

8

Mark the fixed shelf locations onto the inside faces of the cabinet sides. The fixed shelves should be centered at any place where two horizontal door edges meet. Drill countersunk pilot holes through the outside faces of the side panels; the holes should meet with the centers of the top and bottom panels and the fixed shelves.

(continued)

9

Assemble each cabinet box with glue and 2" screws, starting with the side, top, and bottom panels and the fixed shelves. Before the glue sets up, attach the back panel with glue and 1¼" screws. Align the edges of the box with the back panel as you work to ensure the box is square.

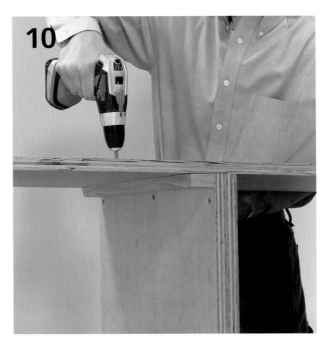

10

For cabinets over 30" wide, build double-layer fixed shelves with glue and 1¼" screws driven up through the bottom layer. This construction adds strength for the long span. Support the shelves with 1 × 2 cleats glued and screwed to the side and back panels. Also screw through the side and back panels into the shelf edges.

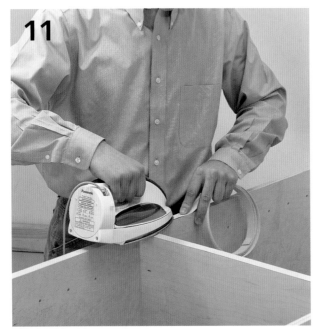

11

If desired, cover the front edges of the cabinet boxes with iron-on veneer edge tape that matches the plywood veneer. Slightly roundover the edges of the applied tape with sandpaper. Finish all exposed cabinet surfaces as desired, and apply at least a good seal coat to hidden surfaces to protect against moisture.

12

Set each cabinet in place so its front edges overhang the base and top frames by ½". Align the side edges of adjacent cabinets and fasten them together with 1¼" screws. Anchor the cabinets to the base and top frames with 2½" screws using shims to fill any gaps between the top frame and the top of the cabinets.

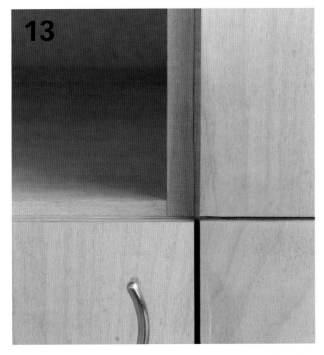

13

Cut the door panels to size from the same plywood used for the cabinet boxes. The doors should overlap the side and top/bottom cabinet panels by ⅝" and overlap any fixed shelf by ⁵⁄₁₆" (or stop ¹⁄₁₆" back from the center of doubled shelves). Apply veneer edge tape and finish the doors as desired.

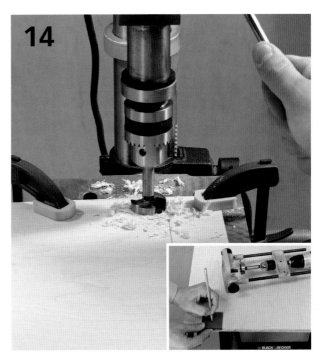

14

Drill holes for the cabinet hinges. Use a Forstner bit and drill with a drill guide (or a drill press) to make the hinge-cup holes. Follow the hinge manufacturer's specifications for hole sizes and placement. *Tip: You can buy a kit that includes the cup-hole bit and a template for marking the hinge holes (inset photo).*

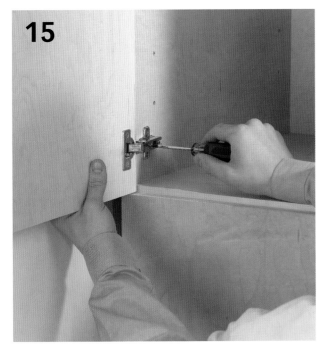

15

Mount the doors to the cabinet side panels following the manufacturer's directions. Adjust the hinges as needed so all gaps are even and the doors close properly. Install handles or pulls onto the doors. Add the adjustable shelves.

16

Option: Cut strips of ¼" veneer plywood to fit the gaps along the top, bottom, and sides of the cabinets. Install 1 × 2 or 2 × 2 backing along the sides, ½" from the cabinets' front edges. Fasten the trim to the base/top frames and the backing with 1" brads.

CUSTOM LAUNDRY CENTER

Many laundry rooms—or set-aside laundry areas in larger rooms—lack two vitally important features: organization and lighting. This laundry center answers both needs in style. This is a self-contained built-in that functions like a room within a room, adding both storage space and task lighting for what can otherwise be a disagreeable task. It is built from a base cabinet and butcher block countertop on one side of a 24-inch-wide, 7-foot-tall stub wall, and a bank of wall cabinets on the other side of the wall. The cabinets are designed to fit above a washer and dryer combo, although you may need to adjust the measurements to accommodate your particular washer and dryer.

The structure includes a ceiling with light fixtures mounted over both sides, and a switch wired into the stub wall to control the lights. The walls are built from inexpensive wall sheathing and, along with the

ceiling, are clad with easy-to-wash tileboard that adds brightness while contrasting with the maple wood of the cabinets. The edges of the center are trimmed with clear maple.

Tools ▸

Tape measure	Hammer or
Level	pneumatic nailer
Pencil	Jigsaw
Square	Circular saw
Power drill and bits	Miter saw
Powder-actuated	Eye and ear
nailer	protection
	Work gloves

This sharp cabinet configuration not only helps you get your laundry room in order, but it also adds a good deal of style and practical lighting.

Materials & Cutting List

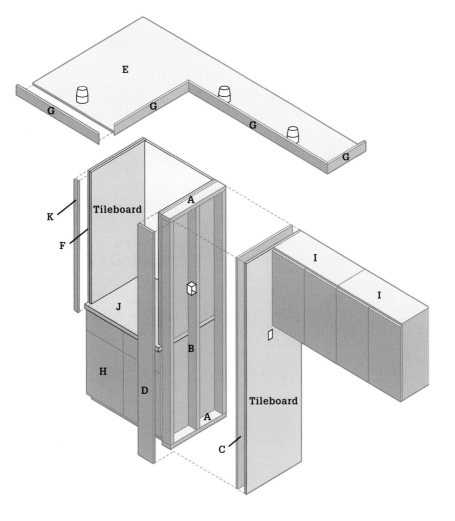

(1) 4 × 8 × ½ plywood or OSB (wall sheathing)
(1) 4 × 8 × ¾ plywood or OSB (ceiling)
(3) 4 × 8 sheets tileboard with an 8'. inside corner strip and panel adhesive
(3) Recessed canister light with trim kit
(1) Clothes rod (24") with mounting hardware
1 × 2, 1 × 4 and 1 × 6 maple for trim
32"-wide base cabinet
Butcher block countertop for base cabinet
(2) 30" 2-door uppers
Electrical box, switch, 14/2 romex, switch plate
End panel for upper cabinets (if unfinished)
Panel adhesive
Drywall or deck screws
Nails
(4) 1½ × 3½ × 96 pine

Part	No.	Desc.	Size	Material
A	2	Cap/sill plate	1½ × 3½ × 23¾"	2 × 4
B	3	Stud	1½ × 3½ × 79"	2 × 4
C	1	Full wall	½ × 23¾ × 81¾"	Sheathing
D	1	Wall cap	¾ × 5½ × 79"	Maple 1 × 6
E	1	Ceiling	¾ × 24 × 100"*	Sheathing
F	2	Half wall	½ × 23¾ × 43"	Sheathing
G	4	Top trim	¾ × 5½ × cut to fit	Maple 1 × 6
H	1	Base cabinet	34½" h × 36" w	Stock cabinet
I	2	Wall cabinets	12 × 30 × 30"	Stock cabinets
J	1	Countertop	1½ × 25 × 36	Countertop
K	1	Trim	¾ × 1½ × 43"	1 × 2

*Can be pieced together from two boards joined above A

169

HOW TO BUILD A LAUNDRY CENTER

Attach the base plate for the stub wall perpendicular to the wall, allowing space between the stub wall and the corner for your base cabinet. Use pressure-treated wood if your laundry is in the basement and use pressure-treated lumber for the base plate and attach it by driving concrete nails with a powder-actuated nailer for a concrete floor.

After toenailing the studs to the base plate (and facenailing the stud next to the wall if possible), attach the cap plate, making sure the studs are vertical.

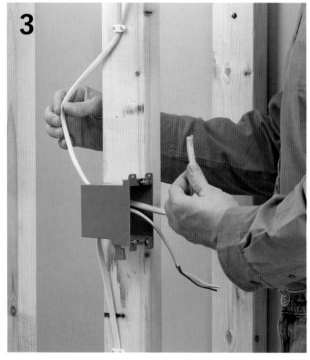

Run cable and install boxes for the light fixtures. Hire an electrician to do this if you are not experienced with home wiring. *Note: You may need to apply for a permit and have your wiring inspected.*

Install the base cabinet between the stub wall and the corner, making sure it is level and securely attached to at least one wall.

5

Attach the countertop material (butcher block was used here). The countertop should be flush against both walls and it should overhang the base cabinet slightly.

6

Stud location

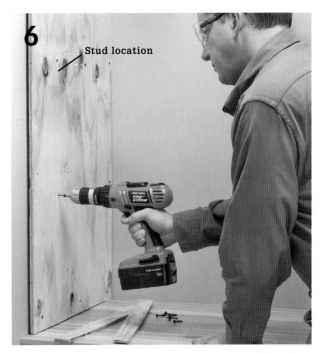

Cut a piece of wall sheathing that's the same width as the stub wall and reaches the same height when placed on the countertop surface. Attach the sheathing to the side of the countertop area. Insert a couple of furring strips between the sheathing and the wall to create airspace.

7

Clad the stub wall on both sides with wall sheathing, making sure to cut out accurately for the switch box. The sheathing on the countertop side should rest on the countertop. Slip shims underneath the wall sheathing on the washer and dryer side so it does not contact the floor.

8

Cut pieces of tileboard to cover the wall surfaces and attach them with panel adhesive. Attach inside corner strips cut to fit at the inside corners of the countertop area. Rub the tileboard aggressively with rags to help seat it.

(continued)

9

Mount the wall cabinets so they are level and their tops are flush with the top of the stub wall and they butt up against the stub wall. Drive screws through the mounting strips and into the wall at stud locations or into ledgers.

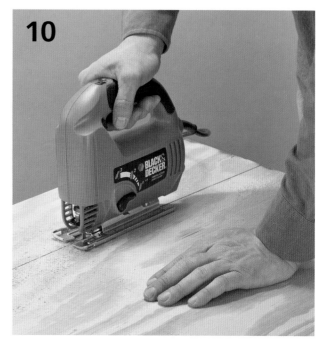

10

It's easiest to cut the ceiling board, attach tileboard, and mount light fixtures before you attach the ceiling assembly to the stub wall and cabinets. Cut the ceiling board to size and shape from a piece of sheathing.

11

Mount the hardware and box for the light fixture to the ceiling panel before you install the ceiling.

12

Set the ceiling panel over the laundry center and attach it with nails or screws driven into the top plate of the stub wall and the cabinet sides.

13

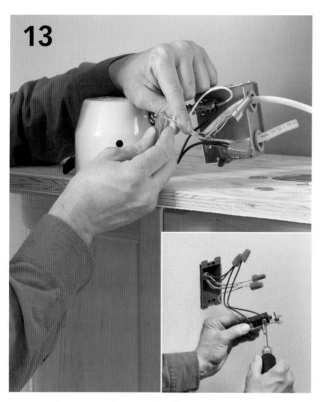

Be sure the power is turned off to the room. Make the wiring connections at the light fixtures and at the switch (inset). Consult an electrician as necessary.

14

Trim out the top of the structure with 1 × 4 hardwood to conceal the gap beneath the ceiling panel. Miter the outside and inside corners as you install the trim. If you prefer, you can use crown molding here.

15

Attach the vertical trim boards, butting them up against the top trim and keeping the bottom slightly above the floor. Apply a finish and top coat to the trim boards as desired.

16

Install your washer and dryer (or have your appliance dealer install them for you). Make sure to follow local codes for water and drain supply and for venting your dryer.

DOUBLE-BOWL VANITY TOP

Side-by-side double sinks are a wonderful addition to bathrooms large enough to accommodate the extra fixture. Often called "his-and-her" sinks, double sinks can be indispensable in a busy bathroom serving a large household, or for a couple whose schedules put them in the master bath at the same time each day.

The first issue to consider in adding a double sink is available space. You need to maintain the minimum required space around the sink, including 30 inches of clear space in front of the sink (but no less than 21 inches) and 30 inches from the center of one sink to the center of the other. Any sink or vanity edge should be at least 4 inches from a side wall, and should not impede door swing.

You'll also want to decide how much plumbing modification you're willing to do. Side-by-side standalone sinks, such as pedestals or wall-mounted models, require new supply and drains. But a double sink vanity like the one shown here can be added simply by using dual-use hardware that splits the existing supply and drain lines.

Tools & Materials ▸

Carpenter's level
Screwdrivers
Power drill
Basin wrench
Stud finder
Adjustable wrench
Hacksaw

Silicone caulk
Dual outlet valves
Braided steel supply lines
P-trap
PVC connections
Plumber's putty
Eye and ear protection

A double-bowl vanity is a useful fixture for accommodating multiple users during rush hour in your bathroom. Most home centers stock a selection of double-bowl options, but for the best variety allow enough time for a custom order (usually 1 to 6 weeks).

DOUBLE DRAINS

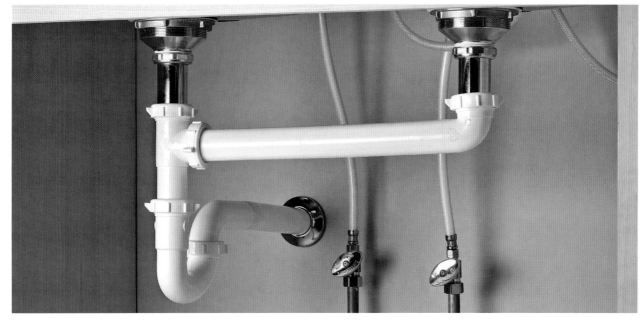

Double-bowl vanities are plumbed very similar to double-bowl kitchen sinks. In most cases, the drain tailpieces are connected beneath one of the tailpieces at a continuous waste T. The drain line from the second bowl must slope downward toward the T. From the T, the drain should have a trap (usually a P-trap) that connects to the trap arm coming out of the wall.

DRAIN IN FLOOR

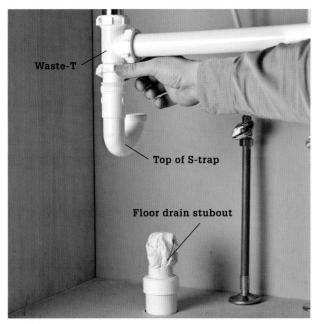

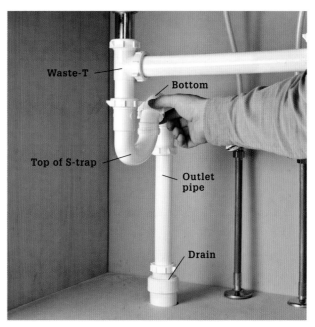

If your drain stubout comes up out of the floor instead of the wall, you'll need an S-trap to tie into it instead of a P-trap. Attach one half of the S-trap to the threaded bottom of the waste-T.

Attach the other half of the S-trap to the stubout with a slip fitting. This should result in the new fitting facing downward. Join the halves of the S-trap together with a slip nut, trimming the unthreaded end if necessary.

HOW TO INSTALL A DOUBLE SINK & VANITY

1

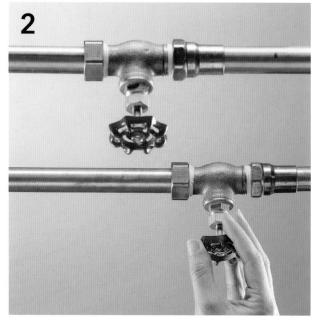

2

Shut off the supply valves located under the sink. Disconnect and remove the supply lines connecting the faucet to the valves. Loosen the P-trap nuts at both ends and remove the P-trap.

Remove the existing countertop and vanity. Turn off the water supply at the main shut-off valve. Drain remaining water by opening the faucet at the lowest point in the house. Use a hacksaw to remove the existing undersink shut-off valves.

3

4

Slide the new dual-outlet valve onto the hot water supply line, pass the nut and compression washer over the pipe, and tighten with a wrench. Install the dual-outlet valve on the cold water supply line in the same way.

Secure the new vanity in place by screwing it to the wall. Lay a bead of caulk along the underside and back edge of the countertop, where it will contact the vanity and wall. Set the countertop in place and check it for level. If your sinks are not integral, install them according to the type of sink you're using.

5

Seat the faucets for the double sinks as you would for a single sink, by applying a bead of putty on the underside of the bases (unless they are to be used with gaskets instead of putty). Secure them in place by tightening the locking nuts on the underside of the faucets.

6

Connect a new PVC P-trap to the undersink drain pipe, and attach a T-connector to the trap. Extend PVC connections to the drain assemblies of both sinks.

7

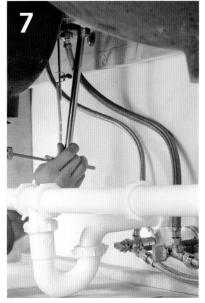

Connect the linkage for the pop-up drain stopper. Connect the braided steel cold water supply lines to the appropriate faucet tailpieces. Once the lines are secure, repeat for the hot water supply lines. Check that all connections are tightened securely.

8

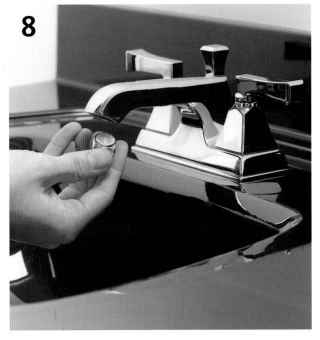

Turn on the main water supply and then turn on the water supply to the faucets. Remove the faucet aerators and run water in the sinks to check the supply lines and drain connections for leaks. Tighten the connections if you find any, and replace the aerators.

Leak Finder ›

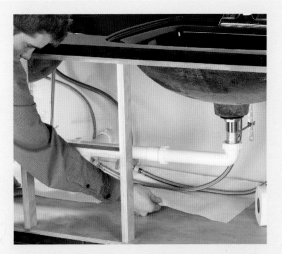

To quickly and easily find an undersink leak, lay bright white pieces of paper, or paper towels, under the pipes and drain connections. Open the water supply valves and run water in the sinks. It should be clear exactly where the water dripped from by the location of any drips on the paper.

BUTCHER BLOCK COUNTERTOPS

Butcher block slabs come in a variety of woods or—since they are made up of small pieces of wood glued together—a combination of different woods. They're available most commonly in maple or oak in end grain, which is composed of vertical pieces of wood, or edge grain and face grain, made up of long strips of wood. Making butcher block can be accomplished as an advanced DIY project, but it's often more cost-effective (and always faster) to purchase pieces in stock sizes and cut them down to fit your kitchen. Because butcher block is ideal for food prep areas but can be impractical near a sink or stove, another option is to install a small section of butcher block in combination with other countertop materials.

Tools & Materials ▸

Carpenter's square	Connector fittings
Forstner bit	Carpenter's square
Drill and bits	Bolt connector hardware
Tape measure	Circular saw with cutting guide
Clamps	Router with piloted roundover bit
Sander	Caulk gun and silicone adhesive
Varnish	Wood screws with fender washers
Scrap wood	Jigsaw with downstroke blade
Tape	Brush and finish material
Silicone adhesive	Faucet and sink
Finish materials	Eye and ear protection

Butcher block countertops enjoy continued popularity because of their natural beauty and warm wood tones.

Butcher block sold by the foot for countertop ranges from 1½ to 3" thick, although some end-grain products, used mostly for chopping blocks, can be up to 5" thick. For residential kitchens, the 1½"-thick material is the most available and most affordable choice. Stock length varies, but 6' and 12' slabs are common. You can also order the material with sink cutouts completed. Premade countertop is sold in the standard 25" depth, but wider versions (30" and 36") for islands are not difficult to find.

Butcher-block countertop material comes presealed, but a finish of varnish or oil, such as mineral or tung oil, is recommended. Seal cut wood around sink cutouts and on trimmed edges to keep it watertight.

A self-rimming sink is the easiest type to mount in a butcher block countertop, but undermount types can look stunning (just make sure to get a perfect seal on the end grain around the sink cutout).

End grain vs. face grain: Traditionally, butcher block countertop surfaces were made with square sections of wood (often maple) oriented with their end grain facing upward. This orientation creates a better, more

durable, knife-friendly cutting surface. For economy, many of today's butcher block sections are edge-glued with exposed edge grain or face grain.

Typical countertop material is 1½" wide and 25" deep, available in a number of lengths from 4' to 12' long.

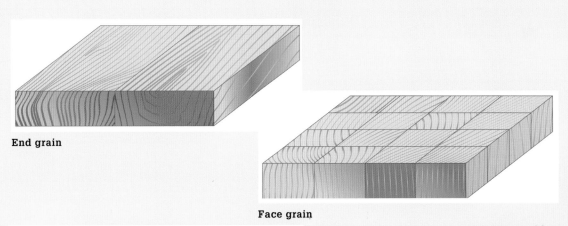

End grain

Face grain

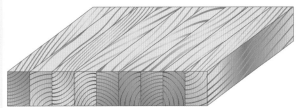

Edge grain

Butcher block that's constructed with the end grain oriented up is the most desirable, but it is relatively hard to find and fairly expensive. Material with the face grain or edge grain facing up is more common and more affordable.

HOW TO BUILD A BUTCHER BLOCK COUNTERTOP

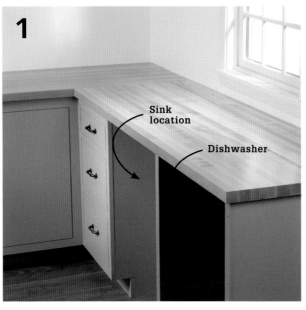

1

Sink location

Dishwasher

Before beginning installation, allow the butcher block to acclimate to your home's moisture level for a couple of days. Wood contracts and expands with moisture and humidity, so it may have warped or expanded during transport. Place it level on the cabinet tops and let it sit until it's settled.

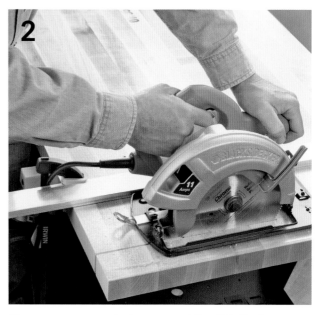

2

Measure your countertop area, adding 1" to the base cabinet depth to allow for overhang. Using a circular saw, cut the piece to size if needed. Butcher block with precut miter corners and cutouts for kitchens is available, but if you're cutting the piece yourself, be sure to apply finish to each new raw edge.

3

Point 3

Point 2

Point 1

Butcher block should be attached using wood screws that allow for some movement. Mark three points in a line on the underside of the countertop, spacing rows of drilling points at 12" intervals.

4

Drill pilot holes for screws at drilling points. Stick tape to the bit 1" from the point to create a depth stop.

5

Drill corresponding holes in the cabinet base that are slotted or at least ⅜" larger than the screws you are using. When driven with a washer under the screw head, screws will be able to move slightly with the wood.

6

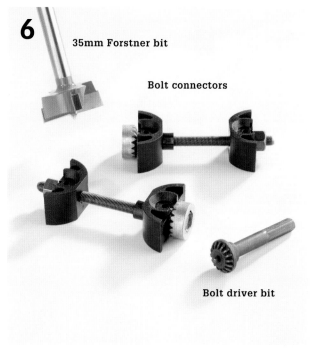

35mm Forstner bit

Bolt connectors

Bolt driver bit

Tip: In most cases butcher block countertops are not mitered at the corners as some other countertop types are. Instead, they are butted at the corners. You also may need to join two in-line pieces with a butt joint. In both instances, use connector fittings.

7

Make butt joints between countertop sections. Lay the two sections of countertop to be joined upside down on a flat worksurface in their correct orientation. Mark drilling points for the connector holes. Drill the holes with a Forstner bit.

8

With the countertop sections roughly in position on the cabinets and flipped right-side up, apply a bead of silicone adhesive near the top of one mating edge.

9

From below, insert the connector bolt so the two heads are flat in the holes and then tighten the bolt with the driver bit (supplied with bolt hardware) to draw the two sections of countertop together. Do not overtighten.

10

Clamp a piece of scrap wood to the end of the countertop so the tops are flush. The scrap wood prevents the router bit from rounding over the corner when the edge of the countertop is profiled.

11

Pull the countertop section away from the wall a few inches and make a roundover cut along the front edges with a piloted roundover bit.

12

Attach the countertop to the cabinet mounting strips by driving screws up through the cabinet strips and into the countertop. The screws should be ¼" shorter than the distance from the bottom of the mounting strips to the top of the countertop. Use 1" fender washers with the screws and snug them up, but do not overtighten. Because of the counterbores and the washers, the countertop will be able to move slightly as it expands and contracts.

13

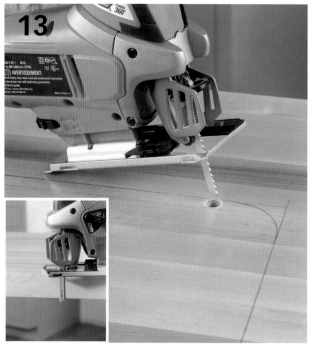

If installing a sink in your countertop, start by outlining the sink in the correct position as recommended in the installation material from the sink manufacturer. Mount a downstroke blade into the jigsaw (inset), and drill a starter hole just inside the sink outline. Make the cutout, taking care to stay just inside the cutting line. If you are installing an undermount sink, smooth the cuts up to the line with a power sander.

Variation: If you're installing an undermount sink, mark a centerpoint for drilling a hole to accommodate the faucet body following the recommendations of the faucet manufacturer. A 1⅜"-dia. hole is fairly standard.

14

Seal the edges of the sink opening with a varnish as instructed by the butcher block manufacturer, or by coating it generously with pure mineral oil or tung oil for a natural finish. Let sit for 15 minutes then wipe off the excess with a clean, lint-free cloth. Let it dry for 48 hours. Repeat six times, letting it dry thoroughly between coats.

15

Add the backsplash of your choice and caulk between the new countertop and the backsplash area with silicone caulk.

16

Install the faucet and sink and make the water supply and drain hookups.

CONCRETE COUNTERTOP

Cast concrete countertops have many unique characteristics. They are durable, heat resistant, and relatively inexpensive (if you make them yourself). But most of all, they are highly attractive and a great fit in contemporary kitchens or bathrooms.

A concrete countertop may be cast in place or formed offsite and installed like a natural stone countertop. Casting offsite makes more sense for most homeowners. In addition to keeping the mess and dust out of your living spaces, working in a garage or even outdoors lets you cast the countertops with the finished surface face down in the form. This way, if you do a careful job building the form, you can keep the grinding and polishing to a bare minimum. In some cases, you may even be able to simply remove the countertop from the form, flip it over, and install it essentially as is.

Tools & Materials ▸

Tape measure	Wire mesh	Black or colored	Bagged concrete mix
Pencil	Pliers	silicone caulk	Paste wax
Circular saw	Concrete mixer	Grinding and polishing	Work gloves and eye
Jigsaw	5-gal. buckets	pads	and ear protection
Power drill and right-	Shovel	Melamine-coated	Dust mask
angle drill guide	Wheelbarrow	particleboard	
Level	Wooden float	Concrete sealer	**If installing sink:**
Carpenter's square	Angle grinder	Coloring agent	Knockout for faucet
Reciprocating saw	Belt sander	Compass	Buffing bonnet
Aviation snips	Automotive buffer	No. 3 rebar	Faucet set
2" coarse drywall	Insulation board	Tie wire	Sink
screws	Plastic sheeting	Panel or silicone	Polyurethane varnish
Deck screws (3, 3½")	Rubber mallet	adhesive	

Building a custom concrete countertop like this is an easier project than you might think. All of the building materials and techniques are covered in this project.

Planning a Concrete Countertop ▸

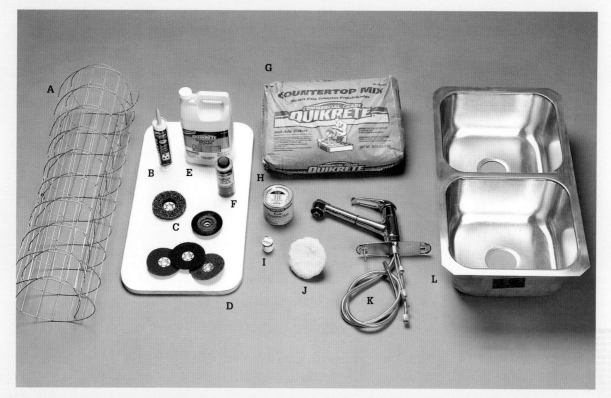

The basic supplies needed to build your countertop form and cast the countertop include: (A) welded wire mesh for reinforcement; (B) black or colored silicone caulk; (C) grinding and polishing pads; (D) melamine-coated particleboard for constructing the form; (E) concrete sealer; (F) coloring agent (liquid or powder); (G) bagged concrete countertop mix or high/early mix rated for 5,000 psi; (H) paste wax; (I) knockout for faucet, if installing sink; (J) buffing bonnet for polisher; (K) faucet set; and (L) sink.

Custom Features: Concrete countertops are normally cast as flat slabs, but if you are willing to put a little more time and effort into it, there are many additional features you can create during the pour. A typical 3"-tall backsplash is challenging, but if you have room behind the faucet you can create a ¾"-tall backsplash shelf in the backsplash area. Or, if you search around for some additional information, you can learn how to cast a drain board directly into the countertop surface. And there is practically no end to the decorative touches you can apply using pigments and inserts.

Estimating Concrete for Countertops: After you design your project and determine the actual dimensions, you'll need to estimate the amount of concrete you'll need. Concrete is measured by volume, in cubic feet; multiply the length by the width and then by the thickness of the finished countertop for volume in cubic inches, then divide the sum by 1,728 for cubic feet. For example,

a countertop that will be 48" long × 24" deep × 3½" thick will require 2⅓ cu. ft. of mixed concrete (48 × 24 × 3.5 / 1,728 = 2⅓) or four 80-lb. bags of countertop mix.

Countertop mix is specially formulated concrete designed for use in either precast or cast-in-place projects. Countertop mix contains additives that improve the workability, strength, and finish of the mix.

HOW TO CAST A CONCRETE COUNTERTOP

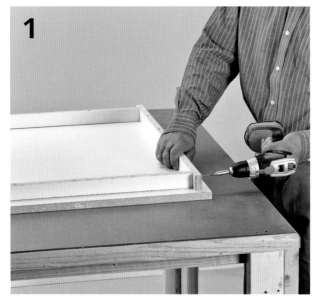

1

Cut 1½"-wide strips of ¾" melamine-coated particleboard for the form sides. Cut the strips to length (26 and 81½" as shown here) and drill two countersunk pilot holes ⅜" in from the ends of the front and back form sides. Assemble the strips into a frame by driving a 2" drywall screw at each pilot hole and into the mating ends of the end form strips.

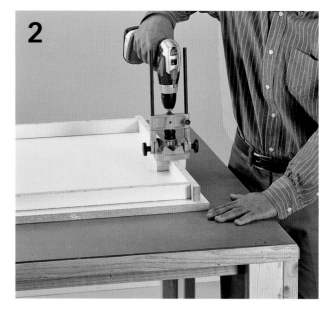

2

Use a power drill mounted in a right-angle drill guide to drill ¼"-dia. guide holes for 3" deck screws at 6" intervals all the way through the tops of the form sides. Countersink the holes so the screw heads will be recessed slightly below the surface.

3

With the base melamine-side up, center the melamine-strip frame pieces on the base. Check the corners with a carpenter's square to make sure they're square. Drive one 3½" deck screw per form side near the middle. The screwheads should be slightly below the top edges of the forms. Check for square again, and continue driving the 3½" screws at 6" intervals through the pilot holes. Check for square frequently. *Note: Do not drive any screws up through the underside of the form base—you won't be able to lift the countertop and access the screws when it's time to strip off the forms.*

4

Make the sink knockout blanks by stacking two pieces of ¾" melamine. The undermount sink we used requires a 20 × 31" knockout with corners that are rounded at a 2" radius. Cut two pieces of ¾"-thick MDF to 20 × 31" square using a tablesaw. With a compass, mark 2"-radius curves at each corner for trimming. Make the trim cuts with a jigsaw. Cut just outside the trim line and sand up to it with a pad sander for a smooth curve.

5

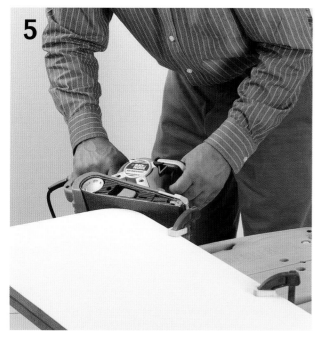

Clamp the two pieces of melamine face-to-face for the knockout and gang-sand the edges and corners so that they're smooth and even. Use a belt sander on a stationary table or an oscillating spindle sander. Don't oversand or the sink knockout will be too small.

6

Because gluing the faces together can add height to the knockout (and cause the concrete finishing tools to bang into it when they ride on the form tops), attach each blank directly to the layer below it using countersunk screws. Keep the edges aligned perfectly, especially if you're planning to install an undermount sink.

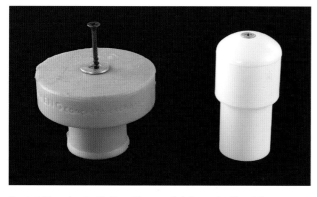

Faucet Knockouts Option: If your sink faucet will not be mounted on the sink deck, you'll need to add a knockout to your form for the faucet hole (best to choose a single-handle faucet), according to the requirements of the manufacturer. You can order knockouts from a concrete countertop supplies distributor, or you can create them with PVC pipe that has an outside diameter equal to the required faucet hole size. To anchor the PVC knockout, cover one end with a flat cap made for that size tubing. Drill a guide hole through the center of the cap so you can secure it with a screw. The top of the cap should be exactly flush with the form sides once it is installed. Before securing, position the knockout next to a form side and compare the heights. If the knockout is taller, file or sand the uncapped end so their lengths match.

7

Seal exposed edges of the sink knockout with fast-drying polyurethane varnish, and then caulk the form once the varnish is dry. Run a very thin bead of colored silicone caulk (the coloring allows you to see where the caulk has been laid on the white melamine) in all the seams and then smooth carefully with your fingertip. In addition to keeping the wet concrete from seeping into gaps in the form, the caulk will create a slight roundover on the edges of the concrete. Caulk around the bottoms of the knockouts as well.

(continued)

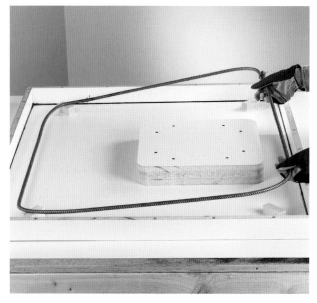

Variation: If your countertop is more than 2" thick, use No. 3 rebar (⅜" dia.) for the primary reinforcement. Do not use rebar on thinner countertops because the rebar will be too close to the surface and can telegraph through. Bend the rebar to fit around the perimeter of the form using a rebar or conduit bender. The rebar needs to be at least 1" away from all edges (including knockouts) and 1" away from the top surface. Tie the ends of the rebar with wire and set it in the form on temporary 1" spacers.

8

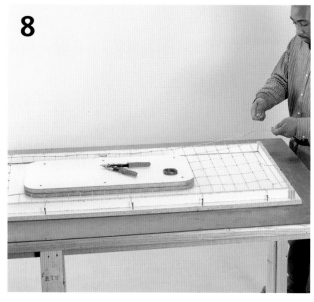

Cut a piece of welded wire (also called rewire) in a 4 × 4" grid so it's 2" smaller than the interior form dimensions. Make a cutout for the sink and faucet knockouts, making sure the rewire does not come closer than 1" to any edge, surface, or knockout. Flatten it as best you can and then hang it with wires that are attached to the tops of the forms with screws (you'll remove the screws and cut the wires after the concrete is placed).

9

Clamp or screw the base of the form to a sturdy workbench or table so it can't move during finishing and curing. Check for level and insert shims between the worktop and the benchtop if needed for leveling. If you're concerned about mess, slip a sheet of 3-mil plastic on the floor under the workbench.

10

Blend water with liquid cement color (if desired) in a 5-gal. bucket prior to adding to the mixer.

11

Slowly pour concrete countertop mix into the mixer and blend for a minimum of 5 minutes. Properly mixed material will flow easily into molds. Add small amounts of water as necessary to achieve the desired consistency.

12

Fill the countertop form, making sure to pack the concrete into corners and press it through the reinforcement. Overfill the form slightly.

13

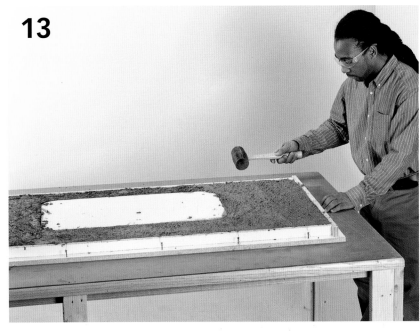

Vibrate the form vigorously as you work to settle concrete into all the voids. You can rent a concrete vibrator for this purpose, or simply strike the form repeatedly with a rubber mallet. If you have a helper and a sturdy floor and worktable, lift up and down on the ends of the table, bouncing it to cause vibrations. Make sure the table remains level when you're through.

14

Strike off excess concrete from the form using a 2 × 4 drawn along the tops of the forms in a sawing motion. If voids are created, pack them with fresh concrete and restrike. Do not overwork the concrete.

(continued)

15

Snip the wire ties holding the rewire mesh once you are certain you won't need to vibrate the form any further. Embed the cut ends attached to the rewire below the concrete surface.

16

Smooth the surface of the concrete with a screed, such as a length of angle iron or square metal tubing. Work slowly with a sawing motion, allowing the bleed water to fill in behind the screed. Since this surface will be the underside of the countertop, no further tooling is required. Cover the concrete with plastic and let dry undisturbed for three to five days.

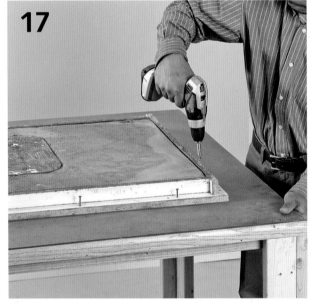

17

Remove the plastic covering and remove the forms. Do not pry against the fresh concrete. In most cases, you'll need to cut apart the sink knockout to prevent damaging the countertop when removing it. Drill a starter hole and then carefully cut up to the edge of the knockout. Cut the knockout into chunks until you can remove it all. The edges of the concrete will be fragile, so be very careful.

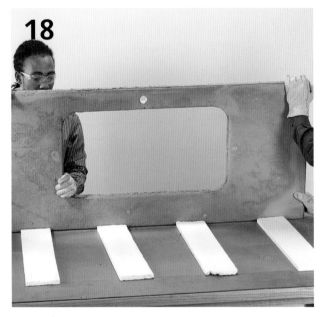

18

Flip the countertop so the finished surface is exposed (you'll need a helper or two). Be extremely careful. The best technique is to roll the countertop onto an edge, position several shock-absorbing sleepers beneath it (rigid insulation board works very well), and then gently lower the countertop onto the sleepers.

19

Grind the countertop surface with a series of increasingly fine grinding pads mounted on a shock-protected 5" angle grinder (variable speed). This is messy work and can require hours to get the desired result. Rinse the surface regularly with clean water and make sure it stays wet during grinding. For a gleaming surface, mount still finer pads (up to 1,500 grit) on the grinder and wet-polish.

20

Clean and seal the concrete with several coats of quality concrete sealer (one with penetrating and film-forming agents). For extra protection and a renewable finish, apply a coat of paste wax after the last coat of sealer dries.

21

Mount the sink (if undermount). Sinks are easier to install prior to attaching the countertop on the cabinet. Attach the sink according to the manufacturer's directions. Undermount sinks like this are installed with undermount clips and silicone adhesive. Self-rimming sinks likely will require some modifications to the mounting hardware (or at least you'll need to buy some extra-long screws) to accommodate the thickness of the countertop.

22

Make sure the cabinet is adequately reinforced and that as much plumbing as possible has been done, and apply a thick bead of silicone adhesive to the tops of the cabinets and stretchers. With at least one helper, lower the countertop onto the base and position it where you wish. Let the adhesive dry overnight before completing the sink and faucet hookups.

GRANITE TILE COUNTERTOPS

Solid granite countertops are hugely popular today, and for good reason: they are stunningly beautiful, amazingly hard and durable, and completely natural. However, they are also expensive and virtually impossible for a do-it-yourselfer to install. Take heart though, there is a way for an enterprising DIYer to achieve the look and feel of natural granite, but at a fraction of the price: granite tile countertops.

You have two basic product options with granite tile. You can use standard granite tiles, which consist of field tiles and edge tiles with square edges that are installed just like ceramic or porcelain tiles are, and finished with thin edge tiles to create the nosing; or you can use granite tiles that are installed with front tiles that feature an integral bullnose that better imitates the look of solid granite. Typically, granite tiles fit together more snugly than ceramic tiles do. This gives you the option of finishing with grout that's the same color as the tiles for a near-seamless appearance.

Layout is the most important step on any tile project, and no less so when working with granite tiles. If tiles need to be cut to fit, it is best to cut the tiles at the center of the installation or the sets of tiles at both ends. This creates a more uniform look. Granite tile can be installed over laminate countertop (not post-form) if you remove the nosing and backsplash first. The laminate substrate must be in good condition with no peeling or water damage.

Tools & Materials ▸

⅝" exterior-grade plywood
¼" tile backer or cementboard
Cementboard screws
Tiles
Tile wet saw with diamond blade
Honing stone
Power drill
Circular saw
Jigsaw
Eye and ear protection
Compass
Utility knife
Straightedge
¼" notched trowel
Modified thinset
Unsanded grout
Grout sealer
Stone sealer
Sponge
Bucket
Rubber gloves
Pry bar
Carpeted mallet

Granite tiles are installed in much the same way as ceramic tiles are, but the ultra-narrow gaps and matching grout mimic the appearance of solid polished granite.

HOW TO INSTALL GRANITE TILE COUNTERTOPS

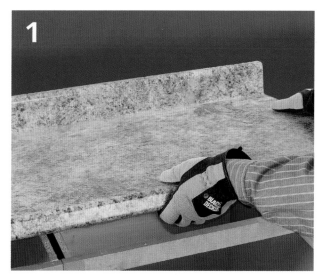

Remove old countertops by unscrewing the countertops from the cabinets. Unscrew the take-up bolts on mitered sections of the countertop. Use a utility knife to cut through any caulk. The countertops should lift off easily; if they don't, use a pry bar to carefully pry them away from the base cabinets. *Note: In some cases you can install the tiles over old laminate countertops.*

Measure the cabinet bank from outside edges to outside edges on all sides and cut a piece of ⅝"-thick exterior-grade plywood to fit. The edges of the plywood should be flush with the outside edges of the cabinet tops. Screw the plywood to the cabinet braces from underneath.

Place the sink upside down in the desired location and trace around it to mark the cutting lines. To create support for the drop-in sink flange, use a compass to trace new cutting lines inside the traced lines (usually ⅝"). See the manufacturer's instructions to confirm dimensions (some sinks come with a template for making the cutout). Use a jigsaw to cut out the sink opening.

Granite tile, like ceramic tile, requires a cementboard or denseboard underlayment layer. Cut the material to the same dimension as the plywood subbase and lay the cementboard over the plywood with the edges flush. From inside the sink base, trace around the sink cutout with a marker. Remove the underlayment and make the cutout with a jigsaw.

(continued)

Apply a ⅛"-thick layer of modified thinset to the top of the plywood using a ¼" notched trowel. Screw the cementboard to the plywood with cementboard screws. Space the screws 4 to 5" apart across the entire surface.

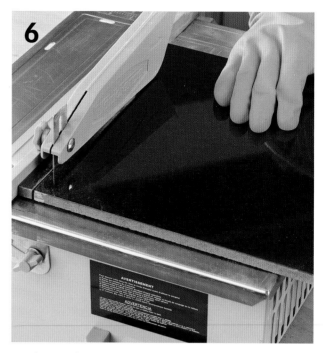

Cut (as needed) and lay out the tiles, beginning with an inside corner if you have one. Arrange tiles for the best color match. Tiles abut directly, with no space for grout. Cut the tiles as necessary to fit. Cut self-edged tiles edge side first. Cut the tiles with the polished side up. Use a fine-honing stone to relieve the cut edge to match the manufactured edges.

VARIATIONS FOR CORNERS & ANGLES

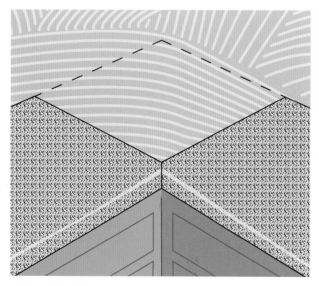

Mitered inside corners are a bit tricky to cut because the mitered point needs to align with the starting point of the bullnose edge. This has the effect of making the corner set back roughly 1".

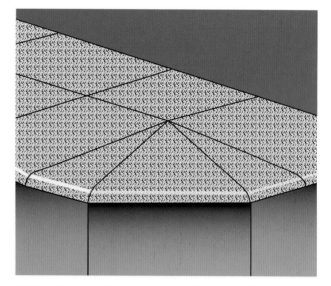

Kitchen islands often have corners that do not form a right angle. In such cases, you can avoid a sharp angle on the countertop by cutting a triangular bullnose piece to fill in.

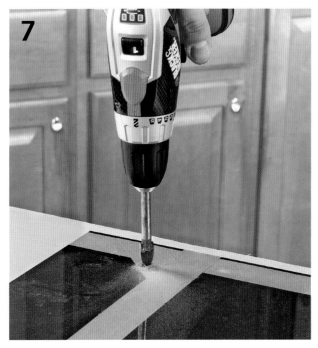

7

Even though the flange of the sink shown here will cover the inside corners in the sink cutout, take care to make a gentle rounded corner cut by drilling at the corner with a ½" masonry bit. Perpendicular corner cuts can lead to cracking. Finish the straight legs of the cutout with a tile saw or a jigsaw with a masonry blade.

8

Start laying tiles. Use modified thinset and a ¼" trowel. If you have an inside corner in your countertop, begin there. Apply thinset at the inside corner, enough to place four or five tiles. Set the left and right inside corner pieces and the first field tile.

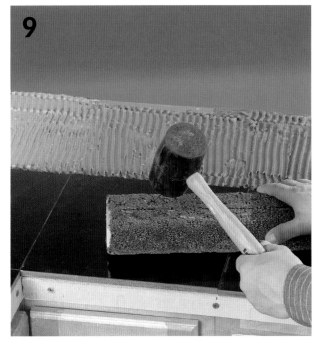

9

Continue setting tiles. Apply the thinset mortar to an area big enough for two to four tiles and place the tiles. Use a 2 × 4 covered with carpeting to set the tiles. Push down on tiles to set, and also across the edges to ensure an even face.

10

After the thinset has dried for at least 24 hours, grout with an unsanded grout. When the grout has dried, seal with natural stone sealer.

BANQUETTE

Almost everyone loves sitting in a booth at a restaurant—why not have one at home? Aside from providing an intimate, cozy setting for eating, games, or homework, a banquette or booth solves a critical space issue. An L-shaped booth eliminates the space needed to pull out chairs on two sides, plus, it allows children to sit closer together. Three kids can occupy booth space that is smaller than that required for two kids on two chairs. This project can create even more usable space if you add a roll-out storage unit under the booth seats.

This project creates an L-shaped, built-in booth in a kitchen corner. It does not show you how to redirect air vents or electrical outlets. Make sure you take into account the thickness of cushion foam if you plan on upholstering the backs. The plans assume you'll use 2-inch foam for seat cushions and back cushions. Thicker cushions will make the bench too shallow. Booth seating is most comfortable if the seats are 16 to 19 inches deep. The total height for the seat should be 18 to 19 inches to fit a standard 29-inch-tall table.

This project is designed to be painted, but if you wish to match your wood kitchen cabinets, you can use veneer plywood. Before beginning to build the

booth, carefully remove the base shoe or molding along both walls using a pry bar. Using a stud finder, mark the stud locations along both walls. Use masking tape to mark the stud locations to avoid marking on the wall surface.

Tools & Materials ▶

Tape measure	2 × 4 lumber
Stud finder	1 × 2 lumber
Pry bar	#8 screws
Circular saw	(1⅝", 2", 2½", 3")
Cordless screwdriver	1½" finish
Carpenter's square	head screws
Level	Finish nails
Bevel gauge	Edge banding
Compass	Trim molding
Jigsaw	Painter's caulk
Hammer	Wood putty
¾" paintable interior	Paint
plywood	Eye and ear protection
Masking tape	Work gloves

HOW TO BUILD A BANQUETTE

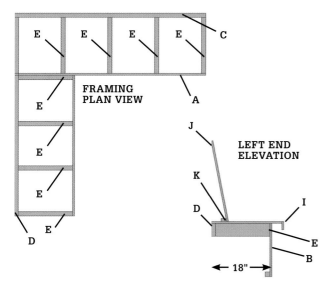

E   E   E   E   C

**FRAMING
PLAN VIEW**

E

A

E

J

**LEFT END
ELEVATION**

K

D   I

E

B

← 18" →

**LEFT SIDE
ELEVATION**

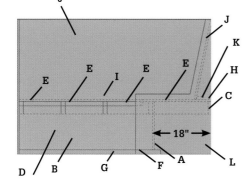

J

J

K

E   E   E

H

E   I   E   C

18"

D   B   G   F   A   L

Cutting List ▸

Key	Part	Size	Material	No.
A	Kickboard, long	15½" × 60"	¾" plywood	1
B	Kickboard, short	15½" × 42"	¾" plywood	1
C	Ledger, long	60"	2 × 4	1
D	Ledger, short	42"	2 × 4	1
E	Braces	16½"	2 × 4	8
F	Cleat, long	60"	2 × 2	1
G	Cleat, short	42"	2 × 2	1
H	Seat, long	22" × 60"	¾" plywood	1
I	Seat, short	22" × 38"*	¾" plywood	1
J	Seat backs	60" × 24"	¾" plywood	2
K	Seat cleats	60"*	1 × 2	2
L	End pieces	20" × 40"*	¾" plywood	2

* cut to fit

1

Cut the kickboards, ledgers, and braces to length.
Attach braces at each end of a ledger using two 2½" screws.
Evenly space the other braces and attach. Attach the
kickboard to the braces using 1⅝" screws. Use a carpenter's or
combination square to make sure all joints are squared.

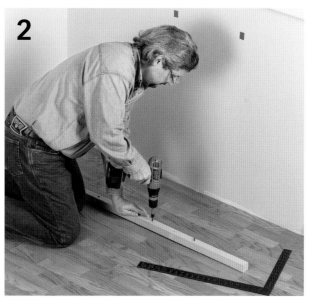

2

Cut the long cleat to length. Measure 18" out from the
wall and draw a line parallel to the wall. Align the cleat with
the inside edge of the line and attach to the floor using
2½" screws.

(continued)

Turn the brace and the kickboard assembly right side up and place against the wall and cleat. Check for level and make sure that the kickboard butts firmly against the cleat. Attach the ledger to the studs using two 3" screws per stud. Attach the kickboard to the cleat using 1⅝" screws.

Assemble the short bench and attach it to the studs and cleat following steps 1 through 3. Make sure the second bench butts firmly against the first bench.

Attach the long bench top using 1⅝" screws. Center the screws over the braces and not the kickboard. Measure from the edge of the long bench to the outside edge of the brace for the exact length of the short bench. Cut and attach the short bench top.

Lean one seat back against the wall so the bottom edge is 6" from the wall. Slide the long back cleat behind the back and mark its location. Use a bevel gauge to determine the edge bevel for the back. Remove the back and bevel the edge with a circular saw or tablesaw.

Attach the cleat to the seat top, using 1⅝" screws. Make sure the cleat is parallel to the wall. Apply edge banding to the top edge of the back. Replace the back and attach it to the cleat using 1⅝" screws. Attach it to the wall studs using 2" screws.

8

Lean the second back against the wall with its base 6" from the wall. Slide the short back cleat behind the back and mark its location. Use a compass to scribe the angle of the long back onto the short back. Cut along this mark using a circular saw. Attach the cleat and seat back as in step 7.

9

Place the end blanks against each end and trace the bench profile. Create a rounded or angular bench end that extends at least 1½" beyond the bench profile. This "lip" will prevent the cushions from slipping off the end. Cut the bench ends using a jigsaw.

10

Before attaching the ends, use a sander to break the pointed bench ends. Apply wood glue to the ends of the bench backs, kickboard, and bench tops. Attach the ends to the braces and bench using finish head screws every 6" to 8". Apply edge banding to the bench ends.

11

Attach the molding of your choice to the front edges of the bench with finish nails. Reattach the base molding if desired, or use trim molding to create panels, as pictured here. Fill all screw holes with wood putty, and sand smooth. Run a bead of painter's caulk along the joint between the bench top and back, the joint where the two bench backs meet, and between the bench back and wall. Smooth with a wet finger. Paint with a high-quality wood primer and satin, semigloss, or gloss paint. Make cushions, if desired.

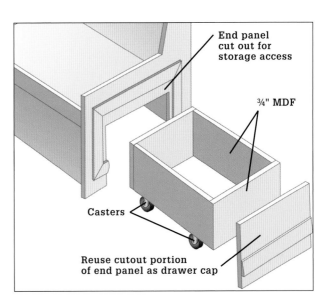

End panel cut out for storage access

¾" MDF

Casters

Reuse cutout portion of end panel as drawer cap

Variation: A wheeled drawer can add some storage space to your banquette. Before attaching the bench end, cut out an opening. Create a box with wheels and a drawer front to fit the opening.

RECESSED CABINET

If you've got a recessed wall area that you're not sure how to use, then a built-in cabinet might be a perfect fit. For example, the set-back space created on one or both sides of a bumped-out fireplace is a perfect spot to install a built-in bookshelf or cabinet.

Building a recessed cabinet is very similar to building a freestanding cabinet. The key difference is that a recessed cabinet must fit perfectly between the side walls. The easiest way to make a cabinet that will fit is to make a basic interior cabinet case that's slightly smaller than the available space and then build a face frame and top cover that will cover the edges of the cabinet and fit snugly against the walls. The secret to achieving a perfect fit is to make the face frame and top slightly oversized and then scribe them to fit against the walls.

You can build a recessed cabinet with or without doors. In the version seen here, glass panel doors were built, but you can also use solid, natural wood veneer or painted plywood panels to conceal the cabinet interior. It is important to purchase tempered glass when you are building glass panel doors. Tempered glass is treated with heat so that if it is broken, it will shatter into small pieces that are less likely to cause serious cuts. It's also stronger. You can't cut it yourself, so be sure to get the size correct when you order it cut-to-fit.

Building this cabinet requires intermediate woodworking skills and a few woodworking power tools, including a tablesaw, miter saw, and router table.

Tools & Materials ▸

Tablesaw
Miter saw
Drill/driver
Pocket hole jig kit
Finish or random-orbit sander
Eye and ear protection
Tape measure
Level
Compass
Finish materials
Wood glue
Work gloves

Doors:
Router table
Rail and stile router bit set
⅜"-rad. rabbet bottom-bearing router bit

Cabinet materials (to make one roughly 4'.-wide × 4'.-tall × 12"-deep cabinet):
(2) 2 × 4 × 8' pine
(1) ¼ × 4 × 8 plain-sawn cherry veneer plywood
(1) ¾ × 4 × 8 plain-sawn cherry veneer plywood

(2) ¾ × 1½" × 8' cherry
(2) ¾ × 2½" × 8'. cherry
(1) ¾ × 5 × 48" cherry
2" flat-head wood screws
2½" flat-head wood screws
3" drywall screws
1¼" fine thread washer-head (pocket) screws
18-ga. × 2" brad nails
(24) ¼"-dia. shelf pins
1" brads

Doors (to make four roughly 11 × 46" doors):
(5) ¾ × 2" × 8' solid cherry
(1) ¾ × 4 × 30 solid cherry
(4 pr.) non-mortise full-wrap hinges
(4) ⅛"-thick tempered glass panels
(4) magnetic door catches
18-ga. × ¾" brad nails

Cutting List

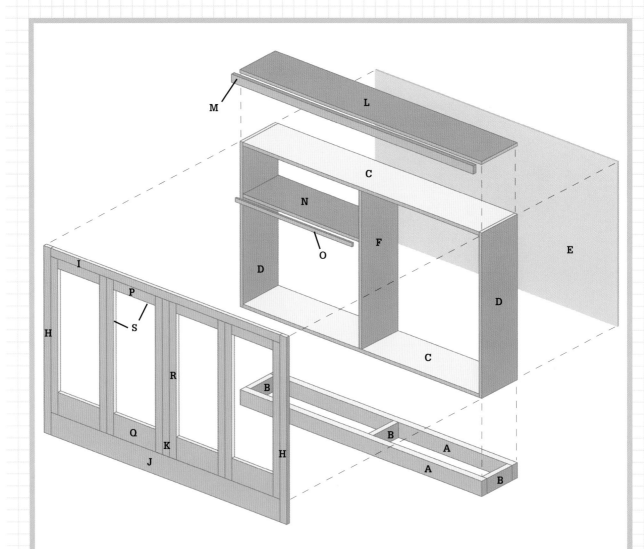

Key	No.	Description	Dimension
Cabinet			
A	2	Base rails	1½ × 3½ × 46"
B	3	Base cross pieces	1½ × 3½ × 8¼"
C	2	Cabinet top and bottom	¾ × 11 × 43½"
D	2	Cabinet sides	¾ × 11 × 48"
E	1	Cabinet back	¼ × 45 × 48"
F	1	Cabinet divider	¾ × 11 × 46½"
G	2	Back cleats (not shown)	¾ × 2½ × 43½"
H	2	Face frame stiles	¾ × 2½ × 51½"
I	1	Face frame top rail	¾ × 2½ × 43"
J	1	Face frame bottom rail	¾ × 4¼ × 43"

Key	No.	Description	Dimension
K	1	Face frame center stile	¾ × 2¾ × 45¼"
L	1	Top	¾ × 11¾ × 48"
M	1	Top front edge	¾ × 1¼ × 48"
N	6	Shelf	¾ × 11 × 43¼"
O	6	Shelf edge	¾ × 1 × 43¼"
P	4	Top rail	¾ × 1⅝ × 6⅝"
Q	4	Bottom rail	¾ × 3⅝ × 6⅝"
R	8	Stiles	¾ × 2 × 44½"
S	16	Glass tack strips	¼ × ¼" × glass perimeter

HOW TO BUILD A RECESSED CABINET

DETERMINE THE CABINET DIMENSIONS

Perhaps the trickiest aspect of building a cabinet that must fit between two walls is calculating the part dimensions so the finished cabinet will fit the space you have. The first step is to measure the width of the space. Walls are seldom plumb, so you must measure the width at several heights above the floor (photo 1). Record the smallest measurement (the narrowest width) and use that dimension to make adjustments to the cutting list (unless your space happens to be 48 inches wide—the width of the cabinet seen here).

Limit the shelf lengths to no more than 30 inches long—any span larger than that and they are likely to sag and break. Shorten shelf lengths in a wide cabinet by dividing the cabinet into multiple sections with vertical divider panels. If the space the cabinet is to be installed in is 32 inches or less, then you will not need a vertical divider. If the space is 32 to 60 inches wide, then you need at least one vertical divider in the center of the cabinet. Install additional vertical dividers if you plan to store heavy objects on the shelves.

MAKE THE BASE

Cut the base frame parts to length and assemble the base with 2½-inch wood screws. Center the base between the side walls and against the back wall. Level the base with shims and then secure it to the back wall (photo 2).

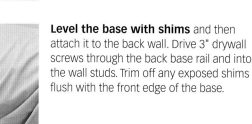

1

Measure the width of the space where the cabinet will be installed. Measure at several heights above the floor and at the front and back of the space. Record and use the smallest measurement.

2

Level the base with shims and then attach it to the back wall. Drive 3" drywall screws through the back base rail and into the wall studs. Trim off any exposed shims flush with the front edge of the base.

(continued)

MAKE THE CABINET FRAME

Cut the cabinet sides, dividers, top, and bottom to size. Bore the shelf-pin holes in the side panels. You can use a manufactured shelf pin jig or use a piece of pegboard as a template to align the holes. Then, cut the back cleats to length. Sand the faces of each part smooth with 150-grit sandpaper. Attach the sides to the top and bottom with 2-inch wood screws. Bore pilot holes before driving screws into plywood edges. Attach the back cleats to the sides and top with 2-inch wood screws. Next, cut a notch to fit around the back cleat in the top of each divider panel. Attach the dividers to the top and bottom with 2-inch screws (photo 3). Cut the back panel to size and attach the back panel to the cabinet frame with glue and brad nails or crown staples (photo 4).

Place the cabinet frame on the base. Center the cabinet on the base and align the front edge of the cabinet with the front edge of the base. Attach the cabinet to the base with 2-inch brad nails. Place shims behind the cabinet at each stud location to fill the gap between the cabinet and wall. Attach the cabinet to the back wall and side walls by driving a screw through the back cleat and side panels into the wall studs (photo 5).

Attach the divider panels to the top and bottom with 2" screws. Use a square to make sure the divider is perpendicular to the top and bottom. Bore a pilot hole and countersink hole for each screw. Drive the screws through the top and bottom.

Attach the back panel with glue and 1" brads or 1" narrow crown staples. Keep the cabinet sides, top, and bottom perpendicular as you attach the back panel.

Attach the cabinet to the wall. Bore a pilot and countersink hole through the back cleat and side panels at each stud location. Place scrap blocks or shims behind each screw hole to fill the gap between the wall and cabinet. Secure the cabinet with 3" drywall screws.

6

Temporarily attach the rails to the cabinet with tape. Then, scribe the stiles to follow the profile of the wall. Hold the stile perpendicular to the rails and against the side wall. Set a compass opening to match the distance that the stile overlaps the ends of the rails.

MAKE THE FACE FRAME & TOP

The face frame and top are made to fit exactly between the walls and will cover the gaps that were left between the cabinet and walls. Cut the face frame stiles and rails to size. Temporarily hold or attach the face frame rails in place against the cabinet frame. Then hold one of the stiles perpendicular to the rails and against the side wall. Scribe the wall profile on the outside edge of the stile (photo 6 and 7). Follow the same process to scribe the other stile. Trim the stiles along the scribe lines. Test the fit of the stiles and trim or sand as necessary to fit. The stiles should fit snugly between the walls and rails. Next, lay out the face frame parts on a flat surface and assemble the frame with pocket screws (photo 8). Sand the face frame smooth.

Attach the face frame to the cabinet frame with glue and a few 18-gauge × 1¼-inch brads. You only need a couple of brads in each piece to hold it securely while the glue cures.

7

Hold the metal point of the compass against the wall and pull the compass down along the wall to trace the profile of the wall onto the face of the stile. The stile must remain perpendicular to the rails as you draw the scribe line.

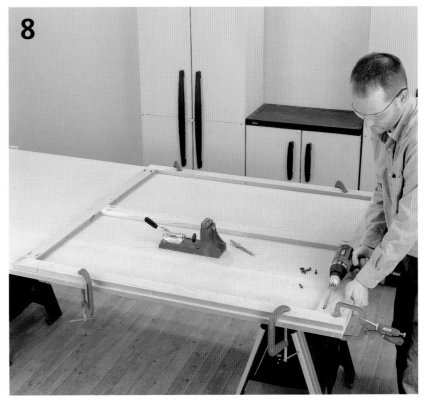

8

Assemble the cabinet face frame with pocket screws. Clamp the parts to a large worksurface to keep them perpendicular as they are connected.

(continued)

The top must fit against three walls. If the walls are perpendicular, then you can simply measure the width of the opening and cut the top panel. But, if the walls are not perfectly square to one another, the easiest way to make a top that fits is to create a template (photo 9). Transfer the template dimensions and cut the top panel.

Cut the top front edge piece the same length as the front edge of the top panel. Attach the top front edge to the top with glue. Clamp the front edge until the glue has cured. Remove the clamps, sand the top assembly and attach the top to the cabinet (photo 10).

Cut the shelf boards and shelf edge to size. Attach the shelf edge to the shelf board, aligning the top edges, with glue. Clean off excess glue and sand the shelves smooth.

Protect the surrounding wall surfaces with masking tape and drop cloths. Apply wood finish or paint to the cabinet and shelves. In this case dark brown oil-base gel stain was applied, followed by three coats of water-base polyurethane. After the finish is dry, attach base molding to match the existing base molding in the room.

BUILD THE DOORS

The first step in building doors is to determine the size of the doors. To prevent sagging, the maximum width of each door should be less than 24 inches If the cabinet opening is greater than 24 inches wide, then use two doors.

The bottom rail is wider than the top rail for two reasons. First, a wider bottom rail gives the door

Tape together pieces of paper or cardboard to make a template for the top. Leave a ⅛" space between the template and the walls. Then, trace the template on the top panel stock and cut out the top.

Attach the top to the cabinet with 1¼" screws. Drive the screws through the underside of the cabinet top panel and into the finished top. Use one screw in each corner and two screws evenly spaced near the front and back of the cabinet.

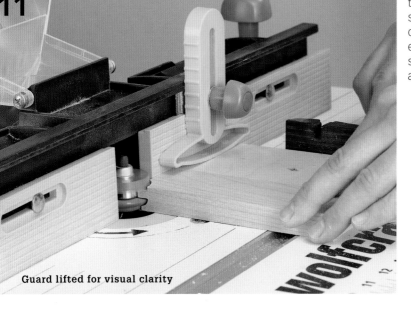

11

Guard lifted for visual clarity

This router bit set cuts a ⅜"–long stub tenon. The extra ¾" necessary for the two stub tenons must be added to the length of the rails. Rout the stub tenons on the ends of the rails. Set the router bit height so the top cutter will mill a ⅛"-deep rabbet above the stub tenon.

12

Rout the groove profile in the inside edges of the rails and stiles. Set the router bit height to align the groove with the stub tenon (inset). Make test cuts in a scrap piece to adjust the bit height for a perfect fit before cutting the actual parts.

good scale by adding a little more visual weight to the bottom of the door. Second, the wider dimension adds more gluing surface, creating a stronger frame to support the glass panel.

Measure the height and width of the face frame openings. Determine the door width and height by subtracting the width of the gaps that must be left around the edges of the doors and between doors (see page 209).

There are several ways to build frame and panel doors. The doors for this cabinet are made using a rail-and-stile (also referred to as a cope-and-stick) router bit set. This set contains two router bits; one bit that cuts the stub tenon in the ends of the rails and another bit that cuts the panel groove and edge profile.

Cut the door parts to size. Then rout the stub tenon profile on both ends of the rails (photo 11). Next, rout the groove profile in the inside edges of the stiles and rails (photo 12). Make test cuts in a scrap piece to adjust the bit alignment.

(continued)

Assemble each doorframe with glue (photo 13). Clamp the frames, checking them for square before the glue sets up. *Note: If you choose to install solid panels rather than glass panels, then install the panels when you assemble the frame.*

The back edge of the groove must be removed to create the rabbet that the glass fits against. Use a router and bottom-bearing rabbet bit to remove the back lip of the groove (photo 14). Use a chisel to clean up the corners of the rabbet that the router bit does not reach.

Hang the doors before you apply the finish and install the glass. These doors are mounted on full wrap-around, no-mortise hinges that offer the no-sag benefits of butt hinges and are easy to install. Attach the hinges to the cabinet and then mount the doors on the hinges (photo 15). Mount magnetic catches on the top rail to keep the doors closed.

After the doors are installed and operating correctly, remove the doors and hardware. Cut ¼ × ¼-inch tack strips to hold the glass panels in the door. Cut enough tack strips to cover the perimeter of all the glass. Sand and finish the doors and tack strips to match the cabinet.

Assemble the doorframe with glue. Measure diagonally across the corners to check the frame for square (or, just use a carpenter's square). If the diagonal measurements are equal, then the frame is square.

Use a bottom-bearing rabbet bit to remove the back lip of the groove. Set the bit depth so that the bearing rides on the front edge or "stick" profile of the door (inset).

Fasten the hinge to the door using the slotted screw holes first. These holes allow you to adjust the door position slightly. Drive screws in the fixed screw holes after the door is positioned correctly in the cabinet. Drill pilot holes for each screw to prevent stripping the screw head, breaking the screws or splitting the door stile.

Install the glass in the doors after the finish is dry. Place a sheet of glass in each door. Cut the tack strips to fit along each side of the glass. Bore ¹⁄₃₂-inch-diameter pilot holes through the tack strips, spacing them 6 inches apart. Place the strips over the glass and drive a 18 gauge × ¾-inch brad nail into each pilot hole (photo 16). After the glass pieces are installed, reinstall the hardware and hang the doors.

Attach the tack strips to hold the glass in the doors. Use a brad push tool to drive the brads or gently tap the brads with a small hammer. Cover the glass with a piece of cardboard to protect it.

Door Dimensions ▸

To prevent sagging, the maximum width of each door should be less than 24". If the cabinet opening is greater than 24" wide, then use two doors.

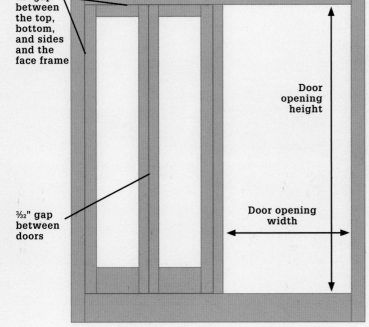

¹⁄₁₆" gap between the top, bottom, and sides and the face frame

³⁄₃₂" gap between doors

Door opening height

Door opening width

Door overall dimensions:

Door width = face frame opening width – side gaps (¹⁄₁₆ sides and ³⁄₃₂ between doors)

Door height = face frame opening height – top and bottom gaps (⅛ total)

Door part dimensions:

Door stile length = height of door

Door rail length = width of door – 2 (stile width) + 2 (tenon length)

WINDOW SEAT

One great way to add cozy charm to a room is to build a window seat. Not only do window seats make a room more inviting, they provide functional benefits as well, particularly when you surround them with built-in shelving. The window seat shown here has a base built from above-the-refrigerator cabinets.

This size provides just the right height (when placed on a 3-inch curb) to create a comfortable seat.

Above the cabinets and flanking each side is a site-made bookcase. A top shelf bridges the two cases and ties the whole thing together—while creating still more space for storage or display.

Tools, Materials & Cutting List

Eye and ear protection
Work gloves
Miter saw
Tablesaw
Circular saw
Pull-type saw
Chisel
Drill/driver
Level
Stud finder
Hammer
Tape measure
Nail set
Pneumatic nailer/compressor
Router
Shooting board
Sander
Shims
Framing square
(2) 15h × 24d × 36w
    stock cabinets
(2) ¾" × 4 × 8' pcs. MDF
    or plywood
Screws/nails
(1) ¼" × 4 × 8'
    birch plywood
Panel adhesive
Caulk
Primer
Paint

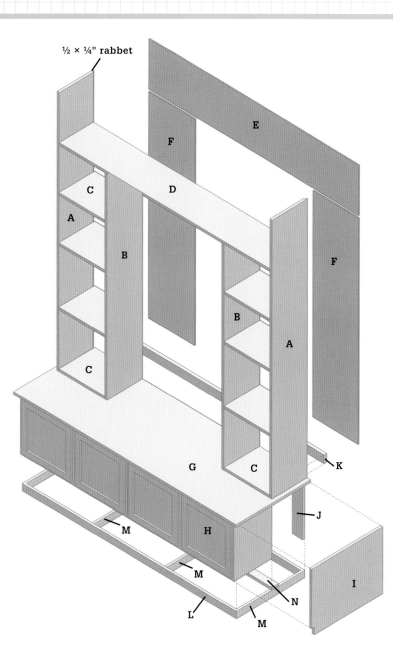

½ × ¼" **rabbet**

Key	No.	Desc.	Size	Material
A	2	Outer standard	¾ × 11½ × 77¼"	MDF
B	2	Inner standard	¾ × 11½ × 63¼"	MDF
C	8	Shelf	¾ × 16½ × 11¼"	MDF
D	1	Top shelf	¾ × 11¼ × 70½"	MDF
E	1	Top backer	¼ × 13¼ × 71⅜"	Plywood
F	2	Backers	¼ × 17½ × 63¼"	Plywood
G	1	Seatboard	¾ × 25 × 74"	MDF

Key	No.	Desc.	Size	Material
H	2	Cabinets	15 h × 36" w	Stock cabinets
I	2	End panel	¾ × 24 × 18"	MDF
J	4	Nailer	¾ × 2½ × 15"	Plywood
K	1	Ledger	¾ × 2½ × 72"	Plywood
L	2	Curb rim	¾ × 3 × 72"	MDF
M	4	Curb strut	¾ × 3 × 22½"	MDF
N	1	Cabinet nailer	¾ × 3 × 72"	MDF

HOW TO BUILD A WINDOW SEAT

1

The key control point for laying this project out is the center of the window sill. Measure and mark it.

2

After striking a level line at cabinet height, measure from the floor in three locations to make sure the cabinets will fit.

3

Strike a plumb line on each edge of the cabinet run. Use a 4' level and strike the line from floor to ceiling.

LAY OUT THE PROJECT

This window seat is integrated with the existing window and trimwork. The key control point for laying out the base cabinets is locating the center of the window opening. It is also important that the cabinets sit level both left-to-right and front-to-back. Level cabinet tops make installing the upper cabinet cases much easier.

Before you begin building, relocate or remove any electrical outlets that'll be covered by the cabinet, according to your local electrical codes. For example, you can't just dead-end wires and leave them buried in a wall. They usually need to be capped and placed in a junction box with a removable faceplate that is accessible (which may mean making a cutout in the back of a cabinet panel).

Mark the center of the window opening on the sill (photo 1). Use a square and a level to transfer that mark down the wall to the cabinet height location. At the height of the cabinets mark a level line. Measure from the floor up to the level line in several locations to make sure the cabinets will fit all along their entire run (photo 2). If they don't fit, make the proper adjustments; that is, raise the line. Cabinets that don't come up to the line must be shimmed so they are level. Using an electronic stud finder, find and mark the wall stud locations beneath the window and on each side in the project area. *Note: You should find jack and king studs directly on either side of the window and a header above the window. Determine the overall span of the cabinets you choose. For the project shown here, the bank will be 6 feet long, measuring from outside-edge to outside-edge. Use a level to mark the outside edges of the cabinet run on the wall. Mark plumb lines down to the floor and up to the ceiling (photo 3).*

INSTALL THE BASE CABINETS

With all the layout lines marked out, the next step is to install the cabinets that form the base of the window seat. This determines the control points for the rest of the project layout. Use a pull-saw and sharp chisel to remove base molding between the vertical layout lines (photo 4).

To elevate the cabinets that will be used for the seat to a more comfortable height, and to create a toe-kick space, build a short curb that matches the footprint of the seat. Since the curb will not be visible, you can use just about any shop scraps you may have to build it. The one shown here is made with MDF sheet stock that is rip-cut into 3-inch-wide strips. Then the curb is assembled into a ladder shape by attaching struts between the front and back curb members with glue and screws (photo 5). Once the ladder is built, set the cabinets on the curb so the cabinet fronts and sides align with the curb. Mark the location of the backs of the cabinets onto the top of the curb and then remove the cabinets. Attach a nailer to the curb just behind the line for the cabinet backs. Then, position the curb tight against the wall in the area where the base molding has been removed. Attach it to the sill plate of the wall with nails or screws.

To support the back edge of the seatboard, attach a ledger to the wall. The top of the ledger (we used a 2½-inch-wide strip of plywood) should be flush with the tops of the cabinets when they are installed on top of the curb. Attach the ledger with panel adhesive and nails or screws driven at stud locations (photo 6). Measure between the top of the curb and ledger and cut a few nailers to this length.

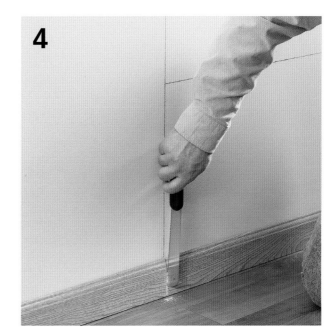

Because a pull-type saw requires almost zero clearance at the bottom of a cut (where it would hit the floor in this application), it's great for removing the base molding so the cabinet carcases fit tight to the wall.

Assemble the curb members into a ladder-like frame and secure the butt joints with glue and screws driven through pilot holes.

Attach a ledger for the back edge of the seatboard to the wall, using panel adhesive and screws driven at stud locations. Tack the ledger in place and then reinforce with wood screws driven at stud locations.

(continued)

Cut nailers to fit between the ledger and the curb and attach them to the wall at the ends of the project area.

For floors that are out of level, shim the cabinets up to the level line to keep them in a level plane.

After clamping the cabinet face-frames together, predrill and fasten them together with screws.

Attach them to the wall at the ends of the project, and add a couple near the center to help support the ledger (photo 7).

Set the cabinets in position on the curb, with the back edges against the nailer. Drive shims between the curb and the floor if necessary to level the cabinets (photo 8). Fasten the cabinets to the nailer strip. Predrill, countersink and fasten the face frames together with screws to form a "gang" of cabinets (photo 9). If you are using cabinets that have no face frames, screw the cabinet sides together as directed by the cabinet manufacturer. Cut off shims as necessary.

If the ends of your window seat are open (that is, they don't butt up against a wall), cut end panels to cover the ends of the cabinets and the open space behind them. Use ¾-inch plywood or hardboard. You may need to remove a sliver of the baseboard on each side so you can butt the panels up against the wall. Attach the panel to the cabinet ends and the curb with panel adhesive.

Cut, rout, and install the seat top. Cutting a 74 × 25-inch blank from MDF (medium-density fiberboard) works well. This will create a 1-inch overhang at the front and sides of the cabinets.

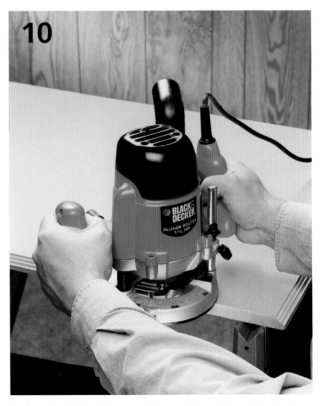

Before installing the seat top, rout a profile on the front and side edges. Don't rout the back.

Use a router and bit with a decorative profile (such as an ogee or a plain roundover) to smooth the hard edge of the MDF (photo 10). Profiling the edge reduces the chance that the edge will chip or crack. Position the seat top on top of the cabinets and the wall ledger and fasten it from the interior of the cabinets using predrilled coarse-threaded drywall screws. A bead of panel adhesive along the top edges of the cabinet and the ledger helps ensure a solid connection.

CUT THE CASE STOCK

The bookcase portion of the window seat can be assembled from sheet stock or solid 1× stock, such as 1 × 12 pine or poplar (pine is cheaper, poplar is stronger and takes paint better) or hardwood like maple, oak, or cherry for staining. Whatever material you choose, install a backer sheet of ¼-inch plywood that fits into rabbets in the backs of the case stock to help ensure square assembly and provide a strong connection point to the wall.

The actual width of 1 × 12 dimension lumber is 11¼ inches, so if using sheet stock, rip all pieces to width. Any edges that face the interior of the room need to be sanded smooth to remove saw marks. Note that it's usually easier to dress the factory edge than the edge cut on-site. Running the pieces on a jointer or router table is a fast, accurate way to dress the edge. A belt sander or finish sander with fine grit paper works too, but be careful not to remove too much stock. Of course, you can also hand sand it.

Cut a ½-inch wide by ¼-inch deep rabbet (see drawing, page 211) on the backs of the standards (photo 11). You can do this with a tablesaw (either make multiple passes on the tablesaw to remove stock or use a stacked dado head cutter blade); using a router with a rabbeting bit; or on a jointer or router table. The remainder of the layout and sizing must be registered from the seat top to accommodate specific site conditions.

INSTALL THE TOP-SHELF BACKER

The remaining measurements for the backer and shelf dimensions are now determined by the distance between your window casing, vertical layout lines, and ceiling height. They must be site-measured for accuracy.

Lay out the top shelf backer (photo 12). It should fit between the ceiling and the top of the window casing—and between your vertical layout lines. To calculate the top shelf backer dimensions, measure between the vertical layout lines. Subtract ⅝ inch. To calculate top shelf backer height, measure from the top of the window casing to the ceiling. Subtract ⅛

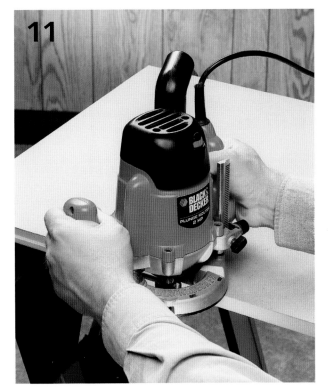

Clamp all work securely before milling the ½ × ¼ rabbet for the backers with a router, which will provide safe, accurate cuts. The remainder of the layout and sizing must be measured from the seat top to accommodate specific site conditions.

Use the layout lines to size the top shelf backer and the backers for the vertical shelf units.

(continued)

13

Marking layout lines all at once using a framing square is a good way to keep lines parallel from shelf-to-shelf. Make sure all bottoms are held flush during the marking procedure.

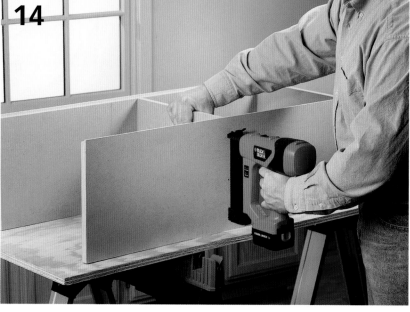

14

Install the shelves between the side standards. Glue the joints and clamp them. Tack them with finish nails. Drill countersink pilot holes and reinforce with three 2½" deck screws at each joint.

inch. Install the top shelf backer tight to the ceiling by fastening to studs with finish nails or screws.

FABRICATE & ASSEMBLE THE BOOKCASES

The bookcases' outside edges run from the seat top to the ceiling. The inside edges run from the seat top to the top of the window casing. Measure and cut each vertical bookcase member to length. On a flat surface, lay all the bottoms of the bookcase members flush and mark out your shelves (photo 13). Use a framing square to mark them. Keep in mind there is a bottom

shelf that sits directly above the seat top. The top shelf is installed later.

Lay out and cut the backer stock. To calculate the width, measure the distance between the window casing and the vertical layout line, minus ⅝ inch. To calculate the height, measure the distance from the seat top to the bottom edge of the top backer and subtract ⅛ inch.

Assemble the cabinet sides and the backers. This is an ideal application for a pneumatic ¼-inch crown stapler, but it can also be done effectively by predrilling

15

Hold the shelf assembly as tight as possible to the window trim, seat top and wall then fasten. Drive at least two or three screws to hold each unit, in addition to nails.

16

For paint grade units, caulk any gaps to make shadow lines disappear. You can caulk the gap on paint grade shelves too. Be extra diligent in wiping down the material after caulking.

and screwing, or by using a pneumatic finish nailer. Use a framing square as a reference to be sure the cabinet carcasses are as square as possible during assembly. Measure, cut, and install shelves at the layout lines (photo 14). Fasten through the cabinet carcass into the shelves. Predrill and countersink if using screws.

INSTALL THE BOOK CASES & TOP SHELF

Butt the left bookcase to the window trim and fasten it to a wall stud with a few screws or nails driven through the backer (photo 15). Make sure the case

sits as tightly to the wall, seat top, and window trim as possible. Expect to make some on-site corrections as necessary to accommodate out-of-plumb walls or other imperfections. Slight gaps can be caulked later. Repeat for the right-side bookcase and then measure, cut, and install the top shelf. If painting, caulk wherever necessary (photo 16). Fill exposed holes for nails and screws, then prime and paint or apply another finish of your choice. Make or buy a comfortable seat cushion. Finally, brew a cup of coffee, grab a good book, and get busy relaxing.

WALL NICHE

A wall niche is kind of cubby hole carved into a stud wall, usually to house display shelving. These days, they are often seen in higher-end housing as prefashioned inserts with an arch shape and Greco-Roman styling, often with classical statuary within the niche sides. The niche shown here is a rather different animal. It is simply a wooden box that you slip into a hole in the wall and then trim out.

A niche creates a perfect spot to stash napkin holders, salt and pepper shakers, and other tableware so your table surface is clear for eating, relaxing or doing a bit of homework.

The steps, skills, and tools described here can be used to create wall niches of various sizes and in numerous locations. It is important to note, however, that these niches are intended for nonload-bearing walls. If the niche you wish to create would involve cutting framing members in a load-bearing wall, consider redesigning the project so you do not have to cut wall studs. Making structural alterations to a load-bearing wall should be done only by qualified professionals.

It's also important to be aware of any electrical wires or gas or water plumbing near your project area.

Check to see if there are light switches or plugs above or below the niche opening before cutting and try to deduce where plumbing might be routed and located.

Safety notice: This project should be installed only in nonload-bearing walls. Do not cut wall studs in load-bearing walls unless you are working with a certified building engineer or licensed contractor.

HOW TO BUILD A WALL NICHE

LAY OUT THE NICHE
Determine that the wall you're cutting into is not a load-bearing or exterior wall. Determine the opening's finished location and height and width. A niche 8 inches tall by 24 inches wide is just the right proportions for most kitchen tables and booths. Use a 2-foot level and mark all four sides of the opening plumb and level at the finished location. These lines are the control points for all other measurements.

Measure ¾ inch out from each control point line (photo 1). Do this at two points on each line and connect the dots using a 2-foot level.

MAKE THE CUTOUT
Check in the basement and adjoining walls for wiring and pipes. Open a preliminary hole with a razor knife to check if you're unsure. Use a drywall saw or reciprocating saw to cut along the cutline. Make the cut as shallow as you can in case there are hidden wires or pipes in the wall.

Remove the drywall, exposing the wall studs. More than likely, you're going to have a wall stud or two somewhere in the middle of the opening. Use a reciprocating saw to remove the studs. Or, you can use a circular saw to start the cut (photo 2), carefully aligning it with the edge of the drywall and using it to cut the stud. Then, finish the cut with a reciprocating saw (photo 3). Be careful not to cut through the drywall on the back side of the cut.

When removing studs, you may pull a fastener through from an adjoining room and have to repair that afterwards. Nails or screws may be penetrating from the other side of the wall into the stud. Carefully remove the stud section. It is likely that removing the stud section will cause the fastener to pull through the opposite side of the wall, so touch-up may be necessary. For most nonload-bearing walls the competed niche box should provide adequate support for the cut studs. But if you are cutting more than one stud, or if you simply want to be certain the niche

Tools, Materials & Cutting List

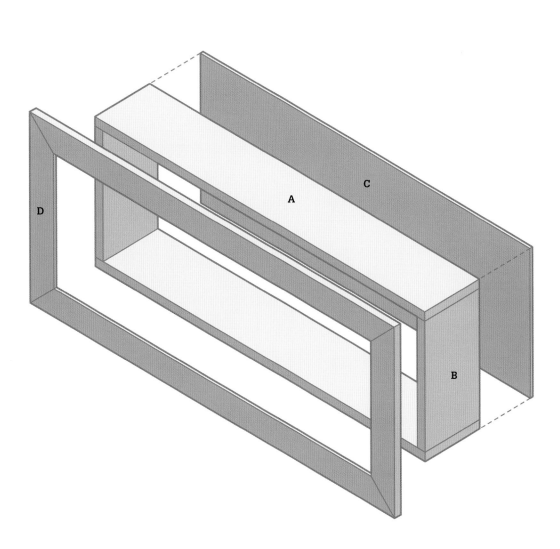

Eye and ear protection
Work gloves
Drywall/plaster
  cutting saw
Reciprocating saw
Cordless drill/driver
Circular saw
Miter saw
Countersink
Finish nails
Glue or panel adhesive
Caulk or adhesive

Sandpaper
Drywall finishing tools
2-ft. level
Aviator snips
1 × 6
Trim-head screws
¼" birch plywood
  scrap
1⅝" drywall screws
Case molding
Paint

Key	No.	Desc.	Size	Material
A	2	Top/bottom	¾ × 3⅝ × 25½"	Hardwood
B	2	Side	¾ × 3⅝ × 8"	Hardwood
C	1	Back	¼ × 9½ × 25½"	Plywood
D	4	Trim	½ × 2⅞" × miter to fit	Case molding

Start your layout by mapping out the niche's finished dimensions, then measure out from there for the rough opening where you will make your cuts. This is the cutline. With electrical power turned off, cut the opening in the wall covering. Use caution in case there are hidden wires or pipes in the area.

Cut as deeply into the wall studs as you can with a circular saw or trim saw.

Use a reciprocating saw to finish the cut. This method is easier on the drywall—especially if the studs back up to another room—and provides a straighter cut.

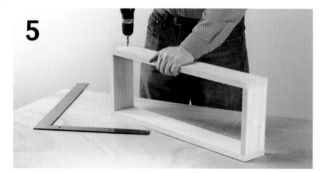

Rip-cut the niche frame boards to width. Cut them so they stop just short of the opposite wallcovering when installed.

Assemble the niche box. Drill countersunk pilot holes for the screws.

Use standard casing to trim out the niche like a picture frame. Preinstalling the trim means you can slip the niche box assembly into the opening. The trim guides how the box sets against the wall, similar to how a prehung door is installed.

box does not sag from downward pressure, make the opening larger and install a double 2 × 4 header over the niche box. This will require considerably more patching of the wall covering, but you may appreciate it for your own peace of mind.

BUILD THE NICHE BOX

Measure the depth of your wall cavity and subtract ⅜ inch from the overall depth to give yourself a little bit of flexibility when installing the niche and to allow for the thickness (¼ inch) of the backer material. This

measurement yields the required width of the boards you'll use to make the niche box. Rip-cut 1 × 6 × 8 lumber to the required width, using a tablesaw or a circular saw with a straightedge guide (photo 4). Cut the frame parts to length.

Fasten top and bottom niche frame parts to the sides with drywall screws driven into countersunk pilot holes (photo 5). Cut the backer board to size and attach it to the back edges of the frame with drywall screws or finish nails. Cut trim moldings (such as door casing or picture frame molding) to fit the niche

Fasten the niche box up into the stud ends with finish nails.

box. For the most satisfying results, choose a molding style and approach that reflects the molding scheme already in the room. Fasten the trim to the niche box with finish nails and glue or panel adhesive (photo 6). Run a small bead of caulk/adhesive on the face of the niche box.

INSTALL THE NICHE BOX

The niche box is fastened through the interior walls of the box to the ends of the stud(s) you removed. It can also be fastened to blocks you install in the wall cavity on each side. Locate each stud and transfer its location to the interior of the box and mark it.

Test-fit the niche box to make sure it lays flat against drywall. When you have established that the fit is good, run a bead of caulk/adhesive on the backsides of the trim pieces.

Insert the niche box into the opening. Press firmly so the trim squeezes into the adhesive.

Predrill holes at stud locations and fasten with a pair of 6d finish nails driven through the frame boards and into the ends of the cut wall studs (photo 7).

Fill and sand fastener holes. Sand and caulk as necessary. Prime and paint or apply another finish of your choice.

Options for Making a Wall Niche ▸

One key to cutting in a wall niche is to understand that you must cut a larger hole in your wall than the finished dimensions of the wall niche. So first, you determine the niche's finished location and opening dimensions and mark them out on the wall. You then measure from those lines so that the niche box fits inside the wall. Although making the niche so it fits precisely within a stud bay has some built-in efficiencies, it is not necessary. As you'll see in this project, as long as you're building in a nonload-bearing wall you can locate your niche just about anywhere you choose. Three options for trimming out a wall niche are described here. The first is to frame a wood niche insert with picture-frame trim. The second is to use a drywall wrap created with blocking inside the wall cavity and finished with joint compound to blend with the surrounding wall. The third option simply involves installing a prefabricated product.

Purchase a prefabricated wall niche from an architectural millwork supplier and install it in a properly sized wall opening.

Build your niche completely out of wood, insert it into a hole cut in the wall and trim it with picture molding (as seen on previous pages).

Frame the niche opening and install a wood shelf at the bottom, then trim out the opening with drywall using common taping and finishing techniques.

FORMAL BOOKCASE

Few furnishings add prestige to a space like a formal floor-to-ceiling bookcase. Typically built from clear hardwood, the classically-designed bookcase delivers a refined, Old World feel. The bookcase shown here is made from red oak plywood and red oak 1× stock and moldings finished with a high gloss urethane. What's also nice about this piece is that it incorporates the wall behind it to balance all that clear hardwood with a splash of color and depth. This is a fixed-shelf design that enables you to build shelves anywhere you like to match your needs. And, because the shelf bays are built in a modular fashion, you can design it to any dimensions you wish.

The formal bookcase shown here is 8 feet long, 8 feet high, and installed on a 12-foot-long wall. Because it's centered in the space, the moldings and sides return to the wall, creating niches on the left and right that are great for decoration. However, this bookcase can be built wall-to-wall if desired. It's a flexible design. Finally, the exact same style shelf can be built to take paint. Instead of using red oak, though, poplar is a great choice for a painted finish.

Tools, Materials & Cutting List

Miter saw
Tablesaw
Circular saw
Router
Drill/driver
Level
Stud finder
Pull saw
Flat bar
Router
Step ladder or work platform
Air nailer
Combination square
Drywall or deck screws
Finish nails
Glue
Finishing materials
Eye and ear protection
Work gloves
Construction adhesive

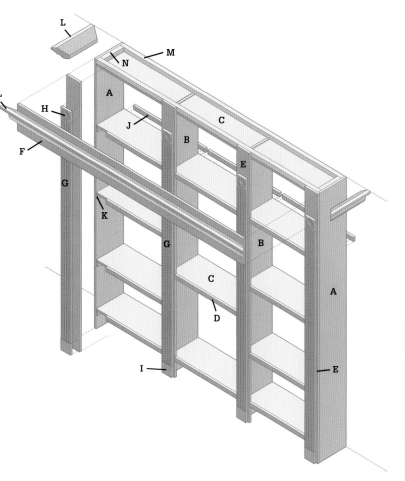

(3) 4 × 8' sheets
   ¾" red oak plywood
(16) 1 × 2" × 8' red oak
(4) 1 × 6" × 8' red oak

(1) 1 × 10" × 8' red oak
(4) ⅝ × 3⅜ × 84"
   oak molding

(4) Rosettes
(4) Plinth blocks
(11) lineal ft. red oak crown molding
(3) 2 × 2" × 8' pine

Key	No.	Desc.	Size	Material	Key	No.	Desc.	Size	Material
A	2	Upright (outer)	¾ × 11½ × 96"	Red oak plywood	**J**	11	Shelf cleat (wall)	¾ × 1½ × 31"	Red oak
B	2	Upright (inner)	¾ × 11½ × 94½"	Red oak plywood	**K**	22	Shelf cleat (side)	¾ × 1½ × 10¾"	Red oak
C	14	Shelf	¾ × 11½ × 31	Red oak plywood					
D	11	Shelf nosing	¾ × 1½ × 31"	Red oak 1 × 2	**L**	3	Crown molding	½ × 3⁵⁄₁₆" × cut to fit	Red oak
E	4	Upright backer	¾ × 5½ × 96"	Red oak 1 × 6	**M**	2	Ceiling cleat (long)	1½ × 1½ × 94½	2 × 2
F	1	Fascia	¾ × 9½ × 96"	Red oak 1 × 10					
G	4	Fluted molding	⅝ × 3⅜ × 78½	Red oak molding	**N**	2	Ceiling cleat (short)	1½ × 1½ × 8½"	2 × 2
H	4	Rosette	¾ × 4 × 4"	Red oak molding					
I	4	Plinth block	¾ × 4 × 4"	Red oak molding					

HOW TO BUILD A FORMAL BOOKCASE

Cut through the base molding at the edges of the project area and remove it so the bookcase can fit tightly up against the wall.

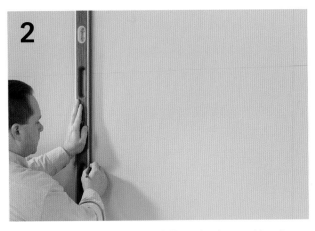

Carefully mark out the plumb lines for the outside edges of the uprights and continue the mark up onto the ceiling.

Use a spacer as a gauge for marking the position of the front edge of the 2 × 2 nailing frame that is attached to the ceiling.

LAY OUT THE PROJECT ON YOUR WALL

This bookcase is designed to be stick-built at your installation site. The best place to begin is by drawing layout lines on the wall. The most important lines mark the locations of the four uprights, which need to be vertical and parallel, and the shelf cleats, which must be horizontal and parallel. Start by locating the centerline for the bookcase installation and marking it on the baseboard and on the wall. Measure out 4 feet on each side of the centerline and make marks for the outside edges of the bookcase. These lines represent the outer faces of the left and right uprights. Using a pull saw, cut and remove the baseboard between the left and right marks. Make your cuts as square as possible (photo 1).

Measure and make a mark at 15½ and 16¼ inches on each side of the centerline, dividing the project area into three equal bays and establishing locations of the ¾-inch-thick uprights.

Measuring up from the floor, mark horizontal shelf cleat locations on the walls at the back of each bay. The cleats should stop at the upright locations so the ¾-inch-thick uprights can fit snugly in between the cleat ends. In the drawing, there is one bottom shelf, set 6½ inches off the floor in all three bays. The left and right bays have shelves 24, 48, and 72 inches up from the floor. The center bay has a single center shelf set at 36 inches off the top of the bottom shelf ledger and a top shelf at 72 inches (see diagram, page 223). Using a 4-foot level, mark horizontal reference lines for the shelf cleats in all three bays. Draw a small "X" below each line as a reminder of which side of the line to fasten the cleat. Then, use the 4-foot level to extend the outlines for the uprights all the way up from the floor to the ceiling (photo 2). These sets of parallel lines should be ¾ inch apart and plumb.

At the ceiling, lay out the location for the 2 × 2 frame that creates nailing surfaces for the outer uprights and the 1 × 6 upright backers that are centered on the front edges of the uprights. The 2 × 2 frame should span from the inside faces of the outer uprights and extend 11½ inches out from the wall (photo 3).

Make a Marking Gauge ▸

Make an 11½"-wide spacer to use as a marking gauge.

4

Attach the 2 × 2 nailing frame to the ceiling at the layout lines, making sure to catch a ceiling joist where possible and using appropriate anchors in spots where no joist is present.

5

Attach all of the shelf cleats to the wall, making sure to preserve an even ¾" gap between cleat ends to make room for the inner uprights.

If you're installing undercabinet lights such as puck lights, locate the center of each bay on the ceiling and mark them for lights. Get a qualified electrician to install the wiring, fixtures, and switches. If you're doing the work yourself, follow local building codes. Pull the wire through the drywall or plaster and pigtail (curl up) for fixture installation later.

INSTALL THE NAILING FRAME

For ease of installation, assemble the 2 × 2 nailing frame on the ground. Use 2½-inch pneumatic finish nails or drywall screws to join the 2 × 2 frame components. Test to make sure the assembly is square. Attach the frame to the ceiling by screwing up through the members at ceiling joist locations (use an electronic stud finder to identify these). Attach the frame to the wall's top plate at the wall/ceiling joint (photo 4). If the ceiling joists are parallel to the wall,

you may need to use toggle bolts or other wall anchors to secure the frame along the front edge.

ATTACH THE SHELF CLEATS TO THE WALL

While plenty of fasteners, including trim-head wood screws or 8d nails, may be dependably used to connect the 1 × 2 red oak shelf cleats to the walls at stud locations, a pneumatic or cordless finish nailer loaded with 2-inch nails is ideal for the task. It eliminates the need to predrill and countersink fasteners, as you would when driving screws or hand-nailing into hardwood. A pneumatic nailer also dispenses fasteners quickly and accurately, making it much easier when you're working alone. Cut and install the cleats at the layout lines. A few dabs of construction adhesive applied to the wall behind the cleats will add even more strength to the connection. Fasten the cleats so the upright returns can be installed around them (photo 5).

(continued)

INSTALL THE UPRIGHTS

Cut the outer uprights (11½ inches wide) to full room height in length. Rest the bottoms on the floor and nail the top ends to the ends of the 2 × 2 nailing frame (photo 6). Also drive 8d finish nails through the uprights and into the ends of the shelf cleats in the outer bays (drill pilot holes first).

Rout a roundover, bead, or chamfer onto each edge of the upright backer if desired (photo 7). Cut the inner uprights (11½ inches wide) to length. They should be 1½ inches shorter than the outer uprights because they butt up against the underside of the 2 × 2 nailing frame on the ceiling. Position the inner uprights between the ends of the shelf cleats that are attached to the wall in each bay. At the ceiling, use a framing square to make sure the inner uprights are perpendicular to the wall and then position a 1 × 6 upright backer over the upright edge. Center the backer on the upright edge and nail it to the 2 × 2 nailing frame. Double check that the upright is perpendicular to the wall by measuring the bays at the wall and at the front of the upright and making sure the measurements are the same. Then drill pilot holes and drive 8d finish nails (or pneumatic nails) through the backer and into the edge of the upright at 12-inch intervals (photo 8). Install both inner uprights.

INSTALL THE SHELVES

The shelves and shelf cleats help stabilize the structure, so install them next. Start by nailing a shelf to the 2 × 2 ceiling frame at the top of each bay (photo 9).

Nail the outer uprights to the ends of the nailing frame attached to the ceiling.

Routing a bead, round over, or chamfer adds nice detail and shadow lines to the upright backers.

Attach the upright backers to the front edges of the inner uprights with pneumatic or hand-driven finish nails.

Attach a shelf board at the top of each bay to conceal the framework attached to the ceiling.

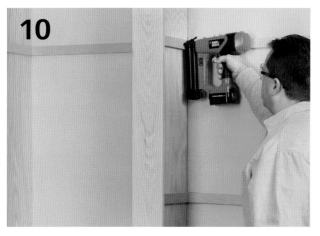

Attach the shelf cleats to the uprights with 1¼" fasteners.

Edge the red oak shelves with 1 × 2 red oak nosing that's bonded to the shelves with glue and finish nails.

Conceal the gap between the top of the bookcase and ceiling with crown molding or sprung cove molding. Installing crown molding can get complicated. Consult a trim carpentry book if you are unsure how to work with crown molding.

Attach the plinth blocks, rosettes and fluted case moldings to compete the trimwork installation.

Attach the short shelf cleats to the sides of the uprights so each shelf is supported on three sides (photo 10). Use a level to make sure the cleats are level and attach them with 1¼-inch finish nails and adhesive.

Cut the remaining shelves to length and set them on the cleats. Cut the 1 × 2 shelf nosing and attach it to the front edges of the exposed shelves, making sure the shelves are flush with the top edge of the nosing (photo 11). Use 4d finish nails driven through pilot holes or pneumatic finish nails to attach the nosing.

ATTACH THE TRIM

Cut the 1 × 10 red oak fascia board the full width of the bookcase and nail it to the top so the ends are flush with the outer faces of the outer uprights. Make sure the fascia board is level before attaching it with nails driven into the tops of the upright backers. Once the fascia board is in place, cut, fit and attach the crown molding and molding return at the top (photo 12).

Install the plinth blocks at the bottom of each upright backer, resting on the floor and centered side to side. Then, attach the rosettes at the top of each upright backer, centered side to side. Measure from the bottom of the rosette to the top of the plinth block and cut fluted case molding to fit. Install with adhesive and nails (photo 13). Fill nail holes, sand, and apply finish. If the installation room has base shoe moldings, you may want to add them to your bookcase for a consistent look.

BOX BEAM SHELVES

If you're looking for a basic starter project that you can finish with your own flourishes and flair, you've come to the right place. This shelf is made from a basic design platform that looks great as is, but it can be easily altered with trim and finish options. In addition to its versatility, this shelf has the benefit that its connection to the wall surface is invisible. The reason is that the "box" has no back and you can slip it over a ledger board fastened to the wall. Fastening through the top of the box holds the assembly securely in place without brackets or even any visible fasteners, creating a tight, integrated look.

As a design element in any living space you can make several Box Beam Shelves and hang them at different heights in a room to create an accent wall. Or, hang several of them at the same level and create a picture rail, of sorts. They're perfect for displaying cherished items and an ideal spot for long, flowing potted plants. Another possibility is to dado in a plate groove for displaying plates and china.

If you want to change the size, shape, and reveals on the basic box you can add different moldings and trim to make it your own. The good news is that the assembly techniques for building the box remain the same. All you need to do is adjust the measurements.

The shelf laid out here is fabricated from MDF and shown painted, but you could make it out of hardwood stock and matching hardwood plywood if you prefer. The basic shelf-box is composed of five pieces: three sides, a bottom, and a top. The shelf is 25½ inches wide, 10¾ inches deep, and 3¼ inches tall. The top shelf panel is a single piece of ¾-inch MDF that is 26½ inches wide and 11¾ inches deep. The ledger is a 2× ripped 1½-inch square.

Tools, Materials & Cutting List

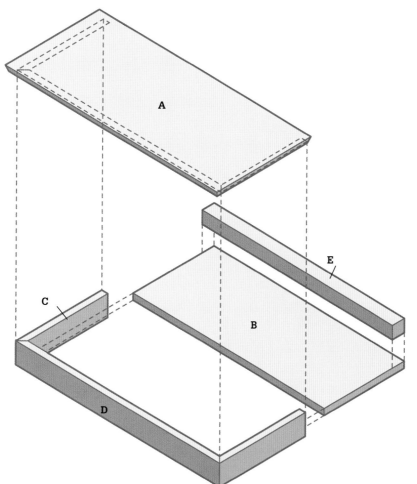

Tools

Tablesaw
Miter saw
Circular saw
Router
Ladder
Level
Cordless drill/driver
Sander or power planer

Materials

¾" MDF
Fasteners
(1) 2 × 4 scrap (at least 24")
(1) tube adhesive caulk
(1) scrap of ¼" plywood

Cutting List

Part	NO.	Desc.	Size	Material
A	1	Top panel	¾ × 11¾ × 26½"	MDF
B	1	Bottom panel	¾ × 10 × 24"	MDF
C	2	Side wraps	¾ × 2½ × 10¾"	MDF
D	1	Front wrap	¾ × 2½ × 25½"	MDF
E	1	Cleat	1½ × 1½ × 23¾"	2 × 4 (or 2 × 2)

HOW TO BUILD BOX BEAM SHELVES

Most power miter saws do not have a 10" cutting capacity. To cut the wide stock for this project, you can either make a portion of the cut on the miter saw then turn the board around so you can finish the cut, or use a circular saw and square-guide.

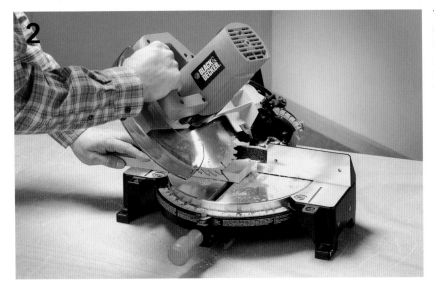

The key to a durable, good-looking assembly is to cut the sides and the front strips that wrap the bottom panel bottom panel accurately. Careful measurement and cutting keeps the miter joints tight and together during assembly.

CUT THE PARTS

The first step is to cut all the pieces on the miter and table saw. If you need to, rough-cut the MDF sheet to size using a circular saw, but make the final cuts with the miter saw and tablesaw. Start by fabricating the shelf's bottom panel. Then, make the pieces for a three-sided (or C-Shaped) shelf box. The pieces will be assembled around the bottom panel. Cut the top-shelf panel. Finally, rip the ledger from a piece of 2× stock. This assembly works best if cutting tolerances are kept tight, so be extra careful with measuring, marking, and cutting.

Cut the bottom panel to size using a sliding power miter saw (or a circular saw and straightedge guide if your miter saw doesn't have a 10-inch cut capacity–photo 1), or a tablesaw. Because the sides and front wrap around the bottom panel, it is the control point for the rest of the layout. Cutting it accurately is important. Be careful to be as exact as you can while cutting. Cut stock for the shelf sides (called the panel wraps) to 2½-inch width and sand, joint, or plane out any saw marks left behind. Also cut the top panel to size.

Rip the ledger to width (1½ inches) and cross-cut it to length. Cut the panel wraps to length using the miter saw (photo 2).

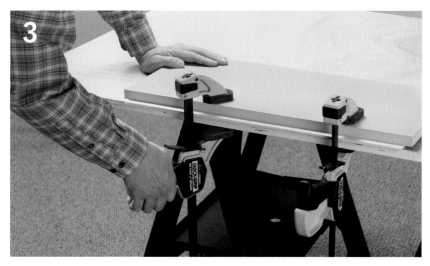

Clamp the bottom panel to the bench to keep it stationary while you fasten the panel wraps around it, enabling you to focus your attention on getting the assembly tight.

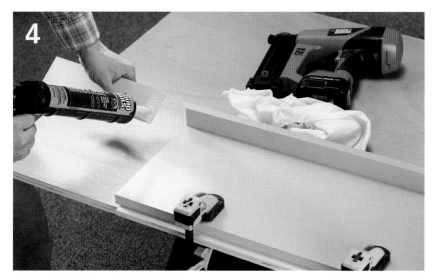

Prior to installing the front panel wrap to the left panel wrap, dab each miter with adhesive caulk.

ASSEMBLE THE PARTS

Assembling the parts square and tight all starts with the bottom panel—it's the guide for getting the miters nice and tight. For fastening, a cordless drill and trim drive screws (pre-drill and countersink all holes) is great. A brad nailer or finish nailer will also work nicely. Should you use a pneumatic tool like this, make sure to drive fasteners straight into the stock. Nails driven at an angle can blow out of the material and are tough to remove.

A good trick for adding shadow lines is to inset the bottom into the panel wraps about ¼ inch. Do this by first screwing a scrap of ¼-inch plywood (cut just a little smaller than the bottom panel's dimensions)

on the bench then clamping the bottom panel over it, propping it up (photo 3). Follow up by wrapping the bottom panel with the panel wraps.

Fasten the left panel wrap to the bottom panel. Use the front panel wrap to guide your exact placement of the left panel wrap. In other words, match up the miters on the front and left panel wraps, then fasten the left panel wrap. Apply adhesive caulk to the left panel wrap miter and the left side miter on the front panel wrap (photo 4), then install the front panel wrap. Make sure to have a damp cloth or sponge to wipe away any squeeze-out. Repeat this process for the right panel wrap and install. Only fasten the bottom edge.

(continued)

Use a router and profiling bit to shape a decorative edge along the front of the top panel (photo 5). Attach the top piece to the box frame. Before fastening, use a combination square and double-check that all reveals are the same (photo 6).

CAULK & FINISH

It's easier to caulk and paint this project in the shop than it is on the wall. Caulk, prime, and paint as desired. A small paint roller sleeve will give a smooth, professional finish (photo 7).

HANG THE SHELF

Installing the Box Beam Shelf on the wall ledger provides an invisible connection. The open back of the shelf slips over a ledger board you fasten to the wall studs. You then drive screws through the shelf panel down into the ledger for a very snug, very secure connection. It may be tempting on some walls to simply use hollow-wall anchors instead of locating and fastening to two studs, but because all the weight of the Box Beam Shelf is out at the front edge, that is not a recommended connection. Besides, at 24 inches long, the ledger for the Box Beam Shelf should cover

Cut a decorative profile along the front edge of the top panel, such as the ogee profile being routed into the top panel here.

Before fastening the top panel on top of the box frame, make sure that the reveals are equal all the way around and that the back is flush to the back edge of the box assembly.

Finishing this Box Beam Shelf in the shop is much easier than finishing it in location. Prop it up on its back edge during finishing so you can access the top, sides, and bottom with a paint brush. Be careful not to knock it over.

Make a solid connection with the studs by driving two screws per stud through the ledger. If the stud is near the end of the ledger, pre-drill and countersink before fastening.

at least two wall studs almost anywhere you put it (especially if your walls have 16 o.c. framing).

Determine the shelf's final location and mark it on the wall. Try to locate it so that the ledger falls over two wall framing members. Strike a level line. Screw the ledger to the wall studs with 3½-inch deck screws (photo 8). Use two screws per stud.

Predrill countersunk pilot holes for at least three deck screws ¾-inch in from the back edge of the top panel. Slip the Box Beam Shelf over the ledger so the back edges are flush against the wall surface. Fasten the shelf to the wall by driving 2-inch deck screws through the pilot holes and into the top of the ledger (photo 9).

Hold the shelf tight to the wall and fasten using at least three 2" deck screws driven through pilot holes and into the tops of the ledger.

"Other Ideas" ▸

One great feature about this shelf design is the numerous ways you can add your own details to it. You can use your table saw to cut in a plate groove in the top shelf panel or apply a molding detail with casing, chair rail or crown under the top shelf panel to provide lift, create texture and add shadow lines. You can add a second top shelf panel a littler larger than the first to create a layered effect. And you can wrap the back with a picture-frame molding. The sky is the limit.

You need to alter the sizes of the shelf box and the top shelf to fit these additions so lay them out carefully before you begin cutting wood. But, because the ledger board connection is strong but small, there is room to move. Here are some ideas to get you started:

PLATE GROOVE

Adding a plate groove is easy and a smart addition if you plan to display plates or other items like framed photos that you intend to lean on the wall. You can cut the grooves in a single pass on your table saw using a dado head cutter, or you can take multiple passes with a standard saw blade to create the groove. Make the groove ¼" to ⅜" wide and ¼" deep. You can even use a router and edge guide to plow a dado into the top of the shelf panel. Tip: When cutting the groove, do not cut all the way up to the ends of the board. That way, the groove will be invisible when viewed from below or straight on. If you cut past the shelf ends you'll be able to see the groove.

MOLDING DETAIL

Adding a basic chair rail molding is the easiest add-on option for the Box Beam Shelf. Depending on the chair rail you choose, you may not even have to alter the measurements on the shelf box, and you can apply the chair rail right to the box. However, if you select a molding that is more than ¾" thick, trim the box size by ¾" so you can keep the top shelf panel's 1" overhang. If you add a molding that's 1" thick or thicker, make the sides of the box 1" shorter and 1" thinner to compensate.

LAYERS

Using two—instead of one—top shelf panels is another simple but interesting way to add detail. Make the second top shelf panel ½" deeper and 1" longer than the original shelf panel shown above. Then, instead of routing a bead on the top of the panel, rout a chamfer on the bottom of each shelf panel to make them look like they are stepped and ascending. Routing a cove is also a nice detail.

PICTURE FRAME

Whichever shelf you build, you can add a picture frame molding to the back of the unit to make the unit look like it is an extension of the wall space. The idea is to use 1 × 4 or MDF ripped to width and wrap the back of the Box Beam Shelf with it. Install the shelf box without the top shelf panel and fasten into the ledger board from the sides. Install the picture frame molding before installing the top shelf panel or any other molding combinations. Also be aware that the picture frame molding adds ¾" to the overall depth of the shelf so you may want to trim a corresponding ¾" off your top shelf panels.

MEDIA BAR

Your snacks and beverages will always be close at hand during the big game when your flat-panel TV is mounted in this media cabinet. It combines the functionality of an entertainment center and the convenience of a mini kitchen. The base and upper cabinets provide storage for your home theater components, movies, games, and snacks. There's also a space between the base cabinets for a small refrigerator or beverage cooler. The counter serves as a perfect serving station or a place to keep a couple additional small appliances, such as a microwave or blender. And, the integrated matching wood wall conceals a structural frame that is easy to mount your TV to and provides a path for cables from the TV to your electronic components in the base cabinet.

This unit may look like a custom-built piece of furniture, but it's actually made from a combination of stock kitchen cabinets and matching cover panels. Building it only requires a few portable power tools and basic building skills.

Tools & Materials ▸

Tablesaw or
   circular saw
   and straightedge
Jigsaw
Drill/driver
Level
2"-dia. hole saw bit
Drill bits (⅛, ¼")
Caulk gun
(5) 2 × 4 × 8'
(2) 1 × 4 × 8'
Screws (1¼, 1⅝,
   2, 2½")
(1) ½" × 4 × 8 finish-
   grade plywood
Panel adhesive
Tape measure

Masking tape
(3) 24" base cabinets
(2) 24" wall cabinets
(1) 25½" × 8'
   countertop
Eye and ear
   protection
Work gloves

Cutting List

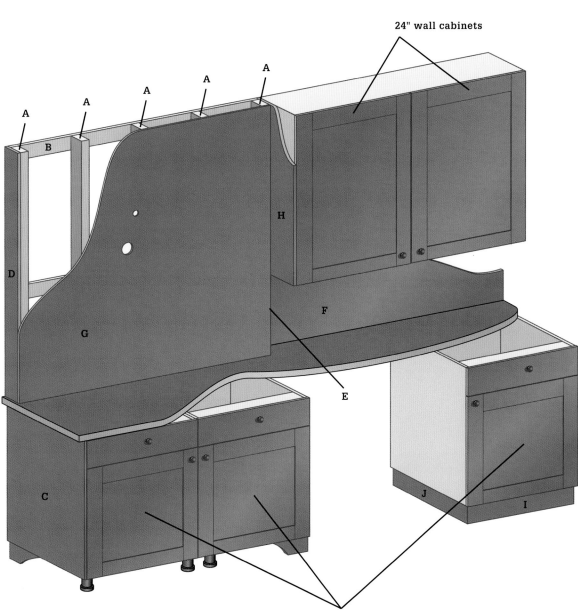

24" wall cabinets

24" base cabinets

Key	NO.	Description	Dimension
A	5	Wall frame studs	1½ × 3½ × 60"
B	3	Wall frame cleats	¾ × 3½ × 47"
C	1	Base cabinet cover panel	½ × 24 × 30"
D	1	Left frame side cover panel	½ × 4¼ × 60"
E	1	Right frame side cover panel	½ × 4¼ × 20"

Key	NO.	Description	Dimension
F	1	Back splash panels	½ × 20 × 48"
G	1	Wall frame front cover panels	½ × 48 × 60"
H	1	Wall cabinet side cover panel	½ × 8⅝ × 40"
I	1	Front toe-kick	½ × 4½* × 24"
J	1 or 2	Side toe-kick	½ × 4½* × 24"

HOW TO BUILD A MEDIA BAR

ROUTE THE WIRING

Install any necessary electrical outlets and home theater cables, such as speaker wire, before you install the cabinets. Install one outlet in the center of the base cabinet refrigerator space and another outlet behind one of the cabinets that will be below the television. You may also want to install one outlet below the wall cabinets (approximately 42 inches above the floor) that will serve appliances that may be used on the countertop. Install the outlet box above the countertop so that it extends ½ inch beyond the drywall and will be flush with the backsplash panel. If you are not familiar with the skills necessary to install the electrical devices, then hire a licensed electrical contractor to handle this work.

INSTALL THE CABINETS & COUNTERTOP

Locate and mark the wall stud locations. Follow the manufacturer instructions to assemble the wall and base cabinet frames if they are not preassembled. If the doors and drawers are not attached to the cabinets, then wait to install them after the cover panels are attached. Install the two wall cabinets. The method you use to attach the cabinets on the wall depends on the type of cabinet construction. In this case a metal bracket is attached to the wall and then the cabinet is fastened to the metal bracket (photo 1).

Cord and cable access holes must be cut in the back and top of the base cabinet that will be installed directly in front of the electrical outlet below the TV. Line up the base cabinets a few feet away from the wall, positioning them in the order that they will be installed. Measure the distance of the wall outlet from the end of the cabinets and from the floor and transfer those measurements to the back of the cabinet to mark the outlet location. Use a jigsaw to cut a 3-inch-wide × 5-inch-tall hole through the cabinet back panel exactly where the outlet will be located. Then cut a 2-inch-wide × 8-inch-long hole through the top spreader at the back of the cabinet (photo 2). Your cables could fit through a smaller hole in the top of the cabinet, but making a larger hole will make routing the cables much easier.

Slide the base cabinets against the wall. Adjust the legs or shim below the cabinets to level the tops of the cabinets. Attach the two adjacent cabinet sides together with the manufacturer-provided connector fasteners or with 1¼-inch screws. Then secure the cabinets to the wall studs with 2½-inch drywall screws.

Cut a notch in the back edge of the countertop that will align with the access hole you cut in the top cabinet spreader. Cut the notch in laminate or wood countertops with a jigsaw (photo 3). Natural stone countertop materials require a diamond abrasive blade and should be cut by a stone countertop fabricator. Attach the countertop to the cabinets (photo 4).

INSTALL THE WALL FRAME & COVER PANELS

Build the wall frame. Cut the 2 × 4 wall frame posts and 1 × 4 cleats to length and assemble them with 2-inch wood screws. Then place the wall frame on the countertop and against the wall cabinet. Secure the wall frame to the room wall (photo 5).

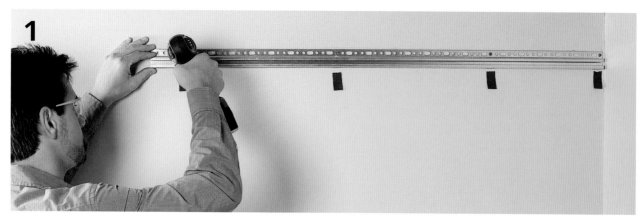

Attach the wall cabinet bracket to the wall as specified in the cabinet installation instructions. Then, fasten the cabinets to the bracket. Attach the cabinets to each other with fasteners provided by the cabinet manufacturer or by driving short screws through the cabinet sides.

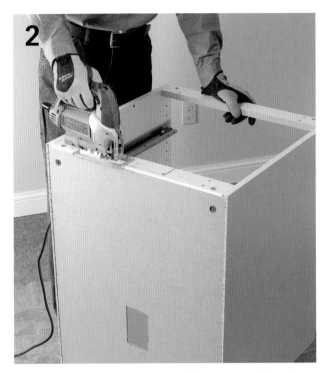

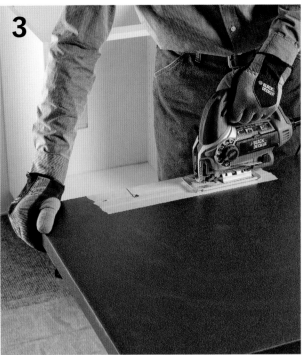

Cut access holes in the base cabinet. Trace outlines for the access holes in the back panel and top spreader on the cabinet that will be installed in front of the wall outlet. Drill ⅜"-dia. saw blade starter holes at each corner of the outline. Use a jigsaw to cut the sides of the hole.

Cut the countertop access hole. Attach masking tape to the countertop to help prevent chipping the surface when it is cut. Mark the access notch outline on the countertop. Cut the notch with a jigsaw.

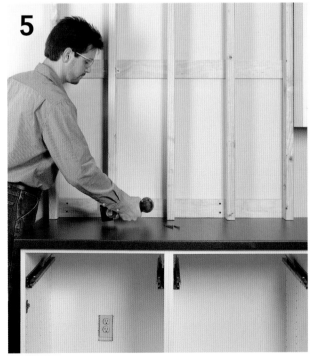

Attach the countertop to the cabinets. Drive 1⅝" screws through the cabinet top and into the countertop. Be careful not to overdrive the screws and break through the top surface of the countertop.

Attach the wall frame to the room wall. Drive 2½" drywall screws through the wall frame cleats and into the room wall studs. Drive three screws into each stud.

(continued)

6

Attach the wall frame side cover panels to the wall frame with panel adhesive and 1⅝" screws. Clamp the panels in position while you drive the screws through the inside face of the wall frame posts. Drill a ⅛"-dia. pilot hole and countersink for each screw ⅛ to ¼" into the 2 × 4 so the screw goes into the plywood about ⅜".

7

Measure the distance from the face of the front panel to the front edge of the wall cabinet. Add the thickness of the door to determine the width of the wall cabinet side cover panel.

Check to make sure all speaker cables or other component cables that are coming from other areas of the room are routed to the area behind the wall frame before concealing that wall with the cover panels. In this case, no additional speakers were installed so no additional speaker cables were routed to the media center. The cables that run between the TV, sound bar speaker, and components in the cabinet are routed after the cabinet construction is complete.

Avoid driving fasteners through the face of the cover panels so that you don't have to fill in or conceal any fastener marks. Each panel is attached with screws and/or panel adhesive. Drive the screws through the inside face of the cabinet or wall frame. Panel adhesive is a type of construction adhesive that has a high initial adhesion and is typically sold in a caulk tube (follow manufacturer application instructions).

Measure the width of the space below the wall cabinets and divide that measurement by two to determine the width of each backsplash panel. Cut the backsplash panels to size. Cut on the back, or apply a strip of masking tape over the cutline and use a plywood cutting blade with a high tooth count (80 tpi tablesaw blade and 60 tpi circular saw blade) to prevent the finished surface from chipping. If there is an outlet installed in the backsplash area, then cut openings in the panel to fit around the wall outlet. Attach the backsplash panels with panel adhesive.

Cut the two frame-side cover panels to size. Cut the cover panels with a tablesaw or circular saw and straightedge guide. Apply panel adhesive to the back face of each panel, clamp them to the wall frame and secure them with screws driven through the frame studs and into the side panel covers (photo 6).

Cut the wall frame front panels to size. The cover panel stock features one finished edge. Install the wall frame front panels with the finished edges on the outside and butt together the unfinished edges at the middle seam. If you are using a cover panel stock that does not feature a finished edge, then you must cover the unfinished edge with heat-activated veneer edge tape or solid wood edging. Attach the panels to the frame with panel adhesive. No screws are used to secure the front panels.

Determine the required width of the wall cabinet side panel (photo 7). Cut the wall cabinet side cover panel to size. Clamp it to the wall cabinet side and attach it by driving 1-inch screws through the inside of the cabinet side. Then attach the base cabinet side panel (photo 8). Finally, attach the toe-kick panels, doors, and drawers.

INSTALL THE COMPONENTS

Follow the manufacturer instructions to install the TV mounting bracket. Drive the mounting bracket anchor screws into the wall frame posts. Next, drill a 2-inch-diameter access hole through the front panel (photo 9). If you are installing a speaker above the TV, then drill a ¾-inch-diameter hole behind the speaker location to route the speaker cable.

Fish the component cables and speaker cable through the access holes and behind the front panels. Follow the manufacturer instructions to secure the TV to the mounting bracket and mount the speaker.

8

9

Attach the wall and base cabinet side panels. Clamp the panel to the cabinet side and drive 1" screws through the inside face of the cabinet side. Then install the toe-kicks.

Use a 2" hole saw to bore an access hole through the wall frame front panel. This hole should be located directly above the notch in the countertop and close to the TV mounting bracket so that the TV will conceal it.

CLUB BAR

Owning your own in-house bar makes a statement about you. For some, it might say "I have arrived and this is my space!" While for others a bar might say "Welcome, friends, our home is your home." And for others, well, let's just say the possibilities are fairly wide-ranging. But whatever story your bar tells—be it one of quiet aperitifs before dining, casual afternoons watching the big game, or raucous evenings of wild revelry—building your bar yourself personalizes the tale and adds a feature to your home that will have a direct impact on how well you enjoy your home life.

The bar shown here is sleekly styled and smartly laid out for the efficient barkeeper. A small refrigerator gives you access to cold drinks and ice while convenient cabinets create excellent storage spots for party favors.

While this is a "dry bar" (no plumbing), the design could be modified in any number of ways to add running water if you wish. All you need to get the party started is a GFCI electrical outlet and the proper floor space.

This compact corner bar design features glossy black MDF aprons with decorative cherry appliqués forming a horizontal grid pattern on the aprons. A cherry plywood bartop sits atop a 2 × 6 L-shaped kneewall, harboring some practical amenities on the bartender side. A flip-up lift gate in the bartop on one end provides pass-through access and can even function as a wait station if you want to get really fancy in your hosting.

The key components—base cabinets, a laminate countertop, the fridge, and the wood for a sleek Asian-inspired style trim-out—set the stage for your next gathering. Let's party.

Club Bar

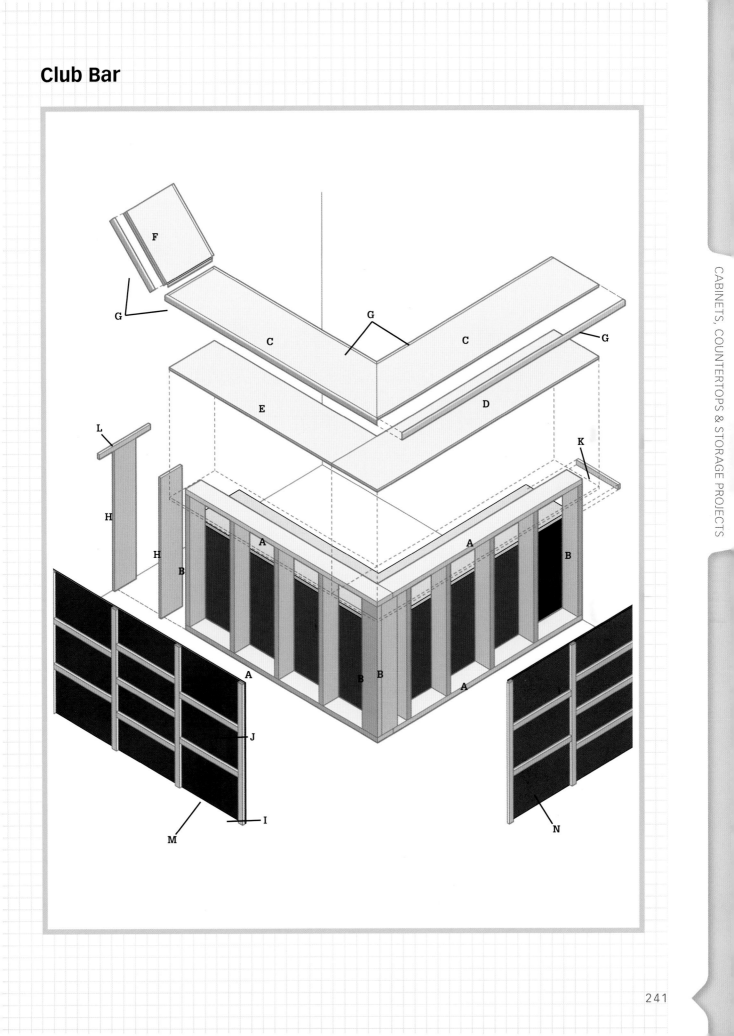

Tools, Materials & Cutting List

Eye and ear protection
Work gloves
Miter saw
Tablesaw
Circular saw
Drill/driver
Level
Stud finder
Router
Pull saw
Flat bar
Pneumatic nailer/compressor
Combination square
(10) 2 × 6" × 8' SPF

(1) ¾ × 4 × 8 particleboard
(1) ¾ × 4 × 8 cherry plywood
   for bartop
(2) 6' strips ½ × 16"
   cementboard
20 sq. ft. 4 × 4 wall tile
Thinset and grout
¾" thick cherry—2 @ 8 × 42"
   (actual)
¾ × 1½" cherry
   approx 80 lineal ft.
(2) ½" × 4 × 8' MDF
24" base cabinet
36" base cabinet—corner

(12" wide doors)
Refrigerator (19w 22d 32¾" h)
Postform countertop
   (mitered, 6' each leg)
16d common nails
Panel adhesive
Deck screws
1½" drywall screws
Finish nails (4d, 6d)
Finishing materials
Glue
Piano hinge
Primer and paint

Key	No.	Desc.	Size	Material
A	4	Sill/header	1½ × 5½ × 68"	2 × 6
B	11	Stud	1½ × 5½ × 38"	2 × 6
C	2	Bartop	¾ × 16½ × 80"	Cherry plywood
D	1	Bar substrate	¾ × 16½ × 80"	Particleboard
E	1	Bar substrate	¾ × 16½ × 65¼"	Particleboard
F	2	Lift gate	¾ × 16½ × 22¼"	Cherry plywood
G	-	Bartop trim	¾ × 1½" × cut to fit	Cherry
H	2	End cap	¾ × 7¾ × 41"	Cherry
I	7	Trim stiles	¾ × 1½ × 41"	Cherry
J	16	Trim rails	¾ × 1½ × cut to fit	Cherry
K	1	Countertop cleat	1½ × 1½ × 22"	2 × 2
L	1	Lift gate stop block	¾ × 1½ × 18"	Cherry
M	1	Apron	½ × 40½ × 68¾"	MDF
N	1	Apron	½ × 40½ × 73½"	MDF

HOW TO BUILD A CLUB BAR

1

Anchor the sill plates for the kneewalls to the floor so they form a right angle at the corner where they meet.

2

Use panel adhesive and deck screws to attach the end kneewall stud to the back wall, attaching at a stud location. If there's no stud, open the wall and insert a horizontal nailer between the nearest studs.

BUILD THE KNEEWALLS

The bar top is supported by a pair of heavy-duty 2 × 6 kneewalls that are anchored to the wall and floor and meet in an L. This configuration presumes that you'll be installing the bar in the corner of the room. If that configuration doesn't work for your space, you can use similar building strategies, but redesign the project as a straight-line or a U-shape bar.

Cut the 2 × 6 sill plates to length (68 inches). Measure out from the corner the distance of the sill plates plus the pass-through opening width plus ¾ inch for the thickness of the end panel (92¾ inches here). Mark a reference line and lay a sill plate at this distance, perpendicular to the back project wall. Arrange the second sill plate so the end overlaps the open end of the first sill plate and the two form a perfect 90-degree angle. Join the corners with screws or a metal connector to keep them from moving during installation, and then anchor the sill plates to the floor. Use 16d common nails or screws (shown in photo 1) and panel adhesive for a wood floor; use a powder-actuated nailer on a concrete floor.

Once the sills are in place, attach the end stud against the back wall. If you are lucky (or planned well) the stud will fall over a wall stud. If the new kneewall falls over a stud bay in the room wall, you'll need to remove some wallcovering and install a nailing cleat between the closest wall studs so you have a very sturdy surface to anchor the end of the wall (photo 2).

Next, make the stud wall corner. Use 16d common nails to toenail the studs to the sill plates (photo 3). Install a stud at the free end of the return, then fill in with evenly spaced intermediate studs spaced no more than 16 inches apart. Cut cap plates the same size as the sill plates and install them with three 16d common nails driven through the tops of the caps and into the end of each wall stud (photo 4). Check each stud with a level before nailing.

MAKE THE APRONS AND TRIM

The decorative front aprons for this bar are made from ½-inch-thick MDF (medium-density fiberboard) panels that have a glossy black finish and are trimmed with strips of cherry arranged in a staggered ladder pattern. If you're feeling ambitious, apply a genuine black lacquer finish. Or, you can come close to the black lacquer look with a quality satin or gloss jet black enamel paint. Either way, for the smoothest possible finish, cut and prepare the panels and spray on the black lacquer finish with an HVLP sprayer. Rip two sheets of ½-inch MDF to 40½ inches wide and then trim them to length to make the bar front panels. Sand the edges to remove any saw marks. Then, apply primer to all faces and edges. When the primer dries, spray black lacquer or paint onto the front face and edges (photo 5). If you do not have access to a good sprayer, use a paint roller with a short-nap sleeve.

(continued)

3

Toenail the corner studs to the sill plates. Use a level to make sure the studs are vertical.

4

Complete the framing for the L-shaped kneewall section. For extra strength, drive a few 3" deck screws through the studs where they meet at the corner.

5

For the smoothest possible finish, spray the front apron panels with an HVLP sprayer. Apply the paint or lacquer over primer, in thin coats.

6

Prepare at least 80' lineal of ¾ × 1½" hardwood stock to trim out the aprons and edges of the bartop.

After installation, the black aprons will be decorated with a grid made from strips of cherry. You can use dimensional 1 × 2 cherry for this, but you'll save a lot of money and get better edges if you purchase random width cherry, then plane and joint it to thickness and rip it to width (photo 6). For the project shown here, you'll need at least 40 lineal feet of stock for the apron trim, plus another 40 feet for the bar countertop edging.

Sand the edges of the cherry trim to remove saw marks and smooth the surfaces. Apply a clear protective wood finish, such as wipe-on polyurethane varnish, to half the stock for use as apron trim (photo 7). The

other half of the stock will be used for edging the countertop. You'll need to cut an edge profile in this stock and attach it to the countertop before finishing it.

INSTALL THE KNEEWALL COVERINGS
The front faces of the L-shaped kneewall are covered with the aprons and apron trim. The back sides (the bartender view) can be covered with just about anything you wish. We used a cement board backer and some wall tile for a nice looking wall covering that's durable and easy to clean. It's easier to install these wallcoverings before the bartop has been installed.

You don't need to create full toe-kick recesses at the bottoms of the apron panels, although you certainly can if you wish. But it is a good idea to install the MDF aprons so they are not in contact with the floor, especially if your installation is going into a basement or any other area that may be subject to moisture problems. The easiest way to do this is simply to cut a piece of ¼-inch-thick sheet stock scrap and slip it up against the sill plate. Then, test the fit of the apron panels. Trim if needed, then apply beads of panel adhesive to the front edges of the wall frame members (photo 8) and attach the aprons with a pneumatic nailer and 2½-inch finish nails (photo 9). You can hand-nail them at wall stud locations with 6d finish nails if you prefer. Cover nail heads with wood putty.

Depending on what type of cabinets you're installing, it likely is not necessary to finish the inside faces of the kneewalls lower than the countertop height. For installing wall tile, we cut 16-inch-wide strips of ½-inch-thick cement board and attached them to the wall studs flush with the top of the cap plate (photo 10). Make sure that seams fall over studs.

Install the wall tile (photo 11). We used inexpensive 4 × 4-inch ceramic wall tile set into a layer of thinset adhesive that's troweled onto the cement board. Whichever wall covering you use, it should extend down past the top of the countertop (in this case, the top of the preformed backsplash), and the edges should be covered by the end panel you'll be installing at the free end of the kneewall.

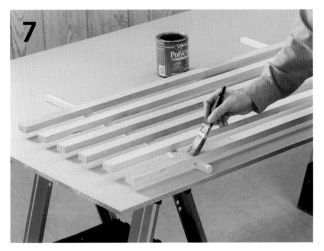

For efficiency, apply a protective finish to the cherry apron trim stock. Dab some finish on the cut ends after you cut each trim piece to length.

Apply panel adhesive to the kneewall studs to strengthen the bond with the black aprons. Slip a ¼-thick spacer beneath each apron to create a gap between the panel and the floor.

Nail the apron panels to the wall studs at 8 to 12" intervals.

Attach cement board strips to the edges of the kneewall framing members as a backer for the backsplash area.

(continued)

Install the inside wallcovering before you cap the wall.

Bond the particleboard subbase directly to the top plates of the kneewalls, taking care to achieve even overhangs of 6" in front and 4" on the bartender side of the walls.

Drive plenty of 2" deck screws to secure the subbase to the walls. The screw heads must be sunk beneath the wood surface.

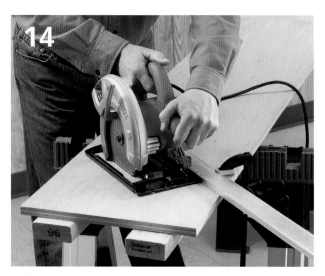

Make 45-degree miter cuts in the bartop top layer using a circular saw and cutting guide.

INSTALL THE BARTOP

The bartop installed here is made of a particleboard subbase that's thoroughly bonded and screwed to the top plates of the kneewall. A cherry plywood top layer then is attached to the narrow particleboard subbase. The subbase is laid out with a butt joint at the corner for ease and for strength, but for a more refined appearance the plywood top is mitered at the corner. When ¾-inch-thick cherry edging is added on all sides, the bartop grows to a finished width of 18 inches (a normal countertop, such as the bartender's countertop on the cabinets below, is 25 inches wide).

Rip the particleboard to 16½ inches wide and then crosscut it to length (one piece is longer so they can be butted together). Attach the strips to the top plates of the kneewalls using panel adhesive and countersunk deck screws (photo 12). Make sure to align the subbase strips carefully. They should overhang the kneewalls by roughly 6 inches in front and 4 inches in back.

Once you have both subbase parts arranged perfectly, drive 2-inch deck screws through the subbase and into the bar wall (photo 13). Be very generous here. If you can't get the screw heads

15

Laminate the top layer of cherry plywood to the subbase with panel adhesives and 1¼" screws driven up through the subbase.

16

Cut a roundover profile in one edge of the cherry edging stock and then cut the parts to length and attach them to the edges of the bartop with nails and glue.

17

Square-cut a piece of 1 × 2 edging to fit exactly between the ends of the roundover edging, and nail and glue it into place.

18

Nail the cherry end panel to the wall end to conceal the stud wall and the edges of the wallcoverings and trim.

to seat beneath the surface of the subbase, drill counter-sunk pilot holes.

Cut the cherry plywood sheet into 16½ inches wide strips, then cut mating miter joints at the ends (photo 14). Take care here: most hardwood plywood has one side that is much nicer, so be sure the cuts are made so the correct faces will be facing up when the bartop is installed. A circular saw with a sharp panel-cutting blade and a straightedge guide may be used to make these cuts.

Attach the top layer of cherry plywood to the subbase with panel adhesive and 1¼-inch wallboard

screws driven up through the subbase and into the underside of the plywood layer (photo 15). Make sure the mitered corner fits together correctly before applying any adhesive or cutting the plywood strips to length *Tip: Wait until the plywood layer is attached to the subbase to cut the strip on the free end to length. That way, you can cut it and the subbase at the same time and ensure that they are exactly flush.*

Check to make sure the edges of the glued-up bartop are smooth and flat, and sand with a belt sander if they are out of alignment or there is a lot of glue squeeze-out (use fine-grit sandpaper to help

(continued)

prevent any splintering of the veneer layer). Mount a ½-inch roundover bit in a router or router table and cut roundover profiles along one edge of the 1 × 2 stock you dressed to use for bartop edging. Attach the edging strips to the countertop with glue and 4d finish nails driven into pilot holes (photo 16). Make sure the tops of the edging boards are flush with or slightly higher than the plywood surface. If necessary, sand the edging until it is flush after you remove the clamps. At the open countertop end, extend the edging ¾ inch past the end of the glued-up layers.

Cut a piece of 1 × 2 edging to fit between the ends of the edging on the open end of the countertop and attach it with glue and finish nails (photo 17). Sand all wood surfaces. Apply multiple coats of very durable, glossy polyurethane varnish to achieve a protective built-up finish. Also paint the underside of the bartop black where it is visible. Build the lift gate section of the countertop as well and finish it the same way, except make it from two layers of cherry plywood and apply a clear finish to both faces.

INSTALL TRIM & HARDWARE
Rip-cut a strip of cherry that's slightly wider than the distance from the tiled wall surface to ¾ inch past the apron fronts (about 8 inches) and then cut it to fit between the floor and the underside of the bartop, which should overhang the end wall stud by ¾ inch or slightly more (photo 18). Cut another identical strip. Attach one strip to the end of the kneewall and attach the other to the wall on the opposite side of the pass-through so the two strips are perfectly aligned.

Cut a strip of 1 × 2 cherry to 18 inches long and attach it to the wall, centered over the 8-inch-wide end panel (photo 19). This strip will function as the stop for the lift gate section of countertop. For consistency, roundover the top edges of the 1 × 2 so it looks like a section of countertop.

Attach a piano hinge to the square-cut mating edge of the lift gate countertop section (photo 20). The barrel of the piano hinge should be oriented upward relative to the bartop surface. Attach the other leaf of the piano hinge to the edge of the main countertop and test to see if it opens and closes easily and is level when open (photo 21).

Cut the cherry trim pieces to size to make the ladder grids that decorate the aprons. Install the strips, following the patterns shown in photo 22. Make sure the ends of the strips are tucked flush against the inside face of the cherry end panel.

INSTALL THE CABINETS
You can appoint the bartender's area of the Club Bar just about any way you wish because the bartop and wall are freestanding, independent structures. We chose to install a couple of base cabinets, a dorm-size refrigerator and an economical, low-maintenance postform countertop. Start by placing the corner cabinet in the corner. Place the 24-inch cabinet to the right of the corner cabinet. Flush up the face frames (if they have them; the ones seen here are frameless)

Attach a 1 × 2 stop block for the lift gate to the wall directly above the wall-mounted end panel.

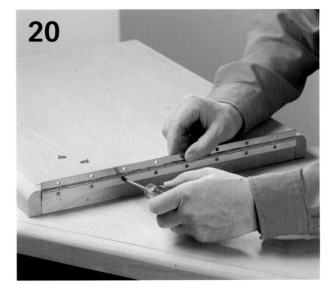

Attach the piano hinge to the lift gate section of the countertop first, then attach the other leaf to the countertop.

21

Attach the lift gate to the countertop and test to make sure it operates smoothly and correctly.

22

Add the decorative cherry strips in a ladder grid pattern, using an air nailer. Start with the vertical strips, then cut the horizontals to fit.

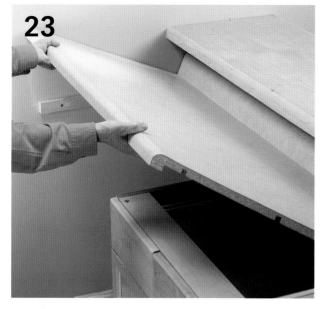

23

Attach a countertop to the base cabinets to create an easy-to-clean worksurface for the bartender.

24

Slide in a refrigerator, kegerator or any appliance you choose.

and clamp the cabinets together with bar clamps. Predrill, countersink, and screw the face frames or cabinets sides together.

Install a countertop for the bartender (photo 23). We chose an inexpensive postform countertop with a precut mitered corner. If you've left one end of the bar open for a refrigerator, install a wall cleat to support the countertop above the refrigerator. Plug

in and slide in your refrigerator (photo 24) and add a couple of strands of holiday lights or any other décor you fancy.

PARTY TIME

Invite friends and family to gather 'round. As they say in Latin: *Res ipsa loquitur:* "The thing speaks for itself." Or, as one of your friends might say: "It's beer-thirty."

WINDOW & DOOR PROJECTS

Windows and doors are the portals to your home lifestyle—the openings that allow air and light into your home and keep your home and its individual rooms secure against intruders and the weather. They are also important décor elements; changing out ho-hum slab doors for elegant panel-and-frame doors, for example, can radically transform the look of any home.

Doors and windows get more stress than almost any structural part of your home, since they are opening and closing constantly and are subject to wear and tear from the outdoor elements. Live in any home long enough and chances are good that you will need to replace or upgrade some or all of the windows and doors.

Window and door projects often come into play during major remodeling projects, such as when previously unused spaces are being converted to living space, or when a major room addition is being constructed. Very often these projects involve framing and installing windows where none existed before. Other space renovation projects, such as remodeling kitchens or bathrooms, may call for the addition of skylights, greenhouse windows, patio doors, or other features.

This chapter offers a wide sampling of window and door projects, ranging from simple replacement to whole-scale framing and installation. While some are common, tried-and-true undertakings, others represent unique window and door projects rarely found in other books.

IN THIS CHAPTER:

PLANNING & PREPARATION

An important early step in your remodeling project is to carefully measure the windows and doors that you wish to replace. You will use these measurements to purchase the new unit, and you must be sure it will fit in the opening.

To finalize your project ideas and make sure they will really work, the next step is to put all the information down on paper. There are two basic types of construction drawings: floor plans and elevation drawings. These drawings may be required if your project needs a building permit.

Floor plans show a room as seen from above. These are useful for showing overall room dimensions, layouts, and the relationship between neighboring rooms. Elevation drawings show a side view of a room, usually with one wall per drawing. Elevations are made for both the interior and exterior of a house and generally show more architectural detail than floor plans.

Both floor plans and elevation drawings provide you with a method for planning and recording structural and mechanical systems for your project. They also help the local building department to ensure your project meets code requirements.

If you will be doing several projects in a short time, you may want to draw a plan of each complete floor of the home. If you're doing one isolated project, you may want to draw the plan of just that room.

To create floor plans, draw one story at a time. First, measure each room from wall to wall. Transfer the room's dimensions onto ¼-inch grid paper, using a scale of ¼ inch = 1 foot Label each room for its use and note its overall dimensions. Include wall thicknesses, which you can determine by measuring the widths of window and door jambs—do not include the trim.

Next, add these elements to your drawings:

- Windows and doors; note which way the doors swing.
- Stairs and their direction as it relates to each story.
- Permanent features such as plumbing fixtures, major appliances, countertops, built-in furniture, and fireplaces.
- Overhead features such as exposed beams or wall cabinets—use dashed lines.
- Plumbing, electrical, and HVAC elements. You may want a separate set of drawings for these mechanical elements and service lines.
- Overall dimensions measured from outside the home. Use these to check the accuracy of interior dimensions.

To create elevation drawings, use the same ¼ inch = 1 foot scale, and draw everything you see on one wall (each room has four elevations). Include:

- Ceiling heights and the heights of significant features such as soffits and exposed beams.
- Windows, including the height and width of the sills and tops of the openings.
- Doors, including the heights (from the floor to the top of the opening) and widths.
- Trim and other decorative elements.

When your initial floor plans and elevations are done, use them to sketch your remodeling layout options. Use tissue overlays to show hidden elements or proposed changes to a plan. Photographs of your home's interior and exterior may also be helpful. Think creatively, and draw many different sketches; the more design options you consider, the better your final plans will be.

When you have completed your remodeling plans, draft your final drawings and create a materials list for the project.

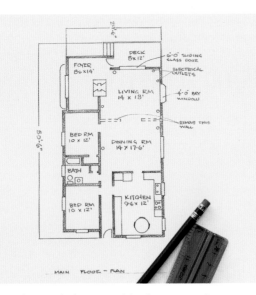

A floor plan can help you envision how a new door or window will impact the living space and traffic patterns.

MEASURING WINDOWS & DOORS

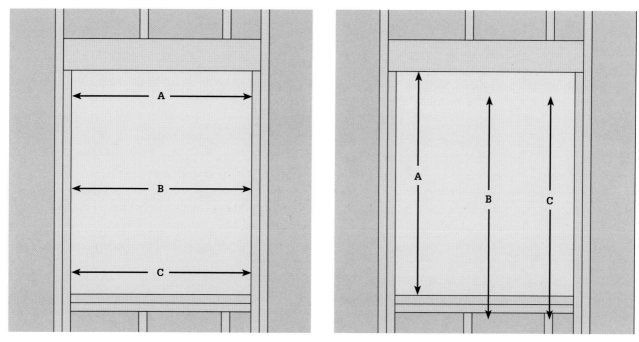

Determine the exact size of your new window or door by measuring the opening carefully. For the width (left), measure between the jack studs in three places: near the top, at the middle, and near the bottom of the opening. Use the same procedure for the height (right), measuring from the header to the sill near the left edge, at the middle, and near the right edge of the opening. Use the smallest measurement of each dimension for ordering the unit.

WORKING WITH PLANS

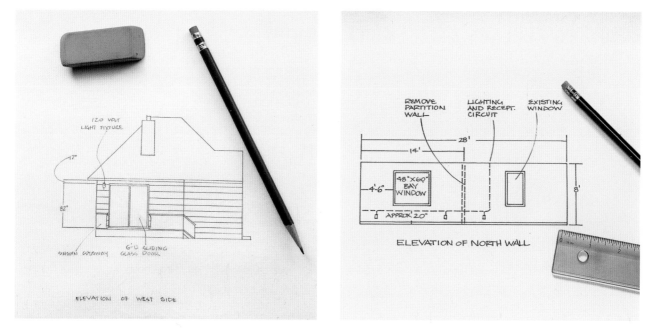

Create elevation drawings showing a side view layout of windows and doors, as viewed from both inside and outside the home. Indicate the size of windows and doors, ceiling heights, and the location of wiring and plumbing fixtures.

REPLACING BASEMENT WINDOWS

Replacing an old and underperforming basement window can accomplish much in conjunction with your basement remodeling project. Newer windows can allow more light in while keeping drafts out. They may have ventilation capabilities that older fixed windows lack. They can offer better security, especially if you install a glass block window that does not let people see inside but still allows light into the room.

Most home centers sell basement windows in standard 32-inch-wide sizes (standard heights are 13, 15, 17, 19, and 23 inches). The main types are awning windows that are hinged on top, hopper windows that are hinged on the bottom, and fixed windows. Some glass block or acrylic block fixed windows include a ventilation opening in lieu of one of the blocks.

If your basement window opening is not a standard size, you have three options. You can have a window custom-made (not as expensive as it sounds), you can remove the old window and enlarge the opening, or you can shrink the opening by using thicker lumber for the rough frame.

Basement windows are the only source of natural light, but they also can allow cold air or even intruders to enter. If you are remodeling your basement, it makes sense to update old windows with new ones that offer better energy efficiency and security.

HOW TO REPLACE A BASEMENT WINDOW

Remove the old window and inspect the rough frame. If it shows signs of rot, remove the frame by cutting the sill and header in half and prying the halves out. Cut new frame members from pressure-treated dimension lumber.

Install the new rough frame using a powder-actuated tool to drive masonry nails. Apply several thick beads of caulk to the concrete surfaces first to create a good seal. The header and sill should run the full width of the opening and be installed before the side members. Caulk around the frame edges and paint the frame with exterior primer.

Position the new window unit in the opening and test it with a level. Use shims to raise it so it is not resting on the sill. Adjust it so the gaps are even on the sides. *Tip: You may find it easier to adjust and install the window frame if you remove the glass sash first.*

Attach the window frame to the rough frame opening with screws driven through the jambs. Often, the screw is accessed through a hole in the inner jamb layer. Arrange shims so the screws will pass through them. Do not overdrive screws—it can pull the window frame out of square.

Fill gaps between the rough window frame and the new window unit with minimal expanding spray foam. Do not spray in too much—it can distort the frame when it dries.

Install stop molding on both sides of the window to cover gaps between the window and the rough frame. Paint the stop molding and frame to match your trim color.

NEW WINDOW SASH

If you're looking to replace or improve old single- or double-hung windows, consider using sash-replacement kits. They can give you energy-efficient, maintenance-free windows without changing the outward appearance of your home or breaking your budget.

Unlike prime window replacement, which changes the entire window and frame, or pocket window replacement, in which a complete window unit is set into the existing frame, sash replacement uses the original window jambs, eliminating the need to alter exterior or interior walls or trim. Installing a sash-replacement kit involves little more than removing the old window stops and sashes and installing new vinyl jamb liners and wood or vinyl sash. And all of the work can be done from inside your home.

Most sash-replacement kits offer tilt features and other contemporary conveniences. Kits are available in vinyl, aluminum, or wood construction with various options for color and glazing, energy efficiency, security features, and noise reduction.

Nearly all major window manufacturers offer sash-replacement kits designed to fit their own windows. You can also order custom kits that are sized to your specific window dimensions. A good fit is essential to the performance of your new windows. Review the tips shown on the next page for measuring your existing windows, and follow the manufacturer's instructions for the best fit.

Tools & Materials ▸

Tape measure	Jamb-liner brackets
Sill-bevel gauge	1" galvanized roofing nails
Flat pry bar	Fiberglass insulation
Scissors	Finish nails
Screwdriver	Wood-finishing materials
Nail set	Torpedo level
Sash-replacement kit	Eye and ear protection

Upgrade old, leaky windows with new, energy-efficient sash-replacement kits. Kits are available in a variety of styles to match your existing windows or to add a new decorative accent to your home. Most kits offer natural or painted interior surfaces and a choice of outdoor surface finishes.

HOW TO INSTALL A NEW WINDOW SASH

Measure the width of the existing window at the top, middle, and bottom of the frame. Use the smallest measurement, then reduce the figure by ⅜". Measure the height of the existing window from the head jamb to the point where the outside edge of the bottom sash meets the sill. Reduce the figure by ⅜".
Note: Manufacturers' specifications for window sizing may vary.

Check for a straight, level, and plumb sill, side, and head jambs using a torpedo level. Measure the frame diagonally to check for square (if the diagonal measurements are equal, the frame is square). If the frame is not square, check with the sash-kit manufacturer: Most window kits can accommodate some deviation in frame dimensions.

Carefully remove the interior stops from the side jambs, using a putty knife or pry bar. Save the stops for reinstallation.

With the bottom sash down, cut the cord holding the sash, balancing weight on each side of the sash. Let the weights and cords fall into the weight pockets.

(continued)

Lift out the bottom sash. Remove the parting stops from the head and side jambs. (The parting stops are the strips of wood that separate the top and bottom sash.) Cut the sash cords for the top sash, then lift out the top sash. Remove the sash-cord pulleys. If possible, pull the weights from the weight pockets at the bottom of the side jambs, then fill the weight pockets with fiberglass insulation. Repair any parts of the jambs that are rotted or damaged.

Position the jamb-liner brackets, and fasten them to the jambs with 1" galvanized roofing nails. Place one bracket approximately 4" from the head jamb and one 4" from the sill. Leave 1/16" clearance between the blind stop and the jamb-liner bracket. Install any remaining brackets, spacing them evenly along the jambs.

Position any gaskets or weatherstripping provided for the jamb liners. Carefully position each liner against its brackets and snap it into place. When both liners are installed, set the new parting stop into the groove of the existing head jamb, and fasten it with small finish nails. Install a vinyl sash stop in the interior track at the top of each liner to prevent the bottom sash from being opened too far.

Set the sash control mechanism, using a slotted screwdriver. Gripping the screwdriver firmly, slide down the mechanism until it is about 9" above the sill, then turn the screwdriver to lock the mechanism and prevent it from springing upward. The control mechanisms are spring-loaded—do not let them go until they are locked in place. Set the mechanism in each of the four sash channels.

Install the top sash into the jamb liners. Set the cam pivot on one side of the sash into the outside channel. Tilt the sash, and set the cam pivot on the other side of the sash. Make sure both pivots are set above the sash control mechanisms. Holding the sash level, tilt it up, depress the jamb liners on both sides, and set the sash in the vertical position in the jamb liners. Once the sash is in position, slide it down until the cam pivots contact the locking terminal assemblies.

Install the bottom sash into the jamb liners, setting it into the inside sash channels. When the bottom sash is set in the vertical position, slide it down until it engages the control mechanisms. Open and close both sashes to make sure they operate properly.

Reinstall the stops that you removed in step 1. Fasten them with finish nails, using the old nail holes, or drill new pilot holes for the nails.

Check the tilt operation of the bottom sash to make sure the stops do not interfere. Remove the labels, and clean the windows. Paint or varnish the new sashes as desired.

FRAMING & INSTALLING WINDOWS

Correct framing techniques will ensure ease of installation and keep your windows operating smoothly.

Many windows must be custom-ordered several weeks in advance. To save time, you can complete the interior framing before the window unit arrives, but be sure you have the exact dimensions of the window unit before building the frame. Do not remove the outside wall surface until you have the window and accessories and are ready to install them.

Follow the manufacturer's specifications for rough opening size when framing for a window. The listed opening is usually 1 inch wider and ½ inch taller than the actual dimensions of the window unit. The following pages show techniques for wood-frame houses with platform framing.

If your house has balloon framing where wall studs pass continuously from one floor to the next, use the method shown on page 262 to install a header. Consult a professional to install a window on the second story of a balloon-framed house.

If your house has masonry walls or if you are installing polymer-coated windows, you may want to attach your window using masonry clips instead of nails.

If your home's exterior has siding, see pages 282, 284, and 322 to 323 for tips on removing these surfaces and making the opening.

Tools & Materials ▶

Tape measure	Self-adhesive flashing
Pencil	10d common nails,
Combination square	1" galvanized
Hammer	roofing nails
Level	Shims
Circular saw	2× lumber
Handsaw	⅛" plywood
Pry bar	Building paper
Nippers	Drip edge
Drill	10d galvanized
Reciprocating saw	casing nails
Stapler	8d casing nails
Nail set	Fiberglass insulation
Caulk gun	Paintable silicone caulk
Zip tool	Eye and ear protection
Chisel	

HOW TO FRAME A WINDOW OPENING

Prepare the project site and remove the interior wall surfaces (page 262). Measure and mark the rough opening width on the sole plate. Mark the locations of the jack studs and king studs on the sole plate. Where practical, use the existing studs as king studs.

Measure and cut the king studs, as needed, to fit between the sole plate and the top plate. Position the king studs and toenail them to the sole plate with 10d nails.

Check the king studs with a level to make sure they are plumb, then toenail them to the top plate with 10d nails.

Measuring from the floor, mark the top of the rough opening on one of the king studs. This line represents the bottom of the window header. For most windows, the recommended rough opening is ½" taller than the height of the window frame.

Measure and mark where the top of the window header will fit against the king studs. The header size depends on the distance between the king studs. Use a carpenter's level to extend the lines across the old studs to the opposite king stud.

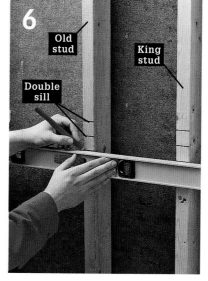

Measure down from the header line and mark the double rough sill on the king stud. Use a carpenter's level to extend the lines across the old studs to the opposite king stud. Make temporary supports if removing more than one stud.

(continued)

7

Bottom
of sill

Set a circular saw to its maximum blade depth, then cut through the old studs along the lines marking the bottom of the rough sill and along the lines marking the top of the header. Do not cut the king studs. On each stud, make an additional cut about 3" above the sill cut. Finish the cuts with a handsaw.

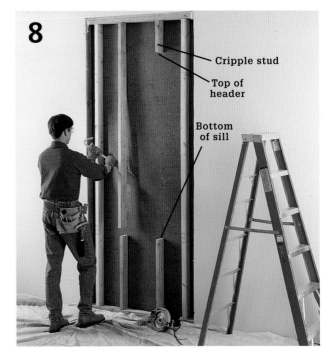

8

Cripple stud

Top of
header

Bottom
of sill

Knock out the 3" stud sections, then tear out the old studs inside the rough opening, using a pry bar. Clip away any exposed nails, using nippers. The remaining sections of the cut studs will serve as cripple studs for the window.

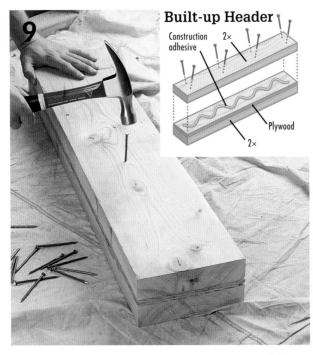

9

Built-up Header

Construction
adhesive

2×

Plywood

2×

Build a header to fit between the king studs on top of the jack studs, using two pieces of 2× lumber sandwiched around ½" plywood.

10

Cut two jack studs to reach from the top of the sole plate to the bottom header lines on the king studs. Nail the jack studs to the king studs with 10d nails driven every 12". *Note: On a balloon-framed house the jack studs will reach to the sill plate.*

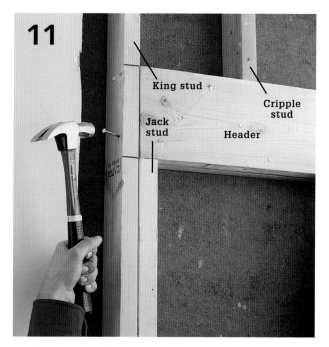

Position the header on the jack studs, using a hammer if necessary. Attach the header to the king studs, jack studs, and cripple studs, using 10d nails.

Build the rough sill to reach between the jack studs by nailing a pair of 2 × 4s together. Position the rough sill on the cripple studs, and nail it to the jack studs and cripple studs with 10d nails.

HOW TO INSTALL A REPLACEMENT WINDOW WITH A NAILING FLANGE

Remove the existing window (see pages 257 and 258), and set the new window into the rough opening. Center it left to right, and shim beneath the sill to level it. On the exterior side, measure out from the window on all sides, and mark the siding for the width of the brick molding you'll install around the new window. Extend layout lines to mark where you'll cut the siding.

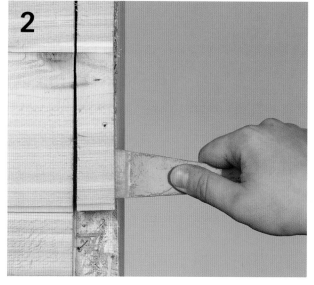

Remove exterior siding around the window area to expose the wall sheathing. Use a zip tool to separate vinyl siding for removal or use a pry bar and hammer to remove wood clapboard. For more on removing exterior surfaces, see pages 282, 284, and 322 to 323.

(continued)

Cover the sill and rough opening framing members with self-adhesive, rolled flashing. Apply additional strips of flashing behind the siding and up the sill flashing. Finish flashing with a strip along the header. The flashing should cover the front edges and sides of the opening members.

Apply a bead of silicone caulk around the back face of the window flange, then set it into the rough opening, centering it side-to-side in the opening. Tack the window in place by driving one roofing nail partway through the top flange. On the interior side, level and plumb the window, using shims to make any necessary adjustments.

Tack the window to the header at one end of the nailing flange, using a 1" galvanized roofing nail. Drive a roofing nail through the other top corner of the flange to hold the window in place, then secure the flange all around the window with more roofing nails. Apply strips of rolled, self-adhesive flashing to cover the window flanges. Start with a strip that covers the bottom flange, then cover the side flanges, overlapping the bottom flashing and extending 8 to 10" above the window. Complete the flashing with a strip along the top, overlapping the side flashing.

Install a piece of metal drip edge behind the siding and above the window. Secure it with silicone caulk only.

Cut and attach brick molding around the window, leaving a slight gap between the brick molding and the window frame. Use 8d galvanized casing nails driven into pilot holes to secure the brick molding to the rough framing. Miter the corner joints. Reinstall the siding in the window installation area, trimming as needed.

Use high-quality caulk to fill the gap between the brick molding and the siding. On the interior side, fill gaps between the window frame and surrounding framing with foam backer rod, low-expansion foam, or fiberglass insulation. Install the interior casing.

Tip Installation Variation: Masonry Clips ▸

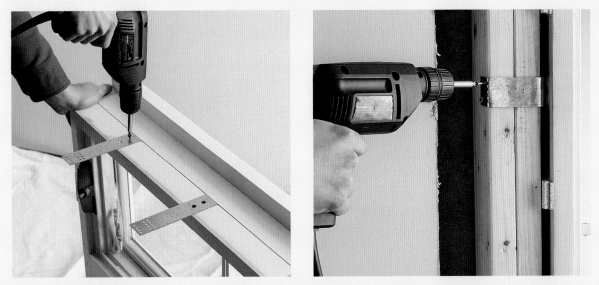

Use metal masonry clips when the brick molding on a window cannot be nailed because it rests against a masonry or brick surface. The masonry clips hook into precut grooves in the window jambs (above, left) and are attached to the jambs with screws. After the window unit is positioned in the rough opening, the masonry clips are bent around the framing members and anchored with screws (above, right). *Note: Masonry clips can also be used in ordinary lap siding installations if you want to avoid making nail holes in the smooth surface of the brick moldings. For example, windows that are precoated with polymer-based paint can be installed with masonry clips so that the brick moldings are not punctured with nails.*

HOW TO INSTALL A ROUND-TOP WINDOW

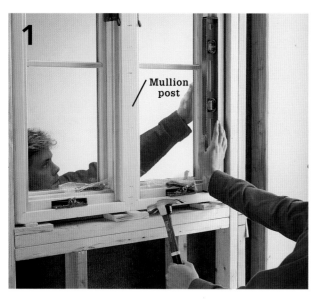

Mullion post

Remove the exterior wall surface as directed on pages 282, 284, and 322 to 323, then test-fit the window, centering it in the rough opening. Support the window with wood blocks and shims placed under the side jambs and mullion post. Check to make sure the window is plumb and level, and adjust the shims, if necessary.

Trace the outline of the brick molding on the wood siding. Remove the window after finishing the outline. *Note: If you have vinyl or metal siding, you should have enlarged the outline to make room for the extra J-channel moldings required by these sidings.*

Tips for Framing a Round-Top Window ▸

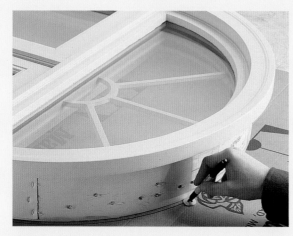

Create a template to help you mark the rough opening on the sheathing. Scribe the outline of the curved frame on cardboard, allowing an extra ½" for adjustments within the rough opening. A ¼ × 1¼" metal washer makes a good spacer for scribing the outline. Cut out the template along the scribed line.

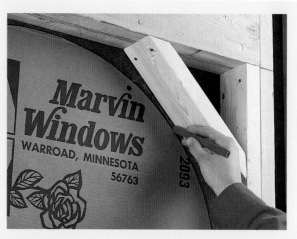

Tape the template to the sheathing, with the top flush against the header. Use the template as a guide for attaching diagonal framing members across the top corners of the framed opening. The diagonal members should just touch the template. Outline the template on the sheathing as a guide for cutting the exterior wall surface.

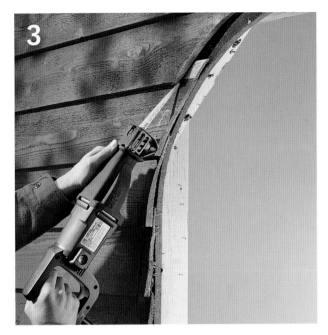

Cut the siding along the outline just down to the sheathing. For a round-top window, use a reciprocating saw held at a low angle. For straight cuts, use a circular saw adjusted so the blade cuts through only the siding. Use a sharp chisel to complete the cuts at the corners.

Cut 8"-wide strips of building paper and slide them between the siding and sheathing around the entire window opening. Bend the paper around the framing members and staple it in place. Work from the bottom up, so each piece overlaps the piece below. *Note: You can also use adhesive-backed, rolled flashing instead of building paper.*

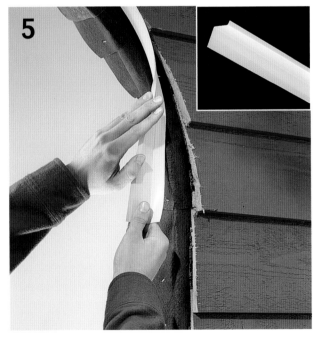

Cut a length of drip edge to fit over the top of the window, then slide it between the siding and building paper. For round-top windows, use flexible vinyl drip edge; for rectangular windows, use rigid metal drip edge (inset).

Insert the window in the opening, and push the brick molding tight against the sheathing. Nail through the brick molding, as usual, to secure the window in the opening.

INSTALLING AN EGRESS WINDOW

An egress window brings a pleasant source of natural light and ventilation to a dark, dank basement. More importantly, it can provide a lifesaving means of escape in the event of a fire. Before you proceed with this project, read more about building code issues regarding basement egress on page 15. Contact your local building department to apply for the proper permits and to learn more about the code requirements for your area.

As long as the window opens wide enough to meet minimum standards for egress, the particular window style is really up to you. Casement windows are ideal, because they crank open quickly and provide unobstructed escape. A tall, double-hung window or wide sliding window can also work. Select a window with insulated glass and clad with vinyl or aluminum for durability; it will be subject to humidity and temperature fluctuations just like any other above-grade window in your home.

The second fundamental component of a basement egress window project is the subterranean escape well you install outside the foundation. There are several options to choose from: prefabricated well kits made of lightweight plastic that bolt together and are easy to install; corrugated metal wells that are a lower-cost option; or, a well built from scratch using concrete, stone, or landscape timber.

Installing an egress window involves four major steps: digging the well, cutting a new or larger window opening in the foundation, installing the window, and, finally, installing the well. You'll save time and effort if you hire a backhoe operator to excavate the well. In most cases, you'll also need a large concrete saw (available at most rental stores) to cut the foundation wall.

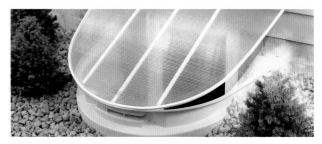

Replacing a small basement window with an egress window is a big job, but it is required if you want to convert part of a basement into livable space, especially a bedroom.

Tools & Materials ▸

Tape measure	Window well
4' level	and window
Stakes and string line	Pea gravel
Shovel	Plastic sheeting
Colored masking tape	Self-tapping
Hammer drill with ½"	masonry screws
dia. × 12- to 16"-	2× pressure-treated
long masonry bit	lumber
Masonry saw	Shims
Hand maul	Insulation materials
Cold chisel	Concrete sleeve anchors
Trowel	Quick-curing concrete
Miter saw	3½" deck screws
Hammer	Foam backer rod
Drill/driver, hammer	Tamper
Caulk and caulk gun	Eye and ear protection
Gloves	Dust mask

HOW TO INSTALL AN EGRESS WINDOW & WINDOW WELL

Lay out the border of the window well area with stakes and string. Plan the length and width of the excavation to be several feet larger than the window well's overall size to provide extra room for installation and adjustment.

Excavate the well to a depth 6 to 12" deeper than the well's overall height to allow room for drainage gravel. Make sure to have your local public utilities inspect the well excavation area and okay it for digging before you start.

Measure and mark the foundation wall with brightly colored masking tape to establish the overall size of the window's rough opening (here, we're replacing an existing window). Be sure to take into account the window's rough opening dimensions, the thickness of the rough framing (usually 2x stock), and the width of the structural header you may need to build. Remember also that sill height must be within 44" of the floor. Remove existing wall coverings inside the layout area.

If the floor joists run perpendicular to your project wall, build a temporary support wall parallel to the foundation wall and 6 to 8' from it. Staple sheet plastic to the wall and floor joists to form a work tent that will help control concrete dust.

(continued)

5

Drill reference holes at each bottom corner with a hammer drill and long masonry bit. These holes will provide reference points for cutting from both sides, ensuring clean breaks.

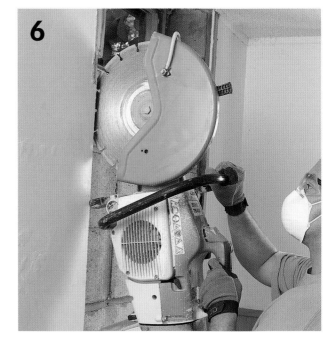

6

Equip a masonry cutting saw (or large angle grinder) with a diamond blade and set it for a ½" cut to score the blocks first. Then reset the saw to full depth and make the final bottom and side cuts through the blocks. Wear a tight-fitting particle mask, ear and eye protection, and gloves for all of this cutting work; the saw will generate a tremendous amount of thick dust. Feed the saw slowly and steadily. Stop and rest periodically so the dust can settle.

7

On the outside foundation wall, score the cuts, then make full-depth cuts.

8

Strike the blocks with a hand maul to break or loosen the block sections. When all the blocks are removed, carefully chip away remaining debris with a cold chisel to create flat surfaces.

9

Fill the hollow voids in concrete block walls, with broken pieces of block, then level and smooth the voids by trowelling on a fresh layer of quick-curing concrete. Flatten the surfaces, and allow the concrete to dry overnight.

10

If your project requires a new header above the new window, build it from pieces of 2× lumber sandwiching ½" plywood and fastened together with construction adhesive and 10d nails. Slip it into place and tack it temporarily to the mudsill with 3½" deck screws driven toenail style.

11

Cut the sill plate for the window's rough frame from 2× treated lumber that's the same width as the thickness of the foundation wall. Fasten the sill to the foundation with ³⁄₁₆ × 3¼" countersunk masonry screws. Drill pilot holes for the screws first with a hammer drill.

12

Cut two pieces of treated lumber just slightly longer than the opening so they'll fit tightly between the new header and sill. Tap them into place with a maul. Adjust them for plumb and fasten them to the foundation with countersunk masonry screws or powder-actuated fasteners.

(continued)

13

Apply a thick bead of silicone caulk around the outside edges of the rough frame and set the window in its opening, seating the nailing flanges into the caulk. Shim the window so the frame is level and plumb. Test the action of the window to make sure the shims aren't bowing the frame.

14

Attach the window's nailing flanges to the rough frame with screws or nails, as specified by the manufacturer. Check the window action periodically as you fasten it to ensure that it still operates smoothly.

15

Seal gaps between the rough frame and the foundation with a bead of exterior silicone or polyurethane caulk. If the gaps are wider than ¼", insert a piece of backer rod first, then cover it with caulk. On the interior, fill gaps around the window shims with strips of foam backer rod, fiberglass insulation, or a bead of minimally expanding spray foam. Do not distort the window frame.

16

Fill the well excavation with 6 to 12" of pea gravel. This will serve as the window's drain system. Follow the egress well kit instructions to determine the exact depth required; you may need to add more gravel so the top of the well will be above the new window. *Note: We added a drain down to the foundation's perimeter tile for improved drainage as well.*

17

Set the bottom section of the well into the hole, and position it evenly from left to right relative to the window. Adjust the gravel surface to level the well section carefully.

18

Stack the second well section on top of the first, and connect the two with the appropriate fasteners.

19

Fasten the window well sections to the foundation wall with concrete sleeve anchors driven into prebored pilot holes. You could also use masonry nails driven with a powder-actuated tool.

20

When all the well sections are assembled and secured, nail pieces of trim around the window frame to hide the nailing flange. Complete the well installation by using excavated dirt to backfill around the outside of the well. Pack the soil with a tamper, creating a slope for good drainage. If you are installing a window well cover, set it in place and fasten it according to the manufacturer's instructions. The cover must be removable.

FRAMING A WINDOW IN A GABLE WALL

Although most windows in a home are located in load-bearing exterior walls, standard attic windows are commonly located in gable walls, which often are non-loadbearing. Installing a window in a non-loadbearing gable wall is fairly simple and doesn't require a temporary support for the framing. Some gable walls, however, are load-bearing: A common sign is a heavy structural ridge beam that supports the rafters from underneath, rather than merely at the rafter ends. Hire a contractor to build window frames in load-bearing gable walls. If you aren't certain what type of wall you have, consult a professional.

A common problem with framing in a gable wall is that the positions of the floor joists may make it difficult to attach new studs to the wall's sole plate. One solution is to install an extra-long header and sill between two existing studs, positioning them at the precise heights for the rough opening. You can then adjust the width of the rough opening by installing vertical studs between the header and sill.

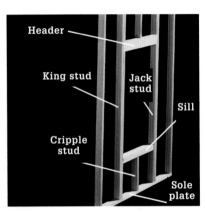

Window frames have full-length king studs, as well as jack studs that support the header. The sill defines the bottom of the rough opening.

> ## Tools & Materials ›

Tape measure
Circular saw
Handsaw
Plumb bob
T-bevel
4' level
Combination square
Reciprocating saw

Framed window or
   door unit
2 × 4 lumber
16d, 10d, and 8d
   common nails
½"-thick plywood
Construction adhesive
Eye and ear protection

HOW TO FRAME A WINDOW IN A GABLE WALL

Determine the rough opening width by measuring the window unit and adding 1". Add 3" to that dimension to get the distance between the king studs. Mark the locations of the king studs onto the sole plate of the gable wall.

Using a plumb bob, transfer the king-stud marks from the sole plate to the sloping top plates of the gable wall.

Cut the king studs to length, angle-cutting the top ends so they meet flush with the top plates. Fasten each king stud in place by toenailing the ends with three 8d nails.

Find the height of the rough opening by measuring the height of the window unit and adding ½". Measure up from where the finished floor height will be, and mark the top of the sill. Make a second mark for the bottom of the sill, 3" down from the top mark.

Measure up from the top sill mark, and mark the height of the rough opening (bottom of header). Make another mark 3½" up, to indicate the top of the header. Using a level, transfer all of these marks to the other king stud and to all intermediate studs.

Draw level cutting lines across the intermediate studs at the marks for the bottom of the sill and top of the header. Cut along the lines with a reciprocating saw, then remove the cutout portions. The remaining stud sections will serve as cripple studs.

Cut the jack studs to reach from the sole plate to the bottom header marks on the king studs. Nail the jack studs to the inside faces of the king studs using 10d common nails driven every 16".

Build a built-up header with 2 × 4s and plywood (page 262). Size it to fit snugly between king studs. Set header on top of jack studs. Nail through king studs into header with 16d nails, then toenail jack studs and cripple studs to header using 8d nails.

Build a sill to fit snugly between jack studs by nailing together two 2 × 4s. Position the sill at the top sill markings, and toenail it to the jack studs. Toenail the cripple studs to the sill. See pages 282, 284, and 322 to 323 to remove the exterior wall surface and pages 263 to 265 to install the window.

GARDEN WINDOWS

Although often found in kitchens, a garden window is an attractive option for nearly any room in your home. Projecting out from the wall 16 to 24 inches, garden windows add space to a room, making it feel larger. The glass roof and box-like design make them ideal growing environments for plants or display areas for collectibles. Garden windows also typically include front- or side-opening windows. These allow for ventilation and are usually available in either awning or casement style.

Home stores often stock garden windows in several common sizes. However, it may be difficult to locate a stock window that will fit in your existing window rough opening. In cases like this you must rebuild the rough opening to the proper size. It may be worth the added expense to custom-order your garden window to fit into the existing rough opening.

The large amount of glass in a garden window has a direct effect on the window's energy efficiency. When purchasing a garden window, as a minimum, look for double-pane glass with low-emissivity (low-E) coatings. More expensive super-efficient types of glass are available for severely cold climates.

Installation methods for garden windows vary by manufacturer. Some units include a nailing flange that attaches to the framing and holds the window against the house. Other models hang on a separate mounting frame that attaches to the outside of the house. In this project, the garden window has a built-in mounting sleeve that slides into the rough opening and is attached directly to the rough framing.

Tools & Materials ▸

Tape measure	2 × 4s
Hammer	Shims
Level	Exterior trim
Framing square	Building paper
Circular saw	3" screws
Wood chisel	Drip edge
Stapler	Construction adhesive
Drill and bits	4d siding nails
Caulking gun	8d galvanized casing nails
Utility knife	Interior trim
Garden window kit	Paintable silicone caulk
Wood strips	Eye and ear protection

A garden window's glass roof makes it an ideal sun spot for houseplants, and it can also help a room feel larger.

HOW TO INSTALL A GARDEN WINDOW

Prepare the project site and remove the interior and exterior trim, then remove the existing window (pages 257 to 258).

Check the rough opening measurements to verify the correct window sizing. The rough opening should be about ½" larger than the window height and width. If necessary, attach wood strips to the rough framing as spacers to bring the opening to the required size.

Use a level to check that the sill of the rough opening is level and the side jambs are plumb. Use a framing square to make sure each corner is square. The rough framing must be in good condition in order to support the weight of the garden window. If the framing is severely deteriorated or out of plumb or square, you may need to reframe the rough opening (pages 261 to 263).

Insert the garden window into the opening, pressing it tight against the framing. Support the unit with notched 2 × 4s under the bottom edge of the window until it has been fastened securely to the framing.

(continued)

5

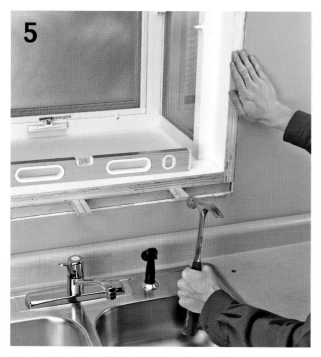

The inside edge of the window sleeve should be flush with the interior wall surface. Check the sill of the garden window for level. Shim beneath the lower side of the sill, if necessary, to make it level.

6

Once the garden window is in place and level, hold a piece of window trim in place along the exterior of the window and trace the outline onto the siding. Remove the window. Cut the siding down to the sheathing using a circular saw.

7

Install strips of building paper between siding and sheathing. Wrap them around the framing and staple them in place. On the sides, work from the bottom up so each piece overlaps the piece below. Reposition the window and reshim. Make sure the space between the window and the siding is equal to the width of the trim on all sides.

8

Drill countersunk pilot holes every 12" to 16" through the window sleeve into the rough header, jack studs, and sill.

9

Insert shims between the window sleeve and rough frame at each hole location along the top and sides to prevent bowing of the window frame. Fasten the window to the framing using 3" screws. Continue checking for level, plumb, and square as the screws are tightened.

10

Locate and mark the studs nearest the edges of the window using a stud finder. Cut two pieces of siding to fit behind the brackets, and tack them in place over the marked studs with 4d siding nails. Position the support brackets with the shorter side against the siding and the longer side beneath the window. Fasten the brackets to the window and the studs using the included screws.

11

Cut a piece of drip edge to length, apply construction adhesive to its top flange, and slide it under the siding above the window. Cut each trim piece to size. Position the trim and attach it using 8d galvanized casing nails driven through pilot holes. Seal the edges of the trim with a bead of paintable silicone caulk, approximately ⅜" wide.

12

Cut all protruding shims flush with the framing using a utility knife or handsaw. Insulate or caulk gaps between the window sleeve and the wall. Finish the installation by reinstalling the existing interior trim or installing new trim.

BAY WINDOWS

Modern bay windows are preassembled for easy installation, but it will still take several days to complete an installation. Bay windows are large and heavy, and installing them requires special techniques.

Have at least one helper to assist you, and try to schedule the work when there's little chance of rain. Using prebuilt bay window accessories will speed your work (see next page).

A large bay window can weigh several hundred pounds, so it must be anchored securely to framing members in the wall and supported by braces attached to framing members below the window. Some window manufacturers include cable-support hardware that can be used instead of metal support braces.

Before purchasing a bay window unit, check with the local building department regarding the code requirements. Many local codes require large windows and low bay windows with window seats to be glazed with tempered glass for safety.

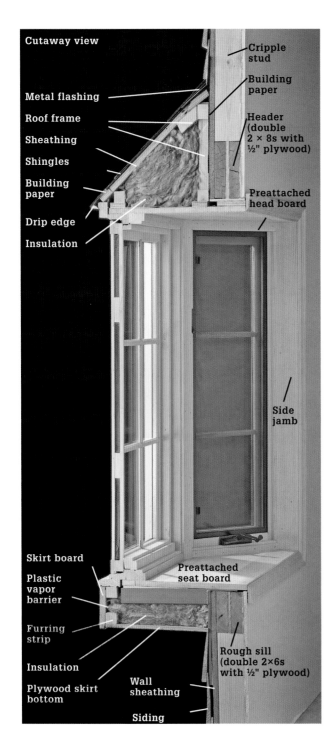

Cutaway view

- Cripple stud
- Building paper
- Header (double 2 × 8s with ½" plywood)
- Metal flashing
- Roof frame
- Sheathing
- Shingles
- Building paper
- Drip edge
- Insulation
- Preattached head board
- Side jamb
- Skirt board
- Plastic vapor barrier
- Furring strip
- Insulation
- Plywood skirt bottom
- Preattached seat board
- Wall sheathing
- Rough sill (double 2×6s with ½" plywood)
- Siding

Tools & Materials ▸

Straightedge
Circular saw
Wood chisel
Pry bar
Drill
Level
Nail set
Stapler
Aviation snips
Roofing knife
Caulk gun
Utility knife
T-bevel
Bay window unit
Prebuilt roof
   frame kit
Metal support
   brackets
2× lumber
16d galvanized
   common nails
16d and 8d
   galvanized
   casing nails

16d casing nails
3" and 2" galvanized
   utility screws
Tapered wood shims
Building paper
Fiberglass insulation
6-mil polyethylene
   sheeting
Drip edge
1" roofing nails
Step flashing
Shingles
Top flashing
Roofing cement
2 × 2 lumber
5½" skirt boards
¾" exterior-grade
   plywood
Paintable silicone caulk
Eye and ear protection

Tips for Installing a Bay Window ▸

Use prebuilt accessories to ease installation of a bay window. Roof frames (A) come complete with sheathing (B), metal top flashing (C), and step flashing (D) and can be special-ordered at most home centers. You will have to specify the exact size of your window unit and the angle (pitch) you want for the roof. You can cover the roof inexpensively with building paper and shingles or order a copper or aluminum shell. Metal support braces (E) and skirt boards (F) can be ordered at your home center if not included with the window unit. Use two braces for bay windows up to 5 ft. wide and three braces for larger windows. Skirt boards are clad with aluminum or vinyl and can be cut to fit with a circular saw or miter saw.

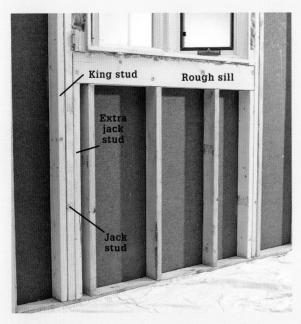

Construct a bay window frame similar to that for a standard window (see pages 261 to 263) but use a built-up sill made from two 2 × 6s sandwiched around ½" plywood. Install extra jack studs under the sill ends to help carry the window's weight.

Build an enclosure above the bay window if the roof soffit overhangs the window. Build a 2 × 2 frame (top) to match the angles of the bay window, and attach the frame securely to the wall and overhanging soffit. Install a vapor barrier and insulation (pages 285, 288, and 289), then finish the enclosure so it matches the siding (bottom).

HOW TO INSTALL A BAY WINDOW

Prepare the project site and remove interior wall surfaces (page 262), then frame the rough opening. Remove the exterior wall surfaces as directed on this page and on pages 284 and 322 to 323. Mark for removal a section of siding directly below the rough opening. The width of the marked area should equal that of the window unit and the height should equal that of the skirt board.

Set the blade on a circular saw just deep enough to cut through the siding, then cut along the outline. Stop just short of the corners to avoid damaging the siding outside the outline. Use a sharp chisel to complete the corner cuts. Remove the cut siding inside the outline.

Position the support braces along the rough sill within the widest part of the bay window and above the cripple stud locations. Add cripple studs to match the support brace locations, if necessary. Draw outlines of the braces on the top of the sill. Use a chisel or circular saw to notch the sill to a depth equal to the thickness of the top arm of the support braces.

Slide the support braces down between the siding and the sheathing. Pry the siding material away from the sheathing slightly to make room for the braces, if necessary. *Note: On stucco, you will need to chisel notches in the masonry surface to fit the support braces.*

Attach the braces to the rough sill with galvanized 16d common nails. Drive 3" utility screws through the front of the braces and into the rough sill to prevent twisting.

Lift the bay window onto the support braces and slide it into the rough opening. Center the unit within the opening.

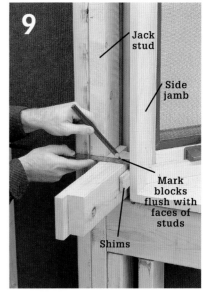

Check the window unit to make sure it is level. If necessary, drive shims under the low side to level the window. Temporarily brace the outside bottom edge of the unit with 2 × 4s to keep it from moving on the braces.

Set the roof frame on top of the window, with the sheathing loosely tacked in place. Trace the outline of the window and roof unit onto the siding. Leave a gap of about ½" around the roof unit to allow room for flashing and shingles.

If the gap between the side jambs and jack studs is more than 1" wide, mark and cut wood blocks to bridge the gap (smaller gaps require no blocks). Leave a small space for inserting wood shims. Remove the window, then attach blocks every 12" along studs.

(continued)

10

Cut the siding just down to the sheathing along the outline using a circular saw. Stop just short of the corners, then use a wood chisel to complete the corner cuts. Remove the cut siding. Pry the remaining siding slightly away from the sheathing around the roof outline to allow for easy installation of the metal flashing. Cover the exposed sheathing with 8"-wide strips of building paper (step 4, page 267).

11

Shim

Brace

Set the bay window unit back on the braces, and slide it back into the rough opening until the brick moldings are tight against the sheathing. Insert wood shims between the outside end of the metal braces and the seat board (inset). Check the unit to make sure it is level, and adjust the shims, if necessary.

12

Anchor the window by drilling pilot holes and driving 16d casing nails through the brick molding and into the framing members. Space nails every 12", and use a nail set to drive the nail heads below the surface of the wood.

13

Blocking

Shim

Jack stud

Drive wood shims into the spaces between the side jambs and the blocking or jack studs and between the headboard and header, spacing the shims every 12". Fill the spaces around the window with loosely packed fiberglass insulation. At each shim location, drive 16d casing nails through the jambs and shims and into the framing members. Cut off the shims flush with the framing members using a handsaw or utility knife. Use a nail set to drive the nail heads below the surface. If necessary, drill pilot holes to prevent splitting the wood.

14

Staple sheet plastic over the top of the window unit to serve as a vapor barrier. Trim the edges of the plastic around the top of the window using a utility knife.

15

Remove the sheathing pieces from the roof frame, then position the frame on top of the window unit. Attach the roof frame to the window and to the wall at stud locations using 3" utility screws.

16

Fill the empty space inside the roof frame with loosely packed fiberglass insulation. Screw the sheathing back onto the roof frame using 2" utility screws.

17

Staple asphalt building paper over the roof sheathing. Make sure each piece of building paper overlaps the one below by at least 5".

18

Cut drip edges with aviation snips, then attach them around the edge of the roof sheathing using roofing nails.

(continued)

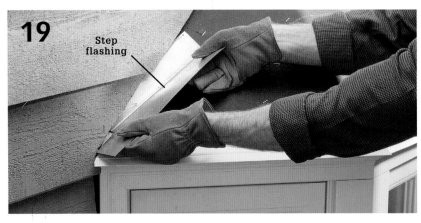

19

Step flashing

Cut and fit a piece of step flashing on each side of the roof frame. Adjust the flashing so it overhangs the drip edge by ¼". Flashings help guard against moisture damage.

20

Trim the end of the flashing to the same angle as the drip edge. Nail the flashing to the sheathing with roofing nails.

21

Cut 6"-wide strips of shingles for the starter row. Use roofing nails to attach the starter row shingles so they overhang the drip edge by about ½". Cut the shingles along the roof hips with a straightedge and a roofing knife.

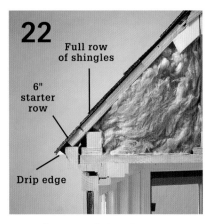

22

Full row of shingles

6" starter row

Drip edge

Nail a full row of shingles over the starter row, aligning the bottom edges with the bottom edge of the starter row. Make sure shingle notches are not aligned.

23

Second step flashing

Install another piece of step flashing on each side of the roof, overlapping the first piece of flashing by about 5".

24

Cut and install another row of full shingles. The bottom edges should overlap the tops of the notches on the previous row by ½". Attach the shingles with roofing nails driven just above the notches.

Continue installing alternate rows of step flashing and shingles to the top of the roof. Bend the last pieces of step flashing to fit over the roof hips.

When the roof sheathing is covered with shingles, install the top flashing. Cut and bend the ends over the roof hips, and attach it with roofing nails. Attach the remaining rows of shingles over the top flashing.

Find the height of the final row of shingles by measuring from the top of the roof to a point ½" below the top of the notches on the last installed shingle. Trim the shingles to fit.

Attach the final row of shingles with a thick bead of roofing cement—not nails. Press firmly to ensure a good bond.

Make ridge caps by cutting shingles into 1'-long sections. Use a roofing knife to trim off the top corners of each piece, so the ridge caps will be narrower at the top than at the bottom.

Install the ridge caps over the roof hips, beginning at the bottom of the roof. Trim the bottom ridge caps to match the edges of the roof. Keep the same amount of overlap with each layer.

(continued)

31

At the top of the roof hips, use a roofing knife to cut the shingles to fit flush with the wall. Attach the shingles with roofing cement—do not use any nails.

32

Staple sheet plastic over the bottom of the window unit to serve as a vapor barrier. Trim the plastic around the bottom of the window.

33

Cut and attach a 2 × 2 skirt frame around the bottom of the bay window using 3" galvanized utility screws. Set the skirt frame back about 1" from the edges of the window.

34

Cut skirt boards to match the shape of the bay window bottom, mitering the ends to ensure a tight fit. Test-fit the skirt board pieces to make sure they match the bay window bottom.

35

Cut a 2 × 2 furring strip for each skirt board. Miter the ends to the same angles as the skirt boards. Attach the furring strips to the back of the skirt boards, 1" from the bottom edges, using 2" galvanized utility screws.

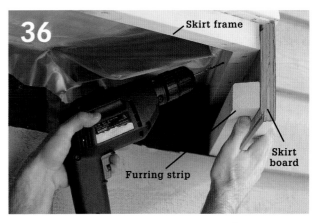

36

Skirt frame

Furring strip

Skirt board

Attach the skirt board pieces to the skirt frame. Drill ⅛" pilot holes every 6" through the back of the skirt frame and into the skirt boards, then attach the skirt boards with 2" galvanized utility screws.

37

Measure the space inside the skirt boards using a T-bevel to duplicate the angles. Cut a skirt bottom from ¾" exterior-grade plywood to fit this space.

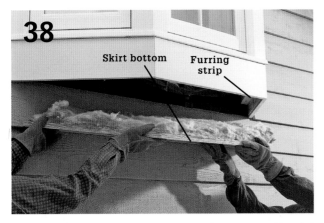

38

Skirt bottom

Furring strip

Lay fiberglass insulation on the skirt bottom. Position the skirt bottom against the furring strips and attach it by driving 2" galvanized utility screws every 6" through the bottom and into the furring strips.

39

Roofing cement

Silicone caulk

Install any additional trim pieces (inset) specified by your window manufacturer using 8d galvanized casing nails. Seal the roof edges with roofing cement, and seal around the rest of the window with paintable silicone caulk. See pages 78 to 79 and 279 to finish the walls.

GLASS BLOCK WINDOWS

Glass block is a durable material that transmits light while reducing visibility, making it a perfect material for creating unique windows. Glass block windows are energy-efficient and work particularly well as accent windows or in rooms where privacy is desired, such as bathrooms.

Glass block is available in a wide variety of sizes, shapes, and patterns. It can be found, along with other necessary installation products, at specialty distributors or home centers.

Building with glass block is much like building with mortared brick, with two important differences. First, glass block must be supported by another structure and cannot function in a load-bearing capacity. Second, glass block cannot be cut, so take extra time to make sure the layout is accurate.

When installing a glass block window, the size of the rough opening is based on the size and number of blocks you are using. It is much easier to make an existing opening smaller to accommodate the glass block rather than make it larger, which requires reframing the rough opening. To determine the rough opening width, multiply the nominal width of the glass block by the number of blocks horizontally and add ¼ inch. For the height, multiply the nominal height by the number of blocks vertically and add ¼ inch.

Because of its weight, a glass block window requires a solid base. The framing members of the rough opening will need to be reinforced. Contact your local building department for requirements in your area.

Use ¼-inch plastic T-spacers between blocks to ensure consistent mortar joints and to support the weight of the block to prevent mortar from squeezing out before it sets. (T-spacers can be modified into L or flat shapes for use at corners and along the channel.) For best results, use premixed glass block mortar. This high-strength mortar is a little drier than regular brick mortar, because glass doesn't wick water out of the mortar as brick does.

Because there are many applications for glass block and installation techniques may vary, ask a glass block retailer or manufacturer about the best products and methods for your specific project.

Glass block windows provide exceptional durability, light transmission, and privacy. New installation products are also making these windows easier for the do-it-yourselfer to install.

Tools & Materials ▸

Tape measure	2 × 4 lumber
Circular saw	16d common nails
Hammer	Glass block perimeter
Utility knife	channels
Tin snips	1" galvanized flat-head
Drill	screws
Mixing box	Glass block mortar
Trowel	Glass blocks
4' level	¼" T-spacers
Rubber mallet	Expansion strips
Jointing tool	Silicone caulk
Sponge	Construction adhesive
Nail set	Mortar sealant
Paintbrush	Eye and ear protection
Caulk gun	

HOW TO INSTALL A GLASS BLOCK WINDOW

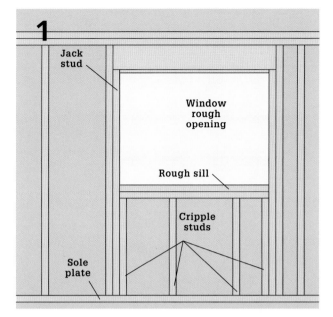

Measure the size of the rough opening and determine the size of the glass block window you will install (opposite page). Reinforce the rough opening framing by doubling the rough sill and installing additional cripple studs. Cut all pieces to size and fasten with 16d common nails.

Cut the perimeter channel to length for the sill and side jambs, mitering the ends at 45°. Align the front edge of the channel flush with the front edge of the exterior wall sheathing. Drill pilot holes every 12" through the channels (if not provided), and fasten the channels in place with 1" galvanized flat-head screws. *Note: Paint screw heads white to help conceal them.*

For the header, cut a channel to length, mitering the ends at 45°, then cut it in half lengthwise, using a utility knife. Align one-half of the channel flush with the exterior face of the sheathing, and fasten in place with 1" galvanized flat-head screws.

Set two blocks into the sill channel, one against each jamb—do not place mortar between blocks and channels. Place a ¼" flat spacer against the first block. Mix glass block mortar and liberally butter the leading edge of another block, then push it tight against the first block. Make sure the joint is filled with mortar.

(continued)

Lay the remainder of the first course, building from both jambs toward the center. Use flat spacers between blocks to maintain proper spacing. Plumb and level each block as you work, then also check the entire course for level. Tap blocks into place using the rubber handle of the trowel—do not use metal tools with glass block. Butter both sides of the final block in the course to install it.

At the top of the course, fill any depression at the top of each mortar joint with mortar and insert a ¼" T-spacer, then lay a ⅜" bed of mortar for the next course. Lay the blocks for each course, using T-spacers to maintain proper spacing. Check each block for level and plumb as you work.

Test the mortar as you work. When it can resist light finger pressure, remove the T-spacers (inset) and pack mortar into the voids, then tool the joints with a jointing tool. Remove excess mortar with a damp sponge or a bristle brush.

To ease block placement in the final course, trim the outer tabs off one side of the T-spacers using tin snips. Install the blocks of the final course. After the final block is installed, work in any mortar that has been forced out of the joints.

9

Expansion strip

Cut an expansion strip for the header 1½" wide and to length. Slide it between the top course of block and the header of the rough opening. Apply a bead of construction adhesive to the top edge of the remaining half of the header channel, and slide it between the expansion strip and header.

10

Clean the glass block thoroughly with a wet sponge, rinsing often. Allow the surface to dry, then remove cloudy residue with a clean, dry cloth. Caulk between glass block and channels and between channels and framing members before installing exterior trim. After brick molding is installed, allow the mortar to cure for two weeks. Apply sealant.

Variation: Glass Block Window Kits ▸

Some glass block window kits do not require mortar. Instead, the blocks are set into the perimeter channels and the joints are created using plastic spacer strips. Silicone caulk is then used to seal the joints.

Preassembled glass block windows are simple to install. These vinyl-clad units have a nailing flange around the frame, which allows them to be hung using the same installation techniques as for standard windows with a nailing flange (pages 263 to 264).

TUBULAR SKYLIGHTS

Any interior room can be brightened with a tubular skylight. Tubular skylights are quite energy-efficient and are relatively easy to install, with no complicated framing involved.

The design of tubular skylights varies among manufacturers, with some using solid plastic reflecting tubes and others using flexible tubing. Various diameters are also available. Measure the distance between the framing members in your attic before purchasing your skylight to be sure it will fit.

This project shows the installation of a tubular skylight on a sloped, asphalt-shingled roof. Consult the dealer or manufacturer for installation procedures on other roof types.

A tubular skylight is an economical way to introduce more sunlight into a room without embarking on a major framing project.

Tools & Materials ▸

Pencil	Reciprocating saw	Wire cutters	Stiff wire
Drill	Pry bar	Utility knife	2" roofing nails or flashing screws
Tape measure	Screwdriver	Chalk	Roofing cement
Wallboard saw	Hammer	Tubular skylight kit	Eye and ear protection

HOW TO INSTALL A TUBULAR SKYLIGHT

Drill a pilot hole through the ceiling at the approximate location for your skylight. Push a stiff wire up into the attic to help locate the hole. In the attic, make sure the space around the hole is clear of any insulation. Drill a second hole through the ceiling at the centerpoint between two joists.

Center the ceiling ring frame over the hole and trace around it with a pencil. Carefully cut along the pencil line with a wallboard saw or reciprocating saw. Save the wallboard ceiling cutout to use as your roof-hole pattern. Attach the ceiling frame ring around the hole with the included screws.

In the attic, choose the most direct route for the tubing to reach the roof. Find the center between the appropriate rafters and drive a nail up through the roof sheathing and shingles.

4

Use the wallboard ceiling cutout, centered over the nail hole, as a template for the roof opening. Trace the cutout onto the roof with chalk. Drill a starter hole to insert the reciprocating saw blade, then cut out the hole in the roof. Pry up the lower portion of the shingles above the hole. Remove any staples or nails around the hole edge.

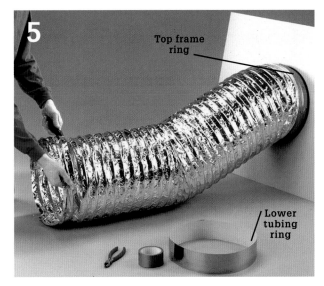

5

Top frame ring

Lower tubing ring

Pull the tubing over the top frame ring. Bend the frame tabs out through the tubing, keeping two or three rings of the tubing wire above the tabs. Wrap the junction three times around with included PVC tape. Then, in the attic, measure from the roof to the ceiling. Stretch out the tubing and cut it to length with a utility knife and wire cutters. Pull the loose end of tubing over the lower ring and wrap it three times with PVC tape.

6

Lower the tubing through the roof hole and slide the flashing into place with the upper portion of the flashing underneath the existing shingles. This is easier with two people, one on the roof and one in the attic.

7

Secure the flashing to the roof with 2" roofing nails or flashing screws. Seal under the shingles and over all the nail heads with roofing cement. Attach the skylight dome and venting to the frame with the included screws.

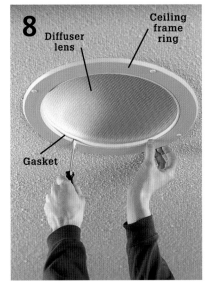

8

Ceiling frame ring

Diffuser lens

Gasket

Pull the lower end of the tubing down through the ceiling hole. Attach the lower tubing ring to the ceiling frame ring and fasten it with screws. Attach the gasket to the diffuser lens and work the gasket around the perimeter of the ceiling frame. Repack any insulation around the tubing in the attic.

FRAMING AN EXTERIOR DOOR

The rough opening for a new exterior door should be framed after the interior preparation work is done, but before the exterior wall surfaces are removed. The methods for framing the opening will vary, depending on what type of construction your house was built with (see photos, below).

Make sure the rough opening is 1 inch wider and ½ inch taller than the dimensions of the door you plan to install, including the jambs, to allow space for adjustment during installation.

Because exterior walls are always load-bearing, the framing for an exterior door requires a larger header than those used for interior partition walls.

Local building codes will specify a minimum size for the door header based on the size of your rough opening.

Always build temporary supports to hold up the ceiling if your project requires that you cut or remove more than one stud in a load-bearing wall.

When you finish framing, measure across the top, middle, and bottom of the door opening to make sure it is uniform from the top to the bottom. If there are major differences in the opening size, adjust the studs so the opening is uniform.

Tools & Materials ▶

Tape measure	Hammer
Pencil	Pry bar
Level	Nippers
Plumb bob	2× lumber
Reciprocating saw	⅜" plywood
Circular saw	10d nails
Handsaw	

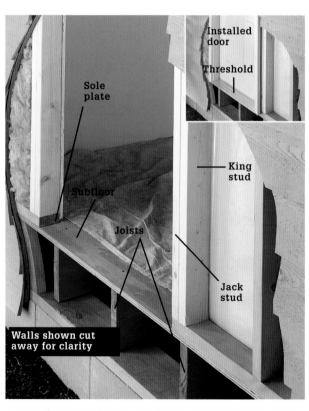

A new door opening in a platform-framed house has studs that rest on a sole plate running across the top of the subfloor. The sole plate is cut away between the jack studs so the threshold for the new door can rest directly on the subfloor.

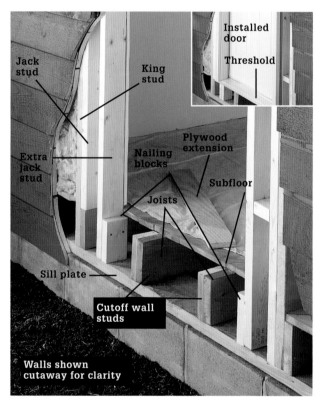

A new door opening in a balloon-framed house has studs extending past the subfloor to rest on the sill plate. Jack studs rest either on the sill plate or on top of the joists. To provide a surface for the door threshold, install nailing blocks, and extend the subfloor out to the ends of the joists using plywood.

HOW TO FRAME AN EXTERIOR DOOR

1

Prepare the project site and remove the interior wall surfaces.

2

Measure and mark the rough opening width on the sole plate. Mark the locations of the jack studs and king studs on the sole plate. (Where practical, use existing studs as king studs.)

3

If king studs need to be added, measure and cut them to fit between the sole plate and top plate. Position the king studs and toenail them to the sole plate with 10d nails.

(continued)

4

Check the king studs with a level to make sure they are plumb, then toenail them to the top plate with 10d nails.

5

Measuring from the floor, mark the rough opening height on one king stud. For most doors, the recommended rough opening is ½" taller than the height of the door unit. This line marks the bottom of the door header.

6

Determine the size of the header needed and measure and mark where the top of it will fit against a king stud. Use a level to extend the lines across the intermediate studs to the opposite king stud.

7

Cut two jack studs to reach from the top of the sole plate to the rough opening marks on the king studs. Nail the jack studs to the king studs with 10d nails driven every 12". Make temporary supports if you are removing more than one stud.

Use a circular saw set to maximum blade depth to cut through the old studs that will be removed. The remaining stud sections will be used as cripple studs for the door frame. Note: Do not cut king studs. Make additional cuts 3" below the first cuts, then finish the cuts with a handsaw.

Knock out the 3" stud sections, then tear out the rest of the studs with a pry bar. Clip away any exposed nails using a nippers.

Build a header to fit between the king studs on top of the jack studs. Use two pieces of 2× lumber sandwiched around ½" plywood. Attach header to the jack studs, king studs, and cripple studs using 10d nails.

Use a reciprocating saw to cut through the sole plate next to each jack stud, then remove the sole plate with a pry bar. Cut off any exposed nails or anchors using a nippers.

FRENCH DOORS

French doors are made up of two separate doors, hinged on opposing jambs of a doorway. The doors swing out from the center of the doorway and into or out from a room. Like most doors, French doors are typically sold in prehung units, but are also available separately. They are generally available only in wood with a variety of designs and styles to choose from.

Before purchasing a prehung French door unit, determine the size of doors you will need. If you are planning to install the doors in an existing doorway, measure the dimensions of the rough opening from the unfinished framing members, then order the unit to size—the manufacturer or distributor will help you select the proper unit.

You can also pick the prehung unit first, then alter an existing opening to accommodate it (as shown in this project). In this case, build the rough opening a little larger than the actual dimensions of the doors to accommodate the jambs. Prehung units typically require adding 1 inch to the width and ½ inch to the height.

If the doorway will be in a load-bearing wall, you will need to make temporary supports (pages 321 to 322) and install an appropriately sized header. Sizing the header (depth) is critical: it's based on the length of the header, the material it's made from, and the weight of the load it must support. For actual requirements, consult your local building department.

When installing French doors, it is important to have consistent reveals between the two doors and between the top of the doors and the head jamb. This allows the doors to close properly and prevents the hinges from binding.

Tools & Materials ▸

Tape measure	Prehung French
Circular saw	door unit
4-ft. level	2 × 4 and 2 × 6 lumber
Hammer	10d & 16d
Handsaw	common nails
Drill	Wood shims
Utility knife	8d finish nails
Nail set	Reciprocating saw
½" plywood	Eye and ear protection

Traditionally, French doors open onto the patio or lush garden of a backyard. But you can create stylish entrances inside your home by bringing French doors to formal dining rooms, sitting rooms, dens, and master suites.

HOW TO INSTALL FRENCH DOORS

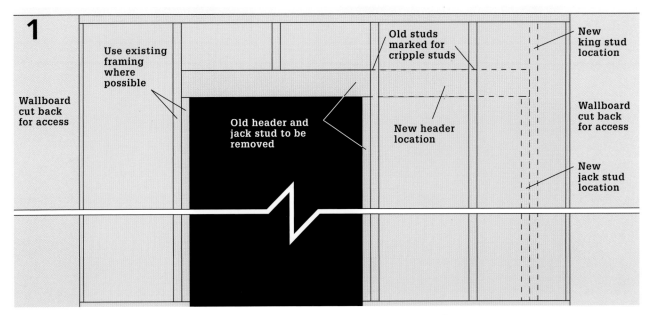

1

Wallboard cut back for access

Use existing framing where possible

Old header and jack stud to be removed

Old studs marked for cripple studs

New header location

New king stud location

Wallboard cut back for access

New jack stud location

Shut off power and water to the area. Remove the wall surfaces from both sides of the wall (page 262), leaving one stud bay open on each side of the new rough opening. Also remove or reroute any wiring, plumbing, or ductwork. Lay out the new rough opening, marking the locations of all new jack and king studs on both the top and bottom plates. Where practical, use existing framing members. To install a new king stud, cut a stud to size and align with the layout marks; toenail to the bottom plate with 10d common nails, check for plumb, then toenail to the top plate to secure. Finally, mark both the bottom and top of the new header on one king stud, then use a level to extend the lines across the intermediate studs to the opposite king stud. If using existing framing, measure and mark from the existing jack stud.

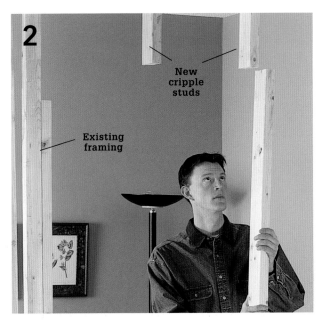

2

New cripple studs

Existing framing

Cut the intermediate studs at the reference marks for the top of the header using a reciprocating saw. Pry the studs away from the sole plates and remove—the remaining top pieces will be used as cripple studs.

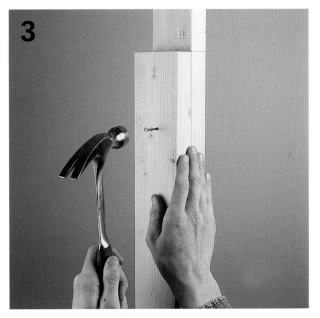

3

To install a jack stud, cut the stud to fit between the sole plate and the bottom of the header, as marked on the king stud. Align it at the mark against the king stud, then fasten it in place with 10d common nails driven every 12".

(continued)

WINDOW & DOOR PROJECTS

301

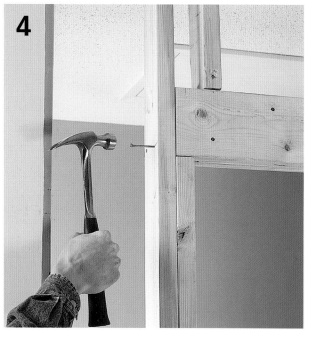

4

Build the header to size (page 12, and page 262, step 9) and install, fastening it to the jack studs, king studs, and cripple studs using 16d common nails. Use a handsaw to cut through the bottom plate so it's flush with the inside faces of the jack studs. Remove the cutout portion.

5

Finish the walls before installing the doors, then set the prehung door unit into the framed opening so the jamb edges are flush with the finished wall surfaces and the unit is centered from side to side.

6

Using a level, adjust the unit to plumb one of the side jambs. Starting near the top of the door, insert pairs of shims driven from opposite directions into the gap between the framing and the jamb, sliding the shims until they are snug. Check the jamb to make sure it remains plumb and does not bow inward.

7

Working down along the jamb, install shims near each hinge and near the floor. Make sure the jamb is plumb, then anchor it with 8d finish nails driven through the jamb and shims and into the framing. Leave the nail heads partially protruding so the jamb can be readjusted later if necessary.

8

Install shims at the other side jamb, aligning them roughly with the shims of the first jamb. With the doors closed, adjust the shims so the reveal between the doors is even and the tops of the doors are aligned.

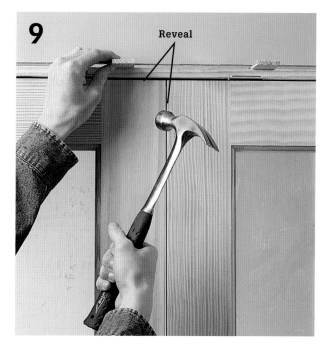

9

Reveal

Shim the gap between the header and the head jamb to create a consistent reveal along the top when the doors are closed. Insert pairs of shims every 12". Drive 8d finish nails through the jambs and shims and into the framing members.

10

Drive all the nails fully, then set them below the surface of the wood with a nail set. Cut off the shims flush with the wall surface using a handsaw or utility knife. Hold the saw vertically to prevent damage to the door jamb or wall. Install the door casing.

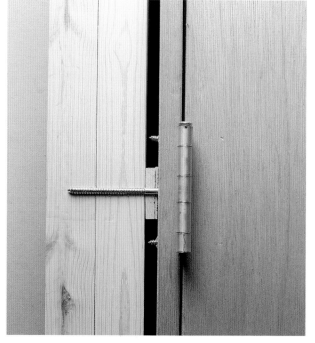

Option: Replace the center mounting screw on each hinge with a 3" wood screw to provide extra support for door hinges and jambs. These long screws extend through the side jambs and deep into the framing members. Be careful not to overtighten screws, which will cause the jambs to bow.

HANGING A NEW DOOR IN AN OLD JAMB

If you've got an unsightly or damaged door to replace but the jamb and trimwork are in good condition, there's no need to remove the jambs. Instead, buy a slab door and hang it in the existing jamb. It's an excellent way to preserve existing moldings and trim, especially if you live in an old home, and you won't have to color-match a new jamb to its surroundings.

If the hinges are also in good condition, you can reuse them as well. This may be particularly desirable in a historic home with ornate hinges. Most home centers stock six-panel slab doors, or you can order them in a variety of styles and wood types. For aesthetic and practical reasons, choose a door size as close to the original door as possible.

The process for hanging the door involves shimming the door into position in the jamb, scribing the ends and edges, and trimming or planing it to fit the opening. You'll also need to chisel hinge mortises in the door edge to accommodate the jamb hinge positions.

This is a project where patience and careful scribing will pay dividends in the end. Have a helper on hand to hold the door in position as you scribe and fit the door in place.

Tools & Materials ▸

Door shims	Power plane or hand plane
Tape measure	Hammer
Compass	Chisel
Combination square	Drill/driver
Utility knife	Hole saw
Circular saw	Spade bit
C-clamps	Slab door
Self-centering drill bit	Hinge screws
Masking tape	Eye and ear protection

Before **After**

Installing a new door in an old jamb dramatically updates the curb appeal of your home.

HOW TO HANG A NEW DOOR IN AN OLD JAMB

Have a helper hold the new door in place against the jamb from inside the room. Slide a pair of thick shims under the door to raise it up slightly off the floor or threshold. Move the shims in or out until the door's top and side rails are roughly even with the jamb so it looks balanced in the opening, then make a mark along the top edge of the the door.

Use pieces of colored masking tape to mark the outside of the door along the hinge edge. This will help keep the door's orientation clear throughout the installation process.

Use a pencil compass, set to an opening of ³⁄₁₆", to scribe layout lines along both long edges of the door and across the top. These lines will create a clear space for the hinges and door swing. If the bottom of the door will close over carpet, set the dividers for ½" and scribe the bottom edge. Remove the door and transfer these scribe lines to the other door face.

Lay the door on a sturdy bench or across a pair of sawhorses with the tape side facing up. Score the top and bottom scribe lines with a utility knife to keep the wood fibers from splintering when you cut across the ends.

(continued)

Trim the door ends with a circular saw equipped with a fine-cutting blade. Run the saw base along a clamped straightedge with the blade cutting 1/16" on the waste side of the layout lines. Check to make sure the blade is set square to the saw base before cutting. Use a power planer or hand plane to plane the door ends to the layout lines.

Stand the door on edge and use a power planer or hand plane to plane down to the edge of the scribe lines. Set the tool for a fine cut; use a 1/16" cutting depth for power planing and a shallower cutting depth for a hand plane. Try to make each planing pass in long strokes from one end of the door to the other.

Shim the door back into position in the jamb with a helper supporting it from behind. Set the door slightly out from the doorstop moldings so you can mark the hinge locations on the door face.

Use a combination square or one of the hinge leaves to draw hinge mortise layout lines on the door edge. Score the layout lines with a utility knife.

9

Cut shallow hinge leaf mortises in the door edge with a sharp chisel and hammer. First score the mortise shape with a straightedge and utility knife or a chisel, then make a series of shallow chisel cuts inside the hinge leaf area. Pare away this waste so the mortise depth is slightly deeper than the hinge leaf thickness.

10

Set the hinges in the door mortises, and drill pilot holes for the hinge screws. Attach the hinges to the door.

11

Hang the door in the jamb by tipping it into place so the top hinge leaf rests in the top mortise of the jamb. Drive one screw into this mortise. Then set the other leaves into their mortises and install the remaining hinge screws.

12

Bore holes for the lockset and bolt using a hole saw and spade bit. If you're reusing the original hardware, measure the old door hole sizes and cut matching holes in the new door, starting with the large lockset hole. For new locksets, use the manufacturer's template and hole sizing recommendations to bore the holes. Install the hardware.

ENTRY DOORS

Few parts of a house have a more dramatic effect on the way your home is perceived than the main entry door. A lovely, well-maintained entryway that is tastefully matched architecturally to the house can utterly transform a home's appearance. In fact, industry studies have suggested that upgrading a plain entry door to a higher-end entry door system can pay back multiple times in the resale of your house. But perhaps more importantly, depending on your priorities, it makes a great improvement in how you feel about your home. Plus, it usually pays benefits in home security and energy efficiency as well.

If you are replacing a single entry door with a double door or a door with a sidelight or sidelights, you will need to enlarge the door opening (see pages 321 to 323). Be sure to file your plans with your local building department and obtain a permit. You'll need to provide temporary support from the time you remove the wall studs in the new opening until you've installed and secured a new door header that's approved for the new span distance (see pages 321 to 322).

The American Craftsman style door with sidelights) installed in this project has the look and texture of a classic wood door, but it is actually created from fiber-glass. Today's fiberglass doors are quite convincing in their ability to replicate wood grain, while still offering the durability and low-maintenance of fiberglass.

Tools & Materials ▸

Tape measure	Framing nails
Level	Finish nails
Reciprocating saw	Nail set
Caulk & caulk gun	Finishing materials
Hammer	Eye and ear protection
Shims	

After

Before

Replacing an ordinary entry door with a beautiful new upgrade has an exceptionally high payback in increased curb appeal and in perceived home value, according to industry studies.

HOW TO REPLACE AN ENTRY DOOR

Remove the old entry door by cutting through the fasteners driven into the jamb with a reciprocating saw (see pages 321 and 322). If the new door or door system is wider, mark the edges of the larger rough opening onto the wall surface. If possible, try to locate the new opening so one edge will be against an existing wall stud. Be sure to include the thickness of the new framing you'll need to add when removing the wall coverings.

Frame in the new rough opening for the replacement door (see pages 49 to 51). The instructions that come with the door will recommend a rough opening size, which is usually sized to create a ½" gap between the door and the studs and header. Patch the wall surfaces.

Cut metal door dripcap molding to fit the width of the opening and tuck the back edge up behind the wallcovering at the top of the door opening. Attach the dripcap with caulk only–do not use nails or screws.

Unpack the door unit and set it in the rough opening to make sure it fits correctly. Remove it. Make sure the subfloor is clean and in good repair, and then apply heavy beads of caulk to the underside of the door sill and to the subfloor in the sill installation area. Use plenty of caulk.

(continued)

5

Set the door sill in the threshold and raise the unit up so it fits cleanly in the opening, with the exterior trim flush against the wall sheathing. Press down on the sill to seat it in the caulk and wipe up any squeeze-out with a damp rag

6

Use a 6' level to make sure the unit is plumb and then tack it to the rough opening stud on the hinge side, using pairs of 10d nails driven partway through the casing on the weatherstripped side of the door (or the sidelight). On single, hinged doors, drive the nails just above the hinge locations. *Note: Many door installers prefer deck screws over nails when attaching the jambs. Screws offer more gripping strength and are easier to adjust, but covering the screw heads is more difficult than filling nail holes.*

7

Drive wood shims between the jamb and the wall studs to create an even gap. Locate the shims directly above the pairs of nails you drove. Double check the door with the level to make sure it is still plumb.

8

Drive shims between the jamb on the latch side of the unit and into the wall stud. Only drive the nails part way. Test for plumb again and then add shims at nail locations (you may need to double-up the shims, as this gap is often wider than the one on the hinge side). Check to make sure the door jamb is not bowed.

9

Drive finish nails at all remaining locations, following the nailing schedule in the manufacturer's installation instructions.

10

Use a nail set to drive the nail heads below the wood surface. Fill the nail holes with wood putty (you'll get the best match if you apply putty that's tinted to match the stained wood after the finish is applied). The presence of the wood shims at the nail locations should prevent the jamb from bowing as you nail.

11

Install the lockset, strikeplates, deadbolts or multipoint locks, and any other door hardware. If the door finish has not been applied, you may want to do so first, but generally it makes more sense to install the hardware right away so the door can be operated and locked. Attach the door sill to the threshold and adjust it as needed, normally using the adjustment screws (inset).

12

Apply your door finish if it has not yet been applied. Read the manufacturer's suggestions for finishing very closely and follow the suggested sequences. Some manufacturers offer finish kits that are designed to be perfectly compatible with their doors. Install interior case molding and caulk all the exterior gaps after the finish dries.

STORM DOORS

Storm doors protect the entry door from driving rain or snow. They create a dead air buffer between the two doors that acts like insulation. When the screen panels are in place, the door provides great ventilation on a hot day. And, they deliver added security, especially when outfitted with a lockset and a deadbolt lock.

If you want to install a new storm door or replace an old one that's seen better days, your first job is to go shopping. Storm doors come in many different styles to suit just about anyone's design needs. And they come in different materials, including aluminum, vinyl, and even fiberglass. (Wood storm doors are still available but not in preassembled form.) All these units feature a prehung door in a frame that is mounted on the entry door casing boards. Depending on the model you buy, installation instructions can vary. Be sure to check the directions that come with your door before starting the job.

Tools & Materials ▸

Drill/driver	Masking tape
Tape measure	Hacksaw
Finish nails	Level
Screwdriver	Primer
Paintbrush	Paint
Hammer	Eye and ear protection

A quality storm door helps seal out cold drafts, keeps rain and snow off your entry door, and lets a bug-free breeze into your home when you want one.

HOW TO INSTALL A STORM DOOR

Test-fit the door in the opening. If it is loose, add a shim to the hinge side of the door. Cut the piece with a circular saw and nail it to the side of the jamb, flush with the front of the casing.

Install the drip edge molding at the top of the door opening. The directions for the door you have will explain exactly how to do this. Sometimes it's the first step, like we show here; otherwise it's installed after the door is in place.

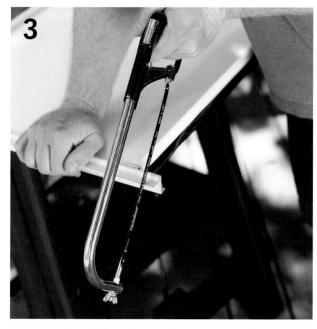

Measure the height of the opening and cut the hinge flange to match this measurement. Use a hacksaw and work slowly so the saw won't hop out of the cut and scratch a visible area of the hinge.

Lift the door and push it tightly into the opening. Partially drive one mounting screw near the bottom and another near the top. Check the door for plumb, and when satisfied, drive all the mounting screws tight to the flange.

(continued)

5

Measure from the doorway sill to the rain cap to establish the length of the latch-side mounting flange.

6

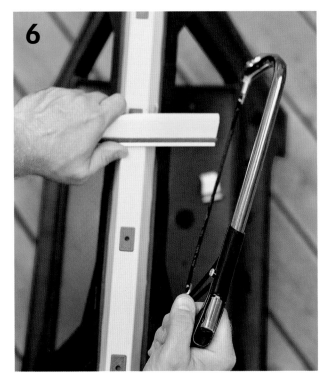

Cut the latch-side flange with a hacksaw. Work carefully so you don't pull out the weatherstripping from the flange channel as you cut. Install the flange with screws.

7

To install the door sweep, slide it over the bottom of the door and install its mounting screws loosely. Make sure the sweep forms a tight seal with the sill, then tighten the screws.

8

Mount the lockset on the door. Tape can help hold the outside hardware in place while you position the inner latch and tighten the screws.

9

Install the strike plates for both the lockset (shown here) and the deadbolt locks. These plates are just screwed to the door jamb where the lock bolt and deadbolt fall. Install the deadbolt.

10

Begin installing the door closer by screwing the jamb bracket in place. Most of these brackets have slotted screw holes so you can make minor adjustments without taking off the bracket.

11

Install the door closer bracket on the inside of the door. Then mount the closer on the jamb bracket and the door bracket. Usually the closer is attached to these with some form of short locking pin.

12

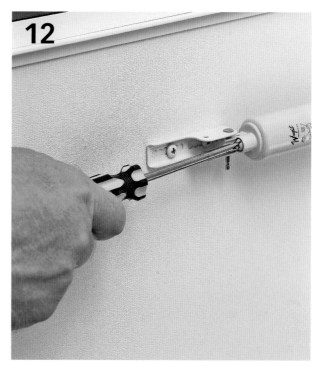

Adjust the automatic door closer so it closes the door completely without slamming it. The adjustment is usually made by turning a set screw in and out with a screwdriver.

ATTIC ACCESS LADDERS

Pull-down attic ladders provide instant access to your attic space, making it easy to store and retrieve items without squeezing through a tight access panel. You can replace an existing access panel with a ladder kit or install the ladder in a more convenient location.

When purchasing an access ladder, consider the amount of use it will get. A basic wooden ladder system may be sufficient for occasional use a few times a year. More frequent use may call for a more sturdy model, such as an aluminum ladder, or a disappearing staircase.

It's important that the ladder you install is the proper size for your ceiling height. Never install one that is shorter than your ceiling height. Compare units for weight load, incline angle, and quality of materials when choosing the right ladder for your home. Although most attic ladders are installed the same way, always follow the manufacturer's directions.

Tools & Materials ▸

Tape measure	2× lumber (for framing
Framing square	and temporary
Pencil	supports)
Wallboard saw	2" and 1¼"
Reciprocating saw	drywall screws
Drill and bits	Casing
Hammer	1 × 4 lumber (for
Hacksaw	temporary ledgers)
Attic access ladder kit	Eye and ear protection
Stiff wire	Dust mask
3" deck screws	

An attic access ladder can turn an otherwise useless space into a handy storage area or roof access.

WINDOW & DOOR PROJECTS

HOW TO INSTALL AN ATTIC ACCESS LADDER

Mark the approximate location for the attic access door on the room ceiling. Drill a hole at one of the corners and push the end of a stiff wire up into the attic. In the attic, locate the wire and clear away insulation in the area. Using dimensions provided by the manufacturer, mark the rough opening across the framing members, using one of the existing joists as one side of the frame. Add 3" to the rough opening length dimension to allow for the headers.

If the width of your ladder unit requires that you cut a joist, build temporary supports in the room below to support each end of the cut joist to prevent damage to your ceiling. Use a reciprocating saw to cut through the joist at both end marks, then remove the cut piece. *Caution: Do not stand on the cut joist.*

Cut two headers to fit between the joists using 2× lumber the same size as your ceiling joists. Position the headers perpendicular to the joists, butting them against the cut joists. Make sure the corners are square, and attach the headers with three 3" deck screws into each joist.

Cut a piece of 2× lumber to the length of the rough opening to form the other side of the frame. Square the corners, and attach the side piece to each header with three 3" deck screws.

(continued)

5

Cut the rough opening in the ceiling using a wallboard saw. Use the rough opening frame to guide your saw blade.

6

Fasten the edges of the wallboard to the rough opening frame using 1¼" screws spaced every 8". Prepare the ladder's temporary support clips according to the manufacturer's directions.

7

If your ladder does not include support clips, attach 1 × 4 boards at both ends of the opening, slightly overlapping the edges, to act as ledgers to support the unit while fastening.

8

With a helper, lift the unit through the opening and rest it on the ledgers. Make sure the unit is square in the frame and the door is flush with the ceiling surface. Shim the unit as needed. *Note: Do not stand on the unit until it is firmly attached to the framing.*

9

Attach the ladder unit to the rough framing with 10d nails or 2" screws driven through the holes in the corner brackets and hinge plates. Continue fastening the unit to the frame, driving screws or nails through each side of the ladder frame into the rough frame. Remove the temporary ledgers or support clips when complete.

10

Open the ladder, keeping the lower section folded back. With the tape measure along the top of the rail, measure the distance from the end of the middle section to the floor on each rail. Subtract 3" and mark the distances on the right and left rails of the third section. Use a square to mark a cutting line across the rails. Place a support under the lower section and trim along the cutting line with a hacksaw. (For wooden ladders, see manufacturer's directions.)

11

Fully extend the ladder and test-fit the adjustable feet on the rails. Adjust the feet so there are no gaps in the hinges and the feet are flush with the floor. Drill through the rails, using a recommended size bit, and attach the adjustable feet with included nuts, washers, and bolts.

12

Install casing around the edges to cover the gap between the ceiling wallboard and the ladder frame. Leave a ⅜" clearance between the door panel and the casing.

WALKOUT PATIO DOORS

A walkout basement without a patio door seems incomplete. Yet many homes with direct access into the basement do not take full advantage of the feature. A sliding or swingout patio door allows several times the amount of natural light into a room that a single door lets in, even if the single door has a large bright panel. If there is a patio or deck on the exterior side of your basement door, enlarging the door will make moving guests and supplies through the doorway much easier and more comfortable.

When choosing a new patio door, you'll need to decide between models with hinged doors that swing out and close together, or ones with sliding door panels. Swinging doors tend to require less maintenance than sliding doors, and they offer better security. Sliding doors are a good choice if ventilation is one of your requirements, because the amount of air they let in is easy to regulate. You can also leave a sliding door open without the wind catching it and causing it to slam or break.

Enlarging a door opening requires that you make structural changes to your house, so it almost always requires a building permit. During construction you will need to provide temporary support to replace the bearing being done by the wall studs you'll need to cut. And when you install the new door, the framed opening must have a substantial header. Check with your local building department for the header requirements. Because basement ceilings may be shorter than 8 feet, you may need to use a header that's fabricated from engineered beams to meet the load-bearing requirements within the available space.

Tools & Materials ▶

Circular saw	Self-adhesive
Reciprocating saw	rubber flashing
with bi-metal blade	Building paper
Handsaw	Drip edge molding
10d, 16d nails	Panel adhesive
2½" deck screws	Fiberglass insulation
½" plywood	Case molding
Hammer	Eye and ear protection

BEFORE AFTER

Replacing a single door with a sliding patio door is a great way to add light to a walkout basement and create an inviting entryway into your home.

HOW TO INSTALL A PATIO DOOR

Build a temporary support wall. Use doubled 2 × 4s (or 4 × 4s) for the top plate and support posts. The wall should extend at least 2' past the planned door opening in each direction and cannot be more than 24" away from the bearing wall. Secure the support wall to the floor and to the ceiling.

Remove the old door and the wallcoverings in the project area. If there are light switches or receptacles in the demolition area, shut off their power supply at the main service panel and then remove cover plates. To remove the old door, take off the case molding and then cut through the nails by sawing between the jambs and the frame with a reciprocating saw and bi-metal blade (inset).

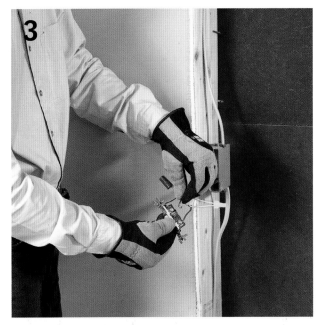

Relocate wiring elements such as switches and receptacles so they are safely outside the new door area. You will need an electrical permit for this and possibly an on-site inspection. If you are not experienced with home wiring, hire an electrician for this part of the job.

Remove wall studs in the project area. If they are difficult to remove, cut them through the center with a reciprocating saw first. Watch out for nails driven in through the exterior side.

(continued)

5

Frame the rough opening so it is sized according to the door manufacturer's recommendation. Install the new king studs if needed and then install the jack studs.

6

Install the new header by driving 16d nails through the king stud and into the ends of the header. You can make your own structural header by sandwiching a strip of ½" plywood between two pieces of dimensional lumber (inset). Assemble the header with construction adhesive and 10d nails or 2½" deck screws. You can also purchase an engineered header.

7

Cut through the exterior wall materials. You can either mark the corners of the framed opening by driving a nail out from the side, or simply use the framed opening as guidance for your reciprocating saw. Also cut through the sole plate at the edges of the opening so the cut end is flush with the jack stud face.

8

Lift the door unit or frame into the opening, with a helper. Test the fit. Trace the edges of the preattached brickmold onto the outside wall, or place a piece of brickmold next to the door and trace around the perimeter to establish cutting lines (inset). Remove the door.

9

Cut along the brickmold cutting lines with a saw set to a cutting depth equal to the thickness of the siding and the wall sheathing. Finish the cuts at the corners with a handsaw. Thoroughly vacuum the floor in the door opening.

10

Seal the framed opening by installing strips of building paper or self-adhesive rubber flashing product. Make sure that the top strip overlaps any seams you create. If the patio door is exposed, attach drip edge molding to the top of the framed opening.

11

Apply a bead of exterior-rated panel adhesive to the door threshold. Also apply adhesive to the back surface of the preattached brickmold or the nailing flange (whichever your door has).

12

Set the door in position so the brickmold or nailing flange is flush against the outside of the framed opening. Center it in the opening, side to side. Tack the door near the top of each side and then check with a level. Install shims where necessary so the door is plumb. Re-hang the door in the frame, if it has been removed.

13

Fill the gaps around the door with minimal expanding foam or with loosely backed fiberglass insulation (foam makes a better seal). Patch the wall and attach case molding (see page 79). If your door does not have preattached brickmold, cut and attach molding on the outside.

ATTIC & BASEMENT PROJECTS

In the quest to find additional living space in an existing home, the first thing to consider is converting unused space in an attic or basement. Such an undertaking is not to be taken lightly, but it is well within reach of any energetic and careful DIYer, and the rewards are substantial. Real-estate agents report that nothing improves the market value of your home like adding a bedroom or bathroom to the basic specs of your home, and adding any living space can help a growing family stay in a home at a fraction of what it would cost to sell and move into a new, larger dwelling.

This chapter alone cannot give you all the information you need to tackle such a major project as converting an attic or basement. You will want to consult the earlier chapters in this book, as many of those projects may well be part of your major construction project. You'll also need to seek out other sources of information, such as good books on wiring, plumbing, and carpentry skills, and practice at those skills. But this book, and especially this chapter, can give you a valuable overview of this kind of work as well as offer some key projects that will make your renovation truly special.

IN THIS CHAPTER:
- Evaluating Your Attic
- Evaluating Your Basement
- Controlling Moisture
- Insulating Basements & Attics
- Framing Soffits
- Stairways
- Building Attic Floors
- Building Attic Kneewalls
- Framing Attic Ceilings
- Adding a Basements Bath
- Installing a Gas Fireplace

EVALUATING YOUR ATTIC

Start your attic evaluation with a quick framing inspection. If the roof is framed with rafters, you can continue to the next test. If it's built with trusses, however, consider remodeling your basement instead. The problem is that the internal supports in trusses leave too little space to work with, and trusses cannot be altered.

The next step is to check for headroom and overall floor space. Most building codes call for 7½ feet of headroom over 50 percent of the "usable" floor space, which is defined as any space with a ceiling height of at least 5 feet Remember that these minimums apply to the finished space—after the flooring and ceiling surfaces are installed. Other things can affect headroom, as well, such as reinforcing the floor frame, and increasing rafter depth for strength or insulation.

You may also find various supports in your attic that are there to strengthen your roof but may limit your space. Collar ties are horizontal boards that join two rafters together in the upper third of the rafter span. They prevent rafter uplift in high winds. Often collar ties can be moved up a few inches but cannot be removed. Rafter ties join rafters in the lower third of their span to prevent spreading. In most attics, the ceiling or floor joists serve as rafter ties. Purlins are horizontal boards that run at right angles to the rafters and are supported by struts. These systems shorten the rafter span, allowing the use of smaller lumber for the rafters. You

Rafter framing creates open space in an attic because the rafters carry most of the roof's weight.

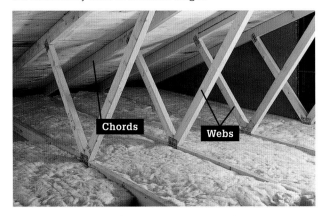

Trusses are made of interconnected cords and webs, which close off most of the attic space.

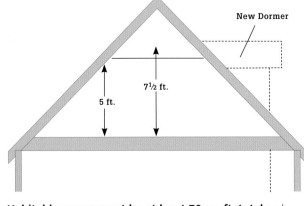

Habitable rooms must be at least 70 sq. ft. total and measure at least 7' in any one direction. To meet headroom requirements, 50% of the usable floor space must have a ceiling height of 7½' You can add to your floor space and headroom by adding protruding windows called *dormers*. In addition to space, dormers add light and ventilation to your attic.

may be allowed to substitute kneewalls for purlins and struts. If you'll need to have any support system altered or moved, consult an architect or engineer.

The rafters themselves also need careful examination. Inspect them for signs of stress or damage, such as cracks, sagging, and insect infestation. Look for dark areas indicating roof leaks. If you find leaks or you know your roofing is past its useful life, have it repaired or replaced before you start the finishing process. And even if the rafters appear healthy, they may be too small to support the added weight of finish materials. Small rafters can also be a problem if they don't provide enough room for adequate insulation.

At this point, it's a good idea to have a professional check the structural parts of your attic, including the rafters and everything from the floor down. In some cases, finishing an attic is like adding a story to your home, which means that the structure must have adequate support for the new space. Attic floors are often built as ceiling frames for the level below and are not intended to support living space. Floors can be strengthened with additional joists, known as sister joists or with new joists installed between the existing ones.

Support for the attic floor is provided by the load-bearing walls below and, ultimately, by the foundation. If these elements can't support the finished attic, they'll need to be reinforced. This may be as simple as strengthening the walls with plywood panels or as complicated as adding support posts and beams or reinforcing the foundation.

In addition to these structural matters, there are a few general code requirements you should keep in mind as you inspect your attic. If you plan to add a bedroom, it will need at least one exit to the outside. This can be a door leading to an outside stairwell or an egress window. Most codes also have minimum requirements for ventilation and natural light, which means you may have to add windows or skylights.

One of the largest expenses of finishing an attic is in providing access: You'll need a permanent stairway at least 36 inches wide, with room for a 36-inch landing at the top and bottom. This is an important planning issue because adding a stairway affects the layout and traffic patterns of the attic as well as the floor below.

Finally, take an inventory of existing mechanicals in your attic. While plumbing and wiring runs can be moved relatively easily, other features, such as chimneys, must be incorporated into your plans. This is a good time to have your chimney inspected by a fire official and to obtain the building code specifications for framing around chimneys.

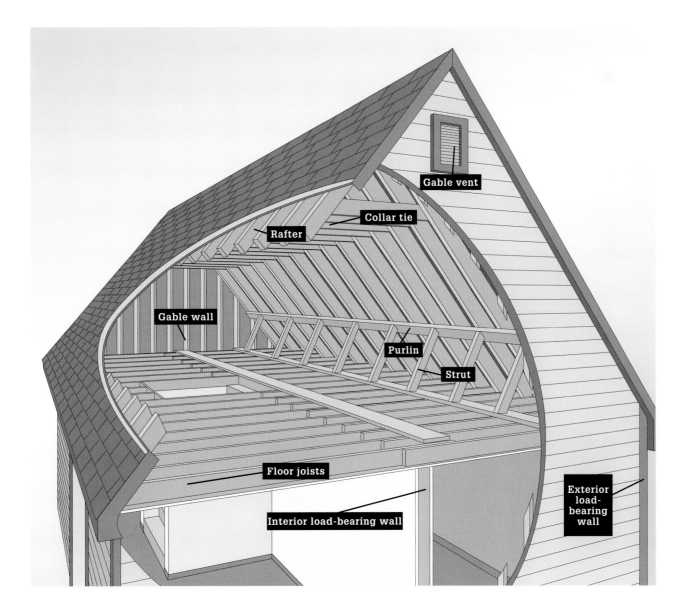

EVALUATING YOUR BASEMENT

The two things that put an end to most basement finishing plans are inadequate headroom and moisture. Begin your evaluation by measuring from the basement floor to the bottom of the floor joists above. Most building codes require habitable rooms to have a finished ceiling height of 7½ feet, measured from the finished floor to the lowest part of the finished ceiling. However, obstructions, such as beams, soffits, and pipes, (spaced at least 4 feet on center) usually can hang down 6 inches below that height. Hallways and bathrooms typically need at least 7-foot ceilings.

While it's impractical to add headroom in a basement, there are some ways of working around the requirements. Ducts and pipes often can be moved, and beams and other obstructions can be incorporated into walls or hidden in closets or other uninhabitable spaces. Also, some codes permit lower ceiling heights in rooms with specific purposes, such as recreation rooms. If headroom is a problem, talk to the local building department before you dash your dreams.

If your basement passes the headroom test, you can move on to the next issue: moisture. For a full discussion on this critical matter, see Controlling Moisture, on page 330. Be aware that moisture problems must be corrected before you start the finishing process.

A well-built basement is structurally sound and provides plenty of support for finished space, but before you cover up the walls, floor, and ceiling, check for potential problems. Inspect the masonry carefully. Large cracks may indicate shifting of the soil around the foundation; severely bowed or out-of-plumb walls may be structurally unsound. Small cracks usually cause moisture problems rather than structural woes, but they should be sealed to prevent further cracking. Contact an engineer or foundation contractor for help with foundation problems. If you have an older home, you may find sagging floor joists overhead or rotted wood posts or beams; any defective wood framing will have to be reinforced or replaced.

Your basement's mechanicals are another important consideration. The locations of water heaters, pipes, wiring, circuit boxes, furnaces, and ductwork can have a significant impact on the cost and difficulty of your project. Can you plan around components, or will they have to be moved? Is there enough headroom to install a suspended ceiling so mechanicals can remain accessible? Or, will you have to reroute pipes and ducts to increase headroom? Electricians and HVAC contractors can assess your systems and suggest modifications.

Aside from being dark and scary places, unfinished basements often harbor toxic elements. One of the most common is *radon*, a naturally occurring radioactive gas that is odorless and colorless. It's believed that prolonged exposure to high levels of radon can cause lung cancer. The Environmental Protection Agency has free publications to help you test for radon and take steps to reduce the levels in your house. For starters, you can perform a "short-term" test using a kit from a hardware store or home center. Look for the phrase "Meets EPA requirements" to ensure the test kit is accurate. Keep in mind that short-term tests are not as

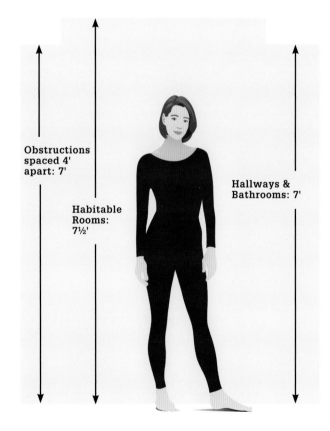

Obstructions spaced 4' apart: 7'

Habitable Rooms: 7½'

Hallways & Bathrooms: 7'

Basement headroom is often limited by beams, ducts, pipes, and other elements. Typical minimums for ceiling height are shown here: 7½' for habitable rooms; 7' for bathrooms and hallways; 7' for obstructions spaced no less than 4' apart.

Rerouting service lines and mechanicals adds quickly to the expense of a project, so consider your options carefully.

Weakened or undersized joists and other framing members must be reinforced or replaced.

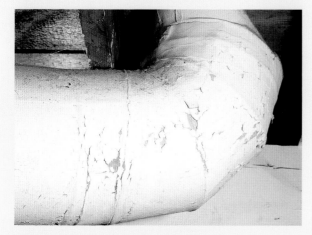

Old insulation containing asbestos poses a serious health risk if it is deteriorating or is disturbed.

Minor cracks such as these in masonry walls and floors usually can be sealed and forgotten, while severe cracking may indicate serious structural problems.

conclusive as professional, long-term tests. If your test reveals high levels of radon, contact a radon specialist.

Another basement hazard is insulation containing asbestos, which was commonly used in older homes for insulating ductwork and heating pipes. In most cases, this insulation can be left alone provided it's in good condition and is protected from damage. If you fear the insulation in your basement poses a hazard, contact an asbestos abatement contractor to have it evaluated or safely removed.

Also check the local codes for exits from finished basements—most codes require two. The stairway commonly serves as one exit, while the other can be a door to the outside, an egress window, or a code-compliant *bulkhead* (an exterior stairway with cellar doors). Each bedroom will also need an egress window or door for escape.

Stairways must also meet local code specifications. If yours doesn't, you'll probably have to hire someone to rebuild it. See page 344 for an overview of typical staircase requirements.

As a final note, if you're planning to finish the basement in a new house, ask the builder how long you should wait before starting the project. Poured concrete walls and floors need time to dry out before they can be covered. Depending on where you live, you may be advised to wait up to two years, just to be safe.

CONTROLLING MOISTURE

Basement moisture can destroy your efforts to create a functional living space. Over time, even small amounts of moisture can rot framing, turn wallboard to mush, and promote the growth of mold and mildew. Before proceeding with your basement project, you must deal with any moisture issues. The good news is that moisture problems can be resolved, often very easily.

Basement moisture appears in two forms: condensation and seepage. Condensation comes from airborne water vapor that turns to water when it contacts cold surfaces. Vapor sources include humid outdoor air, poorly ventilated appliances, damp walls, and water released from concrete. Seepage is water that enters the basement by infiltrating cracks in the foundation or by leeching through masonry, which is naturally porous. Often caused by ineffective exterior drainage, seepage comes from rain or groundwater that collects around the foundation or from a rising water table.

If you have a wet basement, you'll see evidence of moisture problems. Typical signs include peeling paint, white residue on masonry (called efflorescence), mildew stains, sweaty windows and pipes, rusted appliance feet, rotted wood near the floor, buckled floor tile, and strong mildew odor.

To reduce condensation, run a high-capacity dehumidifier in the basement. Insulate cold-water pipes to prevent condensate drippage, and make sure your dryer and other appliances have vents running to the outside. Extending central air conditioning service to the basement can help reduce vapor during warm, humid months.

Crawlspaces can also promote condensation, as warm, moist air enters through vents and meets cooler interior air. Crawlspace ventilation is a source of ongoing debate, and there's no universal method that applies to all climates. It's best to ask the local building department for advice on this matter.

Solutions for preventing seepage range from simple do-it-yourself projects to expensive, professional jobs requiring excavation and foundation work. Since it's often difficult to determine the source of seeping water, it makes sense to try some common cures before calling in professional help. If the simple measures outlined here don't correct your moisture problems, you must consider more

Repairing cracks restores the integrity of concrete foundation walls that leak, but it is often only a temporary fix. Selecting an appropriate repair product and doing careful preparation will make the repair more long lasting. A hydraulic concrete repair product like the one seen here is perfect for basement wall repair because it actually hardens from contact with water.

extensive action. Serious water problems are typically handled by installing footing drains or sump pump systems. Footing drains are installed around the foundation's perimeter, near the footing, and they drain out to a distant area of the yard. These usually work in conjunction with waterproof coatings on the exterior side of the foundation walls. Sump systems use an interior underslab drainpipe to collect water in a pit, and water is ejected outside by an electric sump pump.

Installing a new drainage system is expensive and must be done properly. Adding a sump system involves breaking up the concrete floor along the basement's perimeter, digging a trench, and laying a perforated drainpipe in a bed of gravel. After the sump pit is installed, the floor is patched with new concrete. Installing a footing drain is far more complicated. This involves digging out the foundation, installing gravel and drainpipe, and waterproofing the foundation walls. A footing drain is considered a last-resort measure.

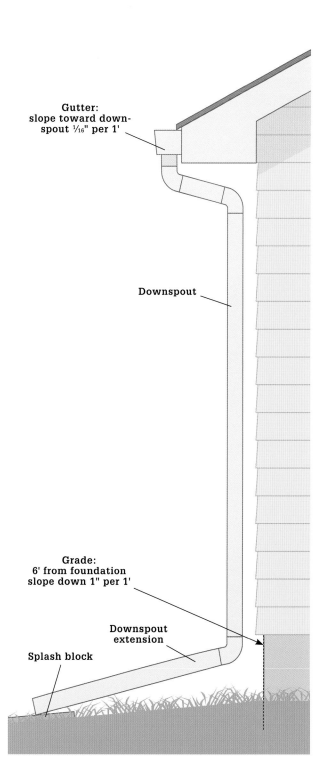

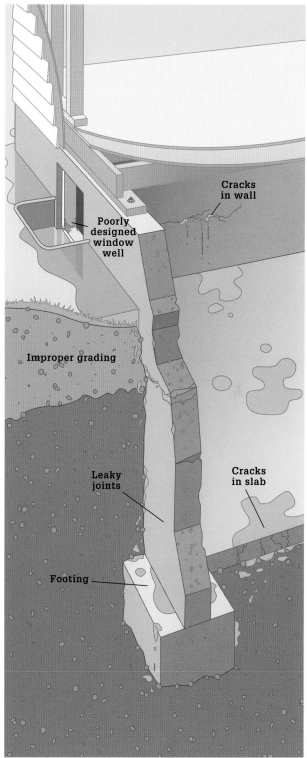

Improve your gutter system and foundation grade to prevent rainwater and snowmelt from flooding your basement. Keep gutters clean and straight. Make sure there's a downspout for every 50' of roof eave, and extend downspouts at least 8' from the foundation. Build up the grade around the foundation so that it carries water away from the house.

Common causes of basement moisture include improper grading around the foundation, inadequate or faulty gutter systems, condensation, cracks in foundation walls, leaky joints between structural elements, and poorly designed window wells. More extensive problems include large cracks in the foundation, damaged or missing drain tiles, a high water table, or the presence of underground streams. Often, a combination of factors is at fault.

HOW TO SEAL CRACKS IN A FOUNDATION WALL

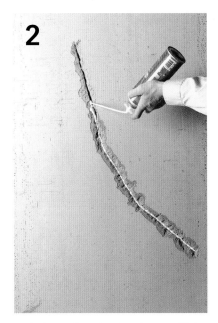

To repair a stable crack, chisel cut a keyhole cut that's wider at the base then at the surface, and no more than ½" deep. Clean out the crack with a wire brush.

To help seal against moisture, fill the crack with expanding insulating foam, working from bottom to top.

Mix hydraulic cement according to the manufacturer's instructions, then trowel it into the crack, working from the bottom to top. Apply cement in layers no more than ¼" thick, until the patch is slightly higher than the surrounding area. Feather cement with the trowel until it's even with the surface. Allow to dry thoroughly.

HOW TO SKIM-COAT A FOUNDATION WALL

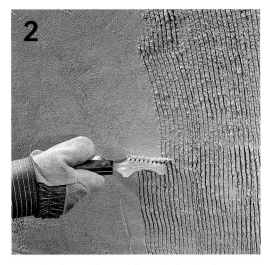

Resurface heavily cracked masonry walls with a water-resistant masonry coating such as surface bonding cement. Clean and dampen the walls according to the coating manufacturer's instructions, then fill large cracks and holes with the coating. Finally, plaster a ¼" layer of the coating on the walls using a square-end trowel. Specially formulated heavy-duty masonry coatings are available for very damp conditions.

Scratch the surface with a paintbrush cleaner or a homemade scratching tool after the coating has set up for several hours. After 24 hours, apply a second, smooth coat. Mist the wall twice a day for three days as the coating cures.

PREVENTING MOISTURE IN BASEMENTS

Waterproof Paint ▸

Masonry paints and sealers, especially those that are described as waterproof, are rather controversial products. Some manufacturers claim that applying a coat of their waterproof paint will create a seal that can hold back moisture, even under light hydrostatic pressure. Others suggest only that their product, when applied to a basement wall, will create a skin that inhibits water penetration from the interior side.

Masonry paints do hold up better on concrete surfaces than other types, largely because they are higher in alkali and therefore less reactive with cement-based materials. But they also can trap moisture in the concrete, which will cause the paint to fail prematurely and can cause the concrete to degrade, especially if the water freezes. Read the product label carefully before applying waterproof paint to your basement walls, and make sure to follow the preparation protocols carefully. If you have a foundation wall with an active water-seepage problem, address the problem with the other methods shown in this section, including grading and gutters. A coat of waterproof paint is not going to make your basement drier.

Clean your gutters and patch any holes. Make sure the gutters slope toward the downspouts at about 1/16" per 1' Add downspout extensions and splash blocks to keep roof runoff at least 8' away from the foundation.

Cover window wells that will otherwise allow water into a basement. Covering them with removable plastic is the easiest way to keep them dry. Covers on egress window wells must be easily removed from inside. If you prefer to leave wells uncovered, add a gravel layer and a drain to the bottom of the well. Clean the well regularly to remove moisture-heavy debris.

DRAINAGE SOLUTION: HOW TO REGRADE

Establish the drainage slope. The yard around your house should slant away from the house at a minimum slope of ¾" per 1' for at least 10'. Till the soil or add new soil around the house perimeter. Drive a wood stake next to the house and another 10' out. Tie a level mason's string between the stakes, and then move the string down at least 2½" at the end away from the house, establishing your minimum slope.

Redistribute the soil with a steel garden rake so the grade follows the slope line. Add topsoil at the high end if needed. Do not excavate near the end of the slope to accommodate the grade. The goal is to build up the yard to create runoff.

Use a grading rake to smooth out the soil so it slopes at an even rate. Drive additional stakes and tie off slope lines as necessary.

Tamp the soil with a hand tamper or plate compactor. Fill in any dips that occur with fresh dirt. Lay sod or plant grass or groundcover immediately.

DRAINAGE SOLUTION: HOW TO INSTALL A DRY WELL

A dry well is a simple way to channel excess water out of low-lying or water-laden areas, such as the ground beneath a gutter downspout. It usually consists of a buried drain tile running from a catch basin positioned at the problem spot, to a collection container some distance away. In the project shown here, a perforated plastic drain tile carries water from the catch basin to a plastic trashcan that has been punctured and filled with stones. The runoff water percolates into the soil as it makes its way along the drain tile and through the dry well.

Set a length of perforated drain tile on the gravel running the full length of the trench. If the trench starts at a downspout, position a grated catch basin directly beneath the downspout and attach the end of the drain tile to the outlet port.

Dig a trench (10" wide, 14" deep) from the area where the water collects to the catch basin location, sloping the trench 2" per 8'. Line the trench with landscape fabric and then add a 1" layer of gravel on top of the fabric.

Dry Wells for Drainage ▸

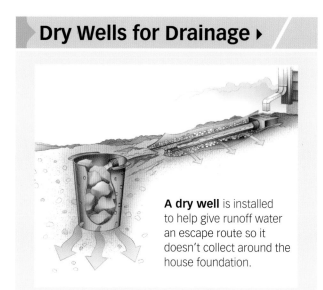

A dry well is installed to help give runoff water an escape route so it doesn't collect around the house foundation.

Install the dry well by digging a hole that's big enough to hold a plastic trash can. Drill 1" holes through the sides and bottom of the can every 4 to 6". Also cut an access hole at the top of the can for the drain tile. Set the can in the hole and insert the free end of the tile. Backfill dirt over the tile and trench and plant grass or cover with sod.

ATTIC & BASEMENT PROJECTS

INSULATING BASEMENTS & ATTICS

Insulating basements is a tricky topic. In colder climates, insulation is necessary for the successful creation of a livable basement room. But the practice is fraught with pitfalls that can cause a host of problems. There are two definites, in any case:

- The exterior is often a better location for new insulation than the interior of basement walls.
- Never insulate a wall that is not dry and well drained.

Almost all of the issues surrounding basement wall insulation have to do with moisture and water vapor. How these issues affect your plans will depend a great deal on your climate, as well as on the specific characteristics of your house, your building site, and whether or not your home was built with foundation drains and a pumping system.

Until recently, basements most often were insulated from the inside because it is easier, faster, and cheaper. A typical installation would be to attach furring strips (2 × 2, 2 × 3, or 2 × 4) to the foundation wall at standard wall stud spacing, and then fill in between the strips with fiberglass insulation batts. A sheet plastic vapor barrier would then be stapled over the insulated wall prior to hanging wallcoverings (usually wallboard or paneling). Experience has shown this model to be a poor method, very frequently leading to moisture buildup within the wall that encourages mold growth and has a negative impact on the indoor air quality. The building materials also tend to fail prematurely from the sustained moisture presence.

If your basement plans require that you insulate the foundation walls, make certain that the walls are dry and that any moisture problems are corrected (see previous section). Then, look first at the exterior.

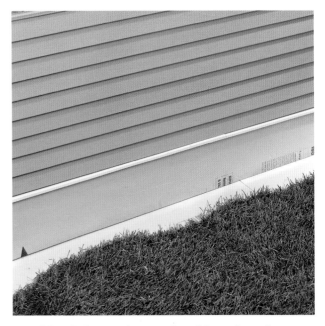

Install insulation on the exterior of the wall, not the interior, whenever possible. Exterior insulation results in a warm wall that will have less of a problem with condensation. The wall also can breathe and dry out more easily if the interior side has no vapor retarder.

Because it is often unnecessary to insulate the full height of the wall, you may find that an exterior apron insulating approach is easier than you imagined (see pages 338 to 339). If your circumstances absolutely require that you insulate inside, use insulating products such as extruded polystyrene or foil-faced isocyanurate that do not absorb water or provide food for mold. You should also keep the wall isolated from the insulation: attach the insulation first, seal it, and then construct a stud wall that has no direct contact with the concrete or concrete block wall (see pages 340 to 341).

High-Efficiency Upgrades ▸

Replace old gas water heaters with high-efficiency models. Not only will this save money on your utilities bill, it will also keep your basement warmer. The more efficient your heater is, the less air it will require for fuel combustion, which means less fresh cold air is drawn into the basement to replace the air consumed by the appliance.

HOW TO INSULATE BASEMENTS & ATTICS

Install rigid foam insulation in basements, both on the exterior and the interior. Extruded polystyrene (sometimes called beadboard) is an economical choice for larger areas, and it forms its own vapor-retarding layer when properly installed and sealed. High-density polystyrene and isocyanurate are denser insulation boards with higher R-values. Isocyanurate usually has one or two foil faces. It is used to seal rim joists but is a good choice for any basement wall location.

Improve insulation and thermal seals in attics and other parts of your house to keep basements warmer in winter. By reducing the amount of warm air that escapes through the roof, you will reduce the amount of cold air that is drawn in through the basement walls to replace the air.

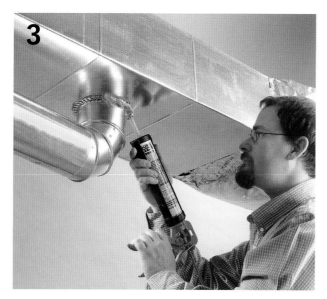

Seal furnace ducts to reduce air leakage. Use a combination of UL 181-rated duct tape (foil tape) and duct mastic. If cold-air return ducts leak, for example, they will draw air from the basement into the air supply system. As with heat loss through the attic, this will cause fresh cold air to enter the basement and lower the ambient temperature.

What Is a Dry Wall? ▸

When building experts warn never to insulate a wall that isn't dry, they have something very specific in mind. A wall that appears dry to the touch may not be classified as dry if it is constantly evaporating small amounts of moisture that will be blocked if you install any kind of vapor retarder (as is likely the case). A dry wall (suitable for interior insulation) is one that is superficially dry to the touch and also meets these criteria:

- Has a positive drainage system capable of removing water that accumulates from any source (this is typically in the form of a sump pump).
- The foundation wall and floor are structured to provide drainage of water away from the house, often through the use of drain tiles and footing drains

ATTIC & BASEMENT PROJECTS

337

INSULATION SOLUTION: EXTERIOR APRON INSULATION

Insulate foundation walls on the exterior side (and not the interior) whenever you can. The easiest way to accomplish this is by installing insulation in the apron area only, so you do not have to excavate all the way to the bottom of the wall. By adding a layer of horizontal insulation in the bottom of the trench, you can realize at least 70 percent of the energy savings of insulating the whole wall, while limiting your digging to 18 inches down and 24 inches out.

Because you will be adding width to the foundation wall by installing exterior insulation, you will need to install flashing to cover the top of the insulation layer and whatever protective wall surface you cover it with. For the project shown here, the insulation is covered with panelized veneer siding over 1-inch-thick rigid foam insulation boards. For extra protection, coat the cleaned walls with a layer of bituminous coating before installing the insulation boards.

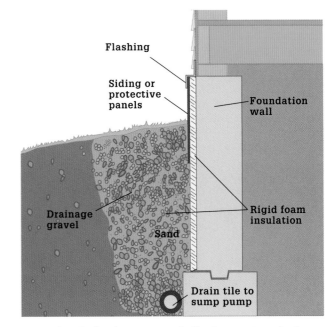

Apron insulation is an easy and effective way to make the basement more comfortable, and save energy without causing any moisture issues.

HOW TO INSTALL APRON INSULATION

Dig an 18 × 24" wide trench next to the wall being insulated. Make sure to first have your local utilities company flag any lines that may be in the area.

Coat the wall with a layer of bituminous coating once you have cleaned it with a hose or pressure washer. The coating simply creates another layer of moisture protection for the basement.

Line the trench with a 2"-thick layer of coarse sand, and then strips of rigid foam insulation. The sand should slope away from the house slightly, and the insulation strips should butt up against the foundation wall.

Install drip edge flashing to protect the tops of the insulation board and new siding. Pry back the bottom edge of the siding slightly and slip the flashing flange up underneath the siding. The flashing should extend out far enough to cover both layers of new material (at least 1½ to 2").

Bond strips of rigid foam insulation board to the foundation wall using a panel adhesive that is compatible with foam. Press the tops of the boards up against the drip edge flashing. When all the boards are installed, tape over the butted seams with insulation tape.

Install siding or another protective layer over the insulation. Here, 2 × 4' faux stone panels are being used. Once the panels are in place, backfill the trench with dirt or gravel. Make sure to maintain minimum slopes for runoff at grade.

INSULATION SOLUTION FOR DRY WALLS: INTERIOR WALL INSULATION

As a general rule, avoid insulating the interior side of your basement walls. It is best to leave breathing space for the concrete or block so moisture that enters through the walls is not trapped. If your exterior basement walls meet the definition of a dry wall (see page 337) however, adding some interior insulation can increase the energy efficiency of your basement. If you are building a stud wall for hanging wallcovering materials, you can insulate between the studs with rigid foam—do not use fiberglass batts and do not install a vapor barrier. If you are building a stud wall, it's a good idea to keep the wall away from the basement wall so there is an air channel between the two.

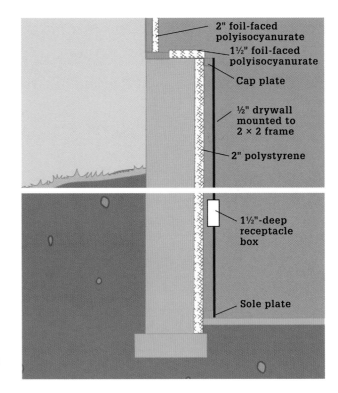

Interior insulation can be installed if your foundation walls meet the conditions for dry walls (see page 337). It is important to keep the framed wall isolated from the basement wall with a seamless layer of rigid insulation board.

HOW TO INSULATE AN INTERIOR BASEMENT WALL

1

2

Begin on the exterior wall by digging a trench and installing a 2"-thick rigid foam insulation board up to the bottom of the siding and down at least 6" below grade. The main purpose of this insulation is to inhibit convection and air transfer in the wall above grade. See pages 338 to 339 for more information on how to use flashing and siding to conceal and protect the insulation board.

Insulate the rim joist with strips of 2"-thick isocyanurate rigid insulation with foil facing. Be sure the insulation you purchase is rated for interior exposure (exterior products can produce bad vapors). Use adhesive to bond the insulation to the rim joist, and then caulk around all the edges with acoustic sealant.

Seal and insulate the top of the foundation wall, if it is exposed, with strips of 1½"-thick, foil-faced isocyanurate insulation. Install the strips using the same type of adhesive and caulk you used for the rim joist insulation.

Attach sheets of 2"-thick extruded polystyrene insulation to the wall from the floor to the top of the wall with construction adhesive. Make sure to clean the wall thoroughly and let it dry completely before installing the insulation.

Seal the gaps between the insulation boards with insulation vapor barrier tape. Do not caulk gaps between the insulation boards and the floor.

Install a stud wall by fastening the cap plate to the ceiling joists and the sole plate to the floor. If you have space, allow an air channel between the studs and the insulation. Do not install a vapor barrier.

FRAMING SOFFITS

Unfinished basements and other areas often contain elements like beams, pipes, and ductwork that may be vital to your house but become big obstacles to finishing the space. When you can't conceal the obstructions within walls, and you've determined it's too costly to move them, hide them inside a framed soffit or chase. This can also provide a place to run smaller mechanicals, like wiring and water supply lines.

You can frame a soffit with a variety of materials including 2 × 2 lumber and 1⅝-inch steel studs. Both work well because they're small and lightweight (though steel is usually easier to work with because it's always straight). For large soffits that will house lighting fixtures or other elements, you might want the strength of 2 × 4s or 3⅝-inch steel studs.

There may be code restrictions about the types of mechanicals that can be grouped together, as well as minimum clearances between the framing and what it encloses. Most codes also specify that soffits, chases, and other framed structures have fireblocking every 10 feet and at the intersections between soffits and neighboring walls. Remember too, that drain cleanouts and shutoff valves must be accessible, so you'll need to install access panels at these locations.

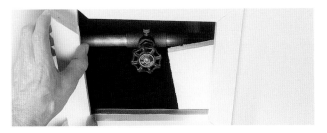

Soffits will require an access panel if they house electrical junction boxes or shutoffs for water or gas supply lines. You can plan these into your framing or create them after the wallcovering is installed, as in the framed opening above. Here, a wood frame is glued to the soffit to create support ledges for the removable wallboard cutout.

A soffit is a bump-out that drops down from the ceiling to conceal ductwork, recessed light fixtures and other obstructions.

VARIATIONS FOR BUILDING SOFFITS

2 × 2 soffit: Build two ladder-like frames for the soffit sides using standard 2 × 2s. Install braces every 16" or 24" to provide nailing support for the edges of the drywall. Attach the side frames to the joists on either side of the obstruction using nails or screws. Then, install crosspieces beneath the obstacle, tying the two sides together.

Simple steel-frame soffit: With ½" drywall, this construction works for soffits up to 16" wide; with ⅝" drywall, up to 24" wide. Use 1⅝, 2½, or 3⅝" steel studs and tracks (see page 41). Fasten a track to the ceiling and a stud to the adjoining wall using drywall screws. Cut a strip of drywall to form the side of the soffit, and attach a steel stud flush with the bottom edge of the strip using Type S screws. Attach the assembly to the ceiling track, then cut and install drywall panels to form the soffit bottom.

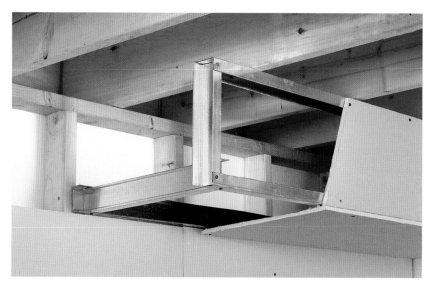

Steel-frame soffit with braces: Use 1⅝, 2½, or 3⅝" steel studs and tracks. Fasten a track to the ceiling and wall with drywall screws. Cut studs to form the side and bottom of the soffit, fasten them to the tracks every 16" or 24" on center, using Type S panhead screws, then join the pieces with metal angle (you can use a steel track cut in half lengthwise). Use a string line and locking clamps to help keep the frame straight and square during construction.

STAIRWAYS

Even though your basement most likely has an existing stairway, this essential element should still be part of your initial planning. Older basement staircases don't necessarily comply with modern building codes, and may need to be upgraded as part of your remodeling project. Making sure that the staircase meets or exceeds local building codes is only common sense; codes governing staircases were established based on time-tested realities about how people walk up and down stairs. Codes focus on safety and comfort, which should be your key concerns in any changes you make to your basement staircase.

Start with the basic measurements. Any staircase serving your basement should be as wide as possible, and comfortable to navigate. Otherwise, even the most beautiful basement rec room or home theater will be uninviting. Although you can build your own staircase (and you'll even find complete kits available that make the process fairly easy and straightforward), chances are that your basement already has a quite serviceable set of stairs. It's easy enough to adapt, upgrade, or renovate what's there, to specifically serve your remodeling goals.

Begin by fixing any obvious problems. Loose banisters or handrails, broken treads, risers, or balusters, or even squeaky stairs, should all be remedied as part of a basement renovation. Small staircase problems can often turn into larger issues, especially when the traffic on the stairs increases.

But even if the existing structure is sound and in good shape, you may want to upgrade some parts of the staircase. A new railing with turned balusters and a detailed banister can bring a fresh new perspective—not only to the staircase, but to the entire basement. Changes like this will probably not challenge your DIY expertise, and can be hugely rewarding.

Bigger changes, including adding a landing, changing the direction of all or part of the staircase, or completely reinforcing the staircase, may call for some professional help. Because staircases are such essential access points, carefully consider the changes you want to make and how likely you are to complete them quickly and completely on your own. If you have doubts, best to call in a pro to help out.

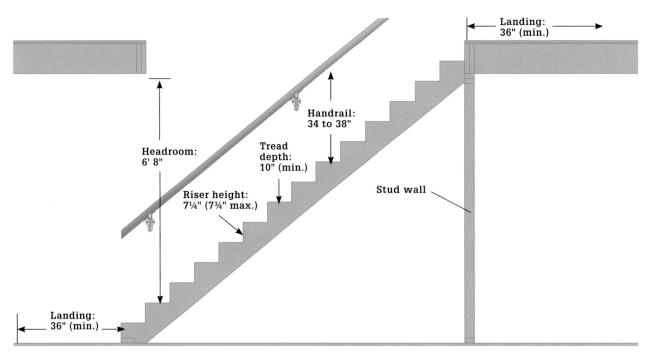

Basement stairs must be wide enough and within the allowable slope for rise and run. They also must have a grippable handrail and a clear landing area of at least 36 × 36" at both the top and bottom. They should be at least 36" wide with a minimum of 6' 8" of headroom. If your house was built prior to the 1960s, there is a good chance the basement stairs don't conform to these standards (they may not even come close). Because you will be creating livable space, most municipalities will require that you upgrade or replace your stairs to meet the above requirements. Even if your local codes don't demand it, however, you should make upgrading your stairs phase one of your project anyway. Safety and convenience are reason enough.

STAIRWAY STYLES

L-SHAPED STAIR

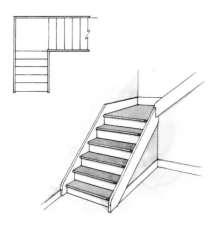

STRAIGHT STAIR WITH OPEN RISERS

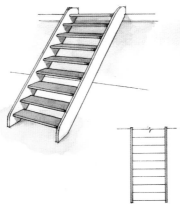

STANDARD SWITCHBACK STAIR

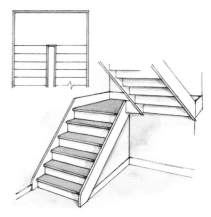

STRAIGHT STAIR

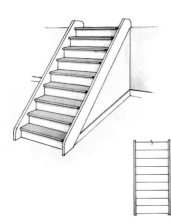

SWITCHBACK STAIR WITH WINDERS

SWITCHBACK STAIR WITH INTERMEDIATE FLIGHT

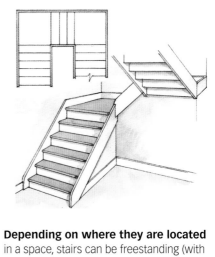

SIDE-FLIGHT STAIR

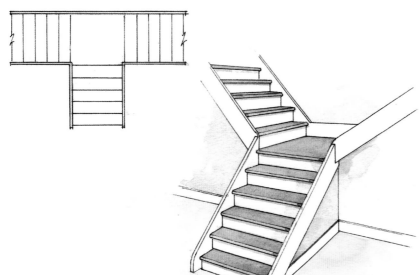

Depending on where they are located in a space, stairs can be freestanding (with no walls on either side) open on one side, or entirely enclosed by walls. As you will see, there are dozens of variations on these common types.

BUILDING ATTIC FLOORS

Before you build the walls that will define the rooms in your attic, you'll need a sturdy floor beneath it all. Existing floors in most unfinished attics are merely ceiling joists for the floor below and are too small to support a living space.

There are several options for strengthening your attic's floor structure. The simplest method is to install an additional, identically sized joist next to each existing joist, connecting the two with nails. This process is known as sistering.

Sistering doesn't work when joists are smaller than 2 × 6s, are spaced too far apart, or where there are obstructions, such as plaster keys, from the ceiling below. An alternative is to build a new floor by placing larger joists between the existing ones. By resting the joists on 2 × 4 spacers, you avoid obstructions and minimize damage to the ceiling surface below. However, be aware that the spacers will reduce your headroom by 1½ inches, plus the added joist depth.

To determine the best option for your attic, consult an architect, engineer, or building contractor, as well as a local building inspector. Ask what size of joists you'll need and which options are allowed in your area. Joist sizing is based on the span (the distance between support points), the joist spacing (typically 16 or 24 inches on center), and the type of lumber used. In most cases, an attic floor must be able to support 40 pounds per square foot of live load (occupants, furniture) and 10 psf dead load (wallboard, floor covering).

The floor joist cavities offer space for concealing the plumbing, wiring, and ductwork servicing your attic, so consider these systems as you plan. You'll also need to locate partition walls to determine if any additional blocking between joists is necessary.

When the framing is done, the mechanical elements and insulation are in place, and everything has been inspected and approved, complete the floor by installing ¾-inch tongue-and-groove plywood. If your remodel will include kneewalls, you can omit the subflooring behind the kneewalls, but there are good reasons not to: A complete subfloor will add strength to the floor, and will provide a sturdy surface for storage.

Tools & Materials ▸

Circular saw	Hammer or nail gun
Rafter square	2 × joist lumber
Drill	2 × 4 lumber
Caulk gun	¾" T&G plywood
16d, 10d, and 8d	Construction adhesive
common nails	2¼" drywall or deck screws
Tape measure	Eye and ear protection

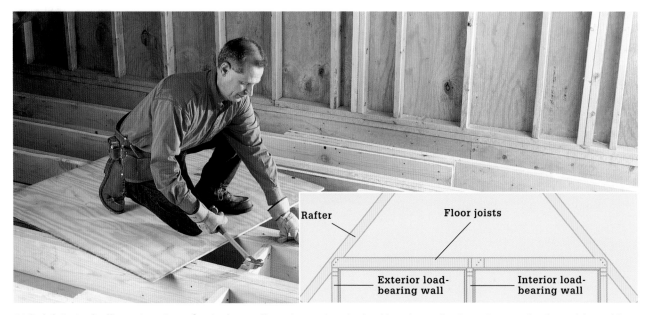

Attic joists typically rest on top of exterior walls and on an interior load-bearing wall, where they overlap from side to side and are nailed together. Always use a sheet of plywood as a platform while working over open joists.

HOW TO ADD SISTER JOISTS

Remove all insulation from the joist cavities and carefully remove any blocking or bridging between the joists. Determine the lengths for the sister joists by measuring the existing joists. Also measure at the outside end of each joist to determine how much of the top corner was cut away to fit the joist beneath the roof sheathing. *Note: Joists that rest on a bearing wall should overlap each other by at least 3".*

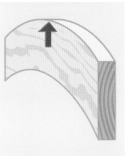

Before cutting, sight down both narrow edges of each board to check for crowning—upward arching along the length of the board. Draw an arrow that points in the direction of the arch. Joists must be installed "crown-up;" this arrow designates the top edge. Cut the board to length, then clip the top, outside corner to match the existing joists.

Set the sister joists in place, flush against the existing joists and with their ends aligned. Toenail each sister joist to the top plates of both supporting walls, using two 16d common nails.

Nail the joists together using 10d common nails. Drive three nails in a row, spacing the rows 12 to 16" apart. To minimize damage to the ceiling surface below caused by the hammering (such as cracking and nail popping), you can use an air-powered nail gun (available at rental stores), or 3" lag screws instead of nails. Install new blocking between the sistered joists, as required by the local building code.

HOW TO BUILD A NEW ATTIC FLOOR

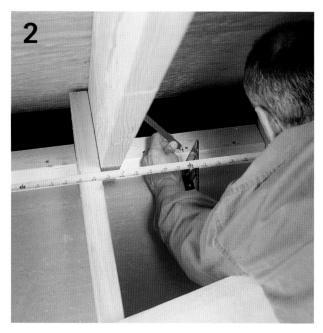

Remove any blocking or bridging from between the existing joists, being careful not to disturb the ceiling below. Cut 2 × 4 spacers to fit snugly between each pair of joists. Lay the spacers flat against the top plate of all supporting walls, and nail them in place with 16d common nails.

Create a layout for the new joists by measuring across the tops of the existing joists and using a rafter square to transfer the measurements down to the spacers. Following 16"-on-center spacing, mark the layout along one exterior wall, then mark an identical layout onto the interior bearing wall. Note that the layout on the opposing exterior wall will be offset 1½" to account for the joist overlap at the interior wall.

To determine joist length, measure from the outer edge of the exterior wall to the far edge of the interior bearing wall. The joists must overlap each other above the interior wall by 3". Before cutting, mark the top edge of each joist. Cut the joists to length, then clip the top outside corners so the ends can fit under the roof sheathing.

Set the joists in place on their layout marks. Toenail the outside end of each joist to the spacer on the exterior wall, using three 8d common nails.

Nail the joists together where they overlap atop the interior bearing wall, using three 10d nails for each. Toenail the joists to the spacers on the interior bearing wall, using 8d nails.

Install blocking or bridging between the joists, as required by the local building code. As a suggested minimum, the new joists should be blocked as close as possible to the outside ends and where they overlap at the interior wall.

HOW TO INSTALL SUBFLOORING

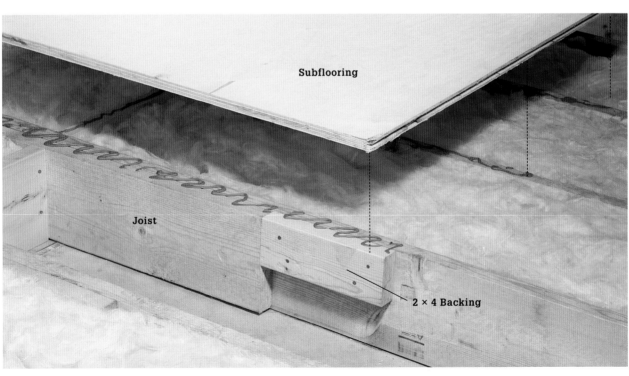

Subflooring

Joist

2 × 4 Backing

Install the subflooring only after all framing, plumbing, wiring, and ductwork is completed and has received the required building inspections. Also install any insulation and complete any caulking necessary for soundproofing. Fasten the sheets with construction adhesive and 2¼" screws, making sure the sheets are perpendicular to the joists and the end joints are staggered between rows. Where joists overlap at an interior bearing wall, add backing as needed to compensate for the offset in the layout. Nail a 2 × 4 or wider board to the face of each joist to support the edges of the intervening sheets.

BUILDING ATTIC KNEEWALLS

Attic kneewalls are short walls that extend from the attic floor to the rafters. They provide a vertical dimension to attic rooms, and without them, attics tend to feel cramped. Kneewalls are typically 5 feet tall, for a couple of reasons: That's the minimum ceiling height for usable floor space according to most building codes, and it defines a comfortable room without wasting too much floor space. The unfinished space behind kneewalls doesn't have to go to waste: It's great for storage and for concealing service lines. To provide access to this space, create a framed opening in the wall during the framing process.

Kneewalls are similar to partition walls, except they have beveled top plates and angle-cut studs that follow the slope of the rafters. The added stud depth created by the angled cut requires a 2 × 6 top plate. Before starting on your kneewall project, it may help to review the techniques for building a partition wall (see pags 39 to 41).

Tools & Materials ▸

Circular saw	T-bevel
Level	2 × 4 and 2 × 6 lumber
Chalk line	16d and 8d common nails
Tape measure	Eye and ear protection
Hammer	

Attic kneewalls are just the right height to be backdrops for furniture, and they make a perfect foundation for built-in storage units.

HOW TO BUILD A KNEEWALL

Create a storyboard using a straight 2 × 4. Cut the board a few inches longer than the planned height of the wall. Measure from one end and draw a line across the front edge of the board at the exact wall height.

At one end of the room, set the storyboard flat against the outer rafter. Plumb the storyboard with a level while aligning the height mark with the bottom edge of the rafter. Transfer the height mark onto the rafter edge, then make a mark along the front edge of the storyboard onto the subfloor. These marks represent the top and bottom wall plates.

3

Holding the storyboard perfectly plumb, trace along the bottom edge of the rafter to transfer the rafter slope onto the face of the storyboard.

4

Repeat the wall-plate marking process on the other end of the room. Snap a chalk line through the marks—across the rafters and along the subfloor. If necessary, add backing for fastening the top plate to the gable wall.

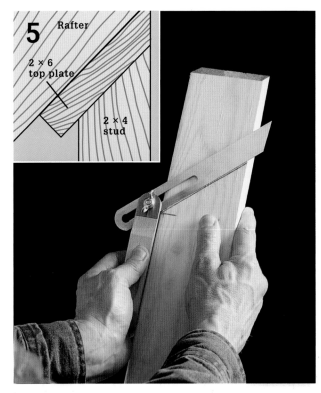

5

Rafter

2 × 6 top plate

2 × 4 stud

To cut a beveled edge on the top wall plate, set a T-bevel to match the rafter-slope line on the storyboard. Use the T-bevel to adjust the blade of a circular saw or tablesaw to the proper angle. Then, bevel-cut one edge of the 2 × 6 top plate. *Note: When the top plate is laid flat across the rafters, the front edge should be perpendicular to the floor.*

6

Mark the stud locations on the wall plates. Install the plates along the chalk lines, fastening them to the rafters and floor joists, respectively, using 16d nails. Measure and cut each stud to fit, angle-cutting the top end so that it meets flush with the top plate. Toenail each stud in place with three 8d nails.

FRAMING ATTIC CEILINGS

By virtue of sloping roofs, most attics naturally have "cathedral" ceilings. It's up to you whether to leave the peaks intact—and apply a finish surface all the way up to the ridge—or to frame in a horizontal ceiling, creating a flat surface that's more like a standard ceiling. Before deciding, consider the advantages and disadvantages of each treatment.

If your attic has collar ties—horizontal braces installed between opposing rafters—your planning should start with those. Are the ties high enough to meet the code requirements for attic headroom? If not, consult an architect or engineer to see if you can move them up a few inches (do not move or remove them without professional guidance). If the ties are high enough, you can incorporate them into a new ceiling or leave them exposed and wrap them with a finish material, such as wallboard or finish-grade lumber. Do not use collar ties as part of your ceiling frame.

A peaked ceiling is primarily an aesthetic option. Its height expands the visual space of the room, and its rising angles provide a dramatic look that's unique in most homes. Because a peaked ceiling encloses the rafter bays all the way up to the ridge, this treatment may require additional roof vents to maintain proper ventilation.

By contrast, a flat ceiling typically offers a cleaner, more finished appearance closer to that of a conventional room, and flat ceilings offer some practical advantages over peaked styles. First, they provide a concealed space above the ceiling, great for running service lines. If there are vents high on the gable walls, this open space can help ventilate the roof (make sure to insulate above the ceiling). The ceiling itself can hold recessed lighting fixtures or support a ceiling fan. And if your plans call for full-height partition walls, you may want a ceiling frame to enclose the top of the wall.

When determining the height of flat-ceiling framing, be sure to account for the floor and ceiling finishes. And remember that most building codes require a finished ceiling height of at least 90 inches.

Tools & Materials ▸

4' level	2 × 4 and 2 × 6 lumber
Chalk line	10d common nails
Circular saw	Eye and ear protection
Hammer	

Flat attic ceilings provide space for recessed light fixtures, vents, and speakers.

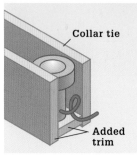

Exposed collar ties can add an interesting architectural element to a peaked ceiling. By adding to the existing ties, you can create a channel for holding small light fixtures.

Collar tie

Added trim

HOW TO FRAME A FLAT CEILING

Make a storyboard for the planned height of the ceiling frame. At one end of the attic, hold the storyboard plumb and align the height mark with the bottom edge of a rafter. Transfer the mark to the rafter. Repeat at the other end of the attic, then snap a chalk line through the marks. This line represents the bottom edge of the ceiling frame.

Using a level and the storyboard, level over from the chalk line and mark two outside rafters on the other side of the attic. Snap a chalk line through the marks. *Note: The storyboard is used merely as a straightedge for this step.*

Cut 2 × 6 joists to span across the rafters, angle-cutting the ends to follow the roof pitch. Check each joist for crowning to make sure you're cutting it so it will be installed with the crowned edge up. Make the overall length about ½" short so the ends of the joists won't touch the roof sheathing.

Nail each joist to the rafters with three 10d common nails at each end. Be sure to maintain 16 or 24" on-center spacing between joists to provide support for attaching wallboard or other finish material.

ADDING A BASEMENT BATH

Abathroom is an essential addition to any basement efficiency apartment because this room is key to making the as useful and independent of the upstairs space as possible. Of course, bathrooms are wonderful basement additions, regardless of what other types of rooms you may be adding.

Many new homes are plumbed with basement stub-outs in place. More likely, you'll need to break up the concrete floor to install a new drain and supply plumbing. With a jackhammer and some help, this is a manageable DIY project.

Because plastic pipes cannot be encased in concrete, they must be laid in granular fill beneath the basement floor. Potential locations for your bathroom are therefore limited by how close the main sewer line is to the floor service where it meets the main drain stack. Check local codes for other restrictions in your area.

Once you've cut into the main waste vent, there can be no drainage in the house until you have fully installed the new branch lines and sealed the joints. Have extra pipe and fittings on hand. Cutting through concrete produces lots of dust. Block off other areas of the basement with plastic sheeting, and wear an approved dust mask or respirator.

A half bath or three-quarter bath (as seen here) is a much-appreciated addition to your basement if you are adding new living spaces elsewhere on the basement level.

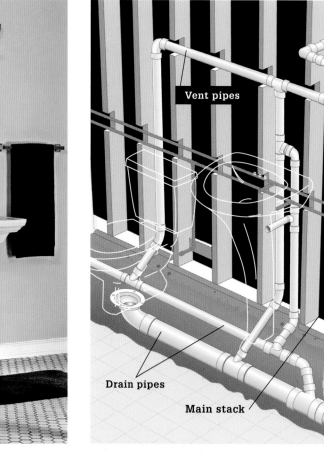

Our demonstration bathroom includes a shower, toilet, and pedestal sink arranged in a line to simplify trenching. A 2" drainpipe services the new shower and sink; a 3" pipe services the new toilet. The drainpipes converge at a Y-fitting joined to the existing main drain. The toilet and sink have individual vent pipes that meet inside the wet wall before extending up into the attic, where they join the main waste-vent stack.

HOW TO PLUMB A BASEMENT BATH

Wet wall location

Mark the proposed location of the bathroom on the basement floor using tape. Include the walls, wet wall, and fixture locations. The easiest configuration is to install all the fixtures against the wet wall, which will contain the water supply and vents. The drain lines should run parallel to the wet wall in the most direct route to the main waste-vent stack. Mark the drain line location (typically around 6" out from the wet wall).

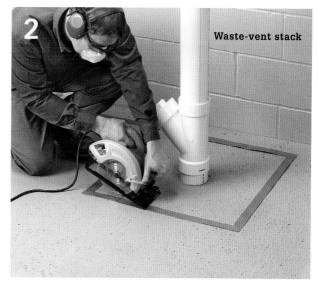

Waste-vent stack

Cut out the area around the main stack. Use a concrete saw or a circular saw with a masonry blade to score a 24 × 24" square cutting line around the waste-vent stack. The cut should be at least 1" deep.

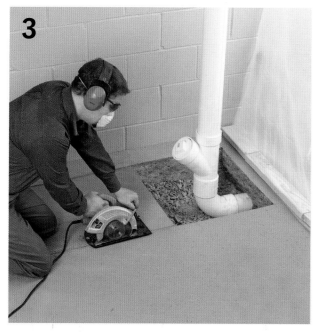

Remove concrete and dirt around the main stack. Using a cold chisel and hand maul, strike along the scored cutting lines to chip out the concrete around the main soil stack. If necessary, break up the concrete within the square so it can be removed. Take care not to damage the pipe. Excavate within the square to determine the depth of the sewer line where it meets the main stack.

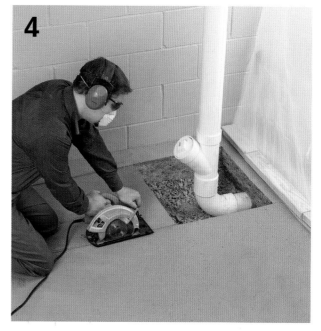

Excavate the drain line trench. Enclose the work area with plastic sheeting to protect the rest of the house from concrete dust. Use a chalk line to lay out a 24"-wide trench centered over the new branch drain location. Score along the lines with a concrete saw or a circular saw with a masonry blade.

(continued)

ATTIC & BASEMENT PROJECTS

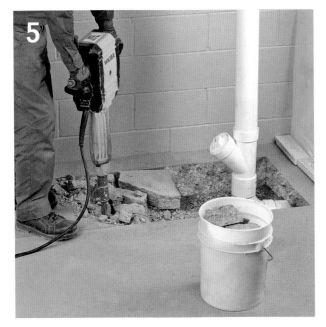

Use a jackhammer to break up the concrete in the trench, taking care not to damage any of the existing plumbing lines. Wear gloves, eye and ear protection, and a dust mask. Remove the concrete for disposal. Remove dirt (technically called granular fill) from the trench, starting at the main waste-vent stack.

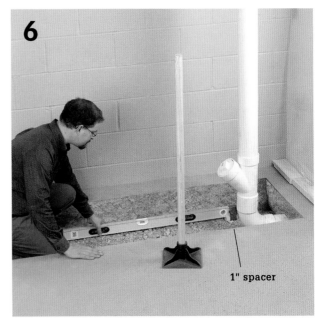

1" spacer

Create a flat-bottomed trench that slopes toward the main stack at ¼" per ft. The soil will hold up the drain lines, so it is important to create an even surface. Use a hand tamper to tamp down the soil if it has been disturbed. Tape a 1" spacer to the end of a 4' level to create a handy measuring tool for checking the proper slope. Set the soil aside to use for backfill.

Cut the drain line or main stack (depending on how deep the drain line is) using a reciprocating saw (or a snap cutter). Support the main waste-vent stack before cutting. Use a 2 × 4 and duct tape for a plastic stack, or riser clamps for a cast-iron stack. If cutting the horizontal drain line, cut as close as possible to the stack.

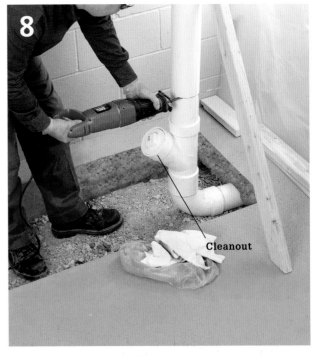

Cleanout

Cut into the stack above the cleanout, and remove the pipe and fittings. Wear rubber gloves, and have a large plastic bag and rags ready, as old pipes and fittings may be coated with sewer sludge. Remember that no wastewater can flow in the house while the pipes are cut open. Turn off the water and drain toilets to prevent accidental use.

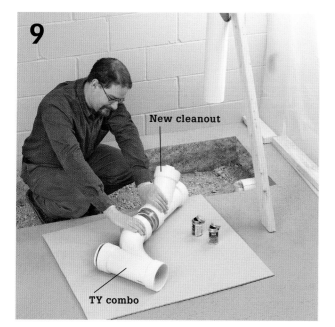

9

New cleanout

TY combo

Cut and test fit a new cleanout and long sweep TY combo assembly, dry-fitting it to the drain stack and the horizontal drain line to the street. Make any needed adjustments and then solvent-glue the fittings and new pipe into a single assembly.

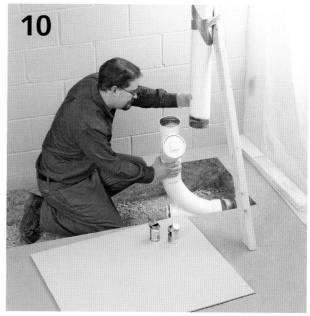

10

Clean the outside of the old pipes thoroughly and apply primer. Also apply primer and solvent glue to the female surfaces of the union fittings in the assembly. Slide the fitting assembly over the primed ends of the drain stack and the drain line at the same time. This requires a little bit of play in one or both of the lines so you can manipulate the new assembly. If your existing pipes will not move at all, you'll need to use a banded coupling on the drain stack to seal the gap.

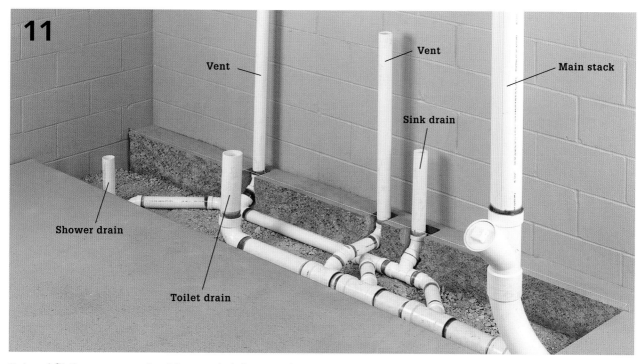

11

Vent

Vent

Main stack

Sink drain

Shower drain

Toilet drain

Cut and fit the components of the new drain line one piece at a time, starting at the stack. Use strings or boards to outline the wet wall, so vent placement is correct. Drain lines underground must be a minimum of 2". Use 3 × 2" reducing Ys to tie the shower drain line and the sink drain line into the toilet drain line. Install vertical drain and vent lines that are long enough to protrude well above the level of the finished floor.

(continued)

12

Check for leaks by pouring water into each new drainpipe. If the joints appear sound, contact your building department and arrange for your inspection (you must do this prior to covering the pipes). Plug the pipe openings with rags to prevent sewer gas from escaping. *Note: Some municipalities require an air test as well.*

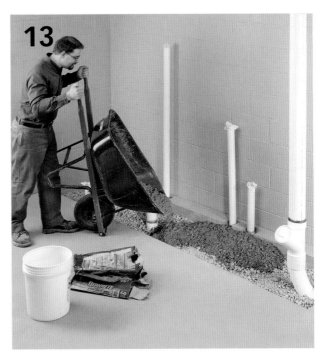

13

Backfill around the pipes with the soil dug from the trench. Mix and pour new concrete to cover the trench, and trowel smooth. Allow the concrete to cure for three days. Some municipalities may require that isolation membrane be wrapped around vertical pipes where they will be surrounded by concrete—check with your local inspector.

14

Build the wet wall from 2 × 6 lumber. The sill plate should be pressure treated, but the other members may be SPF. Notch the sill plate so the vent pipes clear it easily. Use masonry anchors or concrete nails and a powder-actuated nailer to attach the plate.

15

Run 2" vent pipes through notches in the studs. Assemble with vent T and 90° fittings. The 2" pipes are larger than required, but using the same size as the drain lines eliminates the need for reducing fittings and makes for less waste. The 90° fittings are typically less expensive than the vent elbows.

16

Route the vent pipe to a point beneath a wall cavity running from the basement to the attic. Or, if there is another vent line closer that you can tie into, go ahead and do that.

17

Run vent pipe up through the floors above and either directly out through the roof or tie it to another vent pipe in the attic. Remove sections of wall surface as needed to bore holes for running the vent pipe through wall plates. Feed the vent pipe up into the wall cavity from the basement. Wedge the vent pipe in place while you solvent-glue the fittings. Support the vent pipe at each floor with plastic pipe hangers installed horizontally. Stuff fiberglass insulation into holes around pipes. Do not replace any wall coverings until you have had your final inspection.

18

Nail guard

Install the water supply plumbing. Compared to the drain-vent plumbing, this will seem remarkably easy.

Soldering ▸

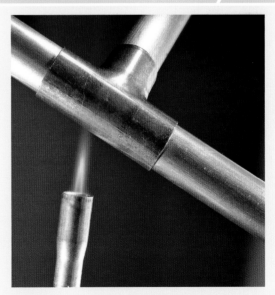

Use caution when soldering copper. Pipes and fittings become very hot and must be allowed to cool before handling.

HOW TO BUILD A BASEMENT BATHROOM

Frame the new walls using pressure-treated sole plates. If walls will contain additional plumbing, build them from 2 × 6 stock.

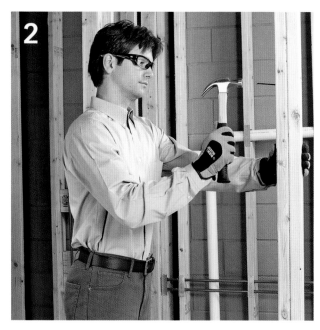

Install framing for the bathroom door (see pages 49 to 51). For economy, a 30"-wide prehung interior door makes sense, but if you want to conserve space consider installing a pocket door. They are fairly common for bathroom applications.

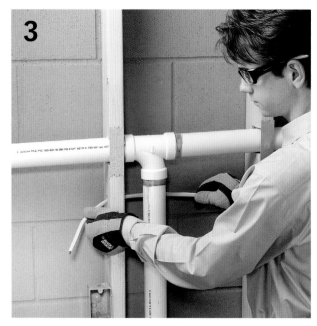

Install 12/2 NM sheathed cable to supply power for a dedicated 20-amp small appliance circuit. Most codes have specific requirements for spacing. The circuit must have GFCI protection. You can wire it with individually protected GFCI receptacles or install a 20-amp GFCI breaker in the main service panel. If you do not have experience with home wiring, hire a professional.

Wire ceiling lights and any wall lights for a lighted medicine chest. Recessed canister lights are a good choice for basements because they don't project down into the room. Have all wiring inspected and approved before you close up the walls.

5

Add ventilation. Basement vents require powered vent fans that can be wall-mounted or ceiling mounted. The ductwork for the fan exhaust is normally routed out through a hole in the rim joist of the house. If the bathroom contains a shower or bathtub, the duct must terminate outdoors. If it is only a half bath some codes allow you to vent into an attic.

6

Install floor coverings (pages 121 to 146). Here, a bed of thinset mortar is being laid for textured porcelain floor tiles. The mortar bed usually can be applied directly to the concrete floor.

7

Trim floor covering materials to fit around drainpipes in the floor, such as the toilet drain stub-out seen here. Complete the floor covering installation.

8

Install the shower pan according to the manufacturer's instructions. Some are set into a bed of mortar or mastic while others are fastened to the wall framing. Trim the drainpipe to the recommended height first (bottom photo) and make all drain connections.

(continued)

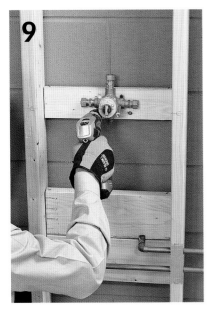

Install shower supply pipes and make hookups to the faucet body. *Note: The easiest shower stalls to install are freestanding, but kits and tileboard units that are installed in framed alcoves are cheaper. Read the directions that come with your stall to see if they recommend installing panels, such as cementboard, as backer before you install the shower.*

Install the shower enclosure kit or make your custom shower surround with tileboard.

Install ceiling coverings. While there are advantages to installing a suspended ceiling or acoustic tile ceiling that's easy to remove for access, mold-resistant wallboard is economical, paintable, and has a finished room feel that the other types lack.

Install wall coverings. Do not use standard wallboard. Use mold-resistant wallboard or cementboard throughout. Do not install a vapor barrier behind the wallboard.

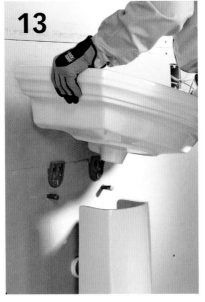

Attach any other wall-mounted fixtures, such as the pedestal sink being hung on a mounting plate above. Do all of the work requiring access to wall or ceiling stud cavities before you install the wall coverings. And don't neglect to have inspections done.

Cover seams and fill holes in the walls and ceiling with fiberglass wallboard tape and joint compound. Sand the compound smooth and apply a coat of wallboard primer.

15

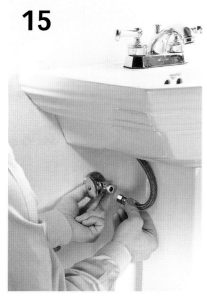

Finish making the supply and drain hookups for the lavatory. Add faucets to all fixtures and test them.

16

Install the toilet after trimming the closet drain pipe to the correct height. Hook up the water supply to the fill valve and then test the operation. Drain times can be a bit slower in basements, and flushes may be weakened slightly by the shallowness of the drain line slopes.

17

Paint the walls and ceiling using a paint with a mold-resistant additive. Paint the ceiling first. For bathrooms, choose a washable, semigloss paint.

18

Hang the entry door and install trim around the door as well as a baseboard trim. You may find it easier to paint or finish the door and trim before installation.

19

Install mirrors, medicine cabinets, towel rods, paper holders, and any other members of the decorative bathroom suite.

20

Attach trim kits and escutcheons to light fixtures and vent fans. Add switch plates and receptacle covers, too. Test all fixtures.

This cozy family room features a vent-free gas fireplace and a brand new patio door that opens out to a lower level walkout patio.

INSTALLING A GAS FIREPLACE

The family room is the only type of room that is actually getting larger as a percentage of the total floorspace in today's new homes. Whether we use it for watching movies, playing games, or just hanging out reading, the family room is an important place in any home. A well-designed family room is spacious, has good light, features comfortable floors, and is easy to clean. It can include a few luxurious features such as a fireplace, a mini-kitchen with snack area, a home theater setup, or a dry bar.

One important consideration when designing a family room is traffic flow. This is especially important if your family room will have exterior access like the walk-out patio door seen here. Try to arrange the room so that a line drawn from the main entry point from upstairs to the exterior door doesn't split the room in two. Be a bit protective of the floorplan so you can set up furniture or arrange activities that can proceed without constant interruptions as other family members move from door to door.

As you design your room, also take into account the electronics that will be set up in your room. Installing high-speed computer/television cable lines, speaker wire, phone lines, and other forms of structured wiring is easiest to do when the walls are uncovered.

The family room seen here features a vent-free gas fireplace. It is not a significant heat source. If you are interested in a fireplace that can provide supplemental heat, install a direct-vent gas fireplace or a woodburning one instead.

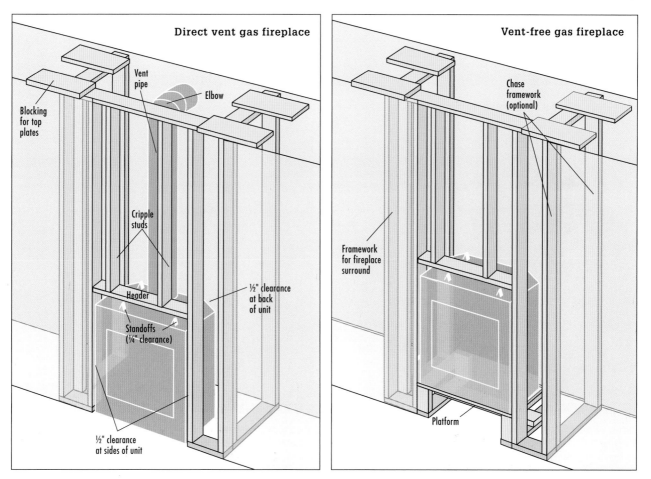

Gas fireplaces come in two types for home use: direct vent (left), which must be exhausted to the home exterior, and vent-free, which do not require venting but must be installed in either an existing firebox or a specially designed firebox that circulates air and exhaust internally. Vent-free models are not currently allowed in the Upper Midwest, California, Alaska, Hawaii, or Canada.

HOW TO BUILD A FAMILY ROOM WITH FIREPLACE

Frame the new walls for the room (see pages 38 to 41). Here, an open area in a walkout basement with a finished exterior wall is being divided into a smaller finished space for a family room with direct access to a patio.

Install wiring cables in the stud walls (see page 40). Because family rooms normally include several types of electronic devices, consider adding multimedia outlets for coaxial cable and speaker cables.

Install fixture boxes for lights keeping the planned ceiling material thickness and installation method in mind. Here, a box is being installed for a 6' section of halogen track lighting to provide adjustable lighting that can be focused on the fireplace mantel.

Frame the opening for the firebox according to the manufacturer's directions and minimum clearances. Because the fireplace surround planned for this room uses 12 × 12" wall tile around the opening, we added full-height studs so the required cementboard backer can be seamed with the wallboard over a stud. A header for the opening is supported by short jack studs at the sides.

5

Construct a support platform for the firebox. Because the firebox will be housed in open space on the other side of the fireplace wall, we were able to get by with a simple wood platform built with 2 × 4s and ¾" plywood.

6

Secure the firebox platform in the wall opening by nailing or screwing it to the studs at the edges of the opening. Some manufacturers may require that you secure the platform to the floor as well.

7

Install wallboard on ceiling. When wallboarding both the ceiling and the walls, it is usually recommended that you do the ceiling first so the vertical panels can be butted up against the ceiling to provide some extra support. If you are hanging a suspended or tile ceiling, wallboard the walls first.

8

Cut cementboard into strips equal in width to the dimension of your tiled surround and attach them to the 2 × 4 nailers bordering the framed firebox opening. It is generally a good idea to predrill for cementboard screws, especially with narrower strips.

(continued)

367

Install mold-resistant wallboard in the rest of the room, keeping the bottom edges at least ½" above the floor. If you have planned your firebox framing properly, all wallboard edges will fall over studs or cross blocks.

Apply joint compound and fiberglass seam tape over seams and cover screwheads with compound. Sand the compound smooth.

Prime and paint the ceiling and the walls. To boost the visual interest of the ceiling, we added some texture to the ceiling paint (above) and applied it with a ⅝" nap roller. The effect is much subtler than the iconic cottage cheese ceiling of the 1960s and 1970s.

Apply a mortar bed for the tile surround using a notched trowel (a ¼" square-notch trowel is typical but check the recommendations on the thinset package label). Apply only as much mortar as you can tile in about 10 minutes. Treating each leg of the square surround separately is a good strategy.

13

Press the surround tiles into the mortar bed and set them by pressing with a short piece of 2 × 4 wrapped in a soft cloth. Most tiles have spacing nubs cast into the edges so setting the gaps between tiles or tile sheets is automatic. If your tiles do not have spacing nubs, use plastic tile spacers available at your tile store. Let the thinset mortar dry overnight once you're finished setting the tiles.

14

Apply dark-tinted grout to the tiles using a grout float. Let the grout harden slightly and then buff off the residue with a soft, clean cloth.

15

Begin adding surround trim. Here, 1 × 4 cherry casing is being attached to wall stud locations. The side casings should be slightly off the floor (if you have not installed flooring yet account for the floor covering thickness) and butted against the tile surround. If you have planned properly, there will be wall studs behind the casing. *Note: We chose 1 × 4 cherry because it is attractive, but also because you can usually buy it dimensioned, planed, and sanded on all sides at the lumberyard. If you have woodworking equipment, use any lumber you like.*

16

Add built-up head casing. The head casing should overhang the side casings by an inch or so. We used a built-up technique to add some depth and profile to the head casing. First, attach a full-width 1 × 4 to the wall. Then, install a 1 × 3 so the ends and top are flush with the ends and top of the 1 × 4. Finally, install a cherry 1 × 2 in the same manner.

(continued)

Cut and install the mantel board. We used another piece of 1 × 4 cherry the same length as the head casings, but if you have access to woodworking tools consider a thicker board for a little more presence. Or, face-glue two 1 × 4s together.

Finish-sand all the cherry and then apply a light wood stain. After the stain dries, topcoat with a cherry-tone or light mahogany wipe-on varnish that will even out the uneven coloration typical with cherry. Fill nail holes with cherry-tinted wood putty.

Set the firebox for the fireplace into the finished surround and check for level. Fasten it to the framing by nailing or screwing through the nailing flange, depending on the manufacturer's recommendations.

Seal the gap around the firebox with high-temperature silicone sealant. Do not use ordinary caulk here because it could melt or even catch fire.

21

Run natural gas supply pipe to within 18" or so of the gas inlet port on the side of the firebox. Attach a stop cock to the supply tube. *Warning: Working with gas pipe and making gas hookups is very dangerous and in many municipalities it may only be done by a licensed professional. Doing the work yourself may also void the warranty on your gas appliance. It is strongly recommended that you hire a professional for this part of the project.*

22

Connect the fireplace to the gas supply with a flexible gas connector tube, making sure to use gas-rated teflon tape to lubricate screw threads on the connector. Restore the gas supply and test all connections with leak detector spray (inset).

23

Install floor coverings. Snap-together laminate planks are easy to install and in general a good choice for basement family rooms (see pages 126 to 129). Trim the laminate planks to fit around the fireplace casings.

24

Install baseboard moldings, lighting trim kits, and any other finishing trim such as door casings. Remember to read the vent-free fireplace manual thoroughly and follow all safety precautions for operation. Have the unit inspected annually to make sure it is still operating properly.

KITCHEN PROJECTS

Other than adding space with an attic or basement conversion (pages 326 to 363) or pulling out the stops to add on a structural room addition (pages 495 to 556), no remodeling project is more complex, or more expensive, than the major remodeling of a kitchen. It can be very rewarding, however. A house with a very old, outdated kitchen will see a dramatic increase in market value with the installation of a new kitchen. Real-estate professionals report that in the right circumstances, homeowners can recoup most or all the cost of the renovation through the increase in their home's value.

But for most people, the true value lies in the improved enjoyment and function of their home once the kitchen undergoes significant remodeling. Although a full tear-out and installation is sometimes done (at great cost), a major kitchen remodeling need not be quite so dramatic. Installing new cabinets and countertops, laying new flooring, replacing old fixtures and appliances, and adding a few custom storage features is within the abilities of patient DIYers and can radically transform any kitchen.

Remember, though, that some kitchen remodels may involve electrical or plumbing upgrades that are beyond the scope of this book. Only very experienced DIYers should consider this kind of work, and only if they have plenty of informational resources at their disposal.

IN THIS CHAPTER:

- Practical Planning Tips
- Slide-Out Storage
- Countertop Selection
- Tile Backsplash
- Stock-Cabinet Island
- Two-Level Tile Island
- Island Vent Hood
- Ranges, Ovens & Cooktops
- Refrigerator Icemaker
- Dishwasher
- Range Hood/Vent Fan
- Drop-in Sink
- Undermount Sink
- Apron Sink

PRACTICAL PLANNING TIPS

There are plenty of practical things to consider before starting a kitchen remodel, but some of the most important involve timing and preparation. In short, the more planning you can do before even touching a tool, the better you will be able to handle the inevitable setbacks. As long as you make sure that it doesn't coincide with major holidays or extended houseguests, a do-it-yourself kitchen remodel doesn't have to take over your life.

The first tip is to be generous when creating a timeline. You never know when ordered parts will be delayed or paint will take twice as long to dry as you estimated. For the most part, the simplest remodel can be completed within a week with more extensive remodels—that involve new cabinets, floors, and professionally installed countertops—taking up to three months to complete. Even if it's a small-scale project, be prepared to not have access to your kitchen while work is being done, since even paint fumes can disrupt daily life for a day or two. One smart solution is to create a temporary kitchen elsewhere in your home where you can plug in a coffeemaker or microwave, or even a mini refrigerator.

Another thing to consider is the need for permits from your local building authority. Familiarize yourself with local codes before you alter anything electrical or structural. For plumbing projects, you'll want to look into the requirements in your area or determine the need for a new line before you get started. As for changes that involve ventilation, you'll want to refer to some of the building codes and guidelines we've included earlier in the book.

Like successful stand-up comedy, successful kitchen remodeling requires impeccable timing. Dedicate a calendar to the projects and be sure to keep it updated. Planning the timing is the only way to keep the amount of time you'll be without a functioning kitchen to a bare minimum, and it will let contractors and tradespeople work more efficiently.

The most important lesson of any DIY project is to know when to call in the professionals. While many of the how-to projects in this book are simply completed by someone with little construction experience, some projects will be more involved than they first appear. For instance, replacing a resilient tile floor may seem like an easy enough project, but the plot thickens when the subfloor is revealed to be in terrible shape and must be torn out and rebuilt. Another time to call in expert assistance is when plumbing or electrical systems are more than twenty years old. Though wires and pipes are meant to last over fifty years, some conditions will cause them to deteriorate, making it tricky to remove them safely. And while many hobbyists can pull off the replacement of upper cabinets with the help of a friend, there are plenty of us who would require a team of carpenters to help hang and install new cabinets.

The how-to lessons in this book have been carefully broken down into step-by-step manuals for each project. Whether you need assistance or have lots of experience at DIY home improvement, the right tools and smart safety precautions make it possible for anyone to achieve dream-kitchen status.

Flextime: Your Little Secret ▶

For added security, it's a good idea to add at least 25% more time to your best guess when determining the overall schedule for your remodeling project. Building in a few flex days as a safeguard against unforeseen problems is also a good idea. However, keep this information to yourself.

If contractors know that your schedule is padded, they may feel free to bump your project for a day or two to squeeze in a smaller rush job for another client. To ensure that your contractors stay on schedule, mark your flex days "cleanup" or "out of town"—don't tell them you've built some extra time into the schedule.

Talk to Building Inspectors ▶

Although building inspectors aren't paid consultants, they can be an excellent design and planning resource. They are your community's field representatives, and their job is to inspect the work done on your project to ensure that it meets building code requirements.

As experts in their respective fields, the building inspector, electrical inspector, and plumbing inspector can give you sound advice on designing your kitchen. Not all inspectors have the time or the willingness to answer a lot of design questions, so make your questions short and specific, and be sure to describe your situation clearly. Also ask if the inspections office provides a pamphlet that summarizes the local code requirements for kitchens.

SLIDE-OUT STORAGE

A base cabinet with slide-out trays or shelves is one of those great modern conveniences that has become standard in new kitchen design. Not only do slide-out trays make reaching stored items easier than with standard cabinet spaces—no more crouching and diving into the deep recesses of cavernous low shelves—they also store more items far more efficiently. With a few shallow trays, a standard base cabinet can hold dozens of food cans and still leave room for tall items like cereal boxes and bags of flour or even deep pots and countertop appliances.

To get the most from your new slide-out system, think carefully about how you will use each tray. Measure the items you're most likely to store together, and let the items dictate the spacing of the trays. Most standard base cabinets are suitable for trays. Wide cabinets (24 inches or wider) without a center partition (middle stile) are best in terms of space usage, but trays in narrow cabinets (18 inches wide) are just as handy. If you have a wide cabinet with a middle stile, you can add trays along one or both sides of the stile. For economy

and simplicity, the trays in this project are made with ¾-inch-thick plywood parts joined with glue and finish nails. If you prefer a more finished look (not that there's anything wrong with the look of nice plywood), you can use 1 × 4 hardwood stock for the tray sides and set a ⅜-inch-thick plywood bottom panel into dadoes milled into the side pieces. Another option is to assemble plywood tray pieces using pocket screws so the screw heads don't show on the front pieces of the trays.

Tools & Materials ▸

Circular saw with straightedge guide or tablesaw	1 × 2 hardwood stock
	¾" finish-grade plywood
	Wood glue
Drill	6d finish nails
Wood screws	Finish materials
Drawer slides (1 set per tray)	Tape measure
	Varnish or polyurethane
Hammer	Eye and ear protection

Slide-out trays eliminate the everyday problem of hard-to-reach and hard-to-see spaces in standard base cabinets. Better still, you can install your trays to accommodate the stuff you use most often.

DRAWER SLIDES

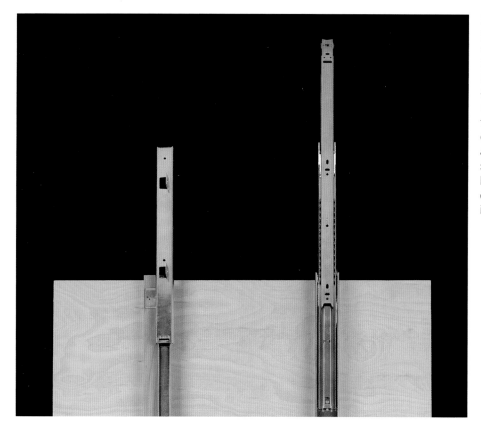

Drawer slides suitable for pullout shelves are commonly available in both standard (left) and full extension (right) styles. Standard slides are less expensive and good enough for most applications. They allow the tray to be pulled out most of the way. Full extension slides are a little pricier than standard slides but they allow the tray to be pulled completely out of the cabinet box for easy access to items in the back.

Spacer strip

Glide-out rail

Spacers must be mounted to the wall cabinets before you can install drawer slides for your slide-out shelves. They are necessary for the drawers to clear the cabinet face frame and the door. For a ¾" spacer, a 1 × 3 or 1 × 4 works well. Paint or finish it to match the cabinet interior.

HOW TO INSTALL SLIDE-OUT CABINET TRAYS

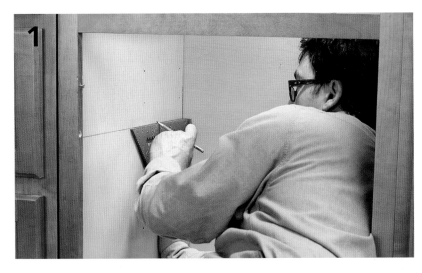

Lay out the tray positions, starting with the bottom tray. Check the drawer slides to see how much clearance you need for the bottom tray. Draw lines on the side panels of the cabinet to represent the bottom edges of the slide supports. Make sure the lines are level and are perpendicular to the cabinet front. Cut the slide supports to length from 1 × 2 hardwood stock (or any hardwood ripped to 1½" wide).

Mount the supports to the side panels of the cabinet with glue and screws driven through countersunk pilot holes. *Note: Depending on the overhang of the cabinet face frames, you may need thicker support stock to provide sufficient clearance for the trays and slide rails.*

Install the drawer slides flush with the bottom edges of the slide supports using the provided screws. Assemble the two halves of each slide, and then measure between the drawer side pieces (rails) to find the exact width of each tray. Plan the depth of the trays based on the cabinet depth.

Cut the bottom piece for each tray from ¾" plywood 1½" smaller than the planned width and depth of the finished tray. Rip four ¾"-wide pieces for the sides, front, and back of each tray. Cut the side pieces to length, equal to the depth dimension of the bottom piece. Cut the front and back pieces 1½" longer than the width of the bottom.

Build the trays with glue and 6d finish nails or pneumatic brads. Fasten the sides flush with the bottom face and front and back edges of the bottom piece, and then add the front and back pieces. Sand any rough surfaces, and finish the trays with two or three coats of polyurethane or other durable varnish. If desired, you can stain the trays prior to finishing so they match your cabinets.

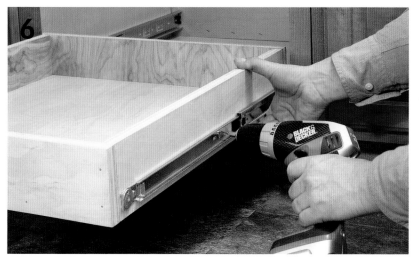

Partially mount the drawer slide rails to one of the trays, following the manufacturer's directions. Test-fit the tray in the cabinet and make any necessary adjustments before completely fastening the rails. Mount the slide rails on the remaining trays and install the trays to finish the job.

COUNTERTOP SELECTION

More than simply a worksurface, a kitchen countertop can dazzle with the look-at-me drama of mottled granite or bring together a country theme with honed soapstone and butcher block. But durability and maintenance (and cost of course) are generally the primary concerns when it comes to countertops.

Some materials, like granite, can withstand the heat of pots and pans, so they are better suited for heavy-duty cooks. Others, including laminate, are affordable options that come in a wide variety of modern colors. There are many choices in countertops, from the less-expensive laminate,

through ceramic and stone tile, to concrete and wood, to high-end granite and marble.

Countertop options for your kitchen depend on how much you are willing to spend, whether you will be doing it yourself or contracting it out, and what look you want to achieve. When choosing countertops, remember that you do not need to have a uniform countertop. Many people choose to use more expensive countertop materials as accents or for islands rather than for the entire kitchen. And last, but not least, if you are inclined toward green remodeling practices, you may find some surprises when you compare countertop materials (see page 385).

Fabricated countertop material like quartz and solid surface is virtually impenetrable to water. If it becomes scratched, minor damage can easily be buffed out.

LAMINATE & POST-FORM

Laminate countertops are formed from layers of resin-saturated paper and plastic that are bonded under pressure, then given a protective coating. The laminate is bonded to a substrate to create the countertop. Also available is through-color laminate, in which the surface color runs all the way through. This product doesn't have the dark edge of standard laminate and does not show surface damage as easily, but it is two to three times more expensive.

The cheapest laminate countertop is ready-made post-form. A post-form countertop comprises a backsplash, counter, and bullnose front apron formed into one seamless piece. Home centers carry post-form countertop options in various lengths and in a few stock colors. You can also have a custom post-form countertop made, which will be slightly more expensive.

One limitation of laminate countertops is that sinks must be drop-in, not undermounted. Though the laminate itself is waterproof, the particleboard or plywood it is attached to will swell if it gets wet. Laminate is also not as heat-proof or scratch-proof as other countertop materials.

TILE

Whether they are ceramic or natural stone, tile countertops are popular, midpriced options. If you like the look of granite but don't want to pay the price, granite tile can create a similar look for substantially less, especially if you do the installation yourself. When selecting tiles for countertops, make sure they are floor tiles—wall tiles will not stand up to the wear and tear of countertop use.

Two major drawbacks of ceramic or stone tile are hardness and grout lines. Glassware and pottery will break and chip readily when knocked or dropped against this surface. Grout lines make the surface uneven and difficult to keep clean, so choose larger tiles to minimize grout lines. Using tiles for a backsplash is an excellent way to get the look of tile near the countertop.

Plastic laminate is bonded to a particleboard subbase with contact cement.

Post-form countertops have a laminate surface that is applied at the factory.

Tiles are set into a bed of thinset mortar troweled onto a cementboard or tilebacker subbase.

SOLID SURFACE

Solid-surface countertops, commonly described by the common brand name Corian™, are popular but more expensive options. With solid color throughout, the pieces are joined with a bonding compound that leaves no visible seam line. Solid-surface countertops can be shaped and inlaid, it comes in many colors and patterns, it is durable, and light damage like scratches can be repaired easily. Solid-surface should not be used as a cutting board, however, and hot pans cannot be placed directly on the surface. Most spills are easily cleaned with soap and water.

Though solid-surface materials are easily worked with standard hand tools, do-it-yourselfers may have difficulty purchasing the materials and bonding agents. If a non-licensed installer installs one of those countertops, the manufacturer will not honor any product warranties.

Solid-surface countertops can be installed on islands or as accents if you don't have the budget to put them everywhere in your kitchen.

QUARTZ SURFACES

Quartz countertops resemble solid-surface countertops in many ways, but they have a higher percentage of mineral material versus plastic resins and binders. Quartz surfaces are manufactured from 93 percent quartz and 7 percent pigments, resins, and binders. Because all quartz surfaces are manufactured using essentially the same equipment and formulas, any difference in appearance among products is due to the type of quartz used.

The quartz surface is unscratchable, non-porous, non-staining, does not need to be sealed, and will not scorch or mar from high heat. Although it is as hard as granite, quartz has more inherent flexibility, so surface cracking does not occur. The surface is cool to the touch, like granite and marble.

Quartz countertops are almost solid granulated and reconstituted quartz (the most common mineral on earth).

STAINLESS STEEL

Although it is slightly more expensive than solid surface or quartz on a per-square-foot basis, stainless steel is a popular countertop material in home kitchens as well as in commercial kitchens. That's because it is an impervious material that doesn't stain, can handle hot pots, and can be fabricated into seamless countertops and sinks. Stainless steel countertops for residential use are usually bonded to plywood or particleboard to quiet the noise and prevent denting. Sinks can either be fabricated as part of the countertop, or, more likely, welded in. Either way, it is a seamless application. The biggest downside is that stainless steel shows fingerprints and watermarks, especially on a polished surface, so it's best to get a matte or satin surface.

Stainless steel countertops normally are bonded to a plywood subbase in residential applications.

BUTCHER BLOCK & WOOD

Advancing technology in wood finishes and sealants have made wood countertops a viable option for kitchen applications. Historically, the amount of water splashed around a sink would ruin a wood surface. The best of the wood options is butcher block, which can be ordered and installed as a relatively easy DIY project. Butcher block is made up of small pieces of wood glued together into a slab. It's generally categorized as either end grain, which is composed of vertical pieces of wood, or edge grain, made of long strips of wood. The thickness of stock slabs can vary, from 1½ inches for the standard countertop to 4 inches for an island or small-section installation. Many people assume that butcher block is convenient because you no longer need cutting boards, but it's a poor idea to use them as direct cutting surfaces. Every nick and cut will collect dirt and will darken differently when the surface is reoiled. Wood, no matter how well it is sealed, expands and contracts in relation to humidity levels, so installation of a wood countertop requires special considerations (see pages 178 to 183).

Butcher block material is sold in standard countertop width and thickness and in varying lengths.

CONCRETE COUNTERTOPS

Concrete has become a very popular, exceptionally dramatic countertop choice. It is a custom option, but is not as expensive as granite. It can be cast in place under certain conditions, but as a moderate to difficult DIY project, it should be created off-site where the dust and chemicals can be easily managed. Concrete can be dyed or stained in many different colors and will accept a virtually unlimited number of finishes. Drainboards can be cast in and ornamental objects can be embedded in the concrete for added functionality or just to make it more unique. Concrete needs to be resealed regularly, or it will permanently stain.

Acidic foods will etch the surface. Like ceramic tile and stone surfaces, it has no give, so expect a greater number of broken glasses and plates. Custom concrete sinks as part of the counter are also possible.

Concrete countertops are cast in forms in a well-ventilated work area and then transported to the cabinets after they are machined and polished.

STONE

Soapstone, slate, marble, and granite are all types of natural stone that are used for countertops. Although they are all quarried stone and are all fairly expensive, they have numerous differences. Soapstone has been used for kitchen countertops and sinks for hundreds of years. Though the stone itself is easily workable with nonspecialized tools, its surface is nonabsorbent and unaffected by either acids or alkalis. The surface will age to a glossy patina, or it can be oiled to achieve this finish. Slate for countertops is durable, hard, and dense. Scratches can be rubbed out, its surface is nonabsorbing and it does not require sealing. Slate comes in shades of green, purple, gray, and black, with a rare red available at a higher cost.

The beauty of marble comes from its veining patterns—unfortunately these are mini fault lines along which the stone will easily break, especially if improperly installed. Some marble is as hard as granite, but most is fairly soft and scratches easily. Granite is the hardest of the stone countertops. It comes in an ever-increasing array of colors—ranging from whites and blacks to pinks, reds, yellows, and greens—as more countries begin exporting their local granites. The main drawback is that it must be sealed to prevent staining.

A big slab of beautiful, natural stone makes an incomparable countertop that is normally at the top of the cost range.

Comparing Countertop Materials ▸

Material	Description	Making it Greener
Plastic Laminate	Paper and resin laminate glued to particle board (or MDF) substrate. Resistant to stains, scratches, and moisture; easy to clean; inexpensive. Surface susceptible to chipping and burning; damage cannot be repaired.	Use formaldehyde-free, recycled-wood substrate and low-VOC adhesive; laminate should be made with recycled paper and water-based resins, if possible.
Paper-resin	Solid slab of paper and resin. Highly workable for custom applications; solid color and same durability throughout slab; resistant to stains and heat. May need periodic cleaning and finishing treatments.	Choose product with high recycled content; purchase from local or regional supplier/fabricator to minimize shipping.
Tile	Ceramic, porcelain, or glass tiles glued to cementboard and wood substrate. Durable and highly heat-resistant; tiles are highly washable; versatile material for custom applications. Grout between tiles is prone to staining and must be sealed periodically.	Use tiles with recycled content or locally produced tiles. Use marine plywood and/or seal plywood to reduce formaldehyde offgassing; set tiles with low-VOC adhesive. Seal grout and tiles (if necessary) with formaldehyde-free, low-VOC sealer.
Glass Composite	Solid slab of glass and resin binder. Durable; unique appearance; heat- and scratch-resistant. May require periodic cleaning and/or sealing treatments.	Choose product with high recycled content. Purchase from local or regional fabricator to minimize shipping.
Butcher Block	Solid-wood strips laminated to form a slab. Natural, renewable material; good surface for cutting; can be refinished. Must be oiled and sealed periodically to maintain appearance.	Choose only FSC-certified wood. Treat surface with food-safe finishes and sealers.
Stainless Steel	Alloy of steel, nickel, and chromium; often glued to wood substrate. Highly durable, rustproof, and easy to clean. Can be scratched and dented.	Recycle the metal if you replace the countertops. Use formaldehyde-free substrate.
Natural Stone	Solid quarried stone slabs or tiles glued to substrate. Durable; heatproof and waterproof. Can chip and crack; some varieties will stain; dark colors make cleaning problematic.	Look for salvaged slabs or buy stone from local quarry.
Engineered Stone	Composite of quartz or other stone, pigments, and polyester resin. Same color and durability throughout slab; doesn't require sealing.	Purchase from a manufacturer in your region and use a local fabricator.
Solid-Surface	Composite of petrochemical-based resins (polyester, acrylic) and bauxite Color and durability consistent throughout material; highly workable and customizable.	Green options are limited; perhaps minimize quantity of countertop.
Concrete	Available in various forms, including poured-in-place concrete, cast concrete, and fiber cement composite materials. Versatile material is highly customizable; durable and heat-resistant. Can be very heavy; prone to cracking, chipping, and staining; must be sealed regularly.	Look for products with high recycled content, such as fly ash (to replace high-embodied energy and aggregates cement). Color material with natural, nontoxic pigments added to concrete mix instead of stains applied to surface.

TILE BACKSPLASH

There are few spaces in your home with as much potential for creativity and visual impact as the space between your kitchen countertop and your cupboards. A well-designed backsplash can transform the ordinary into the extraordinary. Tiles for the backsplash can be attached directly to wallboard or plaster and do not require backerboard. When purchasing the tile, order 10 percent extra to cover breakage and cutting. Remove the switch and receptacle coverplates and install the box extenders to make up for the extra thickness of the tile. Protect the countertop from scratches by covering it with a drop cloth.

Tools & Materials ▸

Level
Tape measure
Pencil
Tile cutter
Rod saw
Notched trowel
Rubber grout float
Beating block
Rubber mallet
Sponge
Bucket

Story stick
Straight 1 × 2
Wall tile
Tile spacers (if needed)
Mastic adhesive
Masking tape
Grout
Caulk
Drop cloth
Sanded grout
Eye and ear protection

Tip ▸

Break tiles into fragments and make a mosaic backsplash. Always use a sanded grout for joints wider than ⅛".

Contemporary glass mosaic sheets create a counter-to-cabinet backsplash for a waterproof, splash-proof wall with very high visual impact.

HOW TO INSTALL A TILE BACKSPLASH

Make a story stick by marking a board at least half as long as the backsplash area to match the tile spacing.

Starting at the midpoint of the installation area, use the story stick to make layout marks along the wall. If an end piece is too small (less than half a tile), adjust the midpoint to give you larger, more attractive end pieces. Use a level to mark this point with a vertical reference line.

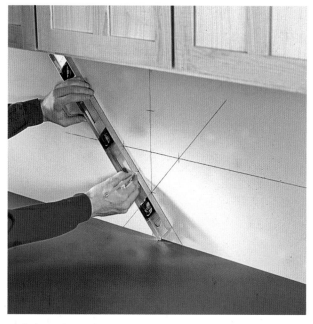

While it may appear straight, your countertop may not be level and therefore is not a reliable reference line. Run a level along the counter to find the lowest point on the countertop. Mark a point two tiles up from the low point and extend a level line across the entire work area.

Variation: Diagonal Layout. Mark vertical and horizontal reference lines, making sure the angle is 90°. To establish diagonal layout lines, measure out equal distances from the crosspoint, and then connect the points with a line. Additional layout lines can be extended from these as needed.

(continued)

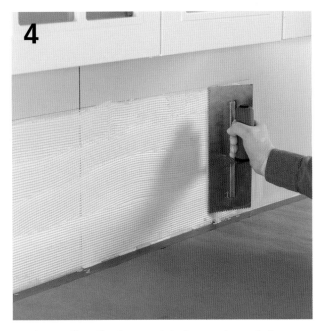

4

Apply mastic adhesive evenly to the area beneath the horizontal reference line using a notched trowel. Comb the adhesive horizontally with the notched edge.

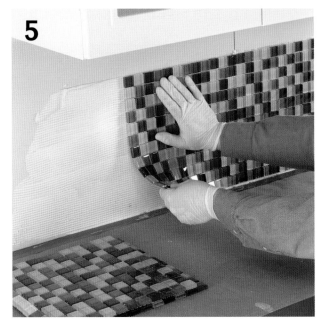

5

Press tiles into the adhesive with a slight twisting motion. If the tiles are not self-spacing, use plastic spacers to maintain even grout lines. If the tiles do not hang in place, use masking tape to hold them in place until the adhesive sets.

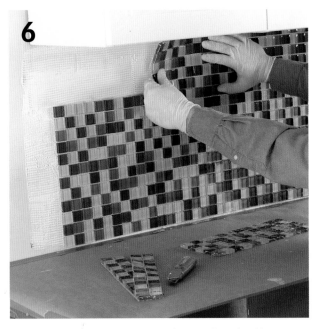

6

Install a whole row along the reference line, checking occasionally to make sure the tiles are level. Continue installing tiles below the first row, trimming tiles that butt against the countertop as needed.

7

Install an edge border if it is needed in your layout. Mosaic sheets normally do not have bullnose tiles on the edges, so if you don't wish to see the cut edges of the outer tiles, install a vertical column of edge tiles at the end of the backsplash area.

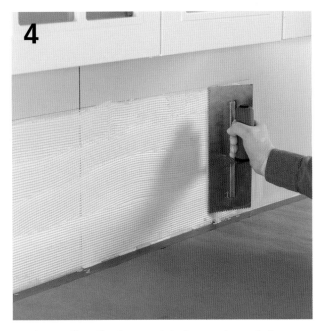

KITCHEN PROJECTS

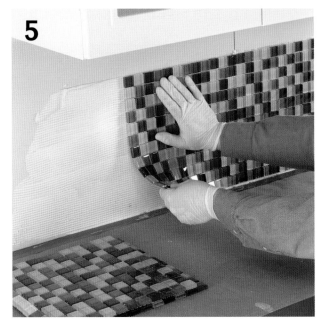

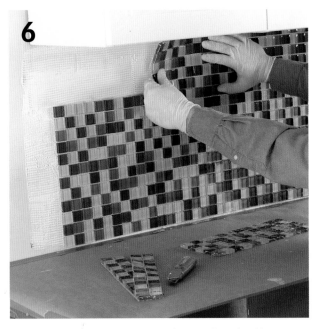

When the tiles are in place, make sure they are flat and firmly embedded by laying a beating block against the tile and rapping it lightly with a mallet. Remove the spacers. Allow the mastic to dry for at least 24 hours, or as directed by the manufacturer.

Mix the grout and apply it with a rubber grout float. Spread it over the tiles, keeping the float at a low 30° angle, pressing the grout deep into the joints. *Note: For grout joints ⅛" and smaller, be sure to use a non-sanded grout.*

Wipe off excess grout, holding the float at a right angle to the tile, working diagonally so as not to remove grout from the joints. Clean any remaining grout from the tiles with a damp sponge, working in a circular motion. Rinse the sponge thoroughly and often.

Clean excess grout with a damp sponge. When the grout has dried to a haze, buff the tile clean with a soft cloth. Apply a bead of caulk between the countertop and the tiles.

STOCK-CABINET ISLAND

Kitchen islands can be created using a whole range of methods, from repurposing an old table to fine, custom woodworking. But perhaps the easiest (and most fail-safe) way to add the conveniences and conviviality of a kitchen island is to make one from stock base cabinets. The cabinets and countertops don't have to match your kitchen cabinetry, but that is certainly an option you should consider. When designing and positioning your new island, be sure to maintain a minimum distance of 3 feet between the island and other cabinets (4 feet or more is better).

Tools & Materials ›

Marker
Drill/driver
2 × 4 cleats
Pneumatic nailer and 2" finish nails or
    hammer and 6d finish nails
2 base cabinets (approx. 36" wide × 24" deep)
Countertop
Drywall screws
Eye and ear protection

Two base cabinets arranged back-to-back make a sturdy kitchen island base that's easy to install. When made with the same style cabinets and countertops as the rest of the kitchen, the island is a perfect match.

HOW TO CREATE A STOCK-CABINET ISLAND

Set two base cabinets back-to-back in position on the floor and outline the cabinet corners onto the flooring. Remove the cabinets and draw a new outline inside of the one you just created to allow for the thickness of the cabinet sides (usually ¾").

Cut 2 × 4 cleats to fit inside the inner outline to provide nailing surfaces for the cabinets. Attach the cleats to the floor with screws or nails. *Tip: Create an L-shaped cleat for each inside corner.*

Join the two base cabinets together by driving 1¼" drywall screws through the nailing strips on the backs of the cabinets from each direction. Make sure the cabinet sides are flush and aligned. Lower the base cabinets over the cleats. Check the cabinets for level, and shim underneath the edges of the base if necessary.

Attach the cabinets to the floor cleats using 6d finish nails. Drill pilot holes for nails, and recess the nail heads with a nail set. Make a countertop (see pages 380 to 385) and install it on top of the cabinets.

TWO-LEVEL TILE ISLAND

Islands are one of the most requested kitchen features. People love them for many reasons, including their value as bi-level counter space. In most cases, the lower level is used as work space and the upper as casual dining space. The upper level provides a little camouflage for the work space, something that's especially welcome in open-plan kitchens where meal preparation areas can be seen from other areas.

When planning casual dining space, remember that designers suggest at least 24 inches per person. For the work space, remember that standard design guidelines recommend at least 36 inches of uninterrupted work space to the side of a sink or cooktop.

On worksurfaces, mosaic and other small tile is rarely the best choice. Larger tile requires fewer grout lines, always a good idea when it comes to cleaning and maintenance. But there is no rule that all three elements of a bi-level island have to use the same material. In fact, projects like this offer wonderful opportunities to mix materials or colors or textures. Choose floor tile or tile made especially for counters and then branch out when it comes to the backsplash. Wall tile and mosaics work beautifully.

Tools & Materials ▸

Tape measure	Paint
Circular saw	Tile spacers
Drill	¾" exterior-grade (CDX)
Utility knife	plywood
Straightedge	4-mil polyethylene
Stapler	sheeting
Drywall knife	Packing tape
Framing square	½" cementboard
Notched trowel	3" deck screws
Tile cutter	Fiberglass mesh tape
Carpeted 2 × 4 mallet	Thinset mortar
Grout float	Grout with latex additive
Sponge	Silicone caulk
Foam brush	Grout sealer
Caulk gun	L-brackets
1 × 2 hardwood	6d finish nails
2 × 4 lumber	Drywall screws
Ceramic tile	Glue
Adhesive	Eye and ear protection

This island adds storage, countertop space, and seating to a kitchen, revealing the truly astonishing transformation this simple yet functional piece can achieve.

HOW TO BUILD A TILED BI-LEVEL ISLAND

Build a 2 × 4 base for the island cabinet by cutting the 2 × 4s to length and joining them in a square frame that lays flat (wide sides down) on the floor. Use metal L-brackets to reinforce the joints. If you don't wish to move the island, fasten the frame to the floor in position with construction adhesive and/or deck screws.

Cut the bottom panels the same dimensions as the base frame from ¾" birch plywood. Attach it to the frame with finish nails. Then, cut the side panels to size and shape and fasten them to the edges with 6d finish nails and adhesive. Slip ¾" shims (scrap plywood works well) beneath the side panels before fastening them.

Cut the 2 × 4 cross supports to length and install them between the side panels at every corner, including the corners created by the L-shape cutout. Use 3" deck screws driven through the side panels and into the ends of the cross supports.

Prime and paint the cabinet interior and exterior.

(continued)

Build a face frame from 1 × 2 hardwood to fit the cabinet front. Attach it to the cabinet with 6d finish nails and hang the cabinet doors (we installed three 13"-wide overlay doors).

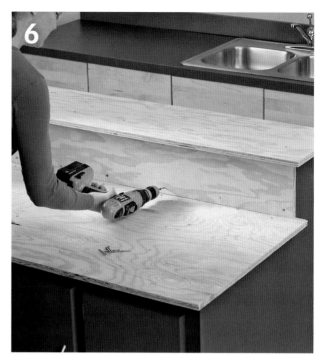

Cut strips of ¾" exterior plywood to make the subbases for the countertops and a backer for the backsplash. The lower counter subbase should overhang by 2" on the front and sides. The upper should overhang 2" on the sides and be centered on the cabinet front to back. Attach the backer and subbases with drywall screws driven down into the 2 × 4 cross supports.

Cut 2" wide strips of plywood for buildup strips and attach to the undersides of the subbases with glue and screws.

Attach the tile backerboard to the counter subbases, the backsplash, and tape seams; cover screw heads with compound (see page 55).

Cut mosaic sheets to fit the backsplash area and attach them with thinset adhesive (see Tile Backsplash, pages 386 to 389).

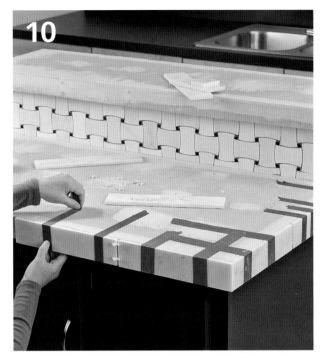

Cut the edge tiles and fasten them around the perimeter of the subbase with thinset adhesive. The tiles should be flush or slightly below the bottoms of the buildup strips and project past the top surfaces so they will be level with the field tiles. If you are not using edge tiles with a bullnose top, install the tiles so they are level with the subbase surface and overhang them with the field tiles.

Install the field tiles for the countertops last (see How to Build a Tile Countertop, pages 192 to 195).

Choose a suitable grout color and apply it to the tile with a grout float. Buff off excess once it has dried. Seal the grout with grout sealer.

ISLAND VENT HOOD

An island vent hood installation is a bit complicated because the unit must be supported from above, and because of the extra ductwork. Before installation, read the manufacturer's instructions carefully for recommended heights for cooktop and hood installation.

Most island vents weigh over 100 pounds, so you will need assistance during parts of the installation. Install the vent hood prior to installing the cooktop, if possible, to prevent damage to the cooktop. If not possible, protect the cooktop and countertop with a heavy moving pad. This installation is vented directly through the roof through attic space above the kitchen. You can also install the ductwork between ceiling joists and out to a side wall, or you can build a soffit around the ductwork. All vent hoods have a maximum permissible length for duct runs. The installation instructions will contain a chart giving equivalent lengths for each type of duct fitting. For example, a 90-degree elbow is the equivalent of 15 feet of round straight duct. A round roof cap is the equivalent of 26 feet of round straight duct.

Shopping Tips ▸

Professional-style cooktops require heavy-duty vent hoods. Check your cooktop manual for venting requirements.

Tools & Materials ▸

Tape measure	Roof vent
Plumb bob	2 × 4 lumber
Ladder	3" #10 wood screws
Wallboard saw	Sheet-metal screws
Drill	Self-sealing roofing nails
Reciprocating saw	NM cable
Screwdriver	Wire connectors
Wire stripper	Tape
6" round duct	Metallic duct tape
Hanger wire	Duct straps
Roofing cement	Eye and ear protection

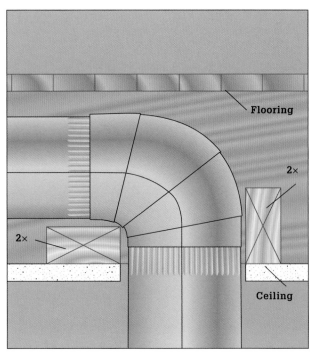

Variation: If you must install ductwork in the ceiling joists, turn one 2 × 4 brace flat to allow the duct to fit between the 2 × 4 and the flooring above.

HOW TO INSTALL AN ISLAND VENT HOOD

Check manufacturer's directions for the distance from the front of the vent to the duct centerline and the necessary vent hood alignment over the cooktop. Use a plumb bob to find the position of the duct centerline over the cooktop. Mark the location of the duct centerline on the ceiling by poking a 12" length of hanger wire through the ceiling. In the attic, pull back the insulation surrounding the wire and the adjoining joists. Center a section of 6" duct over the wire hole and trace around it to mark the cutout for the duct. Using a wallboard saw or a rotary saw, cut out the hole.

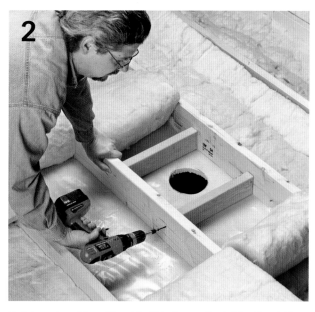

Cut two lengths of 2 × 4 to fit between the joists. Check the manufacturer's instructions for the correct distance between the braces. Place the braces flush against the ceiling top. Drill pilot holes and install with a minimum of two 3" #10 wood screws driven through the joist and into the brace. The cross bracing and the ceiling surface must be level for proper installation of the vent hood. Insert the 6" round duct through the ceiling so it extends down 3 or 4". This must be a female or external connection. Attach lengths of duct until you reach the roof deck.

Draw an outline of the duct on the roof deck. Drill a pilot hole, then saw through the sheathing and roofing material with a reciprocating saw to make the cutout for the vent tailpiece.

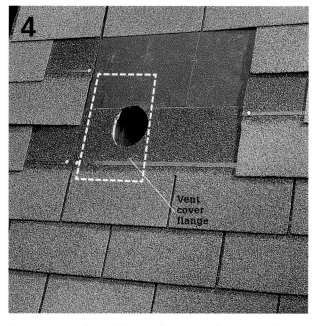

Vent cover flange

Remove a section of shingles from around the cutout, leaving the roofing paper intact. Remove enough shingles to create an exposed area that is at least the size of the vent cover flange.

(continued)

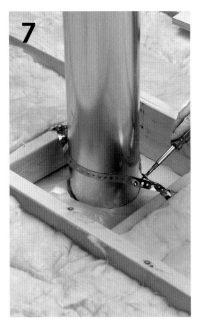

If the hole for the vent does not abut a rafter, attach a 2 × 4 brace between the roof rafters. Attach a hose clamp to the brace or rafter about 1" below the roof sheathing (top). Insert the vent tailpiece into the cutout and through the hose clamp, then tighten the clamp screw (bottom).

Apply roofing cement to the bottom of the vent cover flange, then slide the vent cover over the tailpiece. Nail the vent cover flange into place with self-sealing roofing nails, then patch in shingles around the cover.

Complete installation of the ductwork by securing each joint with self-tapping sheet-metal screws. Wrap each joint with metallic duct tape. Support the duct as it passes through the ceiling with duct straps.

Secure the upper support frame to the ceiling joists or the cross bracing with the screws provided. The screws must be driven into the center of the joists or cross braces. Check to make sure the frame is level in all directions. Insert the lower support frame and secure loosely. Adjust the lower support frame to the desired height above the countertop and tighten the screws. Make sure the support frame is level and plumb.

In the attic, run a branch circuit from a nearby junction box. (This may be a job for an electrician.) Route the cable through the ceiling hole. Pull the cable to reach the junction box, approximately 6" below the frame support. Tape the cable to the frame support.

10

Measure from the bottom of the duct flange in the ceiling to the bottom of the support frame. Add 1" for insertion into the ceiling duct and subtract 1¾" for the hood insertion. (This will vary; check the manufacturer's dimensions.) Cut 6" round duct to this length. Install the duct and attach with sheet-metal screws and metallic duct tape.

11

Slide the top decorative duct cover over the support frame to the ceiling and attach it to the support frame using the supplied decorative screws. Slide the bottom decorative duct cover over the support frame and the top duct cover. Secure with the provided stop screw to hold it in place while the hood is installed.

12

With a helper, lift the hood up to the support frame. Align the hood mounting studs with the support frame holes and guide the hood duct connector into the house duct. Install the nuts and lock washers to the mounting studs and tighten. Check that the hood is level in all directions. Make sure the duct is positioned over the hood connector. Seal the joint with metallic duct tape, not screws.

13

Strip 8" of cable. Thread the cable through a cable clamp and through a knockout into the junction box. Connect the white supply wire to the white vent wire with a wire connector. Connect the black supply wire to the black vent wire. Connect the green or bare supply wire to the green or yellow vent wire. Push the wires into the junction box and replace the cover without pinching the wires. Remove the stop screw and slide down the decorative cover.

RANGES, OVENS & COOKTOPS

Protect your flooring when moving a range, whether it is an old one on the way out or a brand-new one being installed. Typically, ranges have adjustable feet that can gouge floor coverings. A piece of cardboard, tagboard, or a carpet scrap can be slipped under the appliance.

For the most part, installing a new range is simply a matter of positioning it, leveling it, and making sure it is hooked up to a receptacle and gas connection. If you are comfortable working with gas and plumbing, hooking up a gas range or cooktop is not difficult. But in many municipalities only a licensed installer can make gas hook-ups. Ask your local building department if you are unsure (your appliance retailer is also a good source for information).

When moving a range for painting or cleaning, removing it for replacement, or installing a new range, make sure you protect the flooring. Use an appliance dolly to lift a new range from the side only—not the front or the back. If the range will not fit through doors, remove the oven door handle. An electric range or cooktop must have its own dedicated 240-volt circuit. Gas ranges and cooktops also need a grounded 3-hole electrical outlet to power the electronic ignition, clock, and timers.

INSTALLING ELECTRIC RANGES

Receptacles for electric ranges should look like this. They are 50-amp, combination 125/250 volt fittings with a three-slot configuration that will only work with electric range appliance cords. They provide 125-volt power to run lights, clocks, and timers and 250-volt service to the heating elements.

A dedicated circuit with a double pole 50-amp breaker supplies power to the high-voltage receptacle for your electric range. Most codes require 6-gauge copper service entrance round (SER) cable for the circuit. If your circuit does not meet these standards, contact a qualified electrician to upgrade the circuit. *Note: Always shut off power at the main service panel before removing a service panel cover.*

Tips for Installing Gas Ranges ▸

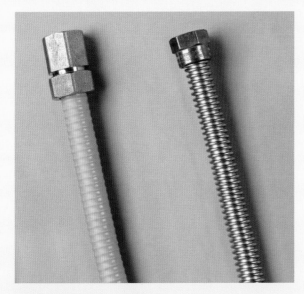

Flexible appliance connectors are required for hooking a gas inlet port up to a gas supply valve. Flexible connectors are usually made of stainless steel, and some areas require that the steel be protected with a PVC coating. These are sold in a variety of lengths. Buy the shortest connector that will reach from the supply valve to the inlet port.

Shut off gas at the nearest in-line shutoff or stopcock valve, as well as the supply valve you will be hooking up to. When closed, a stopcock valve is perpendicular to the gas pipe as seen here.

Use two wrenches to securely attach the appliance connector tube to the gas supply valve. One wrench should be used to hold the tube securely and the other to tighten the male tube coupling onto the female supply valve. Be sure to wrap a layer of gas-rated (yellow) Teflon tape around the supply valve threads before attaching the coupling. Do not overtighten the coupling.

Attach the other end of the flexible appliance connector tube to the gas inlet port in your range or cooktop. Also use yellow Teflon tape to lubricate the threads at this union. Turn on the gas supply and immediately test all connections with leak detector solution. If the connections pass, slide the appliance into position, taking care not to cause stress on or kinks in the connector tube.

REFRIGERATOR ICEMAKER

There's nothing really tricky about installing a refrigerator unless your new model has a built-in icemaker. If your old refrigerator was equipped with an icemaker, you should already have a water supply line running to the refrigerator area. If there is no supply line, contact a plumber to install one for you if you do not know how. Most icemakers either come preinstalled or are purchased as an accessory when you buy your new refrigerator. But if you have an older refrigerator with no icemaker and you'd like it to have one, all is not lost. Inspect the back of the unit, behind the freezer compartment. If your refrigerator has the required plumbing to support an icemaker, you will see a port that is covered with backing. In that case, all you need to do is take the make and model information to an appliance parts dealer, and they can sell you an aftermarket icemaker. Plan to spend $100 to $200.

A built-in icemaker is easy to install as a retrofit appliance in most modern refrigerators. If you want to have an endless supply of ice for home use, you may wonder how you ever got along without one.

Tools & Materials ▸

Screwdrivers	Open-end or adjustable wrench
Nut drivers	Icemaker kit
Needlenose pliers	Saddle valve or T-fitting
Duct or	(for supply tube)
masking tape	Putty knife
Electric drill and	Tape
assorted bits	Eye and ear protection
Channel-type pliers	

How Icemakers Work ▸

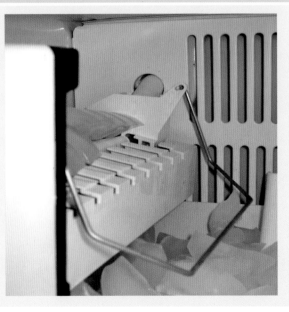

An icemaker receives its supply of water for making cubes through a ¼" copper supply line that runs from the icemaker to a water pipe. The supply line runs through a valve in the refrigerator and is controlled by a solenoid that monitors the water supply and sends the water into the icemaker itself, where it is turned into ice cubes. The cubes drop down into a bin, and as the ice level rises, they also raise a bail wire that's connected to a shutoff. When the bin is full, the bail wire will be high enough to trigger a mechanism that shuts off the water supply.

Aftermarket automatic icemakers are simple to install as long as your refrigerator is icemaker-ready. Buy the correct model for your appliance and do careful installation work—icemaker water supply lines are very common sources for leaks.

HOW TO INSTALL A REFRIGERATOR ICEMAKER

1

Remove all the contents from the refrigerator and freezer compartments and store them in ice chests or in a neighbor's refrigerator. Unplug the unit and pull it out from the wall. Then open the freezer door and remove the icemaker cover plate at the back of the compartment.

2

On the back of the refrigerator, remove the backing or unscrew the icemaker access panel that covers the icemaker port.

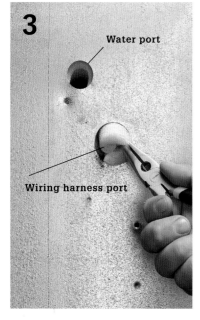

3

Water port

Wiring harness port

Locate and clear the ports. One opening is for the water line. The other is for a wiring harness. Usually, these holes are filled with insulation plugs that keep the cold air inside the freezer from leaking out into the room. Remove these plugs with needlenose pliers.

4

Install the water tube assembly (part of the icemaker kit) in its access hole on the back of the refrigerator. This assembly features a plastic elbow attached to the plastic tube that reaches into the freezer compartment.

5

Hook up the harness. Icemaker kits usually come with a wiring harness that joins the icemaker motor to the power supply wires. Push this harness through the access hole and into the freezer compartment. Seal the hole with the plastic grommet supplied with the harness.

(continued)

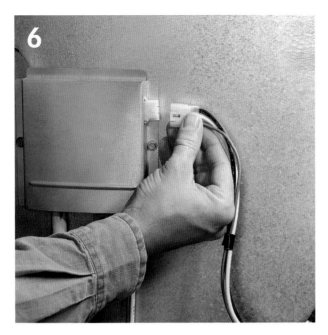

6

Join the end of the icemaker wiring harness to the power connector that was preinstalled on the back of the refrigerator. This connection should be flat against the back. If it isn't, tape it down with duct tape or masking tape.

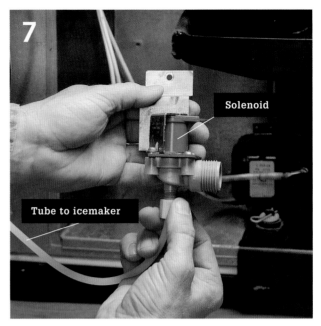

7

Solenoid

Tube to icemaker

Attach the water tube at the top of the refrigerator to the solenoid that is mounted at the bottom with a plastic water line. Run the tube down the back of the refrigerator and attach it to the solenoid valve with a compression fitting. This job is easier to do before you attach the solenoid assembly to the refrigerator cabinet.

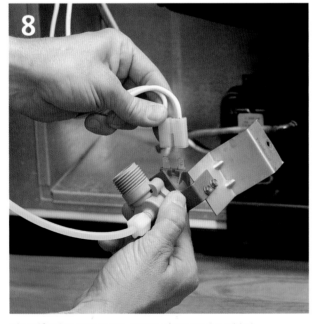

8

Identify the two snap connectors on the wiring harness. One goes to the preinstalled wires on the refrigerator and the other is attached to the solenoid. Just push this second connector onto the brass tabs, usually at the top of the solenoid.

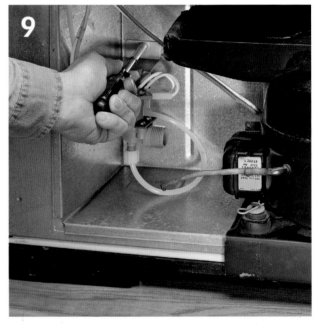

9

Attach the solenoid to a mounting bracket that should be installed on the cabinet wall at the bottom of the refrigerator. Mounting holes may be predrilled in the cabinet for this purpose. But if not, drill holes to match the bracket and the size of the screws. Then attach the bracket and make sure to attach the solenoid ground wire to one of these screws.

Install the water-inlet copper tube once the solenoid is mounted. Attach it by tightening the nut on one end with channel-type pliers. The other end of the tube is held to the refrigerator cabinet with a simple clamp. Make sure the end of this tubing is pointing straight up.

Join the water-inlet tube to the water supply tubing (from the house plumbing system) with a brass compression coupling. Tighten the compression nuts with an open-end or adjustable wrench.

Make sure the water tube and the wiring harness (from the back of the refrigerator) are free inside the freezer compartment. If they are caught on the cabinet, loosen them until they are easily accessible.

Connect the wire harness to the plug on the icemaker unit. Also connect the water supply tube to the back of the icemaker with a spring clip or hose clamp.

Install the icemaker. Remove any small rubber caps that may be installed in the mounting screw holes with a narrow putty knife. Lift the unit and screw it to the freezer wall. The mounting bracket holes are usually slotted to permit leveling the unit. Plug in the refrigerator and test the icemaker.

DISHWASHER

A dishwasher that's past its prime may be inefficient in more ways than one. If it's an old model, it probably wasn't designed to be very efficient to begin with. But more significantly, if it no longer cleans effectively, you're probably spending a lot of time and hot water prerinsing the dishes. This alone can consume more energy and water than a complete wash cycle on a newer machine. So even if your old dishwasher still runs, replacing it with an efficient new model can be a good green upgrade.

In terms of sizing and utility hookups, dishwashers are generally quite standard. If your old machine is a built-in and your countertops and cabinets are standard sizes, most full-sized dishwashers will fit right in. Of course, you should always measure the dimensions of the old unit before shopping for a new one to avoid an unpleasant surprise at installation time. Also be sure to review the manufacturer's instructions before starting any work.

Replacing an old, inefficient dishwasher is a straightforward project that usually takes just a few hours. The energy savings begin with the first load of dishes and continue with every load thereafter.

Tools & Materials ▸

Screwdrivers	Drill	Hose clamps	Bowl
Adjustable wrench	4" of ½" copper tubing	Wire connectors	Eye and ear protection
2' level	Cable connector	Carpet scrap	
⅝" automotive heater hose	Teflon tape		

Efficient Loading ▸

To get the best circulation of water for effective wash action, follow these tips when loading dishes:

- Make sure dishes are loaded so water can reach all of the soiled surfaces.
- Be sure that larger items are not blocking smaller items from the wash action.
- Place all items in both racks so that they are separated and face the center of the dishwasher. This will help to ensure that water reaches all soiled surfaces.
- Place glasses with the open end facing downward to allow proper washing action.
- Do not place glasses over the tines, but between them. This will allow the glasses to lean toward the spray arm and will improve washing. It also promotes drying by reducing the amount of water remaining on the top of the glass after the wash cycle is complete.
- Do not allow flatware to "nest." This prevents proper water distribution between the surfaces.

- Load flatware, except knives, with some handles up and some down to prevent nesting. For safety, knives should always be loaded handles up.

HOW TO REPLACE A DISHWASHER

Shut off the electrical power to the dishwasher circuit at the service panel. Also, turn off the water supply at the shutoff valve, usually located directly under the floor.

Disconnect the old plumbing connections. First unscrew the front access panel. Once the access panel is removed, disconnect the water supply line from the L-fitting on the bottom of the unit. This is usually a brass compression fitting, so just turning the compression nut counterclockwise with an adjustable wrench should do the trick. Use a bowl to catch any water that might leak out when the nut is removed.

(continued)

3

Disconnect the old wiring connections. The dishwasher has an integral electrical box at the front of the unit where the power cable is attached to the dishwasher's fixture wires. Take off the box cover and remove the wire connectors that join the wires together.

4

Disconnect the discharge hose, which is usually connected to the dishwasher port on the side of the garbage disposer. To remove it, loosen the screw on the hose clamp and pull it off. You may need to push this hose back through a hole in the cabinet wall and into the dishwasher compartment so it won't get caught when you pull the dishwasher out.

5

Detach the unit from the surrounding cabinets. Remove the screws that hold the brackets to the underside of the countertop. Then put a piece of cardboard or old carpet under the front legs to protect the floor from getting scratched, and pull the dishwasher out.

6

Prepare the new dishwasher. Tip it on its back and attach the new L-fitting into the threaded port on the solenoid. Apply some Teflon tape or pipe sealant to the fitting threads before tightening it in place to prevent possible leaks.

Lengthening a Discharge Hose ▸

1

If the discharge hose has to be modified to fit onto the disposer port, first insert a 4"-long piece of ½" copper tubing into the hose and hold it in place with a hose clamp. This provides a nipple for the rubber adapter that fits onto the disposer.

2

Clamp the rubber disposer adapter to the end of the copper tubing nipple. Then tighten the hose clamp securely.

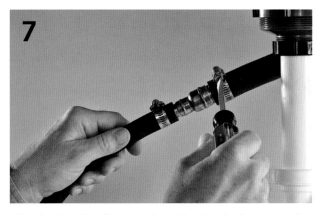

7

Attach a length of new automotive heater hose, usually ⅝" dia., to the end of the dishwasher's discharge hose nipple with a hose clamp. The new hose you are adding should be long enough to reach from the discharge nipple to the port on the side of the kitchen sink garbage disposer.

8

Prepare for the wiring connections. Like the old dishwasher, the new one will have an integral electrical box for making the wiring connections. To gain access to the box, remove the box cover. Then install a cable connector on the back of the box and bring the power cable from the service panel through this connector. Power should be shut off at the main service panel at all times.

9

Install a leveling leg at each of the four corners while the new dishwasher is still on its back. Just turn the legs into the threaded holes designed for them. Leave about ½" of each leg projecting from the bottom of the unit. These will have to be adjusted later to level the appliance. Tip the appliance up onto the feet and slide it into the opening. Check for level in both directions and adjust the feet as required.

10

Once the dishwasher is level, attach the brackets to the underside of the countertop to keep the appliance from moving. Then pull the discharge hose into the sink cabinet and install it so there's a loop that is attached with a bracket to the underside of the countertop. This loop prevents waste water from flowing from the disposer back into the dishwasher.

(continued)

KITCHEN PROJECTS

409

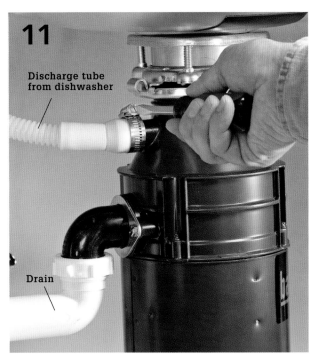

11

Discharge tube
from dishwasher

Drain

Push the adapter over the disposer's discharge nipple and tighten it in place with a hose clamp. If you don't have a disposer, this discharge hose can be clamped directly to a modified sink tailpiece that's installed below a standard sink strainer.

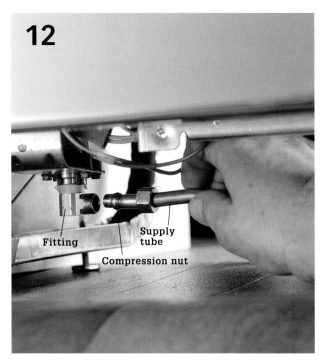

12

Fitting

Supply
tube

Compression nut

Adjust the L-fitting on the dishwasher's water inlet valve until it points directly toward the water supply tubing. Lubricate the threads slightly with a drop of dishwashing liquid and tighten the tubing's compression nut onto the fitting. Use an adjustable wrench and turn the nut clockwise.

13

Complete the electrical connections by tightening the connector's clamp on the cable and then joining the power wires to the fixture wires with wire connectors. Attach the ground wire (or wires) to the grounding screw on the box, and replace the cover.

14

Install the access panel, usually by hooking it on a couple of prongs just below the dishwasher's door. Install the screws (if any) that hold it in place, and turn on the water and power supplies. Replace the toe-kick panel at the bottom of the dishwasher.

RANGE HOOD/VENT FAN

Range hoods are vent fans that are mounted directly over a slide-in range or a cooktop. Some are meant to be seen while others are designed to be hidden in a cabinet or soffit.

Effective ventilation is important for ridding your kitchen of cooking odors, excess moisture (think: mold), smoke, and exhaust fumes from gas burners. If you don't already have a good vent system in place, you should consider installing one to improve your indoor air quality. Recirculating vent fans—those without a duct running outside—also should be replaced, since all they really do is pretend to filter the air before blowing it right back into the kitchen.

The two main types of mechanical ventilation are overhead hoods and downdraft (or cooktop) fans. Overhead systems include the basic under-cabinet types and the higher-end suspended styles with exposed ducting extending from the ceiling. Overheads are more effective and require less suction than downdraft vents, primarily because they work with nature rather than against it: Hot air rises, so all that steam, grease, and fragrant cooking air is easy to capture inside a hood for transfer to the outdoors. Downdraft fans have to work much harder

in reversing the natural flow of air and vapor. Also, many downdraft systems tend to draw heat away from burners (especially gas burners), so your pans don't heat as evenly when the fan is on.

Sizing is important with hood systems. The hood should be at least as wide as, but preferably up to 6 inches wider than, the cooktop and at least 20 inches deep. The power, or capacity, of the fan is another critical factor. Expert recommendations vary. Some say a standard hood fan should move 40 cubic feet per minute for every 12 inches of cooktop width; for example, a 30-inch-wide cooktop gets a 100 cfm fan, which is the minimum required under many building codes. The National Kitchen & Bath Association recommends 150 cfm as a minimum for hood fans.

The manufacturer of your range or cooktop may have its own recommendations. Undersizing a fan results in inadequate ventilation, but oversizing it could potentially lead to a dangerous backdrafting into the home.

HOW TO INSTALL A RANGE HOOD

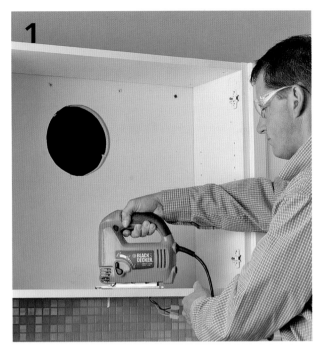

Install the vent duct in the wall first, then cut a hole in the back of the range hood cabinet and mount the cabinet over the duct. Cut a vent hole in the bottom of the cabinet to match the opening on the top of the hood.

Make sure the circuit power is turned off at the service panel, then join the power cable wires to the lead wires inside the range hood. Use wire connectors for this job.

Get someone to help lift the range hood into place and hold it there while you attach it. Drive two screws through both sides and into the adjacent cabinets. If the hood is slightly small for the opening, slip a shim between the hood and the walls, trying to keep the gaps even.

Run ductwork from the cabinet to the exhaust exit point. Use two 45° adjustable elbows to join the duct in the wall to the top of the range hood. Use sheet-metal screws and duct tape to hold all parts together and keep them from moving.

Downdraft cooktop: With a built-in blower unit that vents through the back or bottom of a base cabinet. A downdraft cooktop is a good choice for a kitchen island or peninsula.

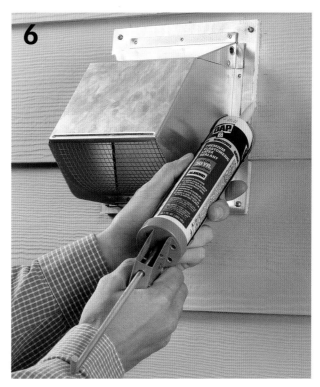

Wall vent: If the duct comes out through the side wall of the house, install a vertical duct cap. Make sure to seal around the perimeter of the cap with exterior caulk.

Ceiling vent: If the duct goes through an overhang soffit, you'll need a transition fitting to connect the round duct to a short piece of rectangular duct. Once these parts are installed, add a protective grille to keep animals and insects from getting into the duct.

Roof vent: For ducts that pass through the roof, cut an access hole through the roofing and sheathing, then install a weatherproof cap on top of the duct and under the roofing shingles. Make a waterproof seal by caulking the cap with plastic roof cement.

DROP-IN SINK

Most drop-in, self-rimming kitchen sinks are easy to install. Drop-in sinks for do-it-yourself installation are made from cast iron coated with enamel, stainless steel, enameled steel, acrylic, fiberglass, or resin composites. Because cast-iron sinks are heavy, their weight holds them in place, and they require no mounting hardware.

Stainless steel and enameled-steel sinks weigh less than cast-iron, and most require mounting brackets on the underside of the countertop. Some acrylic and resin sinks rely on silicone caulk to hold them in place. If you are replacing a sink, but not the countertop, make sure the new sink is the same size or larger than the old sink. All old silicone caulk residue must be removed with acetone or denatured alcohol, or the new caulk will not stick.

Shopping Tips ▸

- When purchasing a sink, you also need to buy strainer bodies and baskets, sink clips, and a drain trap kit.
- Look for basin dividers that are lower than the sink rim—this reduces splashing.
- Drain holes in the back or to the side make for more usable space under the sink.
- When choosing a sink, make sure the predrilled openings will fit your faucet.

Tools & Materials ▸

Caulk gun	Drill
Spud wrench	Mounting clips
Screwdriver	Jigsaw
Sink	Pen or pencil
Sink frame	Wrench
Plumber's putty or silicone caulk	Eye and ear protection

Drop-in sinks, also known as self-rimming sinks, have a wide sink flange that extends beyond the edges of the sink cutout. They have a wide back flange to which the faucet is mounted directly.

HOW TO INSTALL A SELF-RIMMING SINK

1

Invert the sink and trace around the edges as a reference for making the sink cutout cutting lines, which should be parallel to the outlines, but about 1" inside of them to create a 1" ledge. If the sink comes with a template for the cutout, use it.

2

Drill a starter hole and cut out the sink opening with a jigsaw. Cut right up to the line. Because the sink flange fits over the edges of the cutout, the opening doesn't need to be perfect, but, as always, you should try to do a nice, neat job.

3

Attach as much of the plumbing as makes sense to install prior to setting the sink into the opening. Having access to the underside of the flange is a great help when it comes to attaching the faucet body, sprayer, and strainer, in particular.

4

Apply a bead of silicone caulk around the edges of the sink opening. The sink flange most likely is not flat, so apply the caulk in the area that will make contact with the flange.

5

Place the sink in the opening. Try to get the sink centered right away so you don't need to move it around and disturb the caulk, which can break the seal. If you are installing a heavy cast-iron sink, it's best to leave the strainers off so you can grab onto the sink at the drain openings.

6

For sinks with mounting clips, tighten the clips from below using a screwdriver or wrench (depending on the type of clip your sink has). There should be at least three clips on every side. Don't overtighten the clips—this can cause the sink flange to flatten or become warped.

UNDERMOUNT SINK

Undermounted sinks have become quite popular in contemporary kitchens for reasons that are both practical and aesthetic. On the aesthetic side, they look updated and sleek. Practically, they are easier to clean than rimmed sinks because you eliminate that area around the rim seal where stuff always collects.

Most sink manufacturers make sinks that are designed for undermounting, and if you don't mind paying the $100 to $200 premium, a true undermount sink is the best choice. But if your decision-making is driven more by your frugal side, you can undermount a self-rimming (drop-in) stainless steel sink with little difficulty using readily available undermount clips. (Self-rimmers also come in a much wider range of styles). *Note: You can undermount any sink you wish, including heavy cast-iron models, if you support the sink from below instead of hanging it from clips.* Not all countertops are suitable for undermounting a sink. The countertop material needs to be contiguous in nature. That is, the edges that are created when you cut through it need to be of the same material as the surface. Solid-surface, granite, butcher block, and concrete are good candidates for undermounting.

Post-form and any laminated or tiled countertops are not. (Some new products that claim to seal countertop substrate edges around a sink opening are emerging, but are not yet proven or readily available). If you are not able to locate solid-surface seam adhesive or undermount clips, you can use the same installation method for undermounting that is shown in the apron sink mounting project on pages 420 to 423 instead.

Tools & Materials ▸

2HP or larger plunge router	Belt sander
½" template-following router bit	Solid-surface scraps
Roundover bit	Solid-surface seam adhesive with applicator gun
MDF or particleboard for template	Denatured alcohol
Jigsaw	Undermount clips
Drill and bits	Silicone caulk
Abrasive pads	Pipe clamps
Drum sander attachment	Pad sander
Laminate trimmer	Eye and ear protection

HOW TO MAKE A SINK CUTOUT TEMPLATE

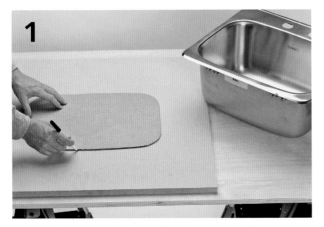

If you are undermounting a self-rimming sink, do not use the sink template provided by the manufacturer. Instead, make your own custom router template to use with a router and pattern-following bit. The template should be sized and shaped so the cutout you make with your pattern-following bit is the same shape and about ⅛" larger than the basin opening in each direction. You can plot the cutout directly onto a piece of MDF, or make a preliminary paper or cardboard template and trace it onto the MDF.

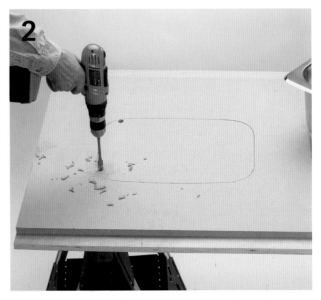

Drill a few starter holes just inside the template outline to create access for your jigsaw blade. If the cutout has sharp radii at the corners, look for a bit or hole-cutter of the same radius and carefully drill out the corners.

3

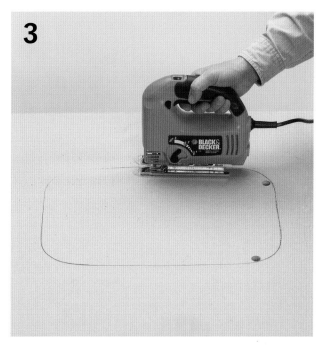

Connect the starter holes by cutting just inside the cutout line with a jigsaw. You can use a straightedge cutting guide for straight runs if you have little confidence in your ability to cut straight.

4

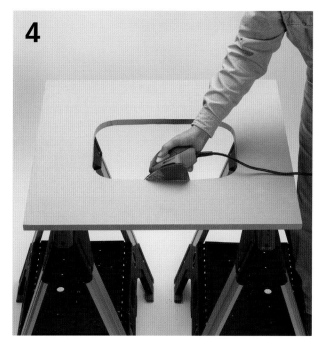

Use a belt sander or pad sander to smooth out the cutting lines and to remove material until the cutout hits the lines precisely. A drum sander attachment mounted in a power drill is useful for smoothing out rounded corners.

HOW TO UNDERMOUNT A SINK

1

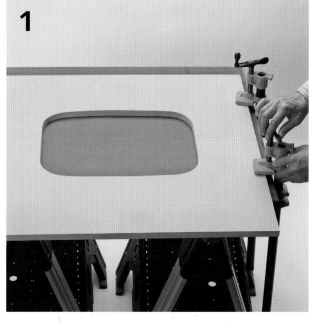

Remove the countertop from the cabinet and transport it to a work area with good light and ventilation. Set the countertop section on sawhorses and then clamp the router template (see previous page) securely so the opening is centered exactly over the planned cutout area. Make sure the router bit won't be cutting into your work area.

2

Use a two-fluted, ⅛" pattern-following bit (preferably carbide tipped) with a ½" shank into a plunge router with a minimum motor size of 2HP. Retract the bit and position the router so the bit is an inch or so away from the edge of the template. Turn the router on and let it develop to full velocity. Then, plunge the router bit into the countertop material until the bit breaks all the way through.

(continued)

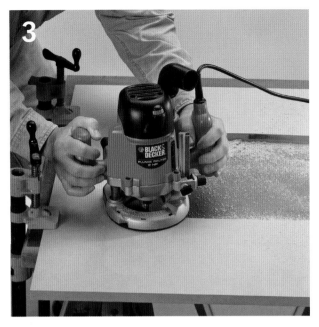

Pull the router bit toward the template edge until the bit sleeve contacts the edge, then slowly cut through the countertop, following the template. Pace is important here: Cutting too fast will cause chatter, cutting too slowly will cause burning or melting. Cut three continuous sides of the opening, hugging the template edge.

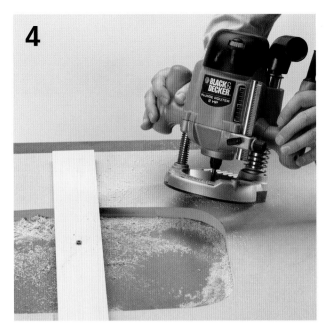

After routing three sides of the opening, stop routing and screw a support board to the waste piece. The ends of the support board should extend onto the template. Position the support so it is near the center, but not in the way for completing the fourth side of the cut. Finish the cut. The support board will prevent the waste from breaking off as the cut nears completion.

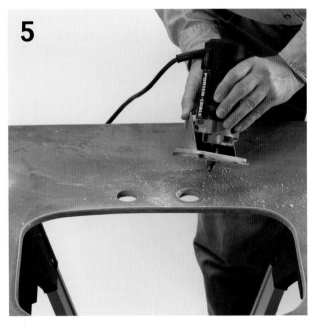

If the sink outline has any chatter or the cutout is not perfectly smooth, make another pass with a straight bit before you remove the template. Remove the template and make a ⅛" roundover cut on both the top and bottom of the sink cutout. If you know exactly where your faucet hole or holes need to be, cut them with a hole saw and round over their tops and bottoms as well.

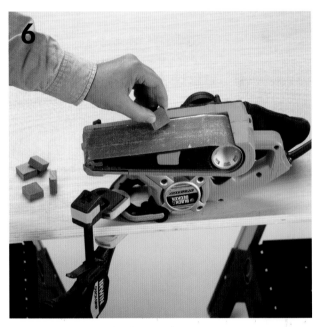

Mount the sink on the countertop before you reinstall it on the cabinet. Cut several 1 × 1" mounting blocks from the solid-surface waste cutout. You'll also need to purchase some seam adhesive to glue the mounting blocks to the underside of the countertop. After they're cut, break all the block edges with a stationary sander or by clamping a belt sander belt-side up and using it as a stationary sander (breaking the edges reduces the chance that the blocks will crack).

7

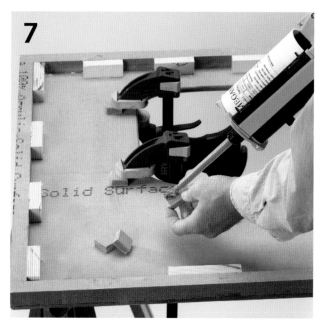

Clean the blocks and the underside of the solid-surface around the cutouts with denatured alcohol. Apply solid-surface seam adhesive to the blocks and bond them to the underside of the countertop, set back ¾" from the cutout. Install three blocks along the long sides of the cutout and two on the front-to-back sides. Clamp the blocks while the adhesive sets up.

8

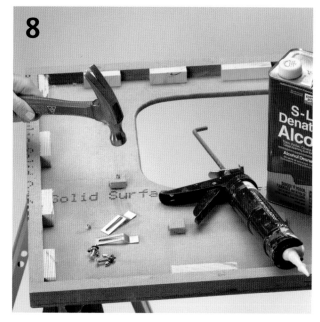

Drill pilot holes, ¼"-dia. × ¾" deep, for the sink clips into each mounting block. The holes should be in the centers of the mounting blocks. Tap the brass inserts for the mounting clips into the holes in the mounting blocks.

9

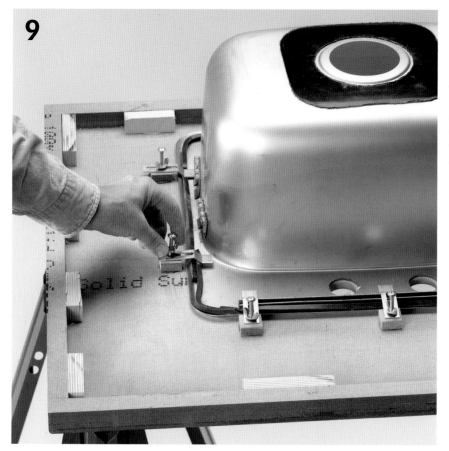

Clean the sink rim and the underside of the countertop with denatured alcohol. When the alcohol has dried, apply a bead of 100% silicone adhesive caulk to the sink rim. Carefully center the sink over the opening and press it in place. Hand-tighten the wing nuts onto the mounting nuts to secure the clips that hold the sink bowl. Replace the countertop and hook up the faucet and drain.

APRON SINK

Despite their vintage look, apron sinks are relative newcomers in modern kitchen design. Also known as farmer's sinks or farmhouse sinks, they are notable for having an exposed front apron that usually projects past the cabinets. Although they can be double-bowl fixtures, most apron sinks are single bowl, and most are made from fireclay (a durable enameled porcelain). Other materials sometimes used for apron sinks include enameled cast iron, copper, stainless steel, and composite. The model seen here, made by Kohler, is a fireclay sink.

Apron sinks typically are not suspended from above as other undermount sinks are: they're just too heavy. Instead, you either attach wood ledgers to the cabinet sides to support a board that bears the sink from below, or you build a support platform that rests on the floor. Either way, the sink is not actually connected to the countertop except with caulk at the seams. As kitchen sinks go, apron sinks are definitely on the high-end side, with most models costing over $1,000. But they create a focal point that makes them rather unique. Plus, they have a warm, comforting appearance that people who own them find appealing.

Apron sinks, also called farmer's sinks or farmhouse sinks, can be nestled into a tiled countertop (called a tile-in) or pressed up against the underside of a solid countertop. Either way, they can be gorgeous.

Tools & Materials ▸

Countertop material	Level	Various screws	Silicone adhesive
Shims	Belt sander	Wood finish	Strainer
Carpenter's square	Pad sander	Brush	Drain tailpiece
Straightedge	Spindle sander	Framing lumber	¾" plywood or MDF
Jigsaw	Router or laminate trimmer	Sheet stock	Eye and ear protection
Tape measure	Drill/driver	Caulk gun	

HOW TO INSTALL AN APRON SINK IN A BUTCHER BLOCK COUNTERTOP

If you are undermounting the sink, outline the sink opening in your countertop material. Plan the opening to create an equal reveal of approximatel ½" on all three sides (which basically means making the opening 1" smaller than the overall sink dimensions). For the 22 × 25" sink seen here, the opening cut into the butcher block is 24" wide and 21" deep (½" reveal in the back plus ½" projection of the sink in front).

Mount a downstroke blade in a jigsaw (see pages 178 to 183 and be sure to read the material on working with butcher block if that is your countertop surface). Cut out the waste to form the sink opening, cutting just inside the cutting lines. Support the waste wood from below so it does not break out prematurely.

Sand up to the cutting lines with a belt sander after the waste is removed. The goal is to create a smooth, even edge.

Sand into the corners of the cutout with a detail sander or, if you own one, a spindle sander (you can mount a small-diameter sanding drum in an electric drill, but be sure to practice first on some scrap wood).

Flip the countertop and sand the cutout along the bottom edges of the opening to prevent any splintering.

Round over the top edges of the cutout with a piloted roundover bit mounted in a small router or a laminate trimmer.

(continued)

Apply several coats of urethane varnish to the exposed wood around the opening. This wood will have a high level of water exposure, so take care to get a good, even coat. Where possible, match the finish of the countertop (if any).

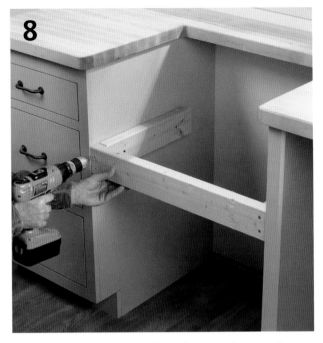

Measure and draw layout lines for a wood support frame to be attached to the adjoining cabinet walls. Attach the frame members (2 × 4) to the cabinet sides first and then face-screw through the front frame member and into the ends of side members.

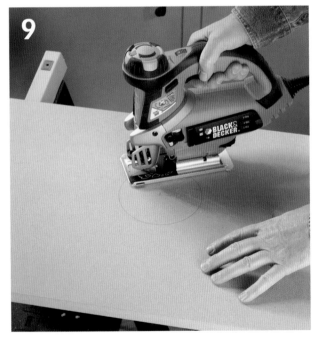

Cut a support platform to size from ¾" plywood or MDF, then layout and cut a drain clearance hole (if your drain will include a garbage disposer, make the hole large enough to accommodate the disposer easily). Also cut holes for the water supply lines if they come up through the floor and there is not enough room between the platform and the wall for the lines to fit.

Remove the countertop section containing the sink cutout, if feasible (if you can't remove the countertop, see sidebar next page). Then, screw the platform to the frame.

11

Set the sink on the platform and confirm that it is level with the cabinet tops by setting a straightedge so it spans the sink opening. If necessary, shim under the sink to bring it to level (if the sink is too high you'll need to reposition the frame members).

12

Apply silicone adhesive to the sink rim and then carefully replace the countertop section before the silicone adhesive sets up. Reattach the countertop.

13

Hook up the drain plumbing and install the faucet. If you are drilling through the countertop material to install a faucet, make sure your installation hole or holes align with the preformed holes in the back flange of the sink.

Option for Unremovable Countertops ▸

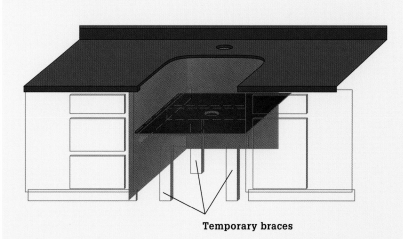

Temporary braces

If you are not able to remove the countertop, you'll need to raise the sink up against the underside of the countertop once you've caulked the rim. Create a 3-piece 2 × 4 frame and platform (as seen in Step 8) but do not attach it to the cabinets. Instead, support the platform with braces. With help, set the sink on the platform and raise it from below after the silicone adhesive has been applied to the sink rim. When the sink rim is tight against the countertop, attach the frame members to the cabinet sides with screws.

BATHROOM PROJECTS

Few rooms in the home get more use from everybody in the family than the bathroom—and no room is subjected to more wear and tear, if for no other reason than the constant presence of moisture. This is one of the major reasons why bathroom remodeling is such a common occurrence.

Another reason is the changing requirements for a bathroom over time. A family room or kitchen serving a young couple can just as easily serve empty nesters, but a bathroom designed for a family with young children may be much different than a bathroom aimed at serving adults—especially as they reach the empty-nest years. A bathtub with watertight wall-surround panels may be ideal for bathing splashing youngsters, but eventually a large, curbless shower might be a better use of that space. A double-sink vanity may give way to an elegant and stylish vessel sink. A bathroom that serves adults rather than kids might be well served with a bidet or private toilet enclosure.

The projects that follow have been chosen largely with this in mind: the ways in which the use of a bathroom changes as your family's needs change. It will serve as useful guide for tailoring your bathroom remodeling project to match your evolving needs.

▌ IN THIS CHAPTER:

- Designing for Accessibility
- Shower Enclosure Kits
- Custom Shower Base
- Curbless Shower
- Alcove Bathtubs
- Three-Piece Tub Surrounds
- Soaking Tubs
- Freestanding Tubs
- Sliding Tub Doors
- Pedestal & Console Sinks
- Wall-Mounted Sinks
- Vessel Sinks
- Bidets
- Vent Fans
- Toilet Enclosure

DESIGNING FOR ACCESSIBILITY

Accessibility has become a key issue not only in the codes that regulate residential bathroom construction, but with almost every feature designed for bathrooms. From toilets to faucets to lighting and beyond, manufacturers are responding to an aging population and the need to accommodate all potential users of a home's bathroom.

Designing bathrooms to accommodate the needs of any individual—including those with mobility limitations and even the severely disabled—is at the heart of what is known as "Universal Design." The term was coined by disabled architect Ronald Mace. The goal? In Mace's words, "The design of products and environments to be usable by all people to the greatest extent possible, without the need for adaptation or specialized design." In practice, that translates to turnkey fixtures that work for able-bodied individuals and those who use a wheelchair or walker alike.

More recently, a focus has been placed on accommodating the 78 million baby boomers who are rapidly aging into a incredibly large elderly population. Studies show that these people want to stay in their homes and remain independent as long as possible. The Aging-in-Place movement has sprung up to facilitate that, and to set guidelines for bathroom design specifically to suit elderly users. But in reality, Aging-in-Place is a subset of Universal Design and it is a difference largely without a distinction. If you take the steps outlined here, and select fixtures and features designed for maximum accessibility, your bathroom will be welcoming and user-friendly now and as you age, and for anyone who might need to use it.

Aging-in-Place bathroom design often deals with remodeling existing spaces to better suit users with age-related mobility issues. Those who can't stand for the span of a shower can take one while sitting in this specially adapted stool. They can use the ergonomic handheld showerhead with a handle that clips onto a nearby grab bar. Even the toilet paper holder has been replaced with one that has a grab bar built in.

UNIVERSAL DESIGN STANDARDS

Bathroom elements that meet the mandates of Universal Design are continually being refined by manufacturers as they respond to legislation such as the ADA (Americans with Disabilities Act) and the needs of an aging population. Design style is inevitably a part of the process. Utilitarian features such as grab bars are increasingly crafted with stunning looks and finishes that make them easy to integrate into even the most sophisticated bathroom style.

Grab bars. The new rule for grab bars is "dual purpose." Towel racks, toilet paper holders, and bathroom shelving are all being crafted with integrated grab bars. Not only does this mean buying and installing one fixture in place of two, it means the grab bars are a blended part of the overall look of the bathroom. Even the grab bars used in bathtubs and showers are seeing style upgrades, with molded finger grips and the same selection of surface finishes that you'll find in other fixtures, such as showerheads and faucets.

Toilets. The key to making this essential fixture comfortable for every potential user lies in seat height. Manufacturers have come up with a multitude of solutions, including power-lift toilet seats, height adapters, higher-than-normal traditional toilets and those that can be adjusted, and wall-mounted toilets that can installed at any height. Grab bars are essential to assist movement on and off any toilet, so it's fortunate that you can find attractive toilet paper holder–grab bar combinations.

Faucets. The first step in making faucets accessible was the use of paddle handles and single-handle faucets that could easily be manipulated by those lacking dexterity, hand strength, or motor skills. Nowadays, technology is aiding people with coordination and hand-strength difficulties in the form of motion-activated and touch-activated faucets. These make using the faucet as easy as moving a hand. They are also a breeze to install.

Bathtubs. The standard bathtub-shower combination can be retrofitted to accommodate limited mobility users with the addition of special stools and handheld showerheads with ergonomic grips. Better yet, consider replacing an existing tub with a walk-in model equipped with a door. These tubs typically have seats at chair height to make the transition into the tub easier. Many also feature jets and heaters to create a luxurious experience. When shopping for a walk-in tub, pay close attention to the contours of the seat and back support. These will be key to how comfortable and supportive the tub is over the course of a nice long soak. Choose a door style that best accommodates the user's preference; available styles open in or out, up or down. The lower the threshold, the better, and the door handle should be easy for the intended user to operate.

Other types of tubs can be made easier to use by locating the controls on the outside edge of the tub or tub deck. This allows the user to fill the tub without leaning over and possibly losing balance.

Understanding Aging in Place ▸

The Aging-in-Place movement shares much with the general Universal Design trend, the key difference being the focus on the needs of the elderly. As we age, we lose strength in our hands, arms, and legs, and often have to deal with nagging chronic injuries associated with aging—arthritis and limited flexibility and mobility chief among those complaints. Many Aging-in-Place changes are focused on accommodating those conditions and preventing any injury that could short-circuit independence.

Lighting. Older people often deal with diminished vision, so effective lighting is key to making Aging-in-Place bathrooms more user-friendly and safer.

This entails a combination of undercabinet and undercounter lighting, baseboard or cove lighting, special shower lights and more powerful ambient lights on the wall and ceiling to dispel any visually confusing shadows.

Nonslip surfaces. Falls are the number-one cause of elderly immobilization and can have serious health ramifications. It's essential that tubs, floors, and shower stalls have truly non-slip surfaces that maintain traction even when wet. This means a slip-resistant glaze or texture on any bathroom flooring, and decals or slip-preventing strips in bathtub-shower combinations.

SHOWER ENCLOSURE KITS

The fastest and easiest way to create a new shower in your bathroom is to frame in the stall area with lumber and wallboard and then install a shower enclosure kit. Typically consisting of three fiberglass or plastic walls, these enclosure kits snap together at the corners and nestle inside the flanges of the shower pan to create nearly foolproof mechanical seals. Often the walls are formed with shelves, soap holders, and other conveniences.

If you are on a tight budget, you can find extremely inexpensive enclosure kits to keep costs down. You can even create your own custom enclosure using waterproof beadboard panels and snap-together connectors. Or, you can invest in a higher-grade kit made from thicker material that will last much longer. Some kits are sold with the receptor (and perhaps even the door) included. The kit shown here is designed to be attached directly to wall studs, but others require a backer wall for support. The panels are attached to the backer with high-tack panel adhesive.

Tools & Materials ▶

Tape measure
Pencil
Hammer
Carpenter's square
Screwdrivers
Pipe wrench
Level
Strap wrench
Adjustable wrench
Pliers
Drill/driver
Center punch
File
Utility knife
Hacksaw
Masking tape

Slicone caulk
   and caulk gun
Shower enclosure kit
Shower door
Showerhead
Faucet
Plumbing supplies
Pry bar
Deck screws
Jigsaw
Large-head
   roofing nails
Eye and ear
   protection

A paneled shower surround is inexpensive and easy to install. Designed for alcove installations, they often are sold with matching shower pans (called receptors). Some include molded-in accessories such as shelves or soap dishes.

HOW TO INSTALL A SHOWER ENCLOSURE

Mark out the location of the shower, including any new walls, on the floor and walls. Most kits can be installed over wallboard, but you can usually achieve a more professional looking wall finish if you remove the wall covering and floor covering in the installation area. Dispose of the materials immediately and thoroughly clean the area.

If you are adding a wall to create the alcove, lay out the locations for the studs and plumbing on the new wood sill plate. Also lay out the stud locations on the cap plate that will be attached to the ceiling. Refer to the enclosure kit instructions for exact locations and dimensions of studs. Attach the sill plate to the floor with deck screws and panel adhesive, making sure it is square to the back wall and the correct distance from the side wall.

Align a straight 2 × 4 right next to the sill plate and make a mark on the ceiling. Use a level to extend that line directly above the sill plate. Attach the cap plate at that point.

Install the 2 × 4 studs at the outlined locations. Check with a level to make sure each stud is plumb and then attach them by driving deck screws toenail style into the sill plate and cap plate.

(continued)

5

Drain location

Cut an access hole in the floor for the drain, according to the installation manual instructions. Drill openings in the sill plate of the wet wall (the new wall in this project) for the supply pipes, also according to the instructions.

6

Install a drain pipe and branch line and then trim the drain pipe flush with the floor. If you are not experienced with plumbing, hire a plumber to install the new drain line.

7

Faucet body

Cross brace

Ball valves

Supply riser

Install new supply risers as directed in the instruction manual (again, have a plumber do this if necessary). Also install cross braces between the studs in the wet wall for mounting the faucet body and shower arm. *Note: Some local codes require that you use gate valve shutoffs, not ball valves.*

8

BLACK & DECKER.

If the supply plumbing is located in a wall (old or new) that is accessible from the non-shower side, install framing for a removable access panel.

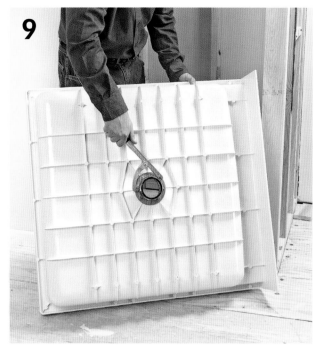

9

Attach the drain tailpiece that came with your shower pan to the underside of the unit, following the manufacturer's instructions precisely. Here, an adjustable spud wrench is being used to tighten the tailpiece.

Option: To stabilize the pan, especially if the floor is uneven, pour or trowel a layer of thinset mortar into the installation area, taking care to keep the mortar out of the drain access hole. Do not apply mortar in areas where the pan has feet that are intended to make full contact with the floor.

10

Set the pan in place, check to make sure it is level, and shim it if necessary. Secure the pan with large-head roofing nails driven into the wall stud so the heads pin the flange against the stud. Do not overdrive the nails.

11

Lay out the locations for the valve hole or holes in the end wall panel that will be installed on the wet wall. Check your installation instructions. Some kits come with a template marked on the packaging carton. Cut the access hole with a hole saw and drill or with a jigsaw and fine-tooth blade. If using a jigsaw, orient the panel so the good surface is facing down.

(continued)

12

Position the back wall so there is a slight gap (about ¹⁄₃₂") between the bottom of the panel and the rim of the pan—set a few small spacers on the rim if need be. Tack a pair of roofing nails above the top of the back panel to hold it in place (or use duct tape). Position both end walls and test the fits. Make clip connections between panels (inset) if your kit uses them.

Clip connectors

13

Remove the end walls so you can prepare the installation area for them. If your kit recommends panel adhesive, apply it to the wall or studs. In the kit shown here, only a small bead of silicone sealant on the pan flange is required.

14

Reinstall the end panels, permanently clipping them to the back panel according to the kit manufacturer's instructions. Make sure the front edges of the end panels are flush with the front of the pan.

15

Once the panels are positioned correctly and snapped together, fasten them to the wall studs. If the panels have predrilled nail holes, drive roofing nails through them at each stud at the panel tops and every 4 to 6" along vertical surfaces.

Install wallcovering material above the enclosure panels and anywhere else it is needed. Use moisture-resistant materials, and maintain a gap of ¼" between the shoulders of the top panel flanges and the wallcovering.

Finish the walls and then caulk between the enclosure panels and the wallcoverings with silicone caulk.

Install the faucet handles and escutcheon and caulk around the escutcheon plate. Install the shower arm escutcheon and showerhead. Add a shower door.

Access panel

Make an access panel and attach it at the framed opening created in step 8. A piece of ¼" plywood framed with mitered case molding and painted to match the wall is one idea for access panel covers.

CUSTOM SHOWER BASE

Building a custom-tiled shower base lets you choose the shape and size of your shower rather than having its dimensions dictated by available products. Building the base is quite simple, though it does require time and some knowledge of basic masonry techniques because the base is formed primarily using mortar. What you get for your time and trouble can be spectacular.

Before designing a shower base, contact your local building department regarding code restrictions and to secure the necessary permits. Most codes require water controls to be accessible from outside the shower and describe acceptable door positions and operation. Requirements like these influence the size and position of the base.

Choosing the tile before finalizing the design lets you size the base to require mostly or only full tiles. Consider using small tile and create a color graduation from top to bottom or in a sweep across the walls. Or, use trim tile and listellos on the walls to create an interesting focal point.

Whatever tile you choose, remember to seal the grout in your new shower and to maintain it carefully over the years. Water-resistant grout protects the structure of the shower and prolongs its useful life.

Tools & Materials ▶

Tape measure
Circular saw
Hammer
Utility knife
Straightedge
Stapler
2' level
Torpedo level
Mortar mixing box
Trowel
Wood float
Felt-tip marker
Ratchet wrench
Expandable stopper
Drill
Tin snips
Torpedo level
Tools and materials
   for installing tile
2 × 4 and 2 × 10
   framing lumber
15# building paper

16d galvanized
   common nails
3-piece shower drain
PVC primer and
   cement
Galvanized finish nails
Galvanized metal lath
Thinset mortar
Thick-bed floor mortar
Latex mortar additive
CPE waterproof
   membrane
   & preformed
   dam corners
CPE membrane
   solvent glue
CPE membrane
   sealant
Cementboard
   and materials
Eye and ear protection

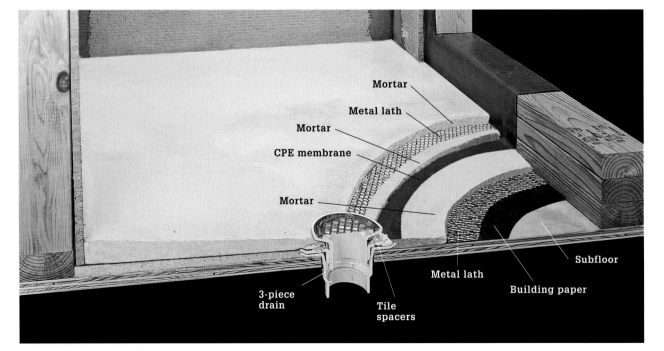

A **custom shower base** is built in three layers to ensure proper drainage: the underlayment, the shower pan, and the shower floor.

BATHROOM PROJECTS

HOW TO BUILD A CUSTOM-TILED SHOWER BASE

Remove building materials to expose subfloor and stud walls. Cut three 2 × 4s for the curb and fasten them to the floor joists and the studs at the shower threshold with 16d galvanized common nails. Also cut 2 × 10 lumber to size and install in the stud bays around the perimeter of the shower base. Install (or have installed) drain and supply plumbing.

Staple 15-pound building paper to the subfloor of the shower base. Disassemble the 3-piece shower drain and glue the bottom piece to the drain pipe with PVC cement. Partially screw the drain bolts into the drain piece, and stuff a rag into the drain pipe to prevent mortar from falling into the drain.

Mark the height of the bottom drain piece on the wall farthest from the center of the drain. Measure from the center of the drain straight across to that wall, then raise the height mark ¼" for every 12" of shower floor to slope the pre pan toward the drain. Trace a reference line at the height mark around the perimeter of the entire alcove, using a level.

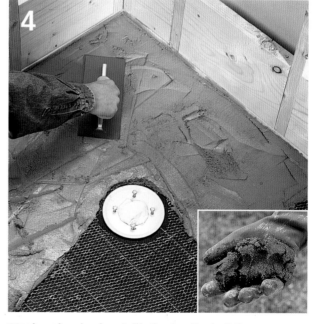

Staple galvanized metal lath over the building paper; cut a hole in the lath ½" from the drain. Mix thinset mortar to a fairly dry consistency, using a latex additive for strength; mortar should hold its shape when squeezed (inset). Trowel the mortar onto the subfloor, building the pre pan from the flange of the drain piece to the height line on the perimeter of the walls.

(continued)

5

Continue using the trowel to form the pre pan, checking the slope using a level and filling any low spots with mortar. Finish the surface of the pre pan with a wood float until it is even and smooth. Allow the mortar to cure overnight.

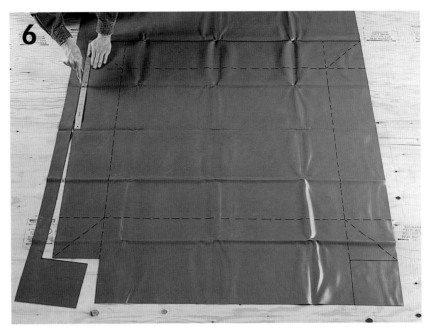

6

Measure the dimensions of the shower floor, and mark it out on a sheet of CPE waterproof membrane, using a felt-tipped marker. From the floor outline, measure out and mark an additional 8" for each wall and 16" for the curb end. Cut the membrane to size, using a utility knife and straightedge. Be careful to cut on a clean, smooth surface to prevent puncturing the membrane. Lay the membrane onto the shower pan.

7

Measure to find the exact location of the drain and mark it on the membrane, outlining the outer diameter of the drain flange. Cut a circular piece of CPE membrane roughly 2" larger than the drain flange, then use CPE membrane solvent glue to weld it into place and reinforce the seal at the drain.

8

Apply CPE sealant around the drain. Fold the membrane along the floor outline. Set the membrane over the pre pan so the reinforced drain seal is centered over the drain bolts. Working from the drain to the walls, carefully tuck the membrane tight into each corner, folding the extra material into triangular flaps.

9

Apply CPE solvent glue to one side, press the flap flat, then staple it in place. Staple only the top edge of the membrane to the blocking; do not staple below the top of the curb, or on the curb itself.

10

Dam corner

At the shower curb, cut the membrane along the studs so it can be folded over the curb. Solvent glue a dam corner at each inside corner of the curb. Do not fasten the dam corners with staples.

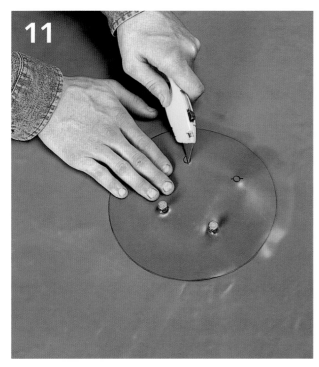

11

At the reinforced drain seal on the membrane, locate and mark the drain bolts. Press the membrane down around the bolts, then use a utility knife to carefully cut a slit just large enough for the bolts to poke through. Push the membrane down over the bolts.

12

Use a utility knife to carefully cut away only enough of the membrane to expose the drain and allow the middle drain piece to fit in place. Remove the drain bolts, then position the middle drain piece over the bolt holes. Reinstall the bolts, tightening them evenly and firmly to create a watertight seal.

(continued)

Test the shower pan for leaks overnight. Fill the shower pan with water, to 1" below the top of the curb. Mark the water level and let the water sit overnight. If the water level remains the same, the pan holds water. If the level is lower, locate and fix leaks in the pan using patches of membrane and CPE solvent.

Install cementboard on the alcove walls, using ¼" wood shims to lift the bottom edge off the CPE membrane. To prevent puncturing the membrane, do not use fasteners in the lower 8" of the cementboard. Cut a piece of metal lath to fit around the three sides of the curb. Bend the lath so it tightly conforms to the curb. Pressing the lath against the top of the curb, staple it to the outside face of the curb. Mix enough mortar for the two sides of the curb.

Overhang the front edge of the curb with a straight 1× board so it is flush with the outer wall material. Apply mortar to the mesh with a trowel, building to the edge of the board. Clear away excess mortar; then use a torpedo level to check for plumb, making adjustments as needed. Repeat for the inside face of the curb. *Note: The top of the curb will be finished after tile is installed (Step 19). Allow the mortar to cure overnight.*

Attach the drain strainer piece to the drain, adjusting it to a minimum of 1½" above the shower pan. On one wall, mark 1½" up from the shower pan, then use a level to draw a reference line around the perimeter of the shower base. Because the pre pan establishes the ¼" per foot slope, this measurement will maintain that slope.

Spread tile spacers over the weep holes of the drain to prevent mortar from plugging the holes. Mix the floor mortar, then build up the shower floor to roughly half the planned thickness of this layer. Cut metal lath to cover the mortar bed, keeping it ½" from the drain (see photo in Step 18).

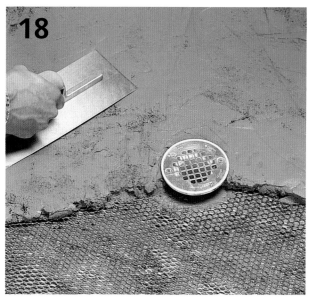

Continue to add mortar, building the floor to the reference line on the walls. Use a level to check the slope, and pack mortar into low spots with a trowel. Leave space around the drain flange for the thickness of the tile. Float the surface using a wood float until it is smooth and slopes evenly to the drain. When finished, allow the mortar to cure overnight before installing the tiles.

Install the tile. At the curb, cut the tiles for the inside to protrude ½" above the unfinished top of the curb, and the tiles for the outside to protrude ⅝" above the top, establishing a ⅛" slope so water drains back into the shower. Use a level to check the tops of the tiles for level as you work.

Bullnose tile

Built-up curb

Shower pan

Mix enough mortar to cover the unfinished top of the curb, then pack it in place between the tiles, using a trowel. Screed off the excess mortar flush with the tops of the side tiles. Allow the mortar to cure, then install bullnose cap tile. Install the wall tile, then grout, clean, and seal all the tile. After the grout has cured fully, run a bead of silicone caulk around all inside corners to create control joints.

CURBLESS SHOWER

Whether it's part of a complete "wet room," or installed as a standalone feature, a curbless shower combines easy access for those with limited mobility, convenience for other users, and a look that is trendy, sophisticated, and attractive. The trick to installing one of these water features is to ensure the moisture stays inside the shower.

Once upon a time, creating a reliably waterproof enclosure for a curbless shower was no small chore. It meant putting a lot of work into creating a custom shower pan. This kind of project was usually above the skill level or desire of the weekend DIYer, and it generally meant hiring a contractor.

Now you can buy curbless shower pan kits that make installation a breeze. The manufacturers have thought through all the issues that can arise and have developed the kits and shower pans to be as foolproof as possible, while also meeting prevailing codes and best standards and practices. Installing a curbless shower using one of these kits is a realistic project for any home handyperson with even moderate DIY skills and a weekend to spare.

These pans come with preconfigured slopes to ensure optimal drainage away from the shower's edges. The product we used for this project, the Tuff Form kit from Access Reliability Center, includes an offset drain hole that offers the option of rotating the pan in the event of a joist or mechanicals that are in the way. This product is offered in nine different sizes and can be cut with a circular saw to just about any shape—including more unusual, curvy shapes for a truly custom look.

Curbless shower pan manufacturers also sell pans with trench drains for an even sleeker look. The pan we used for this project is typical of the prefab curbless pan construction; it can support 1,100 pounds even though the pan itself weighs less than 70 pounds. It sits right on floor joists, with the addition of blocking to support the area around the drain, and to provide nailing surfaces around the edges.

Kits like these offer advantages beyond the ease of installation and a thoughtful configuration of parts. Usually, the plumbing can be completely adjusted and connected from above, so you won't need to work in the basement or a crawl space, or open up a first-floor ceiling to install a second-floor shower. The kits themselves generally include almost everything you'll need for the installation.

Tools & Materials ›

Circular saw	Synthetic paintbrush
Jigsaw	Waterproof latex sealant
Caulking gun	Caulkgun
Torpedo level	Waterproofing tape
Cordless drill and bits	Liquid waterproofing
PVC cement and brush	membrane
Screwdriver	Roller and roller handle
Speed square	Tiles
Screws	Thinset tile adhesive
Putty knife	Notched trowel
Palm sander and	Tile saw
120-grit pad	Adhesive mat
Scissors	Eye and ear protection
Rubber gloves	

A curbless shower kit includes almost everything you need. All you have to supply are some basic tools, the tile, and a little elbow grease.

Wet Rooms and Universal Design ▸

Because a wet room allows the bathroom to be designed with fewer barriers and a single-level floor surface, these rooms are natural partners to a Universal Design approach. If you're thinking about converting a bathroom to a wet room, it's worthwhile to consider a little extra effort to make the space as accessible as possible for the maximum number of users.

Walls. Where codes allow it, consider using thick plywood rather than cementboard for the wall sub-surfaces. Plywood allows for direct installation of grab bars without the need for blocking or locating studs. If you're set on using cementboard, plan out locations for grab bars near toilets, behind and alongside bathtubs, and in showers. Most codes specify that grab bars must be able to support up to 200 pounds—which usually means adding blocking in the walls behind the grab bars.

Shower stall. One of the benefits to adding a curbless shower is easy wheelchair (or walker) access. For maximum accessibility, the shower area should be at least 60" wide by at least 36" deep (60" by 60" is preferable). This allows a wheelchair-bound user to occupy the stall with a helper. And, although the idea is a wide-open shower space, it's always a good idea to add a fold down seat. This allows for transfer from a wheelchair, or a place for someone with limited leg strength and endurance to sit.

HOW TO INSTALL A WATERPROOF SUBBASE FOR A CURBLESS SHOWER

Remove the existing flooring material in the area of the shower pan (if you're remodeling an existing bathroom). Use a circular saw to cut out and remove the subfloor in the exact dimensions of the shower pan. Finish the cuts with a jigsaw or handsaw.

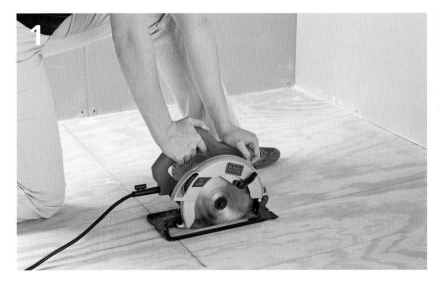

Reinforce the floor with blocking between joists as necessary. Toenail bridge blocking in on either side of the drain waste pipe location, and between joists anywhere you'll need a nailing surface along the edges of the shower pan. If trusses or joists are spaced more than 16" on center, add bridge blocking to adequately support the pan.

(continued)

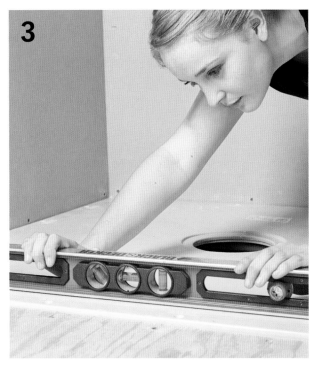

Set the pan in the opening to make sure it fits and is level. If it is not level, screw shims to the tops of any low joists and check again: repeat if necessary until the pan is perfectly level in all directions.

Install or relocate drain pipes as needed. Check with your local building department: if the drain and trap are not accessible from below you may need to have an on-site inspection before you cover up the plumbing.

Check the height of the drainpipe—its top should be exactly 2⅜" from the bottom of the pan—measure down from the top of the joist. If the drainpipe is too high, remove it and trim with a tubing cutter. If it is too low, replace the assembly with a new assembly that has a longer tailpiece.

Lay a thick bead of construction adhesive along the contact areas on all joists, nailing surfaces, and blocking.

7

Set the pan in place and screw it down, using at least 2 screws along each side. Do not overtighten the screws. If you've cut off the screwing flange on one or more sides to accommodate an unusual shape, drill ⅛" pilot holes in the cut edges at joist or blocking locations, and drive the screws through the holes.

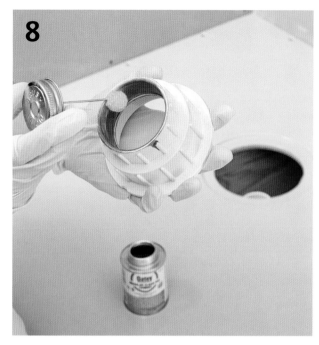

8

Disassemble the supplied drain assembly. Be careful not to lose any of the screws. Place the drain tailpiece on the waste pipe under where the pan's drainhole will be located, and measure to check that it sits at the correct level. Solvent-glue the tailpiece to the end of the waste pipe.

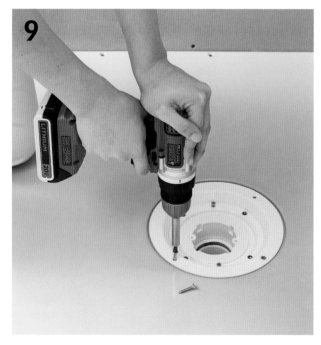

9

Position the supplied gaskets on top of the tailpiece (check the manufacturer's instructions; the gaskets usually need to be layered in the correct order). Set the drain flange piece on top of the tail, and into the drain hole in the pan. Drill ⅛" pilot holes through the flange and into the pan. Screw the flange to the pan.

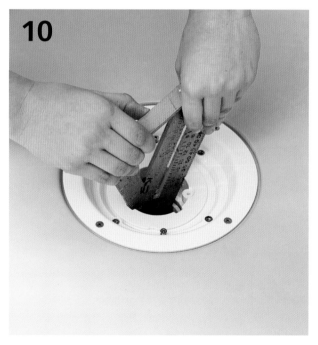

10

Thread the tail top piece into the tail through the drain flange. Use a speed square or other lever, such as spread channel lock pliers, to snugly tighten the tail top piece in place.

(continued)

11

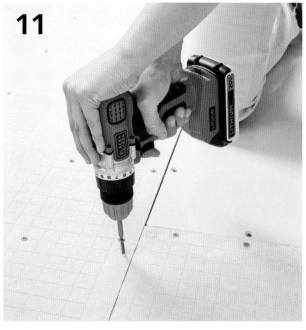

Install tile underlayment for the rest of the project area. If the underlayment is higher than the top of the pan once it is installed, you'll have to sand it to level, gradually tapering away from the pan.

12

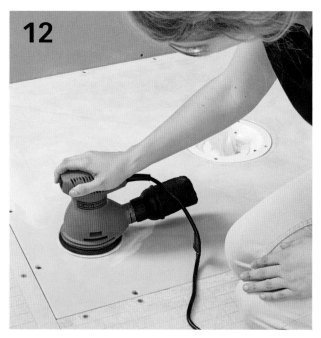

Scrape any stickers or other blemishes off the pan with a putty knife. Lightly sand the entire surface of the pan using 120-grit sandpaper to help the sealant adhere. After you're done sanding, wipe down the sanded pan with a damp sponge. Make sure the entire area is clean.

13

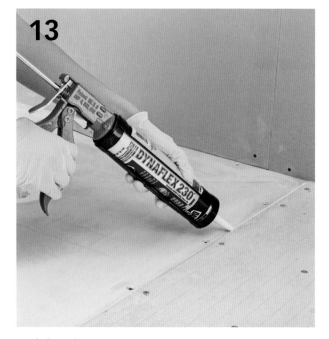

Seal the edge seams at the wall and between the pan and subfloor with waterproof latex sealant. Caulk any pan screw holes that were not used.

14

Cut strips of waterproofing tape to cover all seams in the tile underlayment (both walls and floor). Also cut strips for the joints where walls and floor meet. Open the pail of liquid waterproofing membrane and mix the liquid thoroughly. Beginning at the top and working down, brush a bed of waterproofing liquid over the seams. Before it dries, set the tape firmly into the waterproofing. Press and smooth the tape. Then brush a layer of waterproofing compound over the tape.

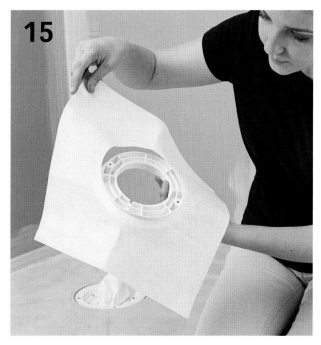

15

Trace a hole in the center of the waterproof drain gasket, using the bottom of the drain clamping donut. Cut the hole out using scissors. Be careful cutting the gasket because it is a crucial part of the drain waterproofing. Check the fit with the gasket against the underside of the clamping donut top flange.

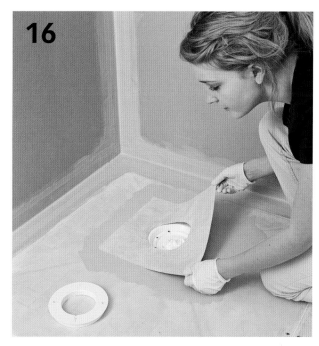

16

Apply a thin coat of the waterproofing compound around the drain hole and to the back of the drain gasket. Don't apply too much; if the waterproofing is too thick under the gasket, it may not dry correctly.

17

Put the gasket in place and brush a coat of the waterproofing over the gasket. Screw the clamping donut in place on the top of the drain and over the membrane. Hand-tighten the bolts and then cover the clamping donut with the waterproofing compound (avoid covering the slide lock for the drain grate).

18

Use a roller to roll waterproofing compound across the walls and over the entire pan surface. The ideal is 4mm thick (about the thickness of a credit card). Allow this first coat to dry for 2 hours, then cover with a second coat. This should conclude the waterproofing phase of the project and you're ready to begin laying tile once the waterproofing compound has dried thoroughly.

HOW TO INSTALL TILE FOR A CURBLESS SHOWER

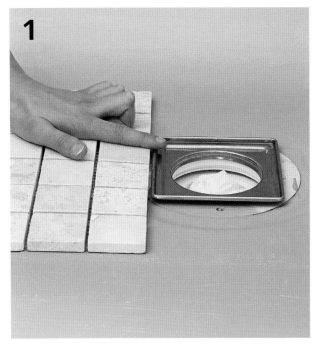

1

Set the floor tile first. Begin by placing a sample of the floor tile directly next to the drain so you can set the drain grate height to match. The adjustable mounting plate for the grate should be flush with the tops of the tile.

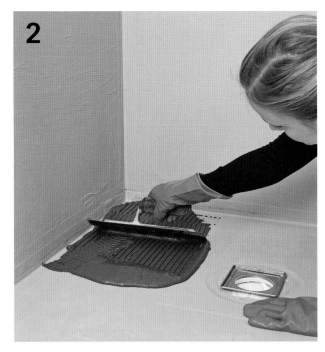

2

Begin laying floor tile in the corner of the shower. Lay a bed of thinset tile adhesive, using a notched trowel. The thinset container should specify the notch size (⅜" square notch is common).

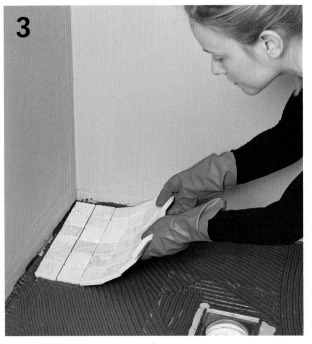

3

Place the corner tile into the bed of thinset and press it to set it. Don't press down too hard or you will displace too much of the material. Continue laying tile, fanning out from the corner toward the drain opening. Leave space around the drain opening as it is likely you'll need to cut tiles to fit.

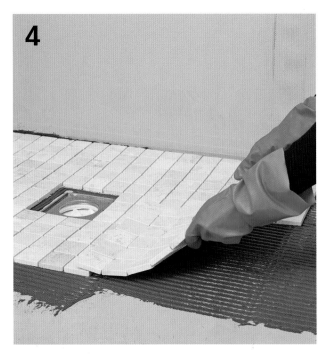

4

Install tile so a small square of untiled area is left around the drain opening (which, in the system seen here, is square, making for an easier cutting job).

5

Mark the tiles that surround the drain opening for cutting. Leave a small gap between the tiles next to the drain grate mounting plate.

6

Cut the tiles along the trim lines using a tile saw. If you are not comfortable using a tile saw, score the tiles and cut them with tile nippers.

7

Apply thinset onto the shower pan, taking care not to get any on the drain grate mounting plate. You may need to use a small trowel or a putty knife to get into small gaps.

8

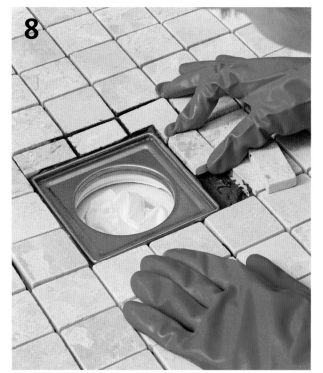

Set the cut tiles around the drain opening, doing your best to maintain even gaps that match the gaps in the rest of the floor. Once you've finished tiling around the drain, complete setting floor tile in the rest of the project area.

(continued)

9

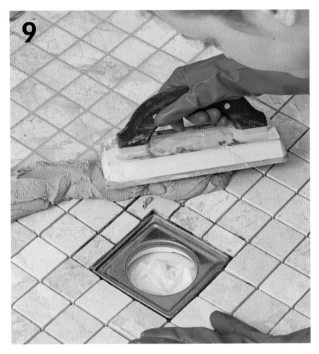

Let the floor tile set overnight and then apply grout. Using a grout sponge, wipe the grout over the gaps so all gaps are filled evenly. After the grout dries, buff the floor with a towel to wipe up excess residue.

10

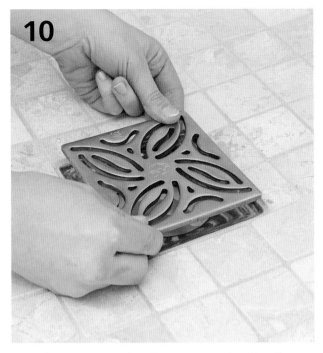

Snap the grate cover into the cover mounting plate (if you've stuffed a rag into the drain opening to keep debris out, be sure to remove it first). The grate cover seen here locks in with a small key that should be saved in case you need to remove the grate cover.

11

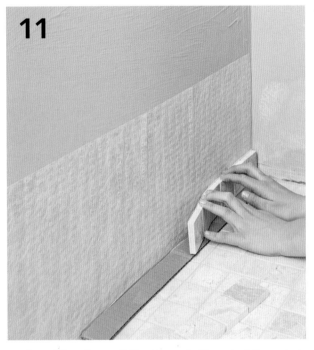

Begin setting the wall tile. Generally, it's easiest if you start at the bottom and work upward. Instead of thinset adhesive, an adhesive mat is being used here. This relatively new product is designed for walls and is rated for waterproof applications. It is a good idea to use a spacer (¼" thick or so) to get an even border at the bottoms of the first tiles.

12

In the design used here, a border of the same mosaic tile used in the floor is installed all around the shower area to make the first course. Dark brown accent tiles are installed in a single vertical column running upward, centered on the line formed by the shower faucet and showerhead. This vertical column is installed after the bottom border.

13

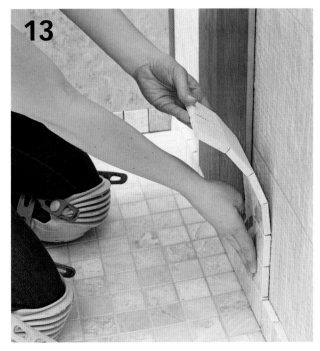

Next, another vertical column of accent tiles is installed on each side of the large, dark tiles. These columns are also laid using the floor tile, which connects the walls and floor visually in an effective way.

14

Finally, larger field tiles that match the floor tile used outside the shower area are installed up to the corner and outward from the shower area. Starting at the bottom, set a thin spacer on top of the border tiles to ensure even gaps.

15

Grout the gaps in the wall tiles. It's usually a good idea to protect any fittings, such as the shower faucet handle escutcheon, with painters tape prior to grouting. If you wish, a clear surround may be installed to visually define the shower area, as in the photo to the right, but because the shower pan is pitched toward the drain it really is not necessary.

ALCOVE BATHTUBS

Tools & Materials ▶

Channel-type pliers
Hacksaw
Carpenter's level
Pencil
Tape measure
Saw
Screwdriver
Drill
Adjustable wrench
Trowel
Shims
Fiberglass insulation
Hammer

Pliers
Galvanized deck screws
Drain-waste-overflow kit
1 × 3, 1 × 4, 2 × 4
    lumber
Galvanized roofing nails
Galvanized roof flashing
Thinset mortar
Plumber's putty
Tub and tile caulk
Propane torch
Eye and ear protection

Most of our homes are equipped with an alcove tub that includes a tub surround and shower. By combining the tub and the shower in one fixture, you conserve precious bathroom floor space and simplify the initial installation. Plus, you only have one bathing fixture that needs cleaning.

But because tub/showers are so efficient, they do get a lot of use and tend to have fairly limited lifespans. The fact that the most inexpensive tubs on the market are designed for alcove use also reduces the average tub/shower lifespan. Pressed steel tubs have enamel finishes that crack and craze; plastic and fiberglass tubs get grimy and stained; even acrylic and composite tubs show wear eventually (and as with other fixtures, styles and colors change too).

Plumbing an alcove tub is a relatively difficult job because getting access to the drain lines attached to the tub and into the floor is often very awkward. Although an access panel is required by most codes, the truth is that many tubs were installed without them or with panels that are too small or hard to reach to be of much use. If you are contemplating replacing your tub, the first step in

the decision process should be to find the access panel and determine if it is sufficient. If it is not (or there is no panel at all), consider how you might enlarge it. Often, this means cutting a hole in the wall on the adjoining room and also in the ceiling below. This creates more work, of course, but compared to the damage caused by a leaky drain from a subpar installation, making an access opening is little inconvenience.

A tub alcove is sized to accept a standard bathtub, usually 5' long in most of North America. A tub with an apron is typical, but you can build out the front instead if you choose.

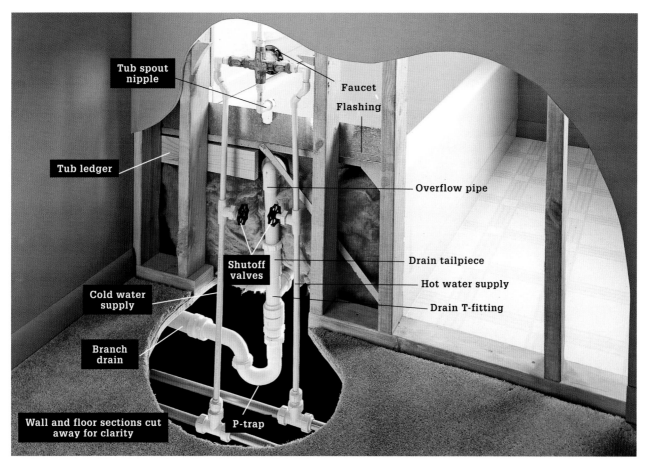

The plumbing for a bathtub includes hot and cold supply pipes, shutoff valves, faucet, and a spout. Supply connections can be made before or after the tub is installed. The drain-waste-overflow system for a bathtub includes the overflow pipe, drain T-fitting, P-trap, and branch drain. The overflow pipe assembly is attached to the tub before installation.

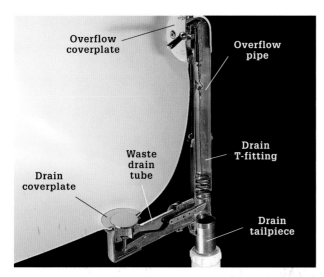

A drain-waste-overflow kit with a stopper mechanism must be attached to the tub before it is installed. Available in both brass and plastic types, most kits include an overflow coverplate, a height-adjustable overflow pipe, a drain T-fitting and tailpiece, a waste drain tube, and a drain coverplate that screws into the drain tube.

Add fiberglass insulation around the body of a steel bathtub to reduce noise and conserve heat. Before setting the tub in position, wrap unfaced batting around the tub, and secure it with string or twine. For showers, deck-mounted whirlpools, and saunas, insulate between the framing members.

HOW TO INSTALL A NEW ALCOVE TUB

Prepare for the new tub. Inspect and remove old or deteriorated wall surfaces or framing members in the tub area. With today's mold-resistant wallboard products, it makes extra sense to go ahead and strip off the old alcove wallcoverings and ceiling down to the studs so you can replace them. This also allows you to inspect for hidden damage in the wall and ceiling cavities.

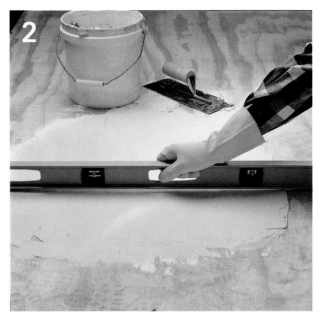

Check the subfloor for level—if it is not level, use pour-on floor leveler compound to correct it (ask at your local flooring store). Make sure the supply and drain pipes and the shutoff valves are in good repair and correct any problems you encounter. If you have no bath fan in the alcove, now is the perfect time to add one.

Check the height of the crossbraces for the faucet body and the showerhead. If your family members needed to stoop to use the old shower, consider raising the brace for the showerhead. Read the instructions for your new faucet/diverter and check to see that the brace for the faucet body will conform to the requirements (this includes distance from the surround wall as well as height). Adjust the brace locations as needed.

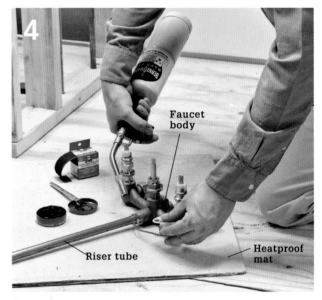

Faucet body

Riser tube

Heatproof mat

Begin by installing the new water supply plumbing. Measure to determine the required height of your shower riser tube and cut it to length. Attach the bottom of the riser to the faucet body and the top to the shower elbow.

BATHROOM PROJECTS

Attach the faucet body to the cross brace with pipe hanger straps. Then, attach supply tubing from the stop valves to the faucet body, making sure to attach the hot water to the left port and cold to the right port. Also secure the shower elbow to its cross brace with a pipe strap. Do not attach the shower arm yet.

Slide the bathtub into the alcove. Make sure the tub is flat on the floor and pressed flush against the back wall. If your tub did not come with a tub protector, cut a piece of cardboard to line the tub bottom, and tape pieces of cardboard around the rim to protect the finish from damage.

Mark locations for ledger boards. To do this, trace the height of the top of the tub's nailing flange onto the wall studs in the alcove. Then remove the tub and measure the height of the nailing flange. Measure down this same amount from your flange lines and mark new ledger board locations.

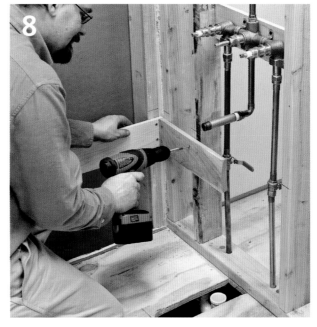

Install 1 × 4 ledger boards. Drive two or three 3"-galvanized deck screws through the ledger board at each stud. All three walls should receive a ledger. Leave an open space in the wet wall to allow clearance for the drain-waste-overflow (DWO) kit.

(continued)

9

Install the drain-waste-overflow (DWO) pipes before you install the tub. Make sure to get a good seal on the slip nuts at the pipe joints. Follow the manufacturer's instructions to make sure the pop-up drain linkage is connected properly. Make sure rubber gaskets are positioned correctly at the openings on the outside of the tub.

10

Drain strainer

Thread the male-threaded drain strainer into the female-threaded drain waste elbow. Wrap a coil of plumber's putty around the drain outlet underneath the plug rim first. Hand tighten only.

11

Attach the overflow coverplate, making sure the pop-up drain controls are in the correct position. Tighten the mounting screws that connect to the mounting plate to sandwich the rubber gasket snugly between the overflow pipe flange and the tub wall. Then, finish tightening the drain strainer against the waste elbow by inserting the handle of a pair of pliers into the strainer body and turning.

12

Place the tub back into the alcove, taking care not to bump the DWO assembly and disturb the connections. You definitely will want a helper for this job. If the drain outlet of the DWO assembly is not directly over the drain pipe when the tub is in position, you'll need to remove it and adjust the drain line location.

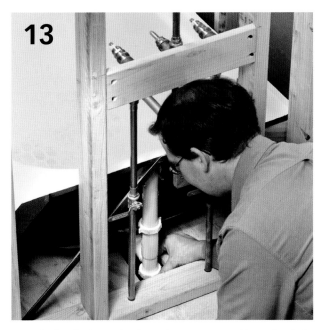

13

Attach **the drain outlet** from the DWO assembly to the drain P-trap. If your alcove walls are covered, you will appreciate that you spent the time to create a roomy access panel for the tub plumbing. Test the drain and overflow to make sure they don't leak. Also test the water supply plumbing, temporarily attaching the handles, spout, and shower arm so you can operate the faucet and the diverter.

14

Drive **a 1½" galvanized roofing nail** at each stud location, just over the top of the tub's nailing flange (inset). The nail head should pin the flange to the stud. For extra protection against moisture penetration, nail strips of metal flashing to the studs so they cover the tub flange.

15

Install **the wallcoverings and tub surround** (see pages 456 to 459 for a three-piece surround installation). You can also make a custom surround from tileboard or cementboard and tile.

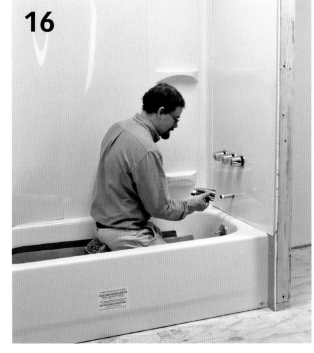

16

Install **fittings.** First, thread the shower arm into the shower elbow and attach the spout nipple to the valve assembly. Also attach the shower head and escutcheon, the faucet handle/diverter with escutcheon, and the tub spout. Use thread lubricant on all parts.

THREE-PIECE TUB SURROUNDS

Tools & Materials ▸

Jigsaw
Hole saw
Drill
Tape measure
Level
Caulking gun
Panel adhesive
Silicone caulk

Adhesive
Screwdriver
Adjustable wrench
Pry bar
Hammer
3-piece tub surround
Eye and ear protection

No one wants bathroom fixtures that are aging or yellowed from years of use. A shiny new tub surround can add sparkle and freshness to your dream bath.

Tub surrounds come in many different styles, materials, and price ranges. Choose the features you want and measure your existing bathtub surround for sizing. Surrounds typically come in three or five pieces. A three-panel surround is being installed here, but the process is similar for five-panel systems.

Surface preparation is important for good glue adhesion. Plastic tiles and wallpaper must be removed and textured plaster must be sanded smooth. Surrounds can be installed over ceramic tile that is well attached and in good condition, but it must be sanded and primed. All surfaces must be primed with a water-based primer.

Three-piece tub surrounds are inexpensive and come in many colors and styles. The typical unit has two end panels and a back panel that overlap in the corners to form a watertight seal. They are formed from fiberglass, PVC, acrylic, or proprietary resin-based polymers. Five-piece versions are also available and typically have more features such as integral soap shelves and even cabinets.

HOW TO INSTALL A THREE-PIECE TUB SURROUND

1

Remove the old plumbing fixtures and wallcoverings in the tub area. In some cases you can attach surround panels to old tileboard or even tile, but it is generally best to remove the wallcoverings down to the studs if you can, so you may inspect for leaks or damage.

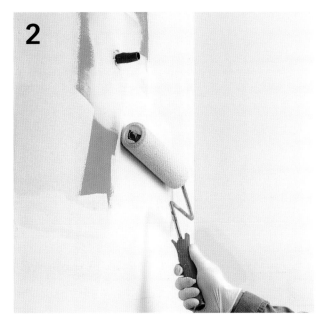

2

Replace the wallcoverings with appropriate materials, such as water- and mold-resistant wallboard or cementboard (for ceramic tile installations). Make sure the new wall surfaces are smooth and flat. Some surround kit manufacturers recommend that you apply a coat of primer to sheet goods such as greenboard to create a better bonding surface for the panel adhesive.

3

Test-fit the panels before you start; the tub may have settled unevenly or the walls may be out of plumb. Check the manufacturer's directions for distinguishing right and left panels. Place a panel in position on the tub ledge. Use a level across the top of the panel to determine if it is level. Create a vertical reference line to mark the edge of the panel on the plumbing end.

Test-fitting ▸

Ensure a perfect fit by taping the surround panels to the walls in the tub area. Make sure the tops are level when the overlap seams are aligned and that you have a consistent gap between the panel bottoms and the tub flange. Mark the panels for cutting if necessary and, once the panels have been removed, make any adjustments to the walls that are needed.

(continued)

4

After performing the testfit, check the fitting instructions to see if you need to trim any of the pieces. Follow the manufacturer's instructions for cutting. Here, we had to cut the corner panels because the instructions advise not to overlap the back or side panel over the corner panels by more than 3". Cut panels using a jigsaw and a fine-tooth blade that is appropriate for cutting fiberglass or acrylic tileboard.

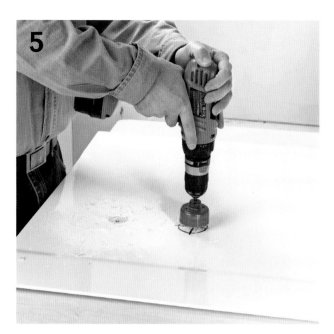

5

Lay out the locations of the faucets, spout, and shower arm. Measure in from the vertical reference line (made in Step 3) and up from the top of the tub ledge. Re-measure for accuracy, as any cuts to the surround are final. Place the panel face-up on a sheet of plywood. Mark the location of the holes. Cut the holes ½" larger than the pipe diameter. If your faucet has a recessed trim plate, cut the hole to fit the recess. Using a hole saw or a jigsaw, cut out the plumbing access holes.

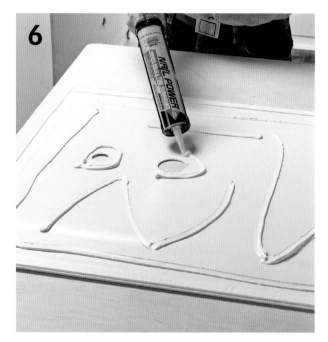

6

Apply the panel adhesive to the back of an end plumbing panel. Circle the plumbing outlet holes 1" from the edge. Follow the manufacturer's application pattern. Do not apply adhesive closer than 1" to the double-sided tape or the bottom edge of the panel.

7

Remove the protective backing from the tape. Carefully lift the panel by the edges and place against the corner and top of the tub ledge. Press firmly from top to bottom in the corner, then throughout the panel.

8

Test-fit the opposite end panel and make any necessary adjustments. Apply the adhesive, remove the protective backing from the tape, and put in place. Apply pressure to the corner first from top to bottom, and then apply pressure throughout.

9

Apply adhesive to the back panel following the manufacturer's instructions. Maintain a 1" space between adhesive tape and the bottom of the panel. Remove protective backing from the tape. Lift the panel by the edges and carefully center between the two end panels. When positioned, firmly press in place from top to bottom.

10

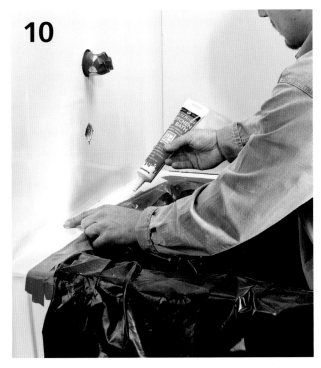

Apply caulk to the bottom and top edges of the panels and at panel joints. Dip your fingertip in water and use it to smooth the caulk to a uniform bead.

11

Apply silicone caulk to escutcheons or trim plates and reinstall them. Allow a minimum of 24 hours for caulk and adhesive to cure thoroughly before using the shower or tub.

SOAKING TUBS

Long a favorite in the Japanese culture, soaking tubs continue to gain fans in America. Although you can soak in any tub, an actual soaking tub is designed so that the bather sits—rather than reclines—immersed in water up to the chin. It usually only takes one long soak for a person to become a devotee of the soaking tub's relaxing benefits.

Traditional soaking tubs are manufactured with sides that can rise 36 inches high or higher; but today's soaking tubs for home use are available in a range of sizes, many with sides around 24 inches deep. (It's crucial for proper soaking that the overflow drain is positioned 20 inches or more from the bottom to allow the tub to be almost completely filled.)

Getting in and out of these types of tubs can be a challenge, which is why they are often installed into a platform built especially for the tub. The platform allows you to sit and then ease into the tub. A wide platform such as the one discussed here leaves plenty of space for candles, bath salts, plants, or other decor- and mood-enhancing additions.

The platform described in the instructions that follow is 22 inches high with a 14-inch wide ledge—comfortably accommodating seating around the tub. The tub itself is 24 inches high, with a 2-inch lip. You can build a platform so that the tub rim fits flush, but a lip is a good idea to keep towels and other items from accidentally sliding off the platform and into the bathwater.

As with other types of tubs, soaking tubs come in a range of styles, shapes, and colors.

A soaking tub needs to be deep, but not necessarily wide. That makes them ideal for long narrow spaces such as this under-window area. Here, a soaking tub with a modest ledge adds big luxury in a small footprint.

Tools & Materials ▸

Plumbing tools & supplies	Cementboard
Tape measure	Hacksaw
Drill	Circular saw
Hammer	Torpedo level
4' level	Thinset mortar
Utility knife	Silicone caulk
2 × 4 lumber	Deck-mount faucet set
2" screws	Soaking tub
1¼" cementboard screws	Tile mortar
Notched trowel	Tile grout
Grout sponge	Grout float
CDX plywood	Ceramic tile
Framing square	(field and bullnose)
	Eye and ear protection

Access Panels ▸

Making the supply and drain hook-ups on a bathtub usually requires access from below or behind the installation area. When installing a drop-in tub in a framed deck platform, you can gain access through the platform apron area, too. If you are hooking up the drain with a slip connection, the Universal Plumbing Code requires that you install a permanent access panel (see page 433) in the wall behind the tub or in the floor and ceiling below. But regardless of codes, you should make a point of creating permanent access to the plumbing hook-ups whenever possible. In the tub installation seen here, a removable access panel on the opposite side of the wet wall provides access to both the drain and supply hookups. This allows the platform deck and apron to be tiled in a contiguous manner. Because the faucet plumbing is readily accessible, each supply tube is connected to a shutoff valve next to the fixture and supply risers are used to bring water to the faucet valve.

HOW TO INSTALL A SOAKING TUB WITH PLATFORM

1

2

Place the tub in position on the subfloor. The tub should be 14½" from the two corner walls, measured from the underside of the tub lip—where the inside edge of the platform deck will run—to wall studs. This allows for ½"-thick wall surface. Shim as necessary to level the tub both ways, or adjust self-leveling feet if tub has them. Hang a plumb bob from the underside of the lip at each corner of tub and mark the subfloor. Check that marks on adjacent corners are the same distance from the wall.

Measure from under the lip edge to the subfloor. This will be the height of the platform wall framing, minus the CDX plywood decking, ½" cementboard, and tile.

3

4

Remove the tub and hammer a nail in at each corner point. Snap chalk lines to represent the inside lines of the inner platform wall. Measure, cut, and align the 2 × 4 sole plates with the chalk lines. Screw all four sole plates for the inside platform wall into position. Check diagonal measurements or use a framing square to ensure the sole plates are square.

Measure and mark 13½" from the inside edge of the open side sole plates, at several points along the plates. These marks will serve as guide points for placing the sole plates of the outside platform walls. Line up the outside edge of the two outer wall sole plates and screw them in place to the subfloor. Measure again to ensure the sole plates are positioned correctly.

5

Measure and cut studs to create the proper platform height. Install studs for both inside and outside platform walls, spacing them every 16". Use L configurations at corners so that the top plates intersect opposite the sole plates. Cut cross braces and screw them in place, staggering with the stud placement.

6

Route supply lines from the wet wall to the location of the deck-mount faucet. The connections will depend on what type of deck-mount faucet you've chosen. Follow the manufacturer's instructions for securing the hot and cold connections for the faucet. If you're unsure of how to plumb the faucet, hire a plumber.

7

Measure and cut CDX plywood for the platform deck (the deck for the two open sides should overhang the outside wall edge by ½" to cover the cementboard that will be used on the walls). Screw the decking into position. If you will be mounting the faucet on the deck, cut holes for the valve handles and spout before screwing down that portion of the deck.

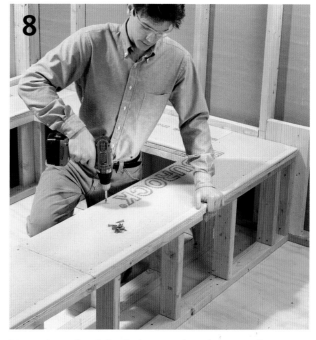

8

Measure and cut the deck cementboard to cover the plywood. Cut to the same overhang as the plywood and drill holes for the faucet if it will be deck-mounted (the one seen here is mounted to the tub deck). Screw cementboard to the plywood deck over top rail and cross braces. Also attach cementboard to the platform aprons.

(continued)

9

Attach wallcoverings in the installation area. Here, six courses of wall tile will be installed on the walls above the tub deck. A strip of cementboard the same width as the total tile height is attached to the wall as a backer for the tile. Then, water-resistant drywall is installed to span from the cementboard to the ceiling to create a smooth, paintable wall surface.

10

Lay tile over the deck surface and the platform aprons using bullnose tile around the two outside edges. Tile on the inside edge of the platform does not need to be finished—it will be covered by the tub lip. Also install wall tiles.

Grout the platform and walls with sanded grout. Buff off excess grout with a coarse rag. Apply a grout sealing product after the grout has dried for several days (this may be done after the tub is installed if you do not want to wait).

11

12

Install the tub. Attach the drain-waste-overflow connection to the tub. Trowel a ½" bed of mortar on the subfloor where the tub bottom will sit (unless manufacturer's directions state otherwise). Set the tub in place in the platform opening, press down into the mortar, and check for level. There should be a very slight gap between tub lip bottom edge and top of tile.

13

Let the mortar bed dry and, working through the open walls and under the platform deck, connect the drain tailpiece to the trap. A large access panel lets you get at both the supply and drain hook ups.

14

Apply a bead of tub-and-tile caulk in the seam between the tub lip and the tiled deck surface. Wet your finger and smooth the bead for a finished look.

FREESTANDING TUBS

Freestanding tubs offer maximum versatility in bathroom design because, theoretically, they can be placed anywhere in the bathroom. They can even be installed in an alcove, in place of an alcove tub. However, because they are attractive from all sides, and one of the key benefits is total access, most homeowners install freestanding tubs with some measure of floor space all around the tub.

Another selling point is the amazing variety among freestanding tubs. Options include the vast array of clawfoot tubs and pedestal tubs in styles from modern to classical. Roll-top freestanding tubs feature a rolled top lip that makes getting into and out of the tub easy. These are often egg-shaped and deep, offering a comfortable soak after a long day. Slipper tubs offer a more dramatic shape, like Cinderella's ball slipper, with a high, sloped back that allows the bather to recline in ultimate comfort.

Clawfoot tubs are a category all their own. Although cast iron is the traditional material for clawfoots, manufacturers also offer easier-to-move acrylic and polymer options. You can pick from many different foot styles, including ball feet, ornamental feet, and, of course, the traditional claw feet. You can also outfit a clawfoot tub with a shower extension on the faucet body, a direct spray "rainwater" head, and a shower ring from which a shower curtain can be hung.

The clawfoot tub seen here is a salvaged, cast-iron rolltop tub. Although the supply of vintage tubs is dwindling, they are still not hard to find and in many cases you can get one for the price of hauling it away (no easy task). Often, the porcelain enamel finish needs refurbishing, which is a job best done by a tub reglazing specialist. The installation process is a fairly simple one. The hardest part is usually running new drain and supply lines under the floor, so if you can place the tub over existing lines, you greatly simplify the installation process.

Regardless of the tub you choose, check with your local building inspector to help you determine whether your floor has adequate structural strength to safely support a freestanding tub. The inspector may suggest (or require) that you have the potential location evaluated by a qualified structural engineer.

Tools & Materials ▸

Adjustable wrench	Cordless drill and bits	Hole saw
Plumber's putty or silicone plumber's grease	Carpenter's level	Eye and ear protection
Teflon tape		

Prepping for a Clawfoot Tub ▸

The actual installation of a clawfoot tub is fairly basic. Success, though, relies on proper preparation so that the tub is positioned just where you want it, and the supply and drain lines are correctly aligned with the tub. Place the tub roughly where you want it and use a stud finder or other method to isolate the floor joists. Determine the location for connections under the floor (new tubs usually come with a template) and mark them by drilling pilot holes all the way through the subflooring. Install new drain and supply plumbing—this is a good time to call in a professional plumber. Finally, lay the finish flooring, if it is not already in place, before installing the tub. Make sure the floor is as level as possible.

HOW TO INSTALL A CLAWFOOT TUB

Position the tub exactly where you'd like it to rest, ideally over existing supply and drain lines. Install the feet first if they were not preattached (inset photo).

Mark locations for supply risers and drain tailpipe on the floor. Drill starter holes and double check below the floor to make sure floor joists will not be directly under the access holes. Use a hole saw slightly wider than each pipe to drill access holes. Install supply lines and drainline.

Install the drain-waste-overflow assembly according to the manufacturer's instructions. With a freestanding tub, it is often easiest to join the assembly parts working upward from the drainpipe connection in the floor. Install the drain flange in the tub, fastening it from the top into the drain shoe. Make the connection to the drain pipe in the floor—if the kit comes with a floor escutcheon that covers the drain connection, make sure it is in place before you attach the tailpipe to the T.

4

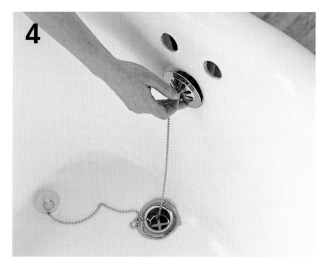

Fasten the overflow cover to the overflow receiver with the bolt or bolts that are provided. Be sure to position the rubber gasket that came with the drain kit so it fits neatly against the tub wall. Do not overtighten the fasteners.

5

Assemble the faucet according to the manufacturer's instructions. Most older clawfoot tubs have a two-valve faucet with a gooseneck spigot that mounts directly to the wall of the tub at the foot end. Many newer freestanding tubs utilize a wall-mounted faucet.

6

Mount the faucet body to the tub wall with the retainer nuts that thread onto the faucet valve stems.

7

Attach the supply risers to the valve inlets for the faucet. Put the supply pipe base escutcheons in place on the floor over the supply line connections. Secure the risers into the supply connections below the floor. Turn on the water supply and test to make sure there are no leaks in any of the pipes or fitting connections, including the drain and overflow.

Feet First ▸

Despite their great weight, it is always a good idea to anchor cast-iron tubs—even a small shift in position can cause the drain or supply connections to fail. Older tubs often have screwholes in the bottoms of the feet so they may be fastened to the floor once the hookups are made. Newer lighter-weight tubs generally use floor pins to stabilize the tub. Some manufacturers recommend using rubber pads and epoxy under each foot, in conjunction with dowels or mounting studs. Some tubs have self-leveling feet, with integral adjustment posts—check and follow the manufacturer's installation instructions.

SLIDING TUB DOORS

Tools & Materials ▸

Tape measure	Masonry bit
Pencil & marker	for tile wall
Hacksaw	Phillips screwdriver
Miter box	Caulk gun
Level	Masking tape
Drill	Silicone sealant
Center punch	Tub door kit
Utility knife blade	Eye and ear protection

Curtains on your bathtub shower are a hassle. If you forget to tuck them inside the tub, water flows freely onto your bathroom floor. If you forget to slide them closed, mildew sets up shop in the folds. And every time you brush against them they stick to your skin. Shower curtains certainly don't add much elegance or charm to a dream bath. Neither does a deteriorated door. Clean up the look of your bathroom, and even give it an extra touch of elegance, with a new sliding tub door.

When shopping for a sliding tub door, you have a choice of framed or frameless. A framed door is edged in metal. The metal framing is typically aluminum but is available in many finishes, including those that resemble gold, brass, or chrome. Glass options are also plentiful. You can choose between frosted or pebbled glass, clear, mirrored, tinted, or patterned glass. Doors can be installed on ceramic tile walls or through a fiberglass tub surround.

A sliding tub door in a metal frame gives the room a sleek, clean look and is just one of the available options.

HOW TO INSTALL SLIDING TUB DOORS

1

Remove the existing door and inspect the walls. Use a utility knife blade to cut sealant from tile and metal surfaces. Do not use a razor blade on fiberglass surfaces. Remove remaining sealant by scraping or pulling. Use a silicone sealant remover to remove all residue. Remove shower curtain rods, if present. Check the walls and tub ledge for plumb and level.

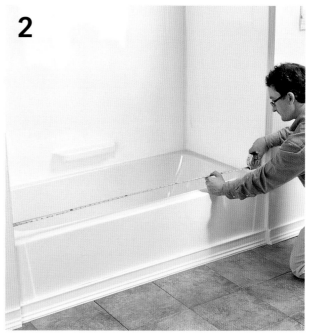

2

Measure the distance between the finished walls along the top of the tub ledge. Refer to the manufacturer's instructions for figuring the track dimensions. For the product seen here, ³⁄₁₆" is subtracted from the measurement to calculate the track dimensions.

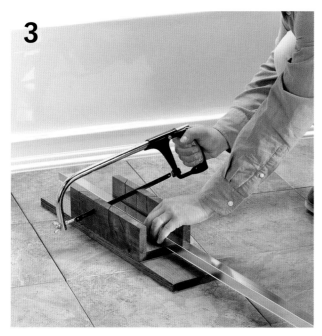

3

Using a hacksaw and a miter box, carefully cut into the track to the proper dimension. Center the track on the bathtub ledge with the taller side out and so the gaps are even at each end. Tape into position with masking tape.

4

Place a wall channel against the wall with the longer side out and slide into place over the track so they overlap. Use a level to check the channel for plumb, and then mark the locations of the mounting holes on the wall with a marker. Repeat for the other wall channel. Remove the track.

(continued)

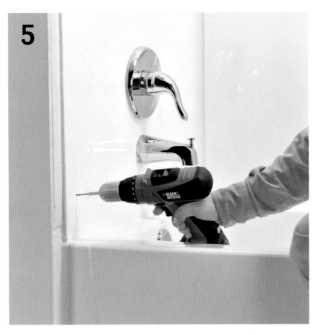

5

Drill mounting holes for the wall channel at the marked locations. In ceramic tile, nick the surface of the tile with a center punch, use a ¼" masonry bit to drill the hole, and then insert the included wall anchors. For fiberglass surrounds, use a ⅛" drill bit; wall anchors are not necessary.

6

Apply a bead of silicone sealant along the joint between the tub and the wall at the ends of the track. Apply a minimum ¼" bead of sealant along the outside leg of the track underside.

7

Position the track on the tub ledge and against the wall. Attach the wall channels using the provided screws. Do not use caulk on the wall channels at this time.

8

At a location above the tops of the wall channels, measure the distance between the walls. Refer to the manufacturer's instructions for calculating the header dimensions. For the doors seen here, the header dimension is the distance between the walls minus ¹⁄₁₆". Measure the header and carefully cut it to length using a hacksaw and a miter box. Slide the header down on top of the wall channels until seated.

9

Mount the rollers in the roller mounting holes. To begin, use the second from the top roller mounting holes. Follow the manufacturer's instructions for spacer or washer placement and direction.

10

Carefully lift the inner panel by the sides and place the rollers on the inner roller track. Roll the door toward the shower end of the tub. The edge of the panel should touch both rubber bumpers. If it doesn't, remove the door and move the rollers to different holes. Drive the screws by hand to prevent overtightening.

11

Lift the outer panel by the sides with the towel bar facing out from the tub. Place the outer rollers over the outer roller track. Slide the door to the end opposite the shower end of the tub. If the door does not contact both bumpers, remove the door and move the rollers to different mounting holes.

12

Apply a bead of silicone sealant to the inside seam of the wall and wall channel at both ends and to the U-shaped joint of the track and wall channels. Smooth the sealant with a fingertip dipped in water.

PEDESTAL & CONSOLE SINKS

Pedestal and console sinks move in and out of popularity more frequently than other types, but even during the times that they aren't particularly trendy they still find a place in many remodels because of their classic and adaptable styling. You'll find them most frequently in small half baths or powder rooms, where their modest footprints make them space-efficient options. Designers are also increasingly using these styles as his-and-her sinks for bathrooms in which the sinks are meant to visually dominate the design.

The primary drawback to pedestal sinks is that they don't offer any storage. Their chief practical benefit is that they conceal plumbing some homeowners would prefer to keep out of sight. Console sinks, with their two front legs and modest apron, offer some space underneath for rolling shelf units or a towel basket.

Pedestal sinks are mounted in one of two ways. Most inexpensive models are hung in much the same way as wall-mounted sinks. The pedestal is actually installed after the sink is hung and its purpose is purely decorative. But other, higher-end pedestal sinks have structural pedestals that bear the weight of the sink. All console sinks are mounted to the wall, although the front legs offer additional support and resistance to users leaning on the front of the sink.

Tools & Materials ▸

Pedestal sink	Basin wrench
2 × 4 lumber	Silicone caulk
Water-resistant drywall	Lag screws
Ratchet wrench	Studfinder
Drill	Eye and ear protection

A console bathroom sink is a wall-mounted lavatory with two front legs that provide back-up support. Many have a narrow apron to conceal the drain trap.

A pedestal sink typically is hung on the wall. The primary function of the pedestal is to conceal plumbing and provide visual appeal.

HOW TO INSTALL A PEDESTAL SINK

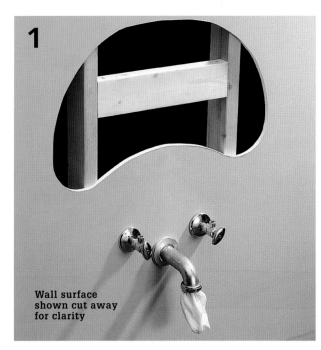

1

Wall surface shown cut away for clarity

Install 2 × 4 blocking between the wall studs, behind the planned sink location. Cover the wall with water-resistant drywall.

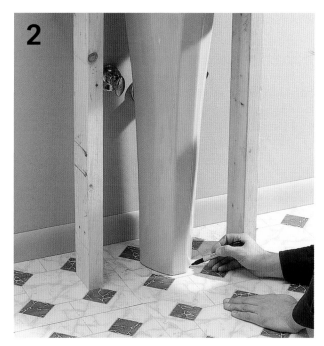

2

Set the basin and pedestal in position and brace it with 2 × 4s. Outline the top of the basin on the wall, and mark the base of the pedestal on the floor. Mark reference points on the wall and floor through the mounting holes found on the back of the sink and the bottom of the pedestal.

3

Set aside the basin and pedestal. Drill pilot holes in the wall and floor at the reference points, then reposition the pedestal. Anchor the pedestal to the floor with lag screws.

4

Attach the faucet, then set the sink on the pedestal. Align the holes in the back of the sink with the pilot holes drilled in the wall, then drive lag screws and washers into the wall brace using a ratchet wrench. Do not overtighten the screws.

5

Hook up the drain and supply fittings. Caulk between the back of the sink and the wall when installation is finished.

WALL-MOUNTED SINKS

There are many benefits to a wall-mounted sink that, depending on your situation and needs, will offset the inherent lack of storage space. In contrast to the footprint of a traditional vanity-mounted sink, wall-mounted units can save space on the sides and in front of the fixture. More importantly, they are an essential addition to a Universal Design bathroom where wheelchair accessibility is a key consideration. It's why these particular fixtures are sometimes called "roll-under" sinks.

All that practicality aside, early models at the lower end of the price spectrum were somewhat unattractive because their designs simply left the drain tailpiece, trap, and supply shut-off valves in plain sight. But there's no need for you to settle for a less-than-handsome wall-mounted sink. Manufacturers have developed two solutions to the problem of exposed plumbing. Some are designed with a bowl that conceals supply line shut-offs, replacing the trap with sleekly designed tailpieces and squared off trap bends. The other solution, and one more widely available, is a wall-mounted pedestal that covers the plumbing. Sinks with this feature are sometimes called "semi-pedestal."

We've opted to illustrate the installation of just such a sink in the instructions that follow. Keep in mind that different manufacturers sometimes use very different mounting procedures. In any case, the idea remains the same: strongly secure the sink to studs or blocking, so that it is completely stable and will not fall.

The most involved part of the installation process is usually rerouting water supply and drain lines as necessary. You should hire a licensed plumber for this if you're not comfortable with the work. Once the plumbing is in place, the installation is quick and easy.

Tools & Materials ▸

Carpenter's level	Standard screwdriver
Adjustable wrenches	Jigsaw
Pipe wrench	Basin wrench
Channel-type pliers	Tape measure
Cordless power drill and bits	Hacksaw
	2 × 8 lumber
Tubing cutting	Eye and ear protection
Phillips screwdriver	

Although a wall-mounted sink offers many benefits—accessibility to wheelchair users among them—there's no need to sacrifice chic style for that functionality.

HOW TO INSTALL A WALL-MOUNTED SINK

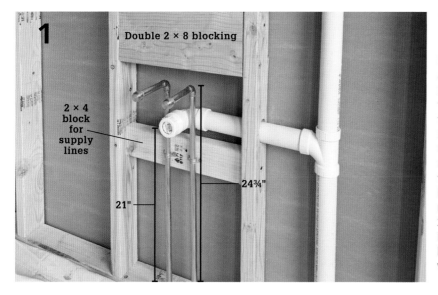

1 Double 2 × 8 blocking

2 × 4 block for supply lines

24¾"

21"

Remove the existing sink if any.
Remove wall coverings as necessary to install blocking for mounting the sink. Reroute water supply and drain lines as necessary, according to the sink manufacturer's directions. The sink in this project required the centerpoints of the waste pipe be 21", and the supply lines 24¾" up from the finished floor. If unsure of your plumbing skills or code requirements, hire a professional plumber for this part of the project. Install blocking between the studs for attaching the mounting bracket for the sink. A doubled 2 × 8 is installed here. Have your plumbing inspected, if required by your municipality, before you install the drywall and finished wall surface.

2

Drill guide holes for the mounting bolts if your sink is a direct-mount model, as this one is. Some wall-hung sinks are hung from a mounting bracket. The bolts used to hang this sink are threaded like lag screws on one end, with a bolt end that projects from the wall. The guide holes should be spaced exactly as the manufacturer specifies so they align with the mounting holes in the back mounting flange on the sink. *Tip: Protect tile surfaces with masking tape in the drilling areas to avoid chip-out.*

3 Doubled nuts to drive bolt into blocking

Drive the threaded mounting bolts (screw end first) into the guide holes. There should be pilot holes (smaller than the guide holes) driven into the blocking. To drive this hardware, spin a pair of nuts onto the bolt end and turn the bolt closest to you with a wrench. Drive the mounting bolt until the end is projecting out from the wall by a little more than 1½". Remove the nuts. Install the pop-up drain in the sink , and then slide the sink over the ends of the mounting bolts so the mounting flange is flush against the wall. You'll want help for this. Thread the washers and nuts onto the ends of the mounting bolts and hand-tighten. Check to make sure the sink is level and then tighten the nuts with a socket or wrench, reaching up into the void between the basin and the flange. Don't overtighten—you could crack the sink flange.
(continued)

4

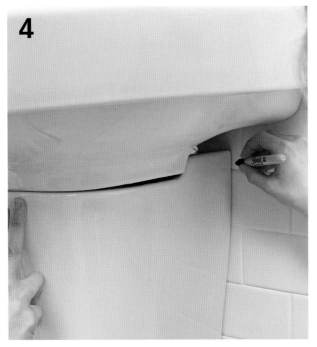

Have a helper hold the sink pedestal (in this model, a half-pedestal) in position against the underside of the sink. Mark the edges of the pedestal on the wall covering as reference for installing the pedestal-mounting hardware. Remove the pedestal.

5

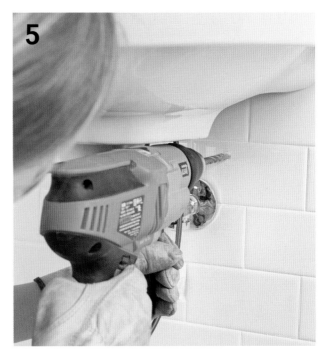

Remove the pedestal and drill the pilot holes for the pedestal-mounting bolts, which work much in the same way as the sink-mounting bolts. Drill guide and pilot holes then drive the mounting bolts, leaving about 1¼" of the bolt end exposed.

6

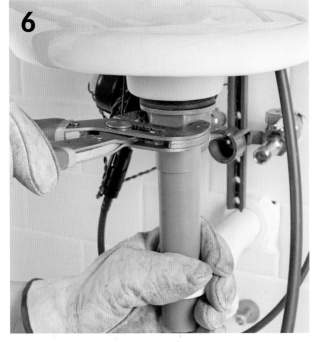

Install the drain and drain tailpiece on the sink. Also mount the faucet body to the sink deck if you have not done so already. Also attach the drain trap arm to the drain stub out in the wall and attach shutoff valves to the drain supply lines. You'll find instructions for doing all of these jobs elsewhere in this book.

7

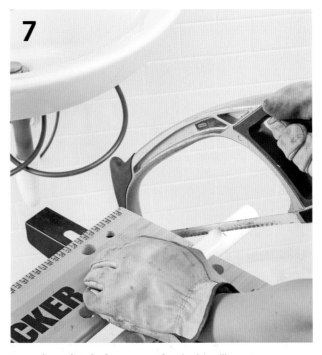

Complete the drain connection by installing a P-trap assembly that connects the tail piece and the trap arm. Also connect the drain pop-up rod that projects out of the tailpiece to the pop-up plunger mechanism you've already installed.

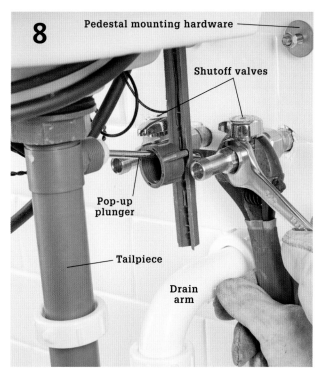

8

Pedestal mounting hardware

Shutoff valves

Pop-up plunger

Tailpiece

Drain arm

Make sure the shutoff valve fittings are tight and oriented correctly, and then hook up the faucet supply risers to the shutoff valves. Turn on the water supply and test.

Leak Finder ▸

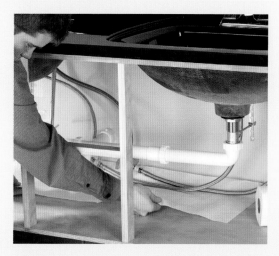

To quickly and easily find an undersink leak, lay bright white paper or paper towels under the pipes and drain connections. Open the water supply valves and run water in the sinks. It should be clear exactly where the water dripped from by the location of the drip on the paper.

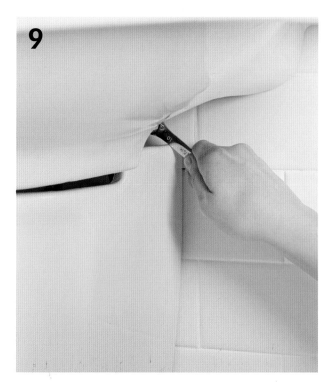

9

Slide the pedestal into place on the mounting studs. Working through the access space under the sink, use a wrench to tighten the mounting nut over the washer on the stud. Carefully tighten the nut until the pedestal is held securely in place. Be careful not to overtighten the nut.

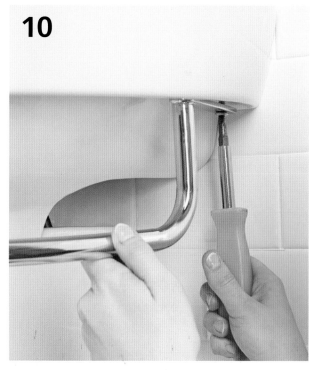

10

Attach the towel bar to the sink by first pushing the well nuts into the holes on the underside of the sink rim. Set the bar in place, and screw in the attachment screws on both sides, just until snug.

VESSEL SINKS

The vessel sink harkens back to the days of washstands and washbowls. Whether it's round, square, or oval, shallow or deep, the vessel sink offers great opportunity for creativity and proudly displays its style. Vessel sinks are a perfect choice for a powder room, where they will have high visibility.

Most vessel sinks can be installed on any flat surface—from a granite countertop to a wall-mounted vanity to an antique dresser. Some sinks are designed to contact the mounting surface only at the drain flange. Others are made to be partially embedded in the surface. Take care to follow the manufacturer's instructions for cutting holes for sinks and faucets.

A beautiful vessel sink demands an equally attractive faucet. Select a tall spout mounted on the countertop or vanity top or a wall-mounted spout to accommodate the height of the vessel. To minimize splashing, spouts should direct flow to the center of the vessel, not down the side. Make sure your faucet is compatible with your vessel choice. Look for a centerset or single-handle model if you'll be custom drilling the countertop—you only need to drill one faucet hole.

Tools & Materials ▸

Pliers	Pop-up drain
Wrench	P-trap and drain kit
Vanity or countertop	Faucet
Vessel sink	Eye and ear protection

Vessel sinks are available in countless styles of materials, shapes, and sizes. Their one commonality is that they all need to be installed on a flat surface.

VESSEL SINK OPTIONS

This glass vessel sink embedded in a "floating" glass countertop is a stunning contrast to the strong and attractive wood frame anchoring it to the wall.

Vessel sinks come in many forms, including the dramatic sloped version here. The modern style fits perfectly with a custom glass counter and sophisticated glass wall tiles.

Vessel sinks don't have to be shaped like a bowl. This rectangular tray sink is a cool alternative to a more common bowl shape and accents the chic, light wood vanity and cabinets in the room.

Vitreous china with a glazed enamel finish is an economical and durable choice for a vessel sink (although it is less durable than stone). Because of the flexibility of both the material and the glaze, the design options are virtually unlimited with vitreous china.

HOW TO INSTALL A VESSEL SINK

Secure the vanity cabinet or other countertop that you'll be using to mount the vessel sink.

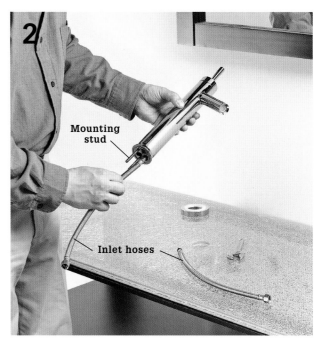

Begin hooking up the faucet. Insert the brass mounting stud into the threaded hole in the faucet base with the slotted end facing out. Hand tighten, and then use a slotted screwdriver to tighten another half turn. Insert the inlet hoses into the faucet body and hand tighten. Use an adjustable wrench to tighten another half turn. Do not overtighten.

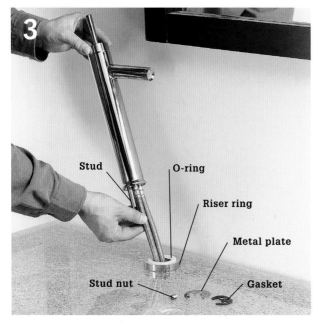

Place the O-ring on top of the riser ring over the faucet cutout in the countertop. From underneath, slide the rubber gasket and the metal plate over the mounting stud. Thread the mounting stud nut onto the mounting stud and hand tighten. Use an adjustable wrench to tighten another half turn.

To install the sink and pop-up drain, first place the small metal ring between two O-rings and place over the drain cutout.

5

Place the vessel bowl on top of the O-rings. In this installation, the vessel is not bonded to the countertop.

6

Put the small rubber gasket over the drain hole in the vessel. From the top, push the pop-up assembly through the drain hole.

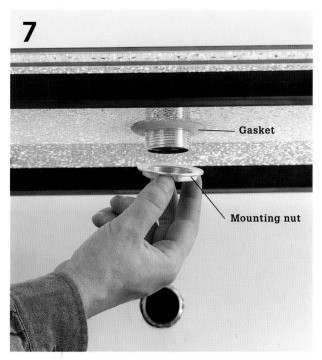

7

Gasket

Mounting nut

From underneath, push the large rubber gasket onto the threaded portion of the pop-up assembly. Thread the nut onto the pop-up assembly and tighten. Use an adjustable wrench or basin wrench to tighten an additional half turn. Thread the tailpiece onto the pop-up assembly.

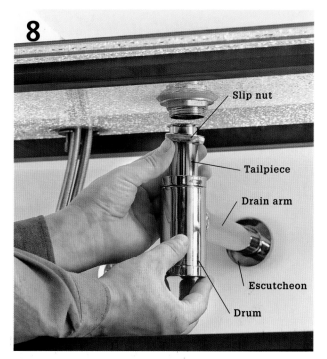

8

Slip nut

Tailpiece

Drain arm

Escutcheon

Drum

Install the drum trap. Loosen the rings on the top and outlet of the drum trap. Slide the drum trap top hole over the tailpiece. Slide the drain arm into the side outlet, with the flat side of the rubber gasket facing away from the trap. Insert the drain arm into the wall outlet. Hand tighten the rings.

BIDETS

Bidets are becoming ever more popular in the United States. Maybe that's because they can give a dream bath that European flare so many of us find alluring. Go to Europe, Asia, or South America and you'll see how much people can come to rely on bidets. Some fans of this bathroom fixture think those who don't use bidets are unhygienic.

With the trend moving toward larger and more luxurious bathrooms, many Americans are becoming intrigued by this personal hygiene appliance. The standard model features hot and cold faucets, and either a movable nozzle located by the faucet handles or a vertical sprayer located near the front of the bowl. Most bidets are outfitted with a pop-up drain. You can also buy a combination toilet and bidet if space is an issue.

Tools & Materials ▸

Tape measure
Drill
Adjustable wrench
Level
Silicone sealant
(2) ⅜" shut-off valves
(2) ⅜" supply lines
P-trap
Tubing cutter
Plumber's putty
Thread tape
Bidet
Bidet faucet
Marker
Eye and ear protection

Installing a bidet is very much like installing a sink. The only difference is that the bidet can have the waste line plumbed below the floor, like a shower. But like sinks, bidets may have single or multiple deck holes for faucets, so be certain to purchase compatible components.

A bidet is a useful companion to a toilet, and it is a luxury item you and your family will appreciate. For people with limited mobility, a bidet is an aide to independent personal sanitation.

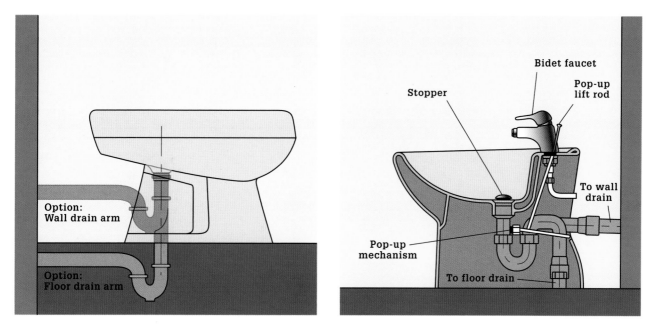

Bidet drains have more in common with sink drains than with toilet drains. Some even attach to a drain arm in the wall, with a P-trap that fits between the fixture drain tailpiece and the arm. Other bidets drain into a floor drain outlet with a trap that's situated between the tailpiece and the branch drain line.

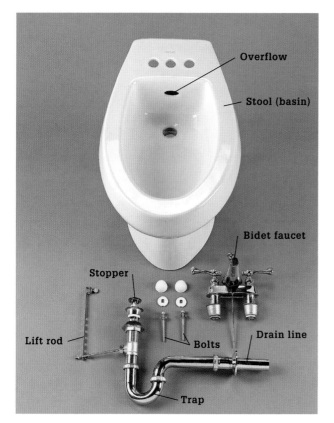

A bidet requires a special faucet that allows you to mix hot and cold water to a temperature you find comfortable. It has a third knob to control the water pressure. The aerator and spout pivot to allow you to adjust the spray to a comfortable height.

You can get all the features of a bidet on your existing toilet with a number of aftermarket bidet seats. These seats feature heaters, sprayers, and dryers in basic or deluxe versions. Installation takes less than an hour and no additional space is needed.

HOW TO INSTALL A BIDET

Rough-in the supply and drain lines according to the manufacturer's specifications. If you do not have experience installing home plumbing, hire a plumber for this part of the job. Apply a coil of plumber's putty to the base of the bidet faucet, and then insert the faucet body into the mounting holes. Thread the washers and locknut onto the faucet body shank and hand tighten. Remove any plumber's putty squeeze out.

Apply a coil of plumber's putty around the underside of the drain flange. Insert the flange in the drain hole, place the gasket and washer, and then thread the nut onto the flange. Do not fully tighten.

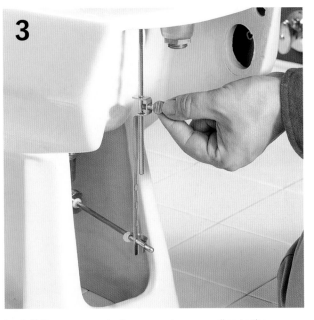

Install the pop-up drain apparatus according to the manufacturer's instructions.

Place the bidet in its final location, checking that supply and drain lines will be in alignment. Mark the locations of the two side-mounting holes through the predrilled holes on the stool and onto the floor.

BATHROOM PROJECTS

Remove the bidet and drill ³⁄₁₆" pilot holes at the marks on the floor. Drive the floor bolts (included with the bidet basin) into the holes. Position the bidet so the floor bolts fit into the bolt holes in the base. Tighten nuts onto the floor bolts.

Connect the water supply risers to the bidet faucet using compression unions. Make sure to hook the hot and cold risers up to the correct ports on the faucet.

Hook up the drain line by attaching the P-trap to the drain tailpiece. The trap is then attached to a branch drain line coming out of the wall or floor in the same manner as a sink drain.

Remove the aerator so any debris in the supply line will clear and then turn on the water and open both faucets. Check for leaks in lines and fix, if found. Assemble the bolt caps and thread them onto the floor bolts. *Note: Do not dispose of paper in the bidet—return to the toilet to dry off after using the bidet for cleaning.*

VENT FANS

For most of us, a dream bathroom does not include foggy mirrors or unpleasant odors. Opening a window, if your bathroom is equipped with one, can help, but vent fans do the best job of clearing the air.

Most vent fans are installed in the center of the bathroom ceiling or over the toilet area. A fan installed over the tub or shower area must be GFCI protected and rated for use in wet areas. You can usually wire a fan with a light fixture into a main bathroom electrical circuit, but units with built-in heat lamps or blowers require separate circuits.

If the fan you choose doesn't come with a mounting kit, purchase one separately. A mounting kit should include a vent hose (duct), a vent tailpiece, and an exterior vent cover.

Venting instructions vary among manufacturers, but the most common options are attic venting and soffit venting. Attic venting routes fan ductwork into the attic and out through the roof. Always insulate ducting in this application to keep condensation from forming and running down into the motor. Carefully install flashing around the outside vent cover to prevent roof leaks.

Soffit venting involves routing the duct to a soffit (roof overhang) instead of through the roof. Check with the vent manufacturer for instructions for soffit venting.

To prevent moisture damage, always terminate the vent outside your home—never into your attic or basement.

You can install a vent fan while the framing is exposed or as a retrofit, as shown in this project.

Tools & Materials ▸

Eye and ear protection	Drill
Flexible dryer vent duct	Hammer
Phillips and straight screwdrivers	Nails
Jigsaw or drywall saw	Wire connectors
Reciprocating saw	Dryer vent clamps
Electrical tester	Vent cover
Exhaust fan unit	Drywall
Drywall screws	4" hole saw

A combination light/vent fan is a great product in powder rooms and smaller baths that to do not generate excessive amounts of air moisture. In larger baths with tubs and showers, install a dedicated vent fan with a CFM rating that's at least 5 CFM higher than the total square footage of the bathroom (inset photo).

BATHROOM PROJECTS

HOW TO REPLACE AN OVERHEAD LIGHT WITH A LIGHT/FAN

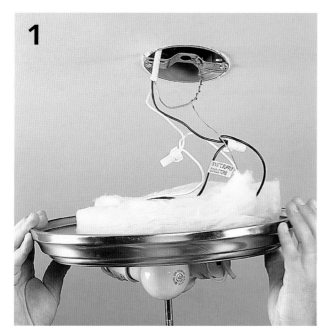

1

Shut off power to the ceiling light at the electrical service panel. Remove the globe and bulb from the overhead ceiling light, and then disconnect the mounting screws that hold the light fixture to the ceiling box.

2

Test the wire connections with a current tester to make sure they are not live, and then disconnect the wires and remove the light fixture. Cap the wire ends.

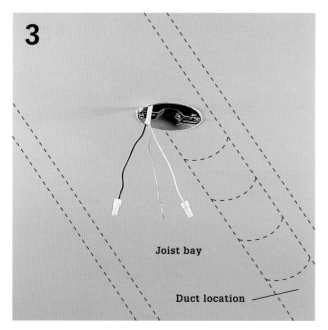

3

Joist bay

Duct location

Plan your exhaust pipe route. In most cases, this means determining the shortest distance between the fan and the outdoors. If the room is located at the top living level, venting through the roof is usually smartest. On lower levels and in basements, you'll need to go through an exterior wall. If you need to route through a wall in a room with a finished ceiling, choose a route that runs through a single ceiling joist bay.

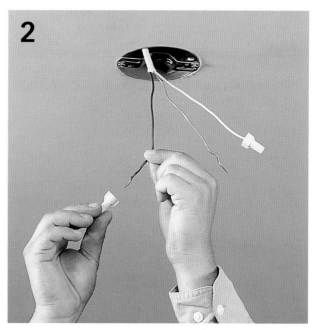

4

Remove ceiling covering in the fan unit installation area and between the joists at the end of the run, next to the wall. You'll need at least 18" of access. If you are running rigid vent pipe or the joist bay is insulated, you'll need to remove ceiling material between the joists for the entire run. Make cuts on the centerlines of the joists.

BATHROOM PROJECTS

(continued)

5

Insert flexible vent tubing into one of the ceiling openings and expand it so the free end reaches to the ceiling opening at the wall. A fish tape for running cable through walls can be a useful aid for extending the tubing.

6

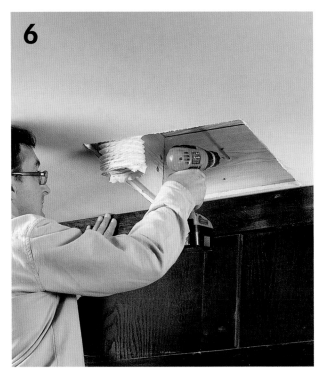

Draw a 4"-dia. circle on the wall framing at the end of the joist bay, marking the exit point for the duct. Choose a long, ¼"-dia. drill bit and drill a hole at the center of the circle. Drill all the way through the wall so the bit exits on the exterior side. This will mark your hole location outside.

7

On the exterior, draw a 4"-dia. circle centered on the exit point of the drill bit. Cut out the opening for the vent cover with a reciprocating saw or a 4" hole saw.

8

Insert the vent cover assembly into the opening, following the manufacturer's directions for fastening and sealing it to the house.

9

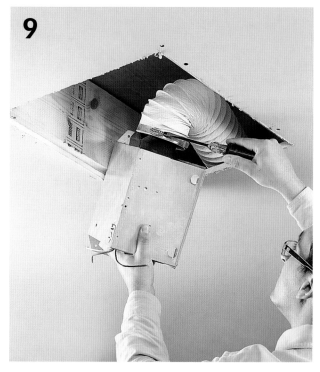

Attach the end of the vent tubing to the outlet on the vent cover unit and secure it with a large pipe clamp.

10

Nail the housing for the light/fan unit to the ceiling joist so the bottom edges of the housing are flush with the ceiling surface.

11

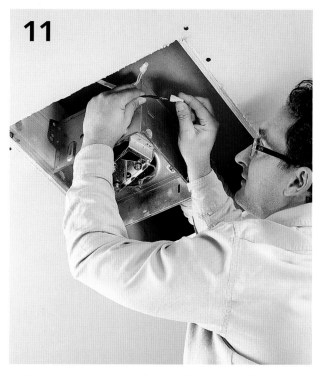

Make the wiring connections in the housing box according to the manufacturer's instructions. In just about every case you should be able to use the existing wires from the original light switch. Once you have connected the wires, restore the power and test the fan.

12

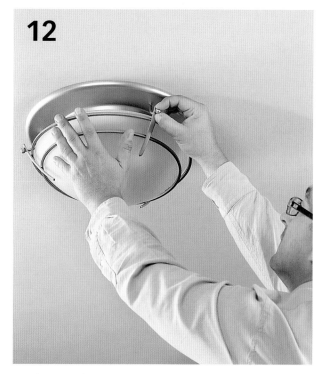

Patch and paint the wall and ceiling in the project area. Mount the light (the model we installed plugs into a receptacle in the fan box), grille, globe, and any other fixture parts.

TOILET ENCLOSURE

One of the best ways to make a busy family bathroom more usable is to enclose the toilet in a room of its own. Toilet enclosures—originally called "water closets" after the cistern they enclosed—make a privacy compartment within the bathroom. This allows one person to shower while the other uses the toilet. It also effectively hides the fixture that most people think is the sore thumb of the bathroom.

Although toilet enclosures are basic structures comprising framed walls and a prehung door, they must be built to maintain adequate spacing around the toilet for maximum comfort and to meet local codes. As a general rule of thumb, you want to leave at least 15 inches from the center of the toilet bowl to the wall surface on either side, and at least 21 inches from the front of the bowl to the door. You may also want to add baffles or soundproofing inside the walls, to make the space as private as possible.

The enclosure shown here includes a combination lighting/ventilation fixture. Both are absolute musts for appropriate hygiene and comfort, even if they are not mandated by local codes. (A window can serve the ventilation function, but you'll still need to install lighting for nighttime use.)

When it comes to toilet enclosures, more room is always better. If you can dedicate extra space to the enclosure, you'll not only make the space more comfortable, you'll be able to add nice finishing touches such as a magazine rack or shelves for candles.

A full enclosure with a door offers the maximum in privacy, but it may be a more extreme solution than you require. A simple partition wall next to the toilet creates a sense of privacy without any claustrophobia.

Tools & Materials ▸

Prehung door unit	Circular saw
Hammer	Drill
16d nails	Drywall
Screwdriver	Handsaw
2 × 4 lumber	Utility knife
Drywall tape	Wall compound
Prehung door	Interior door lockset
Wood shims	Door trim
Quarter-round molding	Silicone caulk
Stud finder	Fiberglass insulation
Level	Eye and ear protection

HOW TO BUILD A TOILET ENCLOSURE

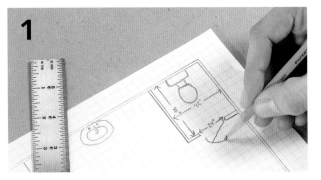

1

Carefully plan out the enclosure. Sketch your plans with exact dimensions to ensure that you allow proper space between toilet and walls, and to ensure door swing won't impede the shower, vanity drawers, or other fixtures.

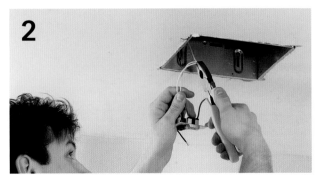

2

Run wiring and ducting for lighting and ventilation as necessary. Install a box for an overhead fixture and run wire for the switch. We installed a combination light/vent fan (see pages 488 to 491) connected to an interior wall switch placed just on the latch-side of the enclosure wall. The fixture can be run off the light switch circuit for the entire bathroom if that circuit has the capacity.

Check existing connection walls for plumb and square.
Cut the sole and top plates accordingly, compensating as
needed for any variances. Place top and sole plates side by
side and mark stud locations, 16" on center.

Secure sole plates to the floor. Plates installed over
resilient flooring as shown here, can be nailed through to
subfloor. When installing over a tile floor, use a masonry bit
to drill pilot holes and then screw through to subfloor. (Over
mosaic floors, it's best to remove the tiles from under the sole
plate and secure the plate directly to subfloor.)

Use a stud finder to locate ceiling joists, and then nail the top plates into place.
Frame out the walls by toenailing studs between top and sole plates as marked.
Frame L-corner for walls, as shown (inset).

Frame the doorway with header,
cripple studs, and jack studs (you should
purchase your prehung door first, so
that you can double-check the opening
measurements against the actual
door unit).   (continued)

7

Hang drywall on the framed walls, inside and out. The enclosure here was clad with standard drywall rather than greenboard, because the walls won't be subjected to any direct moisture contact. If the enclosure abuts a shower or bath, use greenboard or cementboard.

8

Position the prehung door in place. Check that it is oriented correctly, to open out from the enclosure and against a wall, rather than blocking the central space or opening against the vanity.

9

Shim all around the jamb (specifically, behind hinges and lockset location) until the door unit is plumb and square in the opening, and the door opens smoothly. Nail through the door jambs into the framing at the shim points.

10

Saw the shims off flush. Measure, cut, and nail the trim for the door in place. Putty and sand over the nail heads on jambs and casework.

BATHROOM PROJECTS

Use the Wall Cavity ▶

Because the partition wall you've built is essentially empty, it is a good candidate for installing niche fittings that are recessed into the wall. A recessed toilet tissue holder is one easy-to-install fitting. Space will be fairly tight in your enclosure, so using the wall space makes a lot of sense. A wall-niche magazine rack or niche shelving are just two additional ways you may use the wall cavity space.

11

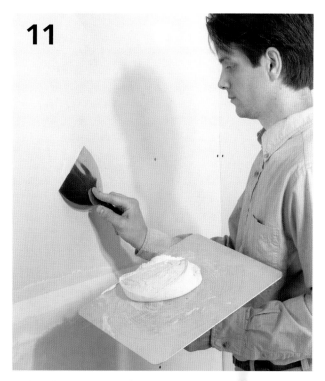

Finish the drywall surfaces with tape and joint compound. Work as neatly as you can to minimize sanding. Seal the new drywall with drywall primer before you paint.

12

Paint the enclosure walls and add any additional elements, including paper holders, grab bars, and shelves or cabinets. The wall area behind the toilet tank is a good spot for installing shallow shelving, but keep it at least 3 ft. above the tank lid.

13

Attach base quarter-round molding on bottom of walls, inside and out (or cove molding if you prefer). Apply a coat of silicone caulk to the bottom of molding before nailing it in place.

ROOM ADDITION PROJECTS

At the very far end of the scale of home-remodeling projects is the construction of a room addition that expands the actual footprint of the house itself. It is one of the most complicated projects a DIYer can hope to undertake—the steps are virtually the same as are used for the construction of an entire home, just on a smaller scale.

While some very skilled DIYers do tackle this kind of sophisticated home-improvement project, most homeowners will want to do some parts of this job, such as the finishing work, but will leave some of the major work to professional contractors. Few DIYers, for example, have the resources to excavate the soil out of large spaces in order to pour foundations.

This final chapter of *The Book of Home Improvement* covers representative stages in the complete construction of a room addition. If you already have a lot of DIY experience and plenty of help, it might be possible to plan, build, and finish a small room addition based on just the information in this chapter. But it's much more likely that this chapter will serve as a helpful overview of the process, one you can use to guide your project as you consult other sources of information and work with a variety of contractors to complete the job.

IN THIS CHAPTER:

- Evaluating Your Site
- Drawing Construction Plans
- Site Preparation
- Pouring a Footing
- Tying into an Existing Foundation
- Laying a Concrete Block Foundation
- Framing the Floor
- Framing a Wall
- Constructing the Addition's Roof
- Installing Asphalt Shingles
- Sheathing Exterior Walls
- Building Wrap
- Installing Siding
- Soffits, Fascia & Gutters
- Installing Windows
- Installing an Entry Door

EVALUATING YOUR SITE

The features of your property play almost as large a part in the planning and design process as the features of your house. Local codes and regulations controlling the size of structures, the maximum percentage of a lot that can be built upon, and the minimum setback requirements are all important determining factors in most addition plans. Along with regulations, your property's topography and exposure should influence the building site. For instance, a yard that slopes severely or has extremely irregular terrain may present challenges to building a room addition foundation. In reviewing your property you also need to check with the local utility companies to determine and mark the location of any buried utilities (call 811). It's far easier to identify these lines prior to construction than it is to repair a ruptured main.

Setback. The setback is the minimum distance that must be maintained between your structure and your property line. Setbacks are established for a number of reasons including safety and clear access to public thoroughfares. Setbacks obviously affect bump-outs and other types of additions that increase the footprint of your structure, but they can also impact garage conversions. If the rules allow for a non-dwelling structure to be close to the property line, converting it to a living space may suddenly violate the setback rules for dwellings.

Easements. You'll also need to take into account any easements on your property. All easements effectively do the same thing: they limit building on parts of your property so that those parts can be accessed by other parties. Common easements include "easements in gross" that allow power, water, and cable companies critical access to utilities on, or crossing, your property. Appurtenances are "easements in common," such as a driveway that crosses your property so that a neighbor can get to theirs. These, like many property easements you'll encounter, are obvious. Others are not. That's why you should check your deed and title for descriptions of property easements before you settle on the final location for your addition.

Code Limitations. Building codes and regulations normally limit how far up you can build, as well as how far out. A local code may allow for an attic conversion that adds dormers, but restricts a second-story addition that raises the height of exterior walls.

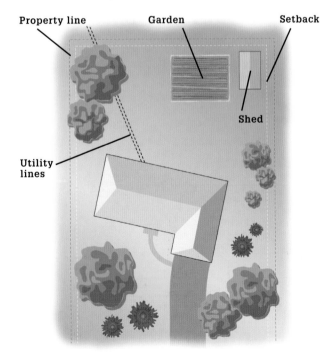

A plan view of your yard that includes all permanent structures will help you determine which codes and regulations will impact your design.

A severe slope in back of this house makes adding on a challenge requiring specialized pier-and-post foundations.

Assessing Your Soil ▸

An important part of evaluating the suitability of your property for a room addition is determining if your soil is going to present any challenges in laying the foundation. Different types of soil can actually add to construction costs because of the extra work required in excavating or reinforcing the foundation. That said, it's always easier to deal preemptively with soil issues as they occur than to fix the many and severe problems unstable soil can create.

The first place to go for information on the soil in your area is your county extension service. They'll be able to give you information about the type of soil in your region. If you don't have a local office, you can contact the United States Department of Agriculture and request a soil map for your area. The type of soil largely determines what problems may occur and what preventative steps are called for.

- **Clay:** Clay shrinks and expands during dry and wet periods more than other soils do. If you have high clay content in your soil, anticipate extra work in laying the foundation. You'll need to spend more time and effort on the drainage system to direct water well away from the area of the foundation.

- **Sand:** Sandy soil is subject to shifting and movement, but is only a serious problem when the sand content is very high, such as along a river or in a coastal area. If you suspect your soil has an unusually high sand content, get a soil analysis. This may lead you to use a different type of foundation for the addition, such as deep piers rather than a poured concrete wall foundation.

- **Muck:** When soil contains large sections of decomposing organic matter, or "muck," the soil base can become quite unstable. If built on, the soil may compress over time, causing detrimental settling in the years to come. If you encounter a lot of muck in excavating a foundation, the most reliable solution is to excavate all of it and replace it with more stable soil. Although this may seem excessive, it's a matter of heading off far worse problems down the road.

Determining what type of soil you'll be dealing with in excavating for a foundation is crucial to planning for an addition. Common types include gravel and sandy gravel (left), sandy (middle), and clay/silt (right).

DRAWING CONSTRUCTION PLANS

Building plans are the roadmap for the journey that leads from that vision of a new and wonderful space in your head to the reality that you'll live with after the construction is completed. How closely the reality matches the vision depends on how detailed, concise, and comprehensive your addition building plans are.

The best way to begin the process is to sketch out a preliminary floor plan yourself. This is easily done with a few basic drafting supplies: a T-square or ruler, an adjustable triangle, grid paper, and a sharp pencil. Take measurements of the existing space that will connect to the addition, or that will be converted, and decide on the measurements of the new space. Now you can rough out the new space on the grid paper.

Use a standard scale of ¼ inch, ½ inch, or 1 inch to 1 foot and start from the exterior walls. Add the locations of doors (marking arcs for the door swing), windows, electrical outlets, plumbing fixtures, and other permanent features such as window seats. Think about where plumbing pipes and heating ducts will go. Finally, add interior walls.

One of the advantages to sketching your own preliminary drawings is that you can play with the dimensions, easily changing floor plan configurations and features to see which suits best. Concerned about light? Sketch in a bay or bow window. Suddenly realize the space is rather long and narrow? Break it up with a framed wall and doorway.

This exercise also gives you the chance to test furniture placement ideas. Cut top-view silhouettes out of construction paper or other thick stock, in shapes representing existing furniture you want to incorporate into the space or pieces you intend to buy. This is a great way to work out details of the floor plan, especially fixture and furniture placements that would present significant problems if discovered later in the construction process.

If you're more inclined to use a mouse than a pencil, you can try drafting your floor plan in one of the many computer-aided design (CAD) programs created just for homeowners. Unless you've had experience with these types of programs, you'll have to spend some time learning the software. However, working with software offers some unique and useful features such as calculating the amount of materials you'll need for the space you design.

Ultimately, no matter how good your drafting skills may be, you'll probably need professionally drawn plans to submit to the building department. Some municipalities allow homeowners to submit plans they've drawn, but most require professionally drafted blueprints and building plans. Although some contractors offer design services, for large, complex projects use an architect to draft your plans. You'll want to select someone who is familiar with the local building department and community.

Drawing preliminary floor plans is your chance to exercise your creativity, try different features and configurations, and get a sense of what the new space will look and feel like.

One of the other benefits of using an architect to create your plans is that he or she will also be able to make suggestions on structural issues you may not have considered.

Whoever drafts the plans will need to include the basic elements required by building departments. These usually entail blueprints that incorporate a site plan, floor plans, elevation drawings where applicable, and a materials list.

- **Site plans** show the addition in relation to the existing property, structures, and surrounding areas. These lay out important dimensions such as the lot size, distance from property setback lines and the position of the structure in relation to existing utilities.
- **Floor plans** are extremely accurate dimensional overviews that clearly show all relevant details such as exact location and dimensions of walls, windows, doors, plumbing, and electrical fixtures.
- **Elevation drawings** show the proposed addition from all sides. Elevation drawings sometimes include cutaway side views, depending on the requirements of the building department and the type of addition or conversion you're proposing.
- **A materials list** is included to show the building authorities that the construction will use only materials that conform to code. (It does not need to list quantities.)

As a collection of highly detailed drawings, the blueprints form specific instructions that you, the builder, and other professionals will follow in constructing the addition. That's why you'll need multiple copies of the blueprints. The building department usually requires that two or more copies be submitted with the permit application, and you'll want contractors and subcontractors to have copies depending on how involved they are (i.e., a plumber installing lines and fixtures for a kitchen and bath). Be sure to forward revised blueprints to everyone whenever changes are made after the initial blueprints are drafted.

A complete set of plans and blueprints drawn by a professional is the gold standard of home design and it will impress your local permit-issuing authorities. But a DIY package can be effective as long as it is put together neatly and with care and includes all of the required elements.

SITE PREPARATION

Before the construction activity gets underway in earnest you should make some site preparations to ensure reasonable access to the work area, as well as to protect your house and grounds from the inevitable stresses of a major construction project. Readying your building site entails moving features and fixtures that are within the borders of the actual job site or the path workers will use to move materials, equipment, and building waste in and out of the work area.

Start by moving the manmade structures. These include outdoor furnishings such as patio tables and chairs, umbrellas, planters, playsets and sandboxes, statuary, and garden ornaments. Prevent any chance of damage by storing these far from the work site, ideally in a protected space such as a garage or shed. In some cases, providing access to the worksite requires removing a fence—temporarily at least.

Remove landscape features as necessary to make runs in parallel construction. Completing a room addition that increases the footprint of your house usually requires that you relocate or remove a landscape feature or two. If a tree or shrub is too large to be moved, you can either remove it, protect it—such as wrapping the trunk of a tree in used tires—or relocate it. You can actually plan the relocation of a tree or large bush as part of the excavation process; a backhoe can do in minutes what might take hours or even days to accomplish by hand. When considering the plants on your lot, begin by looking upward. The altered roofline of a room addition or attic conversion may run right into a large tree branch. It's wise to remedy the situation before, rather than in the middle of construction.

How to Limb a Tree ▸

The best tool for pruning is a telephone. Use it to call an arborist and have them assess the tree and make the appropriate cuts. If you do decide to go it alone, be careful, and follow these basic rules:

- Never cut away more than ⅓ of the tree's branches.
- Start with a shallow undercut several inches away from the branch bark collar—the bulge where the branch meets the trunk. The undercut ensures the bark doesn't peel off as the branch drops.
- Complete the cut from the top to remove the bulk of the branch.
- Make a final cut flush with the outside of the branch bark collar. Do not cut into the collar.
- Leave the wound to heal itself. Don't paint it or add any kind of sealant or preservative.

Start by undercutting from beneath the limb with your bow saw or chain saw.

Finish the cut from above—this keeps the bark from tearing when the limb breaks loose.

Trim the stub from the limb so it's flush with the branch collar.

ROOM ADDITION PROJECTS

Mark underground utilities such as gas and water lines prior to beginning any project that involves digging. Even if lines are indicated on your original plan drawings or site survey, contact the local utilities (call 811) and have them come out to flag the exact location of all lines that are anywhere near the building site. Technicians from the utilities will visit your site and identify the location of underground lines for free.

Mark your property boundaries, whether or not you are expanding outward. Even a small attic conversion will mean a lot of traffic through your yard, with a high potential that pallets of materials will be stationed temporarily on the ground. Marking property lines helps ensure that neither you nor your workers causes any damage to your neighbor's property.

Prepare the interior of the work site, especially if there will be substantial work done inside, as with an attic conversion. Line the pathway in and out of the house by taping down heavy-duty kraft paper from the work area to the nearest exit. You'll also want to partition off any area or room in the house that might be affected by work debris such as dust from sanding drywall joints. Use double layers of thick plastic sheeting to separate the worksite from other areas in the home.

Have all utility lines flagged and marked with spray paint before you dig. Utility companies provide this service free of charge. There is now a national toll-free number in the United States you can call to get referrals for free flagging of utility lines (call 811).

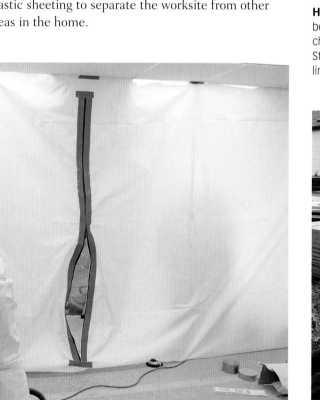

Erect temporary walls to create barriers between the work area and the rest of your house. Heavy duty plastic sheeting is best for this.

Clear the area around the building site to create a staging ground for building materials and temporary storage for excavated dirt. Arrange to have dirt removed as soon as possible. A temporary fence such as a snow fence is required around excavation areas by some codes.

POURING A FOOTING

An addition foundation is laid in stages, each stage building on the previous one. The process starts with excavation of the foundation hole and leveling of the grade on which the foundation will stand. Then the trench for the footing—the solid base for everything that comes after—is dug, and the footing is laid. Finally, the walls are laid or poured and the floor constructed in preparation for the main structure of the addition. If the foundation is developed correctly, the rest of the addition will mesh fluidly with, and last as long as, the existing structure.

The footing is the least visible part of the whole structure, but it's an essential underpinning nonetheless. The footing trench is marked using a plumb line in reference to the corners defined by your original string lines. The trench needs to accommodate a footing that's typically twice as wide as the wall that stands on it, and twice as deep as the wall is wide. The footing can be poured into a cleanly cut trench or, if the soil is not that stable, form boards can be used.

With the footing in place, forms are positioned or, if you're laying a concrete block wall, that process is begun. In either case, the first step is tying into the existing foundation, usually with rebar "pins" that are affixed in holes drilled into the existing foundation. The addition's foundation walls are reinforced throughout, and the floor of the crawlspace or basement is completed with a vapor barrier and, in the case of a basement, a slab. Finally, the floor is built, setting the stage on which the rest of the room addition will take shape.

Tools & Materials ▸

Sledgehammer	Spade or square-edged shovel
Hammer	Bolsters or bricks
Cordless drill	No. 4 rebar
2 × 4s	Steel stakes
Vegetable oil	Eye and ear protection
Metal tie wires	

A concrete footing provides a flat, sturdy surface on which you can stack concrete block foundation walls or pour concrete walls.

HOW TO PREPARE A FOOTING TRENCH

Dig the trench to the plan-specified depth and width. Use a square-end spade to smooth and square the sides of the trench. Thoroughly compact the floor of the trench with a tamper.

Frame the top of the trench with 2 × 4 form lumber. Drive stakes next to the 2 × 4 form boards and attach the boards to the stakes (the round steel stakes seen here are predrilled for deck screws). Level the form boards side-to-side and along their lengths.

Reinforce the footing with No. 4 rebar. Set the rebar on bricks, stones, or use rebar bolsters to raise the rods off the bottom of the trench.

Bind the rebar with metal tie wires to keep the parallel rods from separating when the concrete is poured. Installing a few spacers between rods to keep them separated is also a good idea.

Drive sections of rebar, at least 24" long, into the ground vertically, every 4' and at least 1' from corners. Position the vertical rebar so it will fall in the void areas of concrete blocks. Fill the forms with concrete.

TYING INTO AN EXISTING FOUNDATION

Connecting a new foundation for an addition onto the existing house foundation is an engineering requirement. If you don't physically couple the two foundations, sooner or later you may end up with two separate buildings. By linking the two foundations you take a big step toward ensuring that the construction is structurally sound.

The traditional technique for tying in the new foundation to the old is to drill holes in the existing mating wall, insert rebar "pins" 6 inches to 8 inches deep, securing them in the concrete with epoxy glue. Then it's just a matter of grafting the exposed rebar ties to full lengths of rebar that are installed to reinforce the new foundation when you set up the forms.

This technique was developed for poured foundations, but can also be used with other types. When laying a new foundation of concrete block walls, you can either drill the end blocks to accept the epoxied pins, or you can use special blocks with cavities meant just for this purpose. As you add each course and slip the end blocks onto the pins, tie them to rebar rods positioned vertically through the holes in the blocks, and fill the holes with concrete.

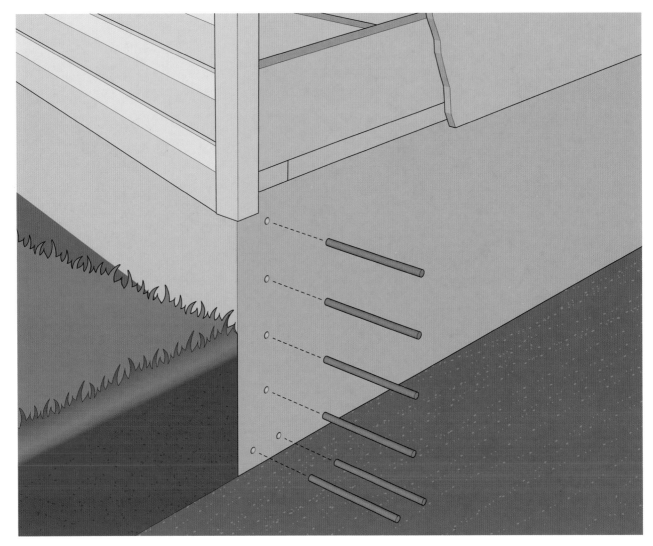

Tie rods cut from No. 4 rebar, usually around 8 to 10" in length, are inserted into holes drilled into the foundation wall and then secured with epoxy glue. The free ends of the tie rods are bound to full-length rebar rods with tie wire.

Tie-in Challenges ▸

In some situations, the traditional method of tying a new foundation wall to an existing one isn't going to work. For instance, if your new foundation wall abuts a concrete block foundation, the existing foundation may be hollow at the points you want to drive the rebar in and set it. If this is the case, you'll have to use one of the many masonry fasteners available (after consulting your local building department for code restrictions, of course). One example is a vertical ladder of fastener strips that are screwed into the existing wall with masonry screws, and locked into the new wall by means of arms that project horizontally from the mounting strips. You'll find other types of wall ties suited to different situations at masonry supply stores. As a last resort—and only if code allows—you can line the joint between the two walls with waterproof expansion material just as you would a large concrete slab. Once the new wall is in place, the joint will tolerate a certain amount of movement while still maintaining a waterproof seal.

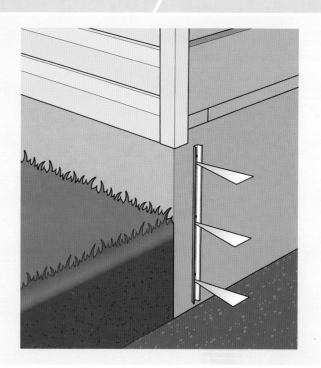

TYING INTO CONCRETE

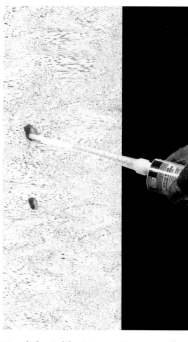

Use a corded hammer drill with a ½" or ⅝" masonry bit to drill access holes for the No. 4 rebar tie rods. Drilling concrete can be a slow job, but do not get impatient and lean too hard on the drill—let the bit do the work.

Use injectable two-part epoxy glue to secure the ends of the rebar tie rods into the holes drilled in your existing foundation wall. Make sure the concrete dust is all cleared from the hole before injecting glue and inserting rods.

LAYING A CONCRETE BLOCK FOUNDATION

Building a concrete block foundation wall is a project even the unskilled home handyman can tackle, because the skills needed are minimal and can be honed through practice. The chief requirement in laying this type of foundation is careful attention to detail, beginning with the measurements.

Although it may seem counterintuitive, the best way to measure for a concrete block wall is from the top down. If you've laid out your string lines correctly, you've already determined the top-of-foundation height; ideally you want the distance down to the footing to equal an exact number of block courses (which, with standard blocks, will be a multiple of eight). Once you've got the measurement right, you can help yourself by working slowly and methodically and following some time-tested rules. When it comes to mortar, be conservative. You should only mix the mortar you'll use in about 30 minutes; if mortar sits around longer than that it

will become difficult to work with. If you're having problems, don't hesitate to mix a new batch of mortar—it should be just stiff enough so that it's not runny. Toss old mortar down the cavities of the wall. Beyond that, follow the steps here and you'll build a sound, plumb and level foundation for your room addition.

Tools & Materials ▸

Eye and ear protection	Level
Circular saw with masonry blade	Mason's jointer
Mason's chisel and maul	Mortar
Sledgehammer	Mortar box
Masonry hoe	1 × 1 piece
Trowel	No. 4 rebar
Plywood	Steel ladder braces
Anchor bolts	

Buttering a concrete block involves laying narrow slices of mortar on the two flanges at the end of the block. It is not necessary to butter the valley between the flanges unless the project calls for it.

HOW TO CUT CONCRETE BLOCK

Mark cutting lines on both faces of the block, and then score ⅛ to ¼"-deep cuts along the lines using a circular saw equipped with a masonry blade.

Use a mason's chisel and maul to split one face of the block along the cutting line. Turn the block over and split the other face.

Option: Cut half blocks from combination corner blocks. Corner blocks have preformed cores in the center of the web. Score lightly above the core, and then rap with a mason's chisel to break off half blocks.

HOW TO MIX MORTAR

Empty mortar mix into a mortar box and form a depression in the center. Add about ¾ of the recommended amount of water into the depression, and then mix it in with a masonry hoe. Do not overwork the mortar. Continue adding small amounts of water and mixing until the mortar reaches the proper consistency. Do not mix too much mortar at one time—mortar is much easier to work with when it is fresh.

Set a piece of plywood on blocks at a convenient height, and place a shovelful of mortar onto the surface. Slice off a strip of mortar from the pile using the edge of your mason's trowel. Slip the trowel point-first under the section of mortar and lift up.

Snap the trowel gently downward to dislodge excess mortar clinging to the edges. Position the trowel at the starting point, and "throw" a line of mortar onto the building surface. Do not get ahead of yourself. If you throw too much mortar, it will set before you are ready.

HOW TO BUILD A BLOCK FOUNDATION WALL

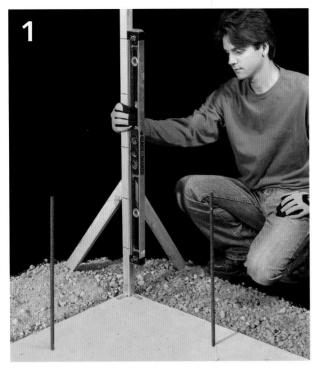

Position story poles at each corner of the foundation. Mark the top line using the string lines as reference, and then mark down 8" for each course of blocks.

Lay the first course in a "dry run" to determine if you'll need to cut or use any special blocks. Use a scrap piece ⅜" thick as a spacer for the mortar joints.

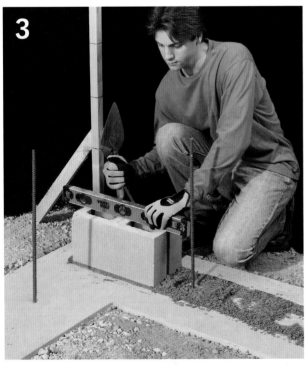

Lay the first block by spreading enough mortar for three blocks in a ladder pattern. Set the corner block in place and check plumb and level against the story pole.

Set the opposite corner block in place and position mason line blocks and guide string. Follow the string in laying the rest of the course.

As you build courses, tie supporting rebar to the footing rebar. Fill the rebar cavities with concrete.

Cut blocks as necessary, scoring on your mark and breaking with a hammer and broad cold chisel. You can also use a grinder equipped with a diamond blade.

Tool the mortar joints with a mason's jointer when the mortar is "thumbprint" ready. Sink anchor bolts for the mudsill into block cavities filled with concrete (inset). Space them roughly every 4'.

Provide additional lateral reinforcement by using steel truss work braces or "ladders" made to lay across the top of a course around the block cavities. These should be used every other course for best effect. Lastly, you can use special metal lath to isolate a course and fill just that course with concrete—a requirement of some codes for the top-most course.

FRAMING THE FLOOR

The floor structure is the stage for the rest of your addition, so take pains to maintain a level surface and solid construction throughout. You'll also make all the construction that follows that much easier, from framing the walls to laying down the final flooring.

Because so much depends on the floor structure, precise measurements are vital. Before you even start framing the floor, re-check level and plumb on the foundation walls and re-measure the existing floor structure. You can adjust to suit minor variations by shimming the mudsill where necessary.

Once you begin building the floor, constantly check level and measurements, and always use sound construction techniques. For instance, never butt floor joists up to one another where the ends meet over a beam. They should overlap to ensure the strongest possible floor structure. And to prevent squeaky floors and add to the integrity, brace with metal X-braces or solid wood blocking between joists even if the codes don't require it for your addition.

Otherwise, you need only follow the plans. If your building plans have been carefully developed, they address code considerations and best standards and practices. Put all the pieces in place accurately and the structural load will be evenly distributed across the floor's surface, guaranteeing a floor that won't sag over time and that provides a comfortable, solid feel underfoot.

Tools & Materials ▶

Hammer
Circular saw
Lag screws
2 × 6s (pressure-treated and not)
Socket wrench

Metal joist hangers
16d nails
10d nails
¾" tongue-and-groove plywood sheets
Eye and ear protection

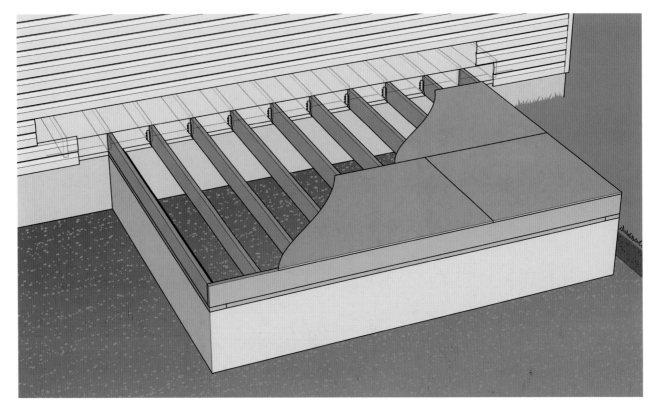

The floor structure for a new addition is not complicated, but making sure it is built correctly and carefully is extremely important.

ROOM ADDITION PROJECTS

HOW TO FRAME A FLOOR

Attach 2 × 6 pressure-treated mudsills to the tops of the foundation walls. They must be positioned flush with the outside edges of the foundation wall. Lay the sills in position so the J-bolts set in the foundation walls mark drilling points in the underside of the sill plates. Drill guide holes for the bolts. Secure the mudsills with the bolts and washers and nuts. *Tip: Add a layer of sill-seal barrier between the sill and the foundation wall.*

Cut the rim joists to length and then toenail them to the mudsill. Align the outside face of each rim joist with the outer edges of the sill plate. Mark the inside face of the mudsill for the joist positions. Use galvanized nails whenever nailing into treated wood.

Nail metal joist hangers to the home's existing rim joist, to support the new joists. In most areas, the joists do not need to be made from pressure treated lumber, but if they do you'll need to use triple-coated, hot-dipped fasteners. Position the hangers 16" on center, unless otherwise designated by code. Remove siding and sheathing as needed to expose the rim joist in the rim joist area.

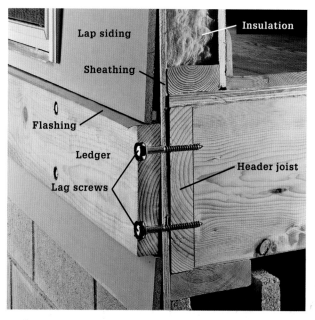

Lap siding

Insulation

Sheathing

Flashing

Ledger

Lag screws

Header joist

Option: In some areas, you may be allowed to remove only the siding and attach a ledger board instead of attaching hangers directly to the house's rim joist.

(continued)

4

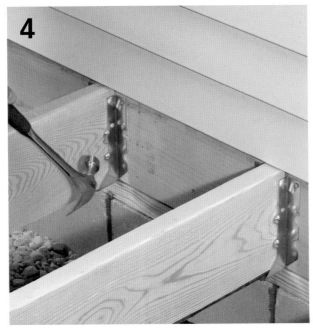

Cut the floor joists to length and set the ends in the hangers, with the other ends resting on the mudsill, flush against the new rim joist. Crown all joists (the bow facing upwards, not sagging down). Secure the joists in the hangers with joist hanger nails or 10d common nails, filling every predrilled nail hole in each hanger. Nail the joists into the hangers and nail the opposite ends to the new rim joist. Check joists for level.

Option: If the subfloor sheets you are installing do not have tongue-and-groove edges, or if you'll need to cut it such that two pieces will meet at a plain butt joint, install blocking to support any seams that will not fall over joists. Blocking also helps stiffen the floor. Use three 16d common nails to attach the end of each piece of blocking to the joists.

5

Install the subfloor sheeting. If you are using sheathing that has no tongue-and-groove edges, install the subfloor so there is a ⅛" expansion gap between panels. Apply a bead of construction adhesive to the tops of the joists before setting each panel. If you have installed nailing blocks, make sure panel seams fall over blocks.

Tongue-and-Groove Sheathing ▸

Subfloor panels must be made of sheathing that is rated for use in a floor system. These may be made either of plywood or oriented strandboards. They are generally ¾" thick (or within a ¹⁄₁₆" or ¹⁄₃₂" of ¾"). Subfloor sheathing often is milled with tongue-and-groove edges that fit together during installation. This provides greater rigidity and reduces bounce. In some cases, using tongue-and-groove sheathing panels can eliminate the need to install nailers between joists if a seam will fall over the spot.

Engineered Lumber ▸

Engineered lumber offers a viable alternative to the dimensional sawn lumber used in the structural members of your floor system. Engineered members, such as beams and truss chords, are constructed from a variety of wood fiber sources—reclaimed wood, mill waste, etc.—that are bonded and manufactured into lumber that performs the same job as their sawn counterparts, only more efficiently. Because engineered lumber uses byproducts that would otherwise have gone into the waste stream, this type of lumber is considered a "green" building option. Engineered components are usually more expensive than sawn pieces, but are lighter and easier to work with. Engineered beams can bear greater amounts of weight than dimensional lumber of the same size, which can sometimes allow you to fit a structural element into a spot that would otherwise be too small.

Two key pieces that can be used in constructing an addition floor are engineered "I" joists or beams, and truss joists.

Engineered I beams come in the same sizes as standard lumber but in the I-form common to steel beams. Light and strong, an entire joist can be carried by a single worker. However, because of their composition, I joists and beams tend to be somewhat "floppy" over their lengths, and are consequently crossbraced more frequently than sawn joists are.

Truss joists are fabricated components with an open-web design similar to the steel joists and beams seen on many bridges. Wooden truss joists are usually constructed of pieces of smaller lumber, such as 2 × 4s. The web design gives the joists exceptional strength and offers more room to run plumbing, wiring and other services through the joists.

Special hangers and braces may be required for engineered lumber, but otherwise the installation process is the same.

Proper floor support is crucial to not only guarantee that the addition's floor doesn't sag or flex, but also to provide necessary structural stability to the whole addition. Building codes and manufacturers instructions will mandate exactly how long you can run an engineered joist.

Engineered lumber usually is made by laminating plywood, OSB or sawn lumber into thick beams with widths corresponding to standard dimensional stock. This beam is made from face-glued strips of plywood and it can span greater distances than a beam of the same width made from solid 2× stock

FRAMING A WALL

Measurements are critical in framing a wall, but the actual components that go into the structure are fairly basic. Refer to your plans and be sure to account for all of the elements of your framed wall, including door and window openings. For any frame carpentry it usually works best to build the wall on the ground or floor, including the sill and cap plates. Then, raise the assembly, position it, and anchor it to the structural members beneath the subfloor.

Tools & Materials ▸

Hammer
Tape measure
Level
Circular saw

Carpenter's pencil
2 × 6 lumber
16d and 10d nails
Eye and ear protection

Hand Nailing ▸

The best hand-nailing technique for joining framing members depends on whether you assemble the framed wall and then raise it, or you add boards one at a time in their final position. If you're assembling the wall on the floor or ground, end-nail the studs to the plates whenever you can (left sample). End-nailed joints, usually made with 10d common nails, are strong and fast to make. To double up wall studs or headers, facenail the parts (right sample) with 8d common nails. Facenailing is also used for attaching jack studs to king studs. To fasten a vertical stud to a top or sole plate that is already in place, toenailing (middle sample) is your best option.

The wall raising is one of the more exciting moments in construction, as the shape of the structure begins to emerge. The basic idea is to build the addition as completely as you can before you cut into the house.

HOW TO FRAME A WALL

Sight down the studs and top and sole plates and replace any with warps or obvious imperfections. Cut the plates and studs to uniform lengths, using a stop block. If you have designed your addition with 8'-tall walls, look for precut 92⅝" studs. *Note: In most climates today, your wall framing members should be made of 2 × 6 lumber, not the 2 × 4 lumber seen here. Code requirements for minimum wall insulation generally require a deeper 2 × 6 stud bay.*

Gang-mark the wall stud locations on the sole and top plates. Cut the plates to length first and clamp the ends together, making sure they are flush. In most cases, the studs should be 16" on center. Draw an X on the side of the marking lines where the stud will fit.

With sole plate lying on-edge, face nail through the sole plate and into the bottoms of the studs. Use two or three 16d common nails per stud. Then, nail the top plate to the other end of the studs so that the wall is framed, lying down.

Build the wall corners. There are several ways you can create interlocking corners so the wall can be attached easily and accurately to the adjoining framed wall. Here, a pair of studs are installed perpendicular to the corner stud to create nailing surfaces for the adjoining wall and for the exterior wall sheathing at the corner.

(continued)

5

Measure the diagonals of the wall to check that it is square. If the diagonal measurements are not identical, use pressure (and clamps if necessary) to pull the wall frame into square. If the diagonals just won't match, measure the wall studs and make sure none of the studs is too long or too short.

6

Raise the first wall. Nail guide blocks to the outside edge of the rim joist to create stops for the soleplate. With a helper, raise the wall into position and check the studs for plumb and the wall for level. If the wall abuts the house make sure it fits cleanly against the wall (the siding should have been removed at the wall tie-in spot by this point).

7

Nail the soleplate to the structural members beneath the subfloor with pairs of 16d common nails spaced every 14" to 16". Attach a 2 × 4 brace to an intermediate stud and anchor the other end to a stake in the ground.

8

Plumb the wall, then nail the corner wall stud to the existing house structure. If you did not plan your addition so the wall meets the house at a house stud location, you'll need to remove the exterior wall sheathing in the installation area and install 2 × 4 or 2 × 6 nailing blocks between the wall studs on each side of the opening.

9

Begin building the second wall. If the wall includes an exterior door, nail king studs into place allowing for the rough-in width of the prehung door unit plus 3" (for the jack studs). Face nail jack studs in place.

Constructing a Header ▸

Door and window openings are wider than normal stud spacing, so they require a head beam, or header, to transfer the overhead weight to the studs at the sides of the opening. Professional builders commonly make their own headers by sandwiching ½" plywood between two 2× pieces. The width of the 2× depends on the width of the opening and how much overhead load the wall carries; check your local codes. The pieces are laminated with construction adhesive and then nailed from both sides to create a strong header that measures exactly as wide as the thickness of a 2 × 4 wall. For 2 × 6 walls, construct a box from parallel 2×s on all sides and fill it with insulation.

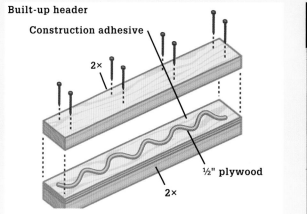

Built-up header

Construction adhesive

2×

½" plywood

2×

(continued)

Place the header on the tops of the jack studs with the ends flush against the king studs. Drive 10d common nails through the king studs and into the header. Then, cut cripple studs to fit between the header and the top plate, maintaining the 16" on center spacing. Toenail the cripple studs into position.

Add extra blocking next to the door opening for improved security.

Jack stud

Window sill

Add framing for windows as needed. Nail king studs into place, allowing for the rough-in width of the window plus 3". Face nail jack studs into place above the sole plate to the bottom of the sill.

Nail a doubled 2 × 4 window sill into place on top of jack studs. Drive 10d common nails through the king studs and into the ends of the double sill.

14

Window header

Nail the window header into position above the top jack studs, face-nailing it through the king studs.

15

Sill

Cripple stud

Header

Nail cripple studs above the header and below the sill, adding more cripples as necessary to maintain at least 16" on center spacing for studs.

16

Tie adjoining wall frames together by nailing them at the corners, and add overlapping top plates to lock the walls together.

CONSTRUCTING THE ADDITION'S ROOF

A well-built roof helps define architectural style while protecting your house from the elements. An addition's roof is no different—it too has to complement the architecture and shield the space below. But the roof on an addition must also link the new space to the existing structure, both visually and structurally.

The first step in effectively making that link is choosing a roof style. Although a basic triangular gable roof is the most common—and one of the easiest to frame—the look or function of your particular addition may be better suited to a more complex hip roof with intersecting planes and multiple valleys, an easy-to-build shed roof with its single sloping plane, or the distinctive gambrel roof that adds two additional angles to the gable's design and increases the attic's head room.

The possibilities increase when you consider the many variations of these basic styles, but the roof you choose for your addition will likely be most influenced by the existing architecture. Because any new roof must complement and tie into existing roof lines, a good design normally matches the addition's roof to the style used on the rest of the house. That's the easiest way to prevent the addition from looking like an afterthought.

Practical considerations also play a big role in roof choice. The most important of these is the angle of the roof's slope, called the pitch. The appropriate pitch for your roof depends on a number of variables, such as rafter size and spacing and local climate conditions. For instance, a more severe pitch is better where heavy snowfall is common but a more moderate pitch will resist high winds better. Pitch is expressed as the "rise" or vertical height in relation to the "run" or span of the roof surface. For instance, a common pitch would be 6-in-12, meaning that the roof slopes 6 inches for every 12 inches of span. Other variables include the depth of the eaves, the soffit style, and end wall overhang, if any. Because your original roof was engineered with these variables in mind, the easiest and most common strategy is to mimic the existing roof and features.

Regardless, the roof details will be worked out in the planning stage and will be detailed in the building plans, according to best practices and code requirements. The plans serve as a roadmap for framing the roof, a process that requires a well-thought-out construction process because it happens mostly in midair. Because the framing members of a roof are usually large and unwieldy, it's unwise to attempt framing even a small roof without at least one or two strong helpers.

Tools & Materials ▸

Carpenter's square	Metal rafter ties
Hammer	Hanger brackets
Tape measure	16d and 8d nails
Carpenter's pencil	2 × 10 ridge board
Jigsaw	2 × 6 joists
Tablesaw	2 × 4s (for ties and blocking)
Circular saw	Building paper
Oriented strandboard	Aviation snips
Drip edge flashing	Eye and ear protection

Roof rafters are usually attached to the wall top plates with a combination of fasteners and metal hangers or ties.

CUTTING THE TEMPLATE RAFTER

Framing the roof will go much quicker if you measure, mark, and cut one rafter, and then use that rafter as a template for laying out the other rafters. All rafters will have top and bottom plumb cuts that are parallel to the roof ridge board, as well as birdsmouth cuts that create an angled notch that fits over the cap plate of the framed wall. Depending on the soffit structure of your roof, you may or may not need a decorative tail cut. The rafter shown here is cut for a 6-in-12 roof pitch.

Birdsmouth cut

Rafter tail

Plumb cut

The two cuts you'll need to make on any rafter are the plumb cuts, which cause the ends of the rafter to be vertical when installed, and the birdsmouth cut, which creates a notch for the rafter to fit over the wall. Some rafter ends also receive a decorative tail cut.

Constructing a Header ▸

For added strength (or as required by code), use metal fasteners or braces to attach the rafters. Always use hardware rated for the size rafters you are using and fasten them securely in place using the recommended fasteners. If you live in a hurricane or earthquake zone, your local codes will have very specific rafter tie requirements that you will need to follow.

HOW TO CUT A TEMPLATE RAFTER

Mark the top plumb cut where the rafter will fit against the ridge board. *Tip: Sight down the rafter to determine which edge, if either, crowns. When installing the rafter, you'll want to position the board with the crown facing in a frown-like orientation—the crown holds up the weight of the roof better.*

Measure and mark the overall length of the rafter, and then mark the bottom plumb cut so it is parallel to, and the same angle as, the top plumb cut.

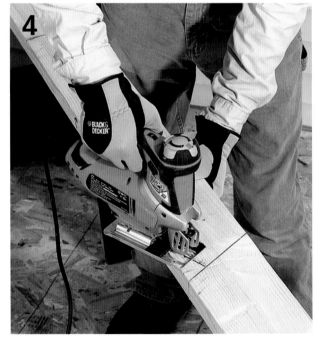

Mark the birdsmouth cut. Measure from top to the outside edge of wall, and mark the birdsmouth plumb cut in from that point. Use the framing square to square and mark off the level cut.

Make the cuts. Use a circular saw to make the plumb cuts and a jigsaw to make the birdsmouth cuts, and then test fit the template rafter. Once it fits perfectly, label it as the template and use it to mark the rest of the rafters.

HOW TO FRAME A ROOF

Mark the positions of the rafters and ceiling joists onto the top plates of the framed walls. Rafters should sit above wall stud location, if possible.

Mark and cut the ends of joists as necessary to match rafter width and roof slope. Mark the first joist in place, then copy the cuts on the remaining rafters.

Toenail the rim joists to the top of the wall and reinforce the connections with metal ties. The ends of the rim joists should be flush with the edges of the front wall and the outer faces should be set back 1½" to create a recess for the vertical rafter supports.

Adjustable Ridge Board Supports ▸

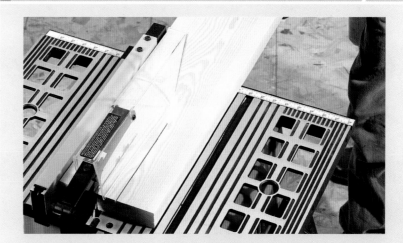

One of the challenges of framing a roof is dealing with large, heavy, and cumbersome framing members. The heaviest is usually the ridge board, which ideally should be in place for the rafters to be installed accurately. But because the ridge board can't simply float in space, it needs to be supported while the rafters are being positioned and attached. Simple 2 × 8 supports nailed to the joist and ridge board can hold the ridge in place with very little flex in the ridge board positioning. To make this "fork" brace, use a tablesaw to cut the shoulders of a notch centered along one end and running down the length of the brace. The notch should be slightly wider than the thickness of the ridge board. Each ridge board brace should be about 10 to 12" longer than the required height of the ridge from the top plate.

(continued)

ROOM ADDITION PROJECTS

Build a pair of temporary ridge board supports to hold the ridge board in place. Cut a notch for the ridge board in the top of each support. The distance from the uncut end of the support to the bottom of the notch should be the planned distance between the tops of the walls and the bottom of the ridge board. Use at least four nails to facenail the supports in place at both ends of the addition. Set the ridge board in position in the supports and tack in place. Install the ceiling joists by toenailing to the top plates of the walls and then reinforcing with metal ties.

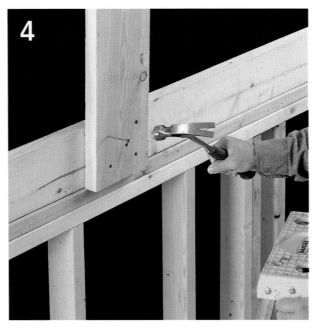

Set a rafter in place against the house siding, making sure it fits cleanly against the ridge board and rests cleanly on the wall. On each side of the ridge, trace the top edges of the rafter onto the siding, then add 2" for sheathing, shingles, flashing, and (for vinyl roofs) J-channel to make cutting lines.

Cut out the siding to make space for the rafter against the wall. *Tip: To cut vinyl siding, reverse the blade direction on a circular saw or cordless trim saw. Once the siding is removed, find the stud locations with a stud finder and mark them.*

Mark, cut, and test fit the gable end rafters to ensure the accuracy of the template. Toenail the rafters to the wall plate and also facenail the rafters next to the house at stud locations.

8

Attach the rafters to the ridge board using hanger brackets. Make sure the distances between rafters are equal, which confirms that the rafters are parallel.

9

Install rafter ties near the tops of the rafters to stiffen the roof structure. Trim the top corners of the 2 × 4 ties first, to match the roof slope.

10

Install 2 × 4 nailers at the front of the roof gables at 16" intervals.

11

If your plans include a gable overhang, or "rake," nail lookouts between the gable-end rafter and the overhang rafter. The lookouts should be installed so their top edges are flush with the rafter tops and they should be cut from the same thickness of 2× stock as the rafters. If your plan includes a fascia, nail the fascia board (or the subfascia) to the rafter ends.

HOW TO INSTALL ROOF UNDERLAYMENT

Nail a full sheet of oriented strandboard (OSB) or exterior-grade plywood rated sheathing to the rafter tops. Make sure the sheathing meets the minimum thickness requirements for your project. Follow the nailing schedules required by your local codes. Spacing of 6" on center is common along the panel edges; 2½" × 8d galvanized box nails are typical when hand-nailing; 0.131" × 2½" clipped head or bent shank nails are used most often for pneumatic nailing. Start at the bottom, gable-end corner.

Start installing the second row of roof sheathing with a half sheet to stagger the joints. Leave a ⅛" gap between sheets to allow for expansion (unless you are using tongue-and-groove sheathing, where the expansion gap sets itself if the panels are installed correctly). *Tip: Tack the corners of the panel by handnailing and then, when the panel is safely in position, use a pneumatic nailer to fill in the field.*

Installing Drip Edge & Building Paper ›

Eave

Rake

The metal drip edge flashing and the building paper are woven together during the installation to create a barrier that sheds water properly. It is important that you install drip edge and building paper in the correct order. First, cut a 45° miter at one end of the drip edge using aviation snips. Place the drip edge along the eaves end of the roof, aligning the mitered end with the rake edge. Nail the drip edge in place every 12". Overlap pieces of drip edge by 2". Install drip edge across the entire eaves, ending with a mitered cut on the opposite corner. Apply felt paper, and ice guard if needed, to the roof, overhanging the eaves by ⅜". Cut a 45° miter in a piece of drip edge and install it along the rake edge, forming a miter joint with the drip edge along the eaves. Overlap pieces by 2", making sure the higher piece is on top at the overlap. Apply drip edge all the way to the peak. Install drip edge along the other rake edges the same way.

Option: Install one or two courses of ice guard membrane at the eave area in colder climates and as required by local codes. This self-adhesive product forms a fully-bonded layer of protection to prevent ice dams from infiltrating beneath the roofcovering as snow melts.

Roll building paper horizontally and install drip edge flashing. Overlap the rows of paper at least 4".

Install building paper on one side of the roof up to the ridge, then cover the other side and overlap ridge by at least 4". Staple down the overlap with a hammer stapler.

Make sure any obstructions or penetrations in the building paper layer are patched over with building paper or with ice guard membrane. You will still need to flash penetrations such as this vent pipe during the roofcovering installation.

INSTALLING ASPHALT SHINGLES

If you want to install asphalt shingles on your roof, then you're in good company. Asphalt shingles, also known as composition shingles, are the roofing of choice for nearly four out of five homeowners in America. They perform well in all types of climate, are available in a multitude of colors, shapes, and textures to complement every housing design, and are less expensive than most other roofing products.

Asphalt shingles are available as either fiberglass shingles or organic shingles. Both types are made with asphalt, the difference being that one uses a fiberglass reinforcing mat, while the other uses a cellulose-fiber mat. Fiberglass shingles are lighter, thinner, and have a better fire rating. Organic shingles have a higher tear strength, are more flexible in cold climates, and are used more often in northern regions.

Although the roofing market has exploded with innovative new asphalt shingle designs, such as the architectural or laminated shingle that offers a three-dimensional look, the standard three-tab asphalt shingle is still the most common, which is the product we're using for this addition. The tabs provide an easy reference for aligning shingles for installation.

To help get the job done faster, rent an air compressor and pneumatic roofing gun. This will greatly reduce the time you spend nailing.

Tools & Materials ›

Aviation snips
Carpenter's square
Chalk line
Flat bar
Roofer's hatchet or
   pneumatic nailer
Utility knife
Straightedge
Tape measure

Building paper
Caulk gun
Flashing
Shingles
Nailing cartridges
Roofing cement
Roofing nails (⅞", 1¼")
Rubber gasket nails
Eye and ear protection

Stagger shingles for effective protection against leaks. If the tab slots are aligned in successive rows, water forms channels, increasing erosion of the mineral surface of the shingles. Creating a 6" offset between rows of shingles—with the three-tab shingles shown above—ensures that the tab slots do not align.

HOW TO INSTALL THREE-TAB SHINGLES

Cover the roof with building paper (page 529) and install drip edge (page 528). Snap a chalk line onto the felt paper or ice guard 11½" up from the eaves edge to mark the alignment of the starter course. This will result in a ½" shingle overhang for standard 12" shingles. *Tip: Use blue chalk rather than red. Red chalk will stain roofing materials.*

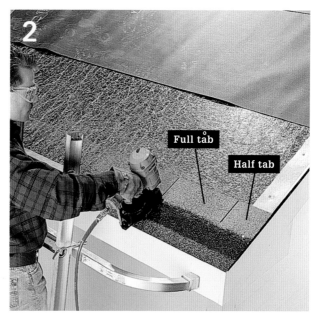

Trim off one-half (6") of an end tab on a shingle. Position the shingle upside down, so the tabs are aligned with the chalk line and the half-tab is flush against the rake edge. Drive ⅞" roofing nails near each end, 1" down from each slot between tabs. Butt a full upside-down shingle next to the trimmed shingle, and nail it. Fill out the row, trimming the last shingle flush with the opposite rake edge.

Apply the first full course of shingles over the starter course with the tabs pointing down. Begin at the rake edge where you began the starter row. Place the first shingle so it overhangs the rake edge by ⅜" and the eaves edge by ½". Make sure the top of each shingle is flush with the top of the starter course, following the chalk line.

Snap a chalk line from the eaves edge to the ridge to create a vertical line to align the shingles. Choose an area with no obstructions, as close as possible to the center of the roof. The chalk line should pass through a slot or a shingle edge on the first full shingle course. Use a carpenter's square to establish a line perpendicular to the eaves edge.

(continued)

Use the vertical reference line to establish a shingle pattern with slots that are offset by 6" in succeeding courses. Tack down a shingle 6" to one side of the vertical line, 5" above the bottom edge of the first-course shingles to start the second row. Tack down shingles for the third and fourth courses, 12" and 18" from the vertical line. Butt the fifth course against the line.

Fill in shingles in the second through fifth courses, working upward from the second course and maintaining a consistent 5" reveal. Slide lower-course shingles under any upper-course shingles left partially nailed, and then nail them down. *Tip: Install roof jacks, if needed, after filling out the fifth course.*

Check the alignment of the shingles after each four-course cycle. In several spots on the last installed course, measure from the bottom edge of a shingle to the nearest felt paper line. If you discover any misalignment, make minor adjustments over the next few rows until it's corrected.

When you reach obstructions, such as dormers, install a full course of shingles above them so you can retain your shingle offset pattern. On the unshingled side of the obstruction, snap another vertical reference line using the shingles above the obstruction as a guide.

Options for Valley Flashing ▸

Here are three options for flashing a valley where two roof planes meet. Closed Valley (left): Create a seamless roof by first laying waterproof membrane in the valley, then mitering shingles at the top and overlapping in the valley. Open Valley (middle): Nail metal flashing down the intersection joint, and overlap shingles from both sides, at least 2". Terminate the flashing at the gutter and lay a bead of roofing cement along the joint between shingles and flashing. W-Flashed Valley (right): Special "W" channel flashing is used where two roofs with different pitches meet. The channel is attached to the roof decks with clips and the clips are bent up at bottom to deflect water back into the flashing.

Shingle upward from the eaves on the unshingled side of the obstruction using the vertical line as a reference for re-establishing your shingle slot offset pattern. Fill out the shingle courses past the rake edges of the roof, then trim off the excess.

Trim off excess shingle material at the V in the valley flashing using a utility knife and straightedge. Do not cut into the flashing. The edges will be trimmed back farther at a slight taper after both roof decks are completely shingled.

(continued)

Install shingles on adjoining roof decks, starting at the bottom edge using the same offset alignment pattern shown in steps 1 to 6. Install shingles until courses overlap the center of the valley flashing. Trim shingles at both sides of the valley when finished.

Install shingles up to the vent pipe so the flashing rests on at least one row of shingles. Apply a heavy double bead of roofing cement along the bottom edge of the flange.

Sleeve

Place the flashing over the vent pipe. Position the flashing collar so the longer portion of the tapered neck slopes down the roof and the flange lies over the shingles. Nail the perimeter of the flange using rubber gasket nails.

Cut shingles to fit around the neck of the flashing so they lie flat against the flange. Do not drive roofing nails through the flashing. Instead, apply roofing cement to the back of shingles where they lie over the flashing.

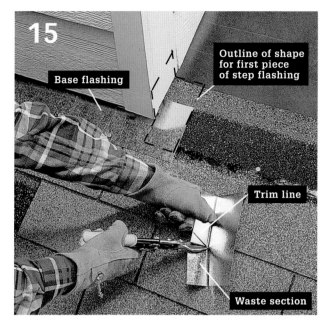

Shingle up to an element that requires flashing so the top of the reveal areas are within 5" of the element. Install base flashing using the old base flashing as a template. Bend a piece of step flashing in half and set it next to the lowest corner of the element. Mark a trim line on the flashing, following the vertical edge of the element. Cut the flashing to fit.

Pry out the lowest courses of siding and any trim at the base of the element. Insert spacers to prop the trim or siding away from the work area. Apply roofing cement to the base flashing in the area where the overlap with the step flashing will be formed. Tuck the trimmed piece of step flashing under the propped area, and secure the flashing. Fasten the flashing with one rubber gasket nail driven near the top and into the roof deck.

Apply roofing cement to the top side of the first piece of step flashing where it will be covered by the next shingle course. Install the shingle by pressing it firmly into the roofing cement. Do not nail through the flashing underneath.

Tuck another piece of flashing under the trim or siding, overlapping the first piece of flashing at least 2". Set the flashing into roofing cement applied on the top of the shingle. Nail the shingle in place without driving nails through the flashing. Install flashing up to the top of the element the same way. Trim the last piece of flashing to fit the top corner of the element. Reattach the siding and trim.

(continued)

When you reach a hip or ridge, shingle up the first side until the top of the uppermost reveal area is within 5" of the hip or ridge. Trim the shingles along the peak. Install shingles on the opposite side of the hip or ridge. Overlap the peak no more than 5".

Cut three 12"-sq. cap shingles from each three-tab shingle. With the back surface facing up, cut the shingles at the tab lines. Trim the top corners of each square with an angled cut, starting just below the seal strip to avoid overlaps in the reveal area.

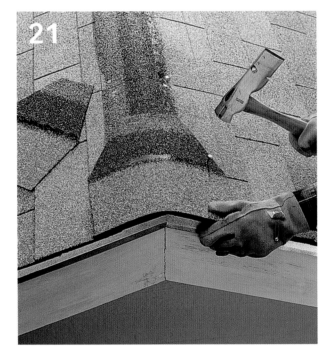

Snap a chalk line 6" down from the ridge, parallel to the peak. Attach cap shingles, starting at one end of the ridge, aligned with the chalk line. Drive two 1¼" roofing nails per cap about 1" from each edge, just below the seal strip.

Following the chalk line, install cap shingles halfway along the ridge, creating a 5" reveal for each cap. Then, starting at the opposite end, install caps over the other half of the ridge to meet the first run in the center. Cut a 5"-wide section from the reveal area of a shingle tab, and use it as a "closure cap" to cover the joint where the caps meet.

23

Shingle the hips in the same manner using a chalk reference line and cap shingles. Start at the bottom of each hip and work to the peak. Where hips join with roof ridges, install a custom shingle cut from the center of a cap shingle. Set the cap at the end of the ridge and bend the corners so they fit over the hips. Secure each corner with a roofing nail, and cover the nail heads with roofing cement.

Option: Install a ridge vent all along the roof ridge to create ventilation. A ridge vent is usually made of a strip of loosely woven batting that allows airflow. This is installed over long slots that are cut into the roof on both sides next to the ridge. Some ridge vents have a granular mineral surface that matches your shingle color preattached; other are designed to be shingled over as you would a normal roof ridge.

24

After all shingles are installed, trim them at the valleys to create a gap that's 3" wide at the top and widens at a rate of ⅛" per foot as it moves downward. Use a utility knife and straightedge to cut the shingles, making sure not to cut through the valley flashing. At the valleys, seal the undersides and edges of shingles with roofing cement. Also cover exposed nail heads with roofing cement.

25

Mark and trim the shingles at the rake edges of the roof. Snap a chalk line ⅜" from the edge to make an overhang, then trim the shingles.

SHEATHING EXTERIOR WALLS

Wall sheathing is the skin that serves as a base for the final siding. There are basically two types of sheathing—structural and non-structural. Structural sheathing supports the framing, increasing the overall strength of the structure. Non-structural sheathing is used where the structure is supported in other ways such as metal ties or let-in boards. The category includes insulation panels and other lightweight alternatives.

Structural sheathing is the option of choice in most additions, and in most cases that means using plywood or oriented strandboard (OSB). Regardless of which you choose, the sheets should be rated for exterior wall use. The most common size is ½ inch, although local code requirements may call for different thicknesses.

Although the standard dimensions for sheets are 4 × 8 feet, you can also purchase 4 × 9 feet, 4 × 10 feet, or even 4 × 12 feet sheets to accommodate your needs. Many people choose to install the panels before raising the walls into position, which makes it easier to work with the large panels, but heavier lifting. Installing the panels after the walls are up, however, makes marking the cuts for window and door openings easier and faster.

Tools & Materials ▸

Hammer	4 × 8 OSTS sheets
Circular saw	2 × 4 blocking
Reciprocating saw	Eye and ear protection
8d nails	

Plywood or OSB panels that are rated for use as wall sheathing are a much better choice for exterior addition walls than insulation boards or other panels that may be allowed but have little or no structural value.

Plywood versus OSB Wall Sheathing ▸

The most common wall sheathing materials are plywood, which is formed of laminated wood layers, and OSB, made of wood strands mixed with adhesive. These two types of sheathing are interchangeable, but in most areas of the country, OSB is cheaper. OSB can also be formed into much larger panels than plywood can, making it a good choice for unusually large wall surfaces. However, plywood absorbs water and dries in a much more efficient and uniform fashion. This means it's a better option in high-moisture areas and as a base for some types of siding such as stucco and wood shingles.

HOW TO INSTALL WALL SHEATHING

Nail the first full panel into place, starting at a bottom corner. If it works for your layout and situation, install the panels horizontally to cut down on trips up and down the ladder. Space nails at 6" intervals around the edges and every 12" in the field.

Start installing the second row of sheathing panels with a half sheet to stagger the joints between panels. Leave a ⅛" expansion gap horizontally and ¹⁄₁₆" gap vertically.

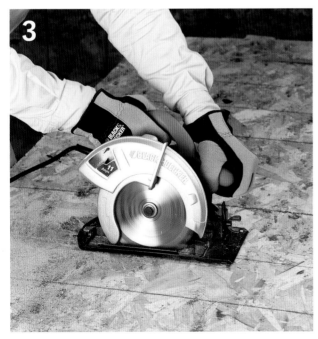

Measure carefully and then mark and cut the openings for windows, doors, and other openings such as vents. In many cases, you may find it easier to trace around framed openings after the sheathing is installed and then cut them out with a reciprocating saw.

Option: Install 4 × 9' sheets of sheathing in installations where the sheathing needs to fill past the wall top plate and up to or near the rafter tops.

BUILDING WRAP

Housewrap is a specially engineered fabric that blocks air and water infiltration from the outside but allows moisture vapor to pass through from the inside. It's best to apply the housewrap before installing windows and doors, but since that's not always possible with a remodeling or siding replacement job, you can cut the housewrap to fit around them. Most siding materials need to be nailed to studs, and the marks on the housewrap identify their locations. Staples are permissible for fastening housewrap, but cap nails are recommended and have better holding power.

Felt paper is not the same as housewrap. It's not necessarily designed to work as an air barrier, and it may absorb water. Do not substitute felt paper when housewrap is supposed to be used.

Tools & Materials ▸

Hammer	Housewrap (3, 5, 9, or
Utility knife	10' widths)
Tape dispenser	Housewrap tape
Cap nails (2 or 3")	Eye and ear protection

Make "martini glass" cutouts in the building wrap for window and vent openings. Fold the flaps inside and staple along studs and sill.

HOW TO INSTALL BUILDING WRAP

Starting 6 to 12" around a corner and 3" over the foundation to cover the sill plate, unroll the housewrap along the side of the house with the printed side facing out. Align the printed stud marks on the housewrap with the stud marks on the sheathing. Keep the roll straight as you unwrap it.

Nail the housewrap every 12 to 18" on the vertical stud lines using cap nails. Keep the housewrap pulled snug as it's unrolled. Cut holes in the housewrap for extrusions such as hose spigots and the electric meter.

When starting a new roll, overlap vertical seams by 6 to 12", aligning the stud marks. Begin the second course by overlapping the bottom course by 6". Once again, make sure stud marks are lined up.

At window and door locations, cut the housewrap at the middle of the nailing flanges. At the bottom, cut the housewrap at the sill. Pull the sill and jamb flashing over the housewrap. Be careful not to slice the nailing flanges and windowsills when cutting the housewrap.

Tape all seams with housewrap tape to assist the vapor seal.

Also apply housewrap tape to accidental tears, and seams around doors, windows, and plumbing and electrical protrusions. Tape the bottom of the protrusion first, then the sides, then place a piece of tape over the top.

INSTALLING SIDING

The best way to seamlessly blend the addition with the rest of the house is to use the exact same siding for the addition. However, the transition will be convincing only if the siding runs from the house to the addition without visual interruption. The following illustrations demonstrate how to integrate your new siding with your old as naturally as possible.

Vinyl, fiber cement, or wood clapboard: Although the mounting method is different for siding and clapboard, the method for incorporating old with new is the same: on parallel walls, remove short end sections and panels, pry up starter strips, and overlap building wrap from the addition onto the old wall. Replace the siding with new full-length pieces that run onto the addition wall. On inside corners, run inside corner trim up the intersection and side the addition as new.

Stucco: Stucco is a difficult material to work with at any time, but blending two stucco walls is a challenge usually best left to a professional. The trick is to score and hammer out several inches at the end of the existing wall. Leave the steel mesh lath, and overlap with the lath from the new wall. Then stucco the joint carefully to avoid cracks.

Brick and stone: There are two methods for incorporating the brick or stone wall of a new wall with an older surface. The most solid connection is made by "toothing" out the existing wall—removing bricks or stones along the edge and cementing in connecting pieces from new wall to old. On irregular stone walls or where you want to save the labor of toothing a brick wall, you can use steel wall ties. These are rails that are attached to the existing wall with tongues that are hooked in and sit between the mortar joints of the new wall.

Shingles and shakes: Pry up shingles 1 foot in from the edge (leaving only whole shingles) at which the parallel addition wall will attach. Overlap addition wall building wrap and begin installing shingles from the exposed part of the existing wall, repeating the existing pattern. Where the walls meet at a right angle use inside corner trim and shingle the addition wall as you would any new construction.

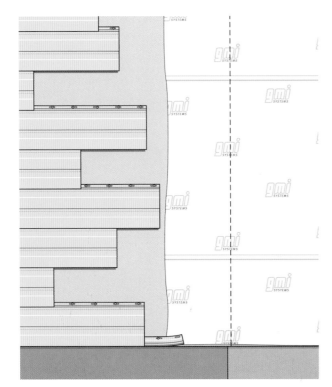

Lap siding to lap siding

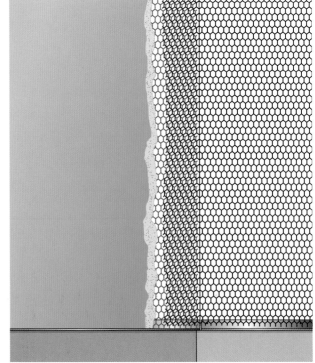

Stucco to stucco

Masonry unit to masonry unit

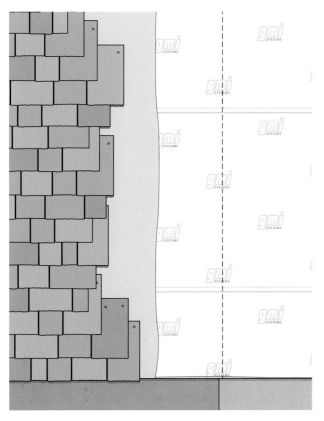

Shingle to shingle

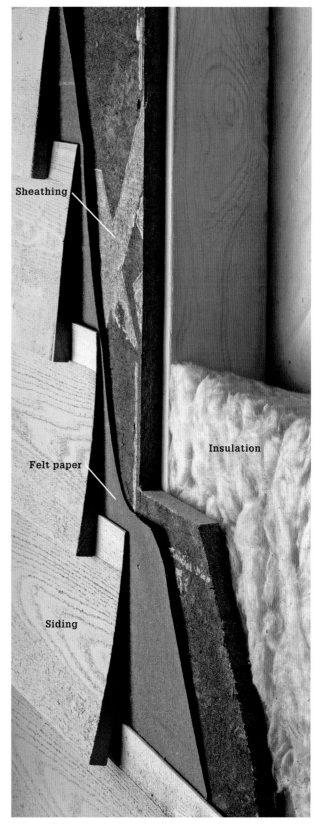

Sheathing

Insulation

Felt paper

Siding

Lap siding, backers for stucco, furring strips for shakes, and any panelized siding products should be attached with fasteners that go through the sheathing and into the wall framing.

HOW TO INSTALL VINYL SIDING

Nail the inside and outside corner posts for the siding into place, starting ¼" below top of corners. Drive nails in on either side of each post and check for plumb, then nail every 8" down the post, overlapping the top pieces. Leave a gap between the nails and the surface of the siding so that the post is loose enough to move slightly.

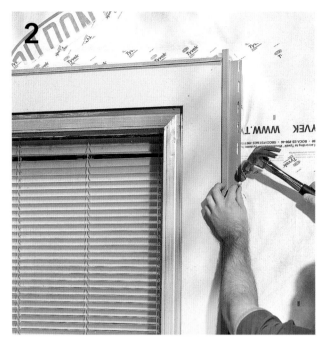

Measure, cut, and nail J-channels in place on either side of windows and doors, in the same manner that you nailed the corner posts, leaving them slightly loose to allow for expansion.

Cut a 1"-long piece of J-channel for the top corner of each window and door. Bend over the flange of each cut corner piece slightly so it fits over the top J-channel and functions as a drip edge.

Measure, cut, and install J-channel along the roof lines. To overlap, cut 1" from the nailing hem. Overlap ¾", leaving ¼" for expansion.

5

At an outside corner, measure up from the point where the bottom edge of the siding will hang to the width of the starter strip minus ¼". Hammer in a nail at this point and repeat at the opposite corner. Snap a chalk line between nails as a reference for starter strips.

6

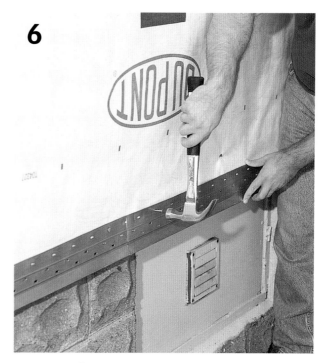

Measure and snap starter strip chalk lines around the other walls of the addition. Position the starter strip so that top edges are even with the reference chalk lines. Fasten the starter strips by hammering nails in the centers of the slots at 10" intervals.

7

Securely lock the first horizontal siding panel into the starter strip. Ensure that the panel is locked in over its entire length before nailing. Nail the first panel to the sheathing. Hammer nails in the centers of slots, leaving a 1/32" gap between the nailheads and the siding surfaces.

8

Check that the panel can move freely from side to side. Continue nailing panels as needed to complete the course. Overlap adjacent panels by approximately 1", or about one-half the length of the notch at the end of the panel.

(continued)

9

Lock and nail the panels for the second course into place. Stagger the panel lengths so that the overlaps are offset by at least 12" from course to course. Check alignment and level after every course and make adjustments as necessary.

10

Measure and cut panels to fit around the openings, leaving an extra ¼" all around for expansion. At cutout areas beneath an opening, punch the upper cut edge of the panel with a snap lock punch and nail through the hole. Install utility trim over the edge.

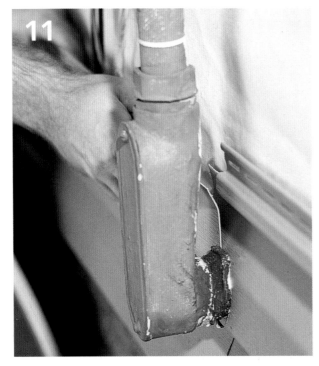

11

Cut slots in the panels to fit around fixtures such as a hose bibb or a service entry cable housing, leaving an extra ¼" around the fixture. Add a decorative trim ring, available at home centers or your siding retailer, for a finished look.

Blending Old & New ▸

Making the siding on your addition blend with the existing siding, and look good in its own right, is mostly a matter of using a few simple design techniques. Overlap panels as far away as possible from doorways and other areas that see significant foot traffic. This will place vertical seams where they are less noticeable. And to keep unsightly seams to a minimum, use panels that are as long as possible and never shorter than 3'.

OTHER TYPES OF LAP SIDING

Wood lap siding comes in wide or narrow strips and is normally beveled. Exterior-rated wood that can be clear coated is common (usually cedar or redwood). Other wood types are used, too, but these are usually sold preprimed and are suitable for painting only.

Fiber-cement lap siding is a relative newcomer but its use is spreading quickly. It is very durable but requires some special tools for cutting and installation.

Starting Wood & Fiber Cement Lap Siding ▸

Attach a starter strip at the base of each wall section. Cut the strip from the top (narrow) edge of the worst-looking pieces of siding. Nail the strip all along the bottom of the wall, keeping a gap of about ⅛" beneath it to limit contact with moisture.

Nail the first course of beveled siding in place. For fiber cement board drive nails only through the area of the siding board that will be overlapped by the next course, which will conceal the nailhead.

SOFFITS, FASCIA & GUTTERS

Some older homes and certain house styles such as Arts & Crafts are designed with open eaves in which the ends of the rafters are exposed. But installing fascia and soffits creates a finished appearance to the roofline.

In addition, modern vinyl soffits offer many advantages over traditional wood styles; they are easy to clean, simple to install, and virtually maintenance-free. Vinyl panels and channels are easily cut to fit with special shears or a saw. The soffit panels come in solid and perforated styles and, although the standard practice is to install one perforated panel for about every three or four solid panels, you can actually create an entire soffit of perforated panels—which will make ordering the materials much easier.

SOFFIT & FASCIA TYPES

Fascia cladding. Clad an existing fascia with aluminum or vinyl, or nail F-channel to the bottom of the fascia if you prefer to maintain the wood surface. You can also select vinyl fascia, with the soffit channel molded into the design.

Metal soffit panels. Nail F-channel to the wall, leaving a small gap between the nailhead and channel to allow for expansion. Soffit panels rest on a fascia cladding ledge and F-channel. A portion of each panel is usually perforated for ventilation.

Wood soffits. Wood panels are custom cut from ¼ or ½" exterior rated plywood. The panels can be nailed to rafter lookouts or set onto narrow ledges similar to F-channels. Vent covers are attached over ventilation holes cut into the panels.

HOW TO INSTALL GUTTERS & DOWNSPOUTS

Mark the starting point of the gutter at one end (or the middle of a long run), and at the low point at the other end, allowing for ¼ to ½" to slope for every 10' of run. Snap a chalk line between the two points.

Attach a drop outlet to the fascia at the low point, preferably with a long deck screw that extends into the rafter end.

Mount hangers for the gutters, beginning at the high-end mark. Mount the hangers approximately every 30" unless directed otherwise by the manufacturer.

Cut the gutter sections and downspouts to fit using a fine-toothed hacksaw. Remove any burrs with fine-grade sandpaper and test-fit the sections.

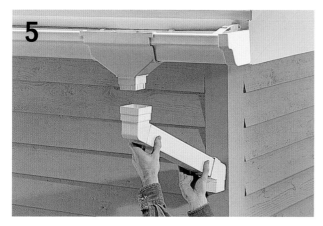

Build the downspout by connecting the pipe sections with elbows to run down the wall. Connect the downspout to the wall with straps spaced approximately at 8' intervals.

Complete the downspout assembly with a final elbow and pipe section, routed onto a splash drain or into a drain culvert so that water drains away from the foundation.

INSTALLING WINDOWS IN AN ADDITION

Preventing water from getting in is one of the most important considerations when installing a window in an addition. The key is to seal all joints around the window and block anyplace the water could wick in. Although caulking can be effective, it's also easy to miss small spots, and caulking will deteriorate over time. That's why builders in wetter parts of the country install plenty of flashing around the window with waterproof membrane. If you want extra protection against water infiltration, start from the bottom, cut strips of self-adhesive waterproof membrane, and apply them under the window, up the sides, and then on top of the window. All seams should face down and the top and bottom strips should run out 6 inches on either side of the window. Repeat the procedure over the nailing flanges.

Tools & Materials ▸

Hammer
Tape measure
Level
Utility knife
Handsaw
Caulk gun
Window
Self-adhesive flashing
Exterior-grade
    silicone caulk
Shims
Flashing
Metal drip edge
Brickmold
Roofing nails
Minimal-expanding
    spray foam
    insulation
Eye and ear
    protection

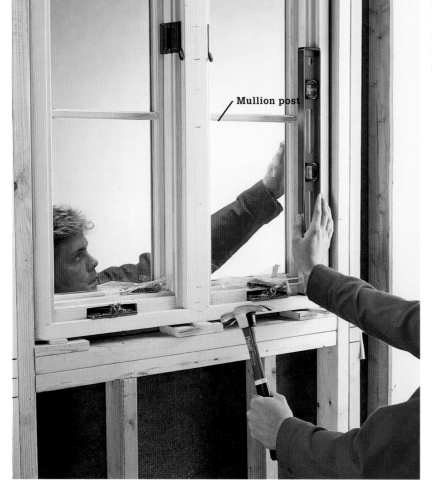

Mullion post

New windows can be installed after the wall framing and sheathing is done. Many builders sheath over the window openings, then cut them out as they install each window, to keep weather and wildlife out.

Green Window Choices ▸

Installing the right windows for your home and region can instantly trim your energy usage. That's why, when choosing windows for an addition, you should always look for the Energy Star label. A designation given by the US Department of Energy, the Energy Star label ensures a window meets or exceeds federal guidelines for home energy efficiency. An even more important gauge than simply looking for an Energy Star label is to read the NFRC label on the window. Specifically, note the U-factor and Solar Heat Gain Coefficient (SHGC) ratings for the window. If you live in a fairly cold region of the country, you want the lowest U-factor you can find, with a moderate to high SHGC. If your home is located in a temperate area with consistently warm temperatures, the SHGC number is the most important one to you, and it should be as low as possible.

NFRC MANUFACTURER
NUMBER 084
976-3-1.000
Model 976 Horizontal Slider Operating, Vinyl,
√8 Glazing, Clear, Air Fill

National Fenestration Rating Council®
CERTIFIED   RES 97

ENERGY PERFORMANCE RATINGS

U-Factor (U.S./I-P)	Solar Heat Gain Coefficient
0.51	**0.65**

ADDITIONAL PERFORMANCE RATINGS

Visible Transmittance	
0.67	—

Manufacturer stipulates that these ratings conform to applicable NFRC procedures for determining whole product performance. NFRC ratings are determined for a fixed set of environmental conditions and a specific product size. NFRC does not recommend any product and does not warrant the suitability of any product for any specific use. Consult manufacturer's literature for other product performance information.
ww nfrc org

MEETS OR EXCEEDS C.E.C.
AIR INFILTRATION STANDARDS

HOW TO INSTALL A WINDOW IN AN ADDITION

Flash the rough sill. Apply 9"-wide self-adhesive flashing tape to the rough sill to prevent moisture infiltration below the window. Install the flashing tape so it wraps completely over the sill and extends 10 to 12" up the jack studs. Fold the rest of the tape over the housewrap to create a 3" overlap. Peel off the backing and press the tape firmly in place. Install tape on the side jambs butting up to the header, and then flash the header.

Caulk the opening. Apply a ½"-wide bead of caulk around the outside edges of the jack studs and header to seal the window flange in the opening. Leave the rough sill uncaulked to allow any water that may penetrate the flashing to drain out.

(continued)

3

Position the window. Set the window unit into the rough opening, and center it side to side. Check the sill for level.

4

Tack the top corners. Drive a roofing nail through each top corner hole of the top window flange to tack it in place. Do not drive the rest of the nails into the top flange yet.

5

Plumb the window. Have a helper hold the window in place from outside while you work inside. Check the window jamb for square by measuring from corner to corner. If the measurements are the same, the jamb is square. Insert shims between the side jambs and rough opening near the top corners to hold the jambs in position. Use additional shims as needed to bring the jamb into square. Recheck the diagonals after shimming.

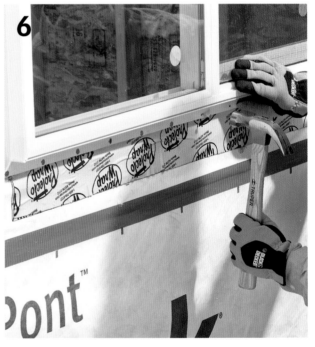

6

Nail the flanges. Drive 2" roofing nails through the flange nailing holes and into the rough sill to secure it. Handnail this flange, being careful not to damage the flange or window cladding.

Flash the side flanges. Seal the side flanges with flashing tape, starting 4 to 6" below the sill flashing and ending 4 to 6" above the top flange. Press the tape firmly in place.

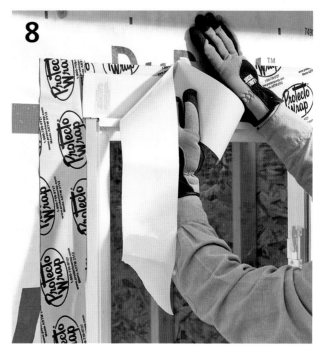

Install the drip cap. Cut a piece of metal drip edge to fit over the top window jamb. This is particularly important if your new window has an unclad wooden jamb with preinstalled brickmold. Set the drip edge in place on the top jamb, and secure the flange with a strip of wide flashing tape. Do not nail it. Overlap the side flashing tape by 6". *Note: If you plan to trim the window with wood brickmold or other moldings, install the drip edge above that trim instead.*

Finish the installation. Cut the shim ends so they are flush with the inside of the wall using a utility knife or handsaw.

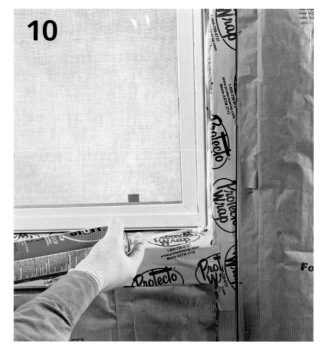

Spray the foam insulation around the perimeter of the window on the interior side.

INSTALLING AN ENTRY DOOR IN AN ADDITION

If your addition is to the front of your house and includes an entry, the new entry door will provide you with a fine opportunity to dress up the house and to integrate the new part with the old. Your choice of exterior door design should be driven by the style of the exterior doors on the existing house. Matching door styles is just one more way of integrating the addition with the design of the house. In addition to the number of panels or other design elements, you'll need to determine whether you want an "inswing" or "outswing" door, and what "hand" it should be. This is a matter of space and precedent. Most exterior doors swing in, but if your addition's space will be small and cluttered, you may want to opt for an outswing door. The "hand" of the door is simply the location of the handle on the side the door swings toward. For example, a left handed inswing door will have the handle on the left side as you face it from inside the space. The hand of the door should be determined by practicality; if there is a perpendicular wall right next to the door, the door should open on the side away from the wall so that visitors don't feel crowded upon entering.

If your addition is in the rear of the house, it may contain an entry door that is less of a design statement than simply a serviceable way to get in and out. The following service door installation includes a fairly plain steel door leading to a workshop addition. If you are installing a fancier front door, the techniques are fundamentally the same.

Tools & Materials ▸

Handsaw
Hammer
Caulk gun
Brick mold
Shims
Prehung exterior door
Minimal-expanding spray foam insulation
Exterior-grade silicone caulk
Galvanized casing nails
Self-adhesive flashing tape
Eye and ear protection

HOW TO INSTALL A PREHUNG ENTRY DOOR IN AN ADDITION

Flash the bottom and sides. Apply two strips of self-adhesive flashing tape to cover the jack studs in the door's rough opening. Cut a slit in the tape and extend the outer ear 4 to 6" past the bottom edge of the header. Fold the tape over the housewrap to create a 3" overlap. Peel off the backing and press the tape firmly in place.

Flash the header. Cover the header with a third piece of self-adhesive flashing tape, extending the ends of the tape 6" beyond the side flashing. Fold the extra tape over the housewrap to form a 3" overlap.

Seal the opening. Apply a ½"-wide bead of caulk up the outside edges of the jack stud area and around the header to seal the brickmold casing.

Position the door in the opening. Set the bottoms of the side jambs inside the rough opening, and tip the door into place. Adjust the door so it's level, plumb, and centered in the opening.

Attach the door. Drive 2½" galvanized casing nails through the brickmold to fasten the door to the jack studs and header. Space the nails every 12".

Shim at the dead bolt and behind the hinges. Insert pairs of shims with the door closed, adjusting the shims in or out until there's a consistent ⅛" gap between the door and the jamb. If your door came with them, insert one long screw at each hinge into the framing. Then fill the gap with foam.

INDEX

H. 7/17